Christian Education for the Local Church

Christian Education for the Local Church

An Evangelical and Functional Approach

Revised Edition

by
H. W. BYRNE, Ed.D.

Author of *A Christian Approach to Education*

Academie
Books Grand Rapids, Michigan
Zondervan Publishing House

ACADEMIE BOOKS are published by Zondervan Publishing House,
1415 Lake Drive, S.E., Grand Rapids, Michigan 49506

CHRISTIAN EDUCATION FOR THE LOCAL CHURCH
Copyright 1963 by
Zondervan Publishing House
Grand Rapids, Michigan
Copyright © 1973 by
The Zondervan Corporation

Library of Congress Catalog Card Number 63-9310

ISBN 0-310-22230-3

To

Sean — My Grandson

Betty — My Daughter

ACKNOWLEDGMENTS

Expressions of appreciation are due, not only to the various publishers who have granted permission to use quotations made, but also to Dr. P. H. Wood, Dr. Edward Simpson, and Dr. Frances Simpson for reading and criticizing the manuscript. A great debt of gratitude is owed to Miss Mary Ann Wagner for typing the manuscript.

Printed in the United States of America

84   85   86   87   88 — 30   29   28   27   26   25   24   23

CONTENTS

Chapter outlines are included at the beginning of each chapter.

LIST OF CHARTS

CHART
PAGE

FOREWORD

There may have been a day and situation in which Sunday School was the most wasted hour in the week, due to ignorance of the task or a careless feeling that anything is good enough for Sunday school. Admittedly, the educational work of the church has been hampered often by confusion, misunderstanding, and mediocrity. Too many have tolerated it as "busy work" for lovely old ladies and chattering children. Some have considered it unnecessary, unscriptural, and unspiritual. A few have eyed it suspiciously as competitive to missions and evangelism. But the current revitalization of Sunday schools is impressing some pessimistic prognosticators that evangelical Christian education is a robust and vigorous child of the church.

If Jesus Christ, the Master Teacher, sent forth disciples to teach all nations; if the apostles, our examples, spent their lives in a teaching ministry; if the Scriptures, our guide, exhort us to teach the precepts of the Lord; if the history of the church indicates the hand of God in blessing upon the teacher; if the pupil, our charge, demands the faithful ministry of teaching; and if the issues at stake are eternal — then certainly it is time for the church to prepare itself for a more effective teaching ministry!

Christian Education for the Local Church is a significant attempt to provide guide lines for improving the educational work of the church. The Scriptural basis and functional approach will be found helpful in clarifying definitions, relationships, objectives, and responsibilities. There is a vast amount of useful material, including wide use of charts and diagrams, and excellent suggestions and samples in the appendix. The soundness of principle and practicality of method will appeal to those actually engaged in some phase of the educational work of the church. Emphasis in matters of administration make this work especially helpful to pastors and other officers responsible for guiding educational programs.

Dr. Byrne is uniquely prepared as an author in this field, having served the Lord in the pulpit, in the classroom, on conference platform, and at the desk. His combination of theological and educational background provide the blend of spiritual life and pedagogical knowledge so necessary for a study of this nature. Student, teacher, officer, and pastor will find herein a wealth of instruction and inspiration which will help him become "apt to teach."

January, 1963

FRANCES F. SIMPSON
EDWARD D. SIMPSON

PREFACE

When the average layman who works in the local church picks up a book on Christian education, he asks himself, "What is in this for me?" One of the motives for this volume was an attempt to answer this question.

The topical treatment of a subject in this field centers the reader's attention on subjects, on things to be done, whereas a functional approach directs attention to objectives, responsibilities and, above all, to people and their duties. Therefore, the approach represented in this work is called "functional" and "evangelical." "Evangelical" focuses attention on Biblical principles. The term "functional" indicates the major thrust of the material presented as follows:

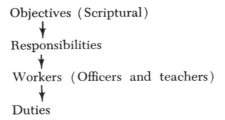

Objectives (Scriptural)

Responsibilities

Workers (Officers and teachers)

Duties

From what has been said, the author hopes that he has designed a book which will prove useful to pastors, boards of Christian education, directors of Christian education, superintendents, teachers and workers involved in the local church program of Christian education. It may also find usefulness as a basic text in total church program in colleges and theological seminaries.

This book is an outgrowth of twelve years in the pastorate, three years teaching in a theological seminary, six years teaching at the college level in the field of Christian education, and wide experience in conferences, classes, and conventions. Almost every major work within the past thirty years was consulted in the preparation of the material contained herein. While much of this material may be considered "ideal," particular effort was made to present realistically a practical down-to-earth program for the local church both large and small. It is felt that most churches can use the suggestions which are made to their own benefit and primarily for the glory of God.

H. W. Byrne
January, 1963

PREFACE TO REVISED EDITION

Every attempt was made in this revised edition to maintain the major thrust of the work with its primary emphasis laid on a "functional" approach to the work of church education. In the decade gone by since the inception of this work changes have taken place in the educational work of the local church. An attempt was made, therefore, to reflect such changes while at the same time maintaining the original advantages of the materials initially presented.

The major addition to the material was made in chapter 7 where a new section on the more creative methods of teaching and learning was included. Here an attempt was made to trace recent trends in educational psychology as well as new developments in learning theory and teaching methodologies. Stress was also laid on the methods employed in open room procedures and team teaching techniques.

Other changes include the updating of the bibliography and an additional appendix which lists some of the more creative methods of teaching and learning in current use.

This revised edition is offered with the hope and prayer that God's people will find in it a tool of greater usefulness in His service.

H. W. BYRNE
February, 1973

THE WORK OF THE CHURCH IN
CHRISTIAN EDUCATION

OUTLINE FOR CHAPTER 1

(Purpose, Pattern, Program)

A. THE CHURCH
  1. Origin of the Church
  2. The Nature of the Church
  3. The Function of the Church
  4. The Purpose of the Church
  5. Objectives of the Church
  6. Teaching Ministry of the Church

B. THE TOTAL CHURCH PROGRAM OF CHRISTIAN EDUCATION
  1. Principles
  2. Purposes and Objectives
  3. Pattern
  4. The Program

C. ORGANIZATION FOR CHRISTIAN EDUCATION IN THE LOCAL CHURCH
  1. Nature and Purpose of Organization
  2. Responsibility for Organizing the Program
  3. Guiding Principles for Organization
  4. Patterns and Plans for Organization
  5. Organizing According to the Scriptural Pattern

D. ADMINISTRATION OF CHRISTIAN EDUCATION IN THE LOCAL CHURCH
  1. Adequate Administration Needed
  2. Functional Administration Necessary

1 | THE WORK OF THE CHURCH IN CHRISTIAN EDUCATION

(PURPOSE, PATTERN, PROGRAM)

A. *The Church*

1. *Origin of the Church.* All Christian ministry for today has been committed to the church. The church began with Jesus Christ. He said, "I will build my church" (Matt. 16:18). From the early days of beginning, He has been engaged in that process (Acts 2:47; Eph. 1:22; 5:23). Someday His task will be completed (Eph. 5:27; Rev. 22:5). Every true Christian feels like the apostle Paul, who said, "For me to live is Christ" (Phil. 1:21). The life of every Christian centers in Christ, for "in him we live, and move, and have our being" (Acts 17:28). For many, it is a debatable question as to just when the church was started, but for all practical purposes, the Day of Pentecost marked its beginning.

2. *The Nature of the Church.* The Greek New Testament records the word "church" as *ecclesia.* It is a derivative of the word *eccletos,* which means "called out" or "called forth," and of *eccaleo,* which means "called out of homes into a public place." Applied to the Christian church, it became known as an assembly of Christian people for worship. These early Christians found fellowship, mutual protection, and service opportunities in the early *ecclesia.*

Membership in the early church was determined by a close, vital relationship to Jesus Christ its Founder. Eligibility was based on a spiritual experience called the "new birth." Baptism was the public testimony to this experience and originally was also a sign of genuine repentance and faith in Christ, which were qualifications for the new birth. Today evangelical believers are obligated to perpetuate this kind of Christianity.

All Christians are, by virtue of the new birth, members of the Body of Christ. This makes the church an *organism,* not an organization. Where an organization is composed of a society of separate individuals enlisted in a common cause, the church is an organism, a *body* of believers so integrated that their relationship to one another is governed by their relation to Christ and directed so as to function toward a common cause.

3. *The Function of the Church.* The function of the church is that of its Founder Jesus Christ. He said, "As my Father hath

sent me, even so send I you" (John 20:21). An obedient church will respond to the authority of its Head and will carry out the commands of its leader.

The birth, life, ministry, death, and resurrection of Jesus Christ laid the foundations upon which the church could build in a lost world. Shortly before taking His leave, Jesus imparted power and authority to His followers to perpetuate His work in the world, looking toward the consummation of all things in the kingdom of God. "Verily, verily, I say unto you, He that believeth on me, the works that I do shall he do also; and greater works than these shall he do; because I go unto my Father" (John 14:12). In His place Jesus promised the presence, purity, and power of His Spirit to assist the church in carrying out the program of Christ in the world (John 14:16, 17, 26; 16:7-16). The result of the coming of the Holy Spirit would be twofold: (1) The church would receive personal and corporate power to witness and proclaim the Gospel to the world (Acts 1:8); and (2) success in this ministry would be achieved in carrying out the Great Commission (Matt. 28:18-20).

Since the church is the repository of the Gospel and the means of its propagation, the true function of the church is to present Christ unto all men. In doing this, the primary function is that of witnessing. "Ye shall be witnesses unto me" (Acts 1:8). Jesus also used other terms which are quite descriptive, "Ye are the light of the world" (Matt. 5:14). The light of Christian truth and holiness as demonstrated by believers is intended to permeate the darkness of ignorance and sin among men. "Ye are the salt of the earth" (Matt. 5:13). The church is to function like salt. It purifies, seasons, and preserves. It is to be noted here in passing that the above functions all have deep educational significance.

4. *The Purpose of the Church.* The purpose of the church is to reveal God through His Son, the Lord Jesus Christ. In doing this, the church virtually takes up the mission of the Lord Jesus Christ Himself who said, "As my Father hath sent me, even so send I you." In His Son, God has given to us a revelation of Himself. This revelation Jesus gave to us in a threefold manner — that of prophet, priest, and king.

As Prophet, Jesus conveys to us a particular message about God, but more than that He discloses the nature of God. He was "The Word made flesh." In Christ we see God in human form. When we see the mind, will, and character of Jesus Christ, we see the mind, will, and character of God. Thus as Prophet, Jesus reveals God to man.

As Priest, Jesus Christ unites and reconciles man to God. He gives first a demonstration of that supreme unity, perfection, and fullness of relationship with God of which our nature is capable. He shows us how we can give perfect homage and obedience to

God. He makes it possible for us to have perfect union with Himself so that we can have union with God. He is our Priest.

As King, Jesus came forth to make His moral claim felt upon our manhood, to redeem and liberate it, to subdue and govern it, in all its parts and faculties. He came to rule first the hearts of men and ultimately to rule the whole world. Thus Jesus is Prophet, Priest, and King.

As Jesus was sent on His prophetic, priestly, and kingly mission, so in His turn He sends out His church in the persons of His disciples. "As my Father hath sent me, even so send I you." The purpose of the church, therefore, is to perpetuate the mission of her Master. She is to perpetuate the prophetic mission of Christ by carrying down through the ages the truth as it was disclosed in Jesus Christ — the truth involved in His person, God and man; the truth about God, which He revealed in His life, His works, His words; the truth about man, his destiny, his capacity, and his sin; the truth about redemption through Jesus Christ. Thus the church is the divinely appointed agency through which the Gospel is proclaimed to the world. The purpose of the church is the purpose of Jesus who said, "The Son of man is come to seek and to save that which was lost" (Luke 19:10). In carrying out this purpose, the work of the church is one of continuing evangelism. This it does through the motivation and power of the Holy Spirit and the command of Jesus as expressed in the Great Commission (Matt. 28:18-20). Teaching is a ministry.

The church is to perpetuate the priestly mission of Jesus. In this its mission is more than in words. "The kingdom of God is not in word, but in power" (I Cor. 4:20). There is the gift of grace, the gift of the Spirit Himself, and the gifts of the Spirit. The church is the channel through which these gifts are dispensed to man. The church becomes one with Him and workers together with Him.

The church also shares the kingly function of Christ. The church is to guide, to discipline, to strengthen, to provide for the various needs of men until they are brought into full obedience to God. There is no expectation, however, of converting the world. This will await the coming of the King. Now the church works with the Spirit in "calling out from among the Gentiles a people for his name" (cf. Act 15:14).

It should be noted at this point that the purpose of the church includes teaching. The church is interested in growth and development along with evangelism and soul winning. It is interested in information as well as investigation and evangelization. The church is to go "into all the world and preach the gospel to every creature" (Mark 16:15). In this way the "body of Christ" will be built up, its membership increased, and the organism completed (Eph. 4:12, 15, 16).

5. *Objectives of the Church.* Having laid the foundations in His life and ministry, the Lord Jesus Christ as Head of the church sent His Spirit on the Day of Pentecost into the hearts of the disciples to bind them into spiritual oneness and to give them the dynamic for carrying out His purposes in the world. In the Acts, the epistles of Paul, and general epistles, we find the record of the early church in carrying forward the purposes of Jesus Christ. We find there too the record of the means whereby the church of today is to continue this ministry. And we see the great continuing goals of the church.

Where the initial purpose of the church begins with the creation and development of Christian character, the goal of the church is *maturity of Christian character.* This provides an individual and character goal for the church. Church members must be Christ-like members. The character of Christ becomes the goal for the individual. Jesus said, "Be ye therefore perfect, even as your Father which is in heaven is perfect" (Matt. 5:48). The secret of Christ-like personality is to be found also in His Words: "Abide in me, and I in you" (John 15:4).

The analysis of the character of Jesus is revealed in the Scriptures. "He that hath seen me hath seen the Father" (John 14:9). Jesus was like God. His godliness was expressed in all areas of His life and conduct. "Jesus increased in wisdom and stature, and in favor with God and man" (Luke 2:52). Here we see the intellectual, physical, social, and spiritual aspects of His character from the human standpoint. Jesus *increased* in all these aspects. The pattern for man therefore, is to become increasingly more Godlike and Christ-like.

The apostle Paul likewise adopted Christ-likeness as the character goal for the Church. "Christ in you, the hope of glory: whom we preach . . . that we may present every man perfect in Christ Jesus" (Col. 1:27, 28). "That ye might be filled with all the fullness of God" (Eph. 3:19). Church members were to be educated to live like Jesus Christ and manifest His truth. The ultimate result of this process is integrated Christian personality, expressed by Paul in II Tim. 3:17: "That the man of God may be perfect, throughly furnished unto all good works." This qualifies man to reveal God.

Objectives for the church, however, reach beyond the individual to society. The true Christian is one who lives in fellowship with other Christians and in harmony with all men. Furthermore, his philosophy of life demands the highest possible degree of social serviceability. Where the social aim of the church stresses individual social development, the *social goal* of the church places emphasis on what Christians can do together for the common welfare. Two agencies are used by God in bringing to realization His social objective: (1) the church, and (2) the kingdom. To this end the church is to form a great missionary society in which the goal is to enlist every disciple of Christ in this body and to develop them into efficient servants. The method to be employed is witnessing and evangelism, expressed in the Great Commission. In order to facilitate this objective, the church, as the kingdom of Christ, moves out into society as a spiritual leaven with a spiritual program called the kingdom of heaven.

The kingdom of God is the ultimate objective for society. Here is where God has perfect control. The theocracy is re-established when the King returns. Perfect love will prevail. In the meantime, while we await for the coming of the kingdom, the child of God is expected to move out into society and prove that the purposes of God can be increasingly effective in human relations. The ultimate results of this kind of living will be a manifestation by individual Christians of the following social characteristics:

1. Perfect brotherly love
2. Sacrificial service
3. Christian culture
4. Good citizenship

Objectives for the church transcend time and earthly existence. The Christian has a perspective for eternity in the return of the Head of the church, the Lord Jesus Christ. This provides hope for the future. It will also create a sense of balance between time and eternity, but at the same time will give added incentive and highest motivation for maximum development and preparation now.

It is possible at this point to summarize the goals of the church in the following manner:

1. Individual personality goal — Christlikeness, godliness
2. The social goal — the church and the kingdom
3. The prophetic goal — the second coming of Jesus Christ

6. *Teaching Ministry of the Church.* The preceding considerations of the origin, nature, function, purpose, and objectives of the church lead one to the certain conclusion that the church has a teaching ministry. The purpose, pattern, and program of Christian education in the local church finds its basis, justification, and amplification in the light of the ministry of the Gospel through the church. The work of the pastor is largely one of a teaching ministry, as we shall see. The Old Testament is replete with instance after instance showing the importance of the teaching ministry. In the New Testament times the early church adopted the synagogue idea. In fact, in Jesus' ministry it is hard to separate preaching and teaching. Early records show that "daily in the temple, and in every house, they ceased not to *teach* and *preach* Jesus Christ" (Acts 5:42). Careful study of Acts 17 reveals that the apostle Paul used both methods, with one method no more important than the

other. We have received a great teaching heritage from our Lord Jesus Christ.

B. THE TOTAL CHURCH PROGRAM OF CHRISTIAN EDUCATION

1. *Principles.* The program of Christian education is determined directly by the nature of the church as discussed above. Christian education is a part of the program of the church. Christian teaching, we have said, is a ministry. Since the church is the divinely appointed agency for the proclamation of the Gospel to the world, it is to the church that we must look for genuine Christian education. God has made His will known in His Word. The Word of God as recorded in the Bible becomes, therefore, the authority and source for the program of Christian education in the local church. The church of today must stick close to the Word of God and the leadership of the Holy Spirit, who is the Divine Superintendent in building God's program of Christian education in the local church. The leadership of the church should expect to find the principles, purposes, objectives, pattern, and program for Christian education in the Word.

The church has an educational responsibility. It is seen first in the obligation to carry out the teaching responsibility embraced by the Great Commission. It is revealed in the obligation to develop Christian personality following the new birth. From the New Testament record we can show that the church is obligated to harbor and protect its membership against heresy and unbelief; we can discover how the early church couched its teachings in doctrinal form for the instruction of the people, being careful, however, to maintain life and power along with precept. We see how standards of social life and ethical conduct were greatly stressed. Where the purpose of the church requires an educational process for its realization, it is further apparent that the method and program of the church are also educational. Thus in one sense of the word the whole church becomes a school whose purpose is to work with God in the creation and development of Christian personality.

It becomes exceedingly clear at this point that all educational agencies which are a part of the church program should be closely integrated in the total program of the church. No part, particularly that of the Sunday School, should be divorced from the overall ministry of the church at large. Christian education is a *part* of the divine program of Christian ministry in the local church. There should be complete integration, correlation, and cooperation from this standpoint.

An examination of the Scriptures provides us with the clues to building a philosophy of Christian education which is functional. The framework which results from this investigation looks like this:

1. In discovering purposes and objectives — follow the Word
2. In establishing the divine pattern — follow the church
3. In building the divine program — follow the pattern

2. *Purposes and Objectives.* Purposes and objectives for Christian education find their roots in the nature and purpose of the church as founded by the Lord Jesus Christ. The source for purposes and objectives today is the Word of God as recorded in the Scriptures, and the needs of man. The average church and Sunday school are inclined to be careless about these things. The result is inefficiency and ineffectiveness. No more profitable exercise can be thought of than for a pastor and his workers to face frankly this important matter.

The word "aim" means *to point so as to hit, to direct efforts.* The word "objective" as here used means *a goal.* Aims and goals are essential in Christian education for a number of reasons. They provide a sense of direction; they give vision and foresight, a basis for standards; they motivate the teaching-learning process. They provide a means of guidance in the selection of materials and methods; they enable both teachers and pupils to evaluate the teaching-learning processes; they save time and provide a sound basis for cooperation. Last, but not least, they provide a basis for integrating and correlating the various factors in the curriculum.

Purposes and objectives have been variously classified. Some refer to them as general and specific; others use the terms ultimate and proximate or immediate. It is not too important how one classifies his purposes, but it is exceedingly important that he be very clear on what they are and how to use them.

An examination of the Scriptural record and the needs of society and the individual makes it possible to discover the general purposes and objectives which guide the whole process of Christian education. They are as follows:

1. Investigation — Find the man (Luke 19:10; John 4:35)
2. Evangelization — Win the man (Luke 19:10 — "save")
3. Identification — Hold the man (Col. 2:5, 7)
4. Information — Build the man (II Peter 3:18)
5. Sanctification — Purify, empower, and fill the man (Acts 15:8, 9; 1:8)
6. Consecration — Use the man (Rom. 12:1, 2)
7. Supervision — Improve the man (II Tim. 2:15)
8. Perfection — Mature the man (II Tim. 3:17)

Investigation is the first great responsibility of workers in Christian education. This was the purpose and program of Jesus who said, "The Son of man is come to seek and to save that which is lost" (Luke 19:10). The Son of Man is come to *seek.* Again He said, "The fields are white already unto harvest" (John 4:35). We have cause to wonder at times if the Christian church has not reversed God's program. Instead of taking the Gospel to the people, great churches and cathedrals have been built with the purpose in mind to entice people to enter a house of God. Today the world is not coming to Christ. We must take Christ to the people. We must join Him in seeking the lost and instructing them in the truth and will of God. We must move out into society as salt and light to love and witness.

After finding the man, it is our responsibility to win that man to Christ and the church. Jesus came to save the lost (Luke 19:10). To Him, a new man makes a new society. A new spirit, not a reconstructed economic order, is the secret. New motives and new attitudes are more important than new methods and activities. Christian people make a Christian society.

Evangelism is the work of an evangelist. It is the message of the "evangel"; it is good news. It means telling, teaching, proclaiming the Gospel in such a way that people will understand it, accept it, and live by it. Evangelism is the work of *all* Christians. "Ye shall be witnesses unto me." "Go ye therefore and teach all nations." Evangelism is the chief work of the Sunday School. In fact, Christian education cannot be Christian unless it is evangelistic. It is winning, keeping, building up in the faith all who are committed to our responsibility. To fail here is to fail in our primary reason for existence and service. Sunday school evangelism, then, is evangelism which comes through Bible teaching. It includes the living of the Christian life. It is graded evangelism; it is personal evangelism. *Evangelization* is a great purpose in Christian education.

After finding the man and winning him to Christ, our purpose is *identification,* to hold the man. "As ye have therefore received Christ Jesus the Lord, so walk ye in him: rooted and built up in him, and established in the faith" (Col. 2:6, 7). The key words here are "rooted" and "established." It is comparatively easy to find and win people to Christ, but it is not so easy to establish them in the faith. This is particularly significant in the field of Christian education in the light of the tremendous drop-out problem which now exists. Someone has stated that we lose 65 per cent of the boys and 75 per cent of the girls from Sunday school ranks by the time they reach 14 years of age. One major denomination made a study of this problem in their churches several years ago and found that out of approximately six million people who started in the early Sunday school grades, only 400,000 remained by the time they reached the adult department. Of course, one can list a variety of causes for this, but it remains on the surface a great problem to be faced in the average church.

One secret of holding power is the development of Christ-like personality. Where the work of evangelism has been completed, this begins to take place. Beyond this, however, we must provide the type of experiences which have holding power. The program should provide Christ-like experiences and activities. These must be attractive, interesting and fruitful.

Again, our purpose is *information*. We are not only interested in finding people, winning them to Christ, and holding them, but we are greatly interested in their intellectual development in the faith. We want to build them up in the most holy faith. Peter admonished the church to "grow in grace, and in the knowledge of the Lord and Saviour Jesus Christ" (II Peter 3:18). It is growth of the best sort; growth in grace and knowledge, growth in character and intellectual breadth. "Ye shall know the truth and the truth shall make you free." It is our responsibility to teach the Word. We need to know our Bibles. While it is true that facts will not save us, nevertheless those Bible facts are important and useful. There is divine power in the Word to build us up and help regenerate a lost humanity. Jesus said, "The words that I speak unto you, they are spirit and they are life." Thus, a part of our ministry is to instill the great ideals and principles of our faith into our pupils, to fix strong convictions, to provide the kind of instruction which will lead to maturity and growth and the ability to meet the problems of life. Christians will seek to sow the seed of the Word everywhere. Systematic, thorough teaching must supplement the pulpit ministry for greatest results. In all this we recognize the presence and power of the Holy Spirit.

Still further, our purpose is *sanctification*. The Christian life is not only a way which leads to truth and destiny, it is a *life*. It is one thing to *know* something, greater to *do* something, but greatest to *be* something. Following conversion and regeneration, there is a life to be lived. We are admonished, therefore, to "walk in the Spirit." To accomplish this, one needs purity of heart and the baptism of the Holy Spirit (Acts 15:8, 9; 1:8). Only in this way will he find the dynamic which is required for successful Christian living and service.

Beyond all this lies another objective, that of *consecration*. Where the elements above have referred largely to the creation and development of Christian character, here emphasis is laid on Christian *service*. Christians are directed to serve the Lord. They are described as ambassadors for Christ, workers together with Him, co-laborers with the Lord. Our people need to be *trained* to do something for the Lord and to do it well (Rom. 12:1, 2). Service-training is the obligation of the church through its program of Christian education. Here the church has failed miserably. We need to give greater stress than ever on service, training, leadership development, and stewardship. Only in this way will the Gospel be extended to the ends of the earth. We must act to meet the needs of the laity of the church whom we have failed. We must plan to use the man for the glory of God. Only in this way can members of the church move out into society to be a blessing and build the kingdom of God among men. Let us not forget that the Sunday school provides the greatest opportunities for putting people to work.

These purposes demand a program of *supervision*. Here stress is laid on improvement. We must learn to do a better job while we are doing it. We are to "study to show ourselves approved unto God, a workman that needeth not to be ashamed, rightly dividing the word of truth" (II Tim. 2:15). The man, the method, and the message must be closely supervised so that a high standard of work will result in quality of service.

Finally, the great objective is *perfection*. "That the man of God may be perfect, throughly furnished unto all good works" (II Tim. 3:17). Our goal is Christian maturity and Christ-likeness, giving the world an expression and demonstration of godliness. Christians with holy hearts endeavor to bring about a Christ-like society.

Every worker in Christian education should know these objectives and have them available for constant reference and use. They should guide teachers in lesson preparation and presentation. They should prove helpful to administrators in policy making, planning, operation, and evaluation. Parents should have them available to use in the home and to direct home-church relationships. The whole educational situation should be directly affected by them. Everyone should be dedicated to their constant realization.

3. *Pattern*. Christian education not only has its purposes and objectives revealed in the Word, but we find there also a demonstration of the process by which these objectives are to be realized. The early church, as recorded in the book of Acts, gives to us an illustration of the pattern by which we are to build. If we follow the pattern, our program will not fail. Under the leadership of the Holy Spirit as the Divine Superintendent of the church, the early church saw that five functions were inherently essential in carrying out the purposes of Jesus and in realizing the objectives of Paul. These functions are recorded for us in Acts 2:41-47. "Then they that gladly received his word were baptized: and the same day there were added unto them about three thousand souls. (vs. 41). And they continued steadfastly in the apostles' doctrine and fellowship, and in breaking of bread, and in prayers" (vs. 42).

1. Evangelism (vs. 41) — "3,000 souls"
2. Education (vs. 42) — "apostles' doctrine"

3. Edification (vs. 42) — "breaking bread and prayers" (worship)
4. Enthusiasm (vs. 42) — "fellowship"
5. Service (vss. 43-47)

The early church practiced these five functions in developing the Body of Christ and in building the kingdom. These functions provide a "block" of Christian service activity. They cover all possible phases of the divine program. Furthermore, these functions were worked in conjunction with one another; they were never divorced in principle or practice. The church of today has had the tendency to place some of these functions into "pigeon holes," trying to separate them one from another. God's design is that all five work vitally in *all* that we do in the field of Christian education. There should be instruction, fellowship, and worship in our evangelism. There should be evangelism, fellowship, and worship in our education. There should be the evangelistic spirit, definite instruction, and the spirit of worship in our fellowship. There should be evangelism, instruction, and fellowship in our worship. Still further, all these functions should be evident in all departments of Christian education. Where each local church has looked at it from this standpoint, it has been able to build a program which was spiritual, comprehensive, well-balanced, and fruitful. Thus in establishing the divine pattern for Christian education in the local church, we must follow the example of the early church.

4. *The Program.* The *basis* upon which the program of Christian education in the local church rests is found in the purpose of the church and the pattern it has laid out for imitation. The great objective is Christian character. It follows naturally then that all activities, materials, methods, and content which go into the program should be bent to the realization of the great objective. In fact the program can be evaluated to the extent by which the purposes are realized in the creation and development of Christian personality. In doing this, both evangelism and teaching are combined into an integrated program of Christian education. Thus, Christian education becomes the very heart of the program of the local church and the primary means by which the goals are reached. The church becomes a great school of Christian living and service.

The program thus becomes the instrument through which the objectives are realized. In this sense, it is virtually a *curriculum*. In fact, the best definition of the program is contained in that word. The *content* of the program or curriculum will consist of all those experiences which will build Christian character and a more Christ-like world. The question arises at this point as to which of these experiences becomes ultimate in the program. For many years philosophers of Christian education have argued over the relative importance of the pupils, the Bible, and society. Students may study various philosophies which stress respectively the importance of these factors. The evangelical Christian recognizes their importance, but must reject all of them as ultimate. Instead, to him, his philosophy is centered in God. It begins with Him. To be genuinely Christian, the program must therefore be Christ-centered. Christ is the power and life of the church. He is also at the center of its program of Christian education. This control He exercises through His Spirit. The other factors find relative significance in their relationship to Him. The Bible becomes the center of subject matter and is the primary source of truth. The pupil becomes the *focus* of the whole process. Then the truth, both living and written, is applied to the social situation. In chart form this philosophy of the Christian program looks like this:

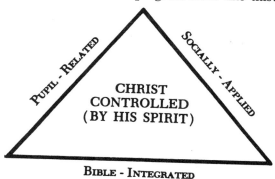

The *elements* of the program are determined by following the revelation of the Scriptures and the pattern set by the early church. This, we have discovered, provides us with a program or curriculum composed of five factors:

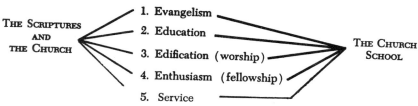

Evangelism is the heart of Christian education. The program, therefore, must contain opportunities for *practicing* evangelism and *studying* evangelism. The Sunday school is perhaps the most fruitful place of evangelism in the church. Many studies have been made to show that approximately three-fourths of the church membership come out of Sunday school ranks. Most of the conversions on record fall into the category of Sunday school age groups, particularly the junior and junior high groups. The task, therefore, is to make Jesus Christ so real that there will be fruit in the power of the Holy Spirit resulting in the salvation of many souls and the extension of this ministry out into a needy world. The strategy of Christian education, therefore, becomes an evangelistic one. Here is where the forces of soul winning and instruction virtually combine into one program. Conversion and regeneration become the door to the process of development of Christian character and Christian service. Where soul winning and instruction have been combined into one dynamic and integrated program, one sees the most fruitful and permanent type of program. Some of the various factors involved in a comprehensive program of evangelism include:

1. Soul winning
2. Enrollment and attendance
3. Follow-up of absentees
4. Religious census
5. Outpost and mission schools
6. Instruction in evangelistic techniques
7. Missions
8. Church membership and Christian life classes
9. Special days
10. Visitation

Every possible channel will be utilized in developing this aspect of the program. There will be evangelism *through parents.* Assistance will be provided to the home in both study and practice so that parents can start at the earliest possible moment the great work of evangelism in the home. There will be evangelism *through the pastor.* He is pastor of the Sunday school as well as of the church. Through preaching, teaching, special classes, personal work, visitation, prayer, and leadership education, the pastor will be greatly utilized in the program. There will be evangelism *through all the workers.* They will be trained for this task. They will visit and do personal work. There will be evangelism *through teachers.* The teacher is an under-pastor, a shepherd of his class. Through personal and intimate contacts the teacher has, next to the parent, perhaps the greatest opportunity. Particular attention should be given, therefore, to providing qualified and consecrated teachers for this task.

The pastor and general superintendent are responsible for promoting an evangelistic program in the Sunday school. Careful plans should be laid to win every scholar to Christ, to train officers and teachers to be evangelistic, and to reach out for new prospects. Prayer lists should be formed, visitation programs planned, and absentees followed up. Let us be thorough in our work to evangelize.

The second major factor in the program is *education.* It is one thing to save a soul; it is another thing to keep him in the faith, to build him up in the faith, to develop Christian character, and to provide a place of service in the kingdom. Once saved, a soul needs to be nourished, fed, enlightened, and given something to do for His Lord. This can be realized only through an effective and efficient *instructional* program. Just as it is logical for the pastor to direct evangelism, so it devolves naturally upon the general superintendent to direct the instructional phase of the program. The pastor, however, is the general supervisor of the total program and works closely with the superintendent in all phases of his work — guiding, advising, and providing general assistance. Care should be taken, however, to see that evangelism is not held separate from the educational phase. The two go together. In fact, we may conclude that the Sunday school is the church itself at work in education and evangelism. It is not merely a part of the church, nor is it merely affiliated with it; it *is* the church at work. The educational phase, therefore, should be expected to find its primary emphasis in the Sunday school, but instruction actually cuts across every division of church life. Some of the various factors involved in a comprehensive program of instruction include:

1. Bible study
2. Christian doctrine
3. Christian ethics
4. Church history, organization, polity
5. Missions
6. Teacher training
7. Leadership education and development
8. Stewardship
9. Social action
10. Techniques of evangelism
11. Worship
12. Fellowship and recreation
13. Prayer
14. Christian home making
15. Christian citizenship
16. Christian culture
17. Service training

Service training needs particular attention at this point. Here the church has failed most often. Participation in service activities has many advantages, among which are contributions to the social happiness of others, character-forming elements, and practical training for the membership in actual practice of gospel truths and obligations.

The third major factor in the program is *edification* or worship. Worship and prayer are vital elements of the local church program and therefore of Christian education. To provide a deeply spiritual atmosphere and yet avoid ritualism and formalism is a big job.

The importance of prayer and communion with God cannot be over-emphasized. We pray, so we evangelize, instruct, and build the program. Our contact and communion with God is our lifeline.

Worship can be defined as a personal experience into which God enters and communion takes place, the result of which is a life changed and enriched in some way. The worshiper becomes aware of God; he gains spiritual insights; he apprehends the will of God more clearly.

The general purposes of worship in the Sunday school are two-fold: (1) to provide for the *act* of worship, and (2) to provide training *for* worship. Here again we see both training and study in this factor. In the act of worship, the pupil must experience two elements: (1) the objective, something given to God, and (2) the subjective, something which takes place within the person. In training, pupils must be taught how to worship and must be prepared for public worship in the morning church service. Here the program should be concerned with the creation of certain concepts, attitudes, appreciations, and aptitudes. In all this, the workers will be led far beyond the mere concept of an "opening exercise" in the Sunday school session. Although everyone is concerned with this element, the pastor and superintendents are directly obligated to give planning, administration, and counsel. Besides the elements just mentioned, some of the factors to be included are:

1. Atmosphere and setting
2. Scriptures
3. Prayer
4. Devotional arts, such as pictures, stories, etc.
5. Offering
6. Liturgy
7. Leadership
8. Training period

Enthusiasm is the fourth factor in the program. Here we are concerned with social life and recreation. From its very beginning in Jesus and His disciples, this factor was evident. The church has always been a particularly intimate group.

The purpose of this element in the program is an educational one, not merely to be used as a propaganda tool or bait for young people. Instead, cultivation of close Christian fellowship will lead to an evangelistic experience, the deepening of heart warmth and mutual appreciation, and the development of Christian personality.

Here, as in the other factors, there should be someone to direct this phase of the work; he may be called a "Superintendent of

Social Life and Fellowship," or something similar. The elements of the program would include some of the following:

1. Burden bearing
2. Recreation
3. Use of leisure time
4. Christian ethics
5. Christian athletics
6. Social etiquette
7. Christian culture
8. Leadership development
9. Personality development; morale building
10. Correlation and integration with other instructional items
11. Cultivation of the Christian spirit

In Ephesians 4:11-13 the apostle Paul calls our attention to the fact that various ministries are required to carry forward the program of the church. The purpose of these ministries is to equip the saints for the work of the ministry. This we see is a ministry of multiplication. Thus the work of the church is not that of one person but of many believers united in a common task as outlined in the pattern above.

The fifth and final program element to be considered is *service*. This word points to ministry. In biblical terms it means "to minister." This is revealed in Luke 4:18: "Jesus came to heal the broken hearted, preach deliverance to the captives, recovery of sight to the blind, to set at liberty them that are bruised." This focuses on the meeting of human need, on serving one's fellowman. It means to help man satisfy his physical and emotional needs, to help solve moral problems, and both intellectual and spiritual difficulties. Such needs may be met by a wide variety of service activities involving people in individual actions, group actions (such as those of departments and classes), and whole church actions. Such ministry is to be conducted in the daily things of life, not merely in times of crisis opportunities, such as deaths, illness, troubled homes and people — although these are to be taken care of. All of the other program elements center here and should be the natural outcome of service in His name to all people everywhere.

The *responsibility* for building such a program lies first of all with the larger church body, with some denominational board. In this case they develop the various curricula and see that materials are created and published. In the *local church* the responsibility is borne by a board of Christian education which builds the total program for the church at large, or by a program committee or executive committee of some kind under the direction of the church governing body. In either case, the local church group responsible should *critically* adopt the denominational program and *adapt* it to its own needs. The various steps involved in this process will be dealt with in a later chapter.

C. ORGANIZATION FOR CHRISTIAN EDUCATION IN THE LOCAL CHURCH

1. *Nature and Purpose of Organization.* Organization has been defined as "the breaking down of the responsibility of the group as a whole into parts which can be assigned to individuals and committees." It provides the framework within which the program can be worked toward the goals set up. There are many good purposes of organization. We organize in the church and Sunday school to harness the power of God. Nothing can be accomplished without God's help and power. But very little can be done without arrangements to harness that power. God uses His power through human instruments. Organization makes possible an intelligent offering of human instrumentality to God for His use. It is a part of the program.

God Himself is a God of organization. Every living thing on earth is beautifully organized. Man himself is an intricate mechanism, the product of the creative power and design of the Creator. The heavens are wonderfully fashioned. The Old Testament record reveals how carefully God organized Israel for her sojourn in the wilderness. The New Testament shows how Jesus went systematically about His task. The early church organized itself for the task committed to it. The apostle Paul carefully organized the churches he established. Organization, however, is not an end in itself, nor does it assure success; but it is God's plan in nature and His will in the spiritual realm.

The benefits derived from good organization are quite evident. It will develop team work and unify the school. It is necessary to have sufficient organization to guarantee regular attendance and proper discipline. It helps to place responsibility. It lays the basis for efficiency and also provides instructional advantages. Without these things pupils cannot be taught properly. It will assist in enlisting members. It makes possible a program to reach out and touch the people. In organizing our forces for the work of Christian education committed to our task, we carry out the Scriptural admonition to "let all things be done decently and in order" (I Cor. 14:40).

2. *Responsibility for Organizing the Program.* The church is represented in the local situation by the congregation. That is where the primary responsibility lies. The program of the congregation is one and the same with that of Christian education. Chris-

tian education should not "take over" the church, but the church should "take *it* over." Ideally, the Sunday school is *in* the church, *of* the church, *for* the church, and *run by* the church. Officers and teachers should be elected by the church (this may be delegated). The Sunday school should be supported by the church and it should report regularly to the church.

Generally, the congregation is represented in its administration by some kind of ruling body which has delegated power from the congregation to conduct the business and administrative affairs of the local church. Some churches call this group the "Official Board"; others use the title "Council of Administration"; still others call it the "Board of Elders," " Board of Deacons," etc. In any case, this body is the administrative agency for the *total* church program. It makes overall provision therefore, for the administration of Christian education. It represents the congregation in receiving reports from all phases of the program of Christian education, particularly from the Board of Christian Education where that body exists.

Many churches place direct responsibility for organizing and building the program of Christian education upon another body called the "Board of Christian Education." This body too has delegated power from the official board to carry on its work, and it is responsible to the church through the ruling body. More will be said about this group in a later chapter where the various steps in building the program are considered. Of course where this board does not exist, someone else must see that proper steps are taken. Small churches should have this board or its equivalent.

The pastor too has direct responsibility in the task of Christian education. He is the administrative leader of the total church. He is responsible to the church. He is specifically responsible for giving guidance and supervision to the total educational program of the church.

Where none of these bodies are present in the local church, some kind of committee — an executive committee or a program committee — must be directly responsible for organizing, planning, and administrating the work of Christian education in the church. It may be, as it is in some of the small churches, that the matter will rest almost entirely on the pastor and Sunday school superintendent. In any case, the program of Christian education should not be neglected. The church ruling body should be careful to delegate someone for this great and important responsibility, even if it is only a committee.

3. *Guiding Principles for Organization.* Because of the great importance attached to Christian education, much study has been given to it. Principles are sufficiently well-known now and are the

common property of everyone. Some of these guiding principles, tested and proved over the years, are:

A. Scriptural
B. Practical
C. Comprehensive
D. Integrated

E. Graded
F. Simplicity and clarity
G. Flexibility
H. Democratic

The organization of the program must be *Scriptural*. This shows that the program must be organized to carry out the purposes of the church. The educational function of the church is clearly revealed, but it is not divorced from the other aspects of the church program. The apostolic church was organized as a unit and each function was integrated with that unit. The common objectives guided the whole process. Elders (also called overseers, bishops, etc.) were given the primary responsibility for instruction (I Tim. 3:2-7; Acts 20:28; I Pet. 5:2, 3). While it is recognized that these officers of the early church had many responsibilities, it is clear that education was one of them. It is also reasonable to conclude that the educational function, in the light of the overall responsibilities of these officers, was shared by those who had delegated authority from them. Undoubtedly, the church council or official board of the average church finds itself operating upon this very principle. Instead of operating without an understanding of their responsibility, the official board should be aware of its educational responsibility and lay out plans for its advancement. This principle, therefore, demands that the authority for organization of Christian education lies with the ruling body of the local church. They make it Scriptural and spiritual.

Organization must be *practical*. It should be designed to meet the needs of people in the church and community. Furthermore, it should meet the needs of the particular group in the local church situation. In this sense every church has an individuality of its own.

Organization must be *comprehensive*. No phase of Christian education should be neglected. There will be provision for administration, instruction, worship, fellowship, and evangelism. All age groups will be included. The program will embrace internal factors and external needs. It will include factors outside the walls of the church. It will have a world vision.

Organization must be *integrated*. This principle calls for two clear-cut requirements: (1) basic union with the primary organization of the congregation, and (2) correlation and interrelationships clearly recognized. This will include the possibility of division within the ranks. This principle also demands that responsbility should be located and centralized in one individual for each unit of the program. Correlation also demands that this responsibility should be distributed as widely as possible so that no one person shall occupy several positions at once.

Organization must be *graded*. If the program is to meet the needs of the people, it must be organized on the level of those needs. It must be adapted to the various age groups involved in it.

Organization should make provision for *simplicity* and *clarity*. Parts of the program should be organized only as they are actually needed in the local situation. Clarity of function and specific tasks which do not overlap should be clearly revealed. The job of each group or part of the program should be clearly seen in its relation to other groups and parts. This will avoid duplication.

Flexibility is needed in the organization. As the program develops, room should be left for expansion. This principle will also allow for making changes in the light of needs as they are discovered in the local situation. It will enable leaders to keep up with progress which is made in the field. Organization, therefore, should serve the needs of the program and be constantly reshaped to meet the demands of growth.

4. *Patterns and Plans of Organization.* Patterns and plans for organizing the program of Christian education are as numerous as there are denominations. Obviously it is impossible at this point to sample all these plans. Instead, we shall try to discover some basic designs which have been used to guide organizational procedures and then submit some suggestions on how to organize with the Scriptural pattern in mind. It is hoped that these suggestions will prove helpful to those who might be setting up a program in a new congregation, to those who might be re-organizing for purposes of growth and efficiency, and to anyone who is interested in practicing good principles in the field.

A survey of practices on the field at the present time reveals a wide variety of procedures. Too often one may find a completely confused situation in many churches. As their programs have grown, they have simply added on organizations and parts of the program with little thought of integration and correlation. The situation which results looks something like this:

CHART 1
A DECENTRALIZED SYSTEM OF ORGANIZATION

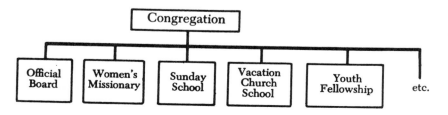

In this plan it is quite obvious that integration is lacking and little correlation is apparent. Whatever relationships might be present undoubtedly would be left up to the alertness of certain officers and workers who see the need.

On the other hand, circumstances have forced some churches to modify their organizations so that more or less by accident they have achieved a partially integrated and correlated plan of organization, somewhat like this:

CHART 2

A PARTIALLY CENTRALIZED SYSTEM OF ORGANIZATION

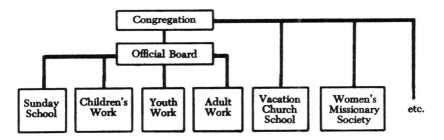

In this plan we have a semblance of centralized control. Here the official board is obviously conscious that it has some administrative responsibility for the total program, but it is apparent that the nature of this responsibility is hazy in this situation.

Some churches which use one of the two plans outlined above have continued to wrestle with the problem of integration. Some have been able to partially solve the problem with the church council plan of procedure. The plan takes the following form:

From this plan one can see an attempt to integrate the various organizations by representation on the church council of the various heads of the groups. Such representatives meet at stated intervals to consider jointly their common objectives and problems. The constitution of the council will vary with the size of the local church. In small churches it may be composed of members of the official board, Sunday school workers, and representatives of the other groups. The pastor serves as chairman. In large churches the membership might be restricted to administrative officers and departmental workers in the Sunday school, plus the presidents or chairmen of the other groups, under the chairmanship of the pastor. In this system it is quite apparent that the council serves in an advisory capacity to the various groups represented in its membership. This group can serve as a clearing house for all parts of the program. Through it the various groups can make their reports to

CHART 3

THE CHURCH COUNCIL SYSTEM OF ORGANIZATION

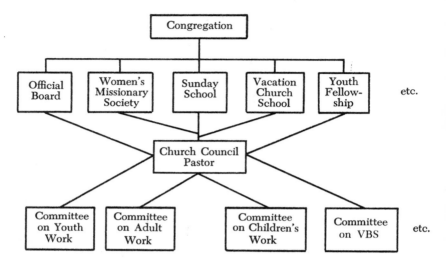

the congregation. The council may make policies, plans, and provisions for building the total program. On the other hand, this group is oversize. This precludes the possibility of detailed planning and evaluation in each of the segments of the program. It does not make for good administration. There is also the strong possibility that the interests of the church at large will be neglected. And it is quite obvious that allocation of authority to proper people in this system is not possible. Responsibility is spread too widely.

Still another plan which is used widely is represented in chart form as follows:

In this plan, the official board is composed of all members of the other boards and certain members at large from the congregation. The pastor is often the chairman and is *ex officio* member of all other boards. The board of trustees in this plan has delegated authority and responsibility for buildings, equipment, and finance. In some cases a board of stewards handles the finances. The board of deacons or stewards handles all other responsibilities, appointing and supervising the work of the Board of Christian Education. That board in turn has delegated authority to handle the entire program of Christian education for the total church.

A modification of this plan places the Board of Christian Education on equal footing with other boards, rather than subject to the board of deacons as shown above. Otherwise, the responsibilities

CHART 4

THE BOARD SYSTEM OF ORGANIZATION

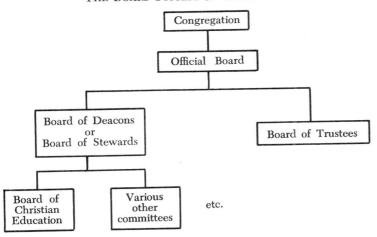

of the Board of Christian Education under this modified plan remain the same. The plan looks like this:

CHART 5

MODIFIED BOARD SYSTEM OF ORGANIZATION

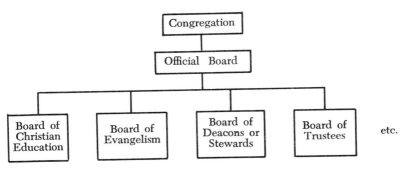

Another system is worthy of mention at this point. For want of a better name, it is called the "Board of Christian Education System of Organization." It appears as follows:

In this plan, the Board of Christian Education has delegated powers to make policies and plans for the total program of Christian education in the local church. It is responsible to the official board and through them to the congregation. The pastor is member *ex officio* of all these committees.

Under this plan the official board nominates the Board of

CHART 6

BOARD OF CHRISTIAN EDUCATION SYSTEM OF ORGANIZATION

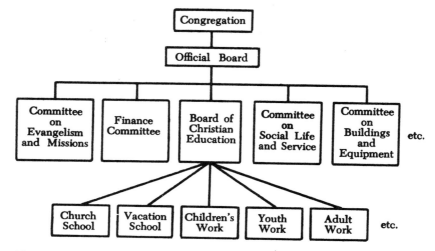

Christian Education and members are elected by the congregation. This plan is perhaps more popular now than any other plan. Nevin C. Harner has outlined certain objections to this plan.[1] (1) Other auxiliaries of the church will not be willing to yield to the supervision of the Board of Christian Education. (2) Christian education is here thought of as *one* task among many to be performed by the church. The primary advantage, on the other hand, lies in an integrated program of Christian education — at least as far as this one phase goes.

The last system, and perhaps the most visionary, to be offered for consideration has been called the "graded church plan." Instead of placing emphasis on tasks to be done, it stresses age groups. The plan looks like this:

CHART 7

THE GRADED CHURCH

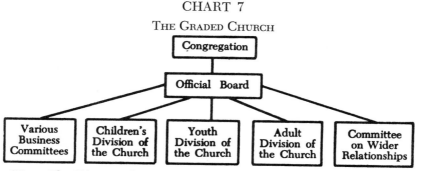

[1]From *The Educational Work of the Church,* copyright, 1939 by Nevin C. Harner, pp. 67, 68. Used by permission of Abingdon Press.

Admittedly this plan has unity. It also provides for a system whereby the whole church becomes organized for the work of Christian education. It calls for the practice of the graded principles in all phases of the work, and therefore separation of the various groups under this plan becomes necessary. It will be noticed also that all the traditional groups and organizations such as the church school, vacation school, etc. — are eliminated. Their functions, however, are retained in the divisional plan.

It is obvious that there are objections to this plan. The principle of true unity and integration is violated by too much decentralizing at the opposite extreme. The traditional groups and organizations have made unquestioned contributions to the life of the church and seemed entrenched to the very end. An administrative difficulty is presented by this plan. The official board simply has too much to do in this system. The various aspects of the program are too vast for one body to handle directly. Furthermore, this plan violates the Scriptural principle of evangelism. No one function, no matter how worthy it may be, must usurp the place of any other function, particularly that of evangelism. This plan lends itself too much to professionalism, and it definitely draws away from the volunteer lay principle of leadership and service. The danger of stratifying the congregation into age groups which likely will never meet is a very real one.

5. *Organizing According to the Scriptural Pattern.* The principle has already been stated that in building the Scriptural program one must follow the Scriptural pattern. This, we have discovered, is found in the example of the church and the requirements of the Word. The clue to the Scriptural plan is to keep ever before us the Biblical objectives for Christian education. These have been listed as evangelism, education, worship, and fellowship. The first responsibility of the church, therefore, is to realize its responsibility through these objectives. The whole process will take the following form:

In this plan the church is clearly in charge of the program of Christian education. This, along with keeping objectives in the forefront, helps to keep the plan Scriptural. The *official board* has delegated authority from the church to organize and administer the entire church program, including education. It is elected by the congregation and supervises the work of all boards and committees of its constituency. Its membership varies with the denomination.

The *pastor* is directly responsible to the congregation and is expected to supervise the total program. He works closely with all boards and committees of the official board. In some instances, he is chairman of the official board.

The *minister of education* is really an associate minister of the congregation. In this capacity he is subject to the authority of the

CHART 8

THE FUNCTIONAL PATTERN FOR ORGANIZATION[2]

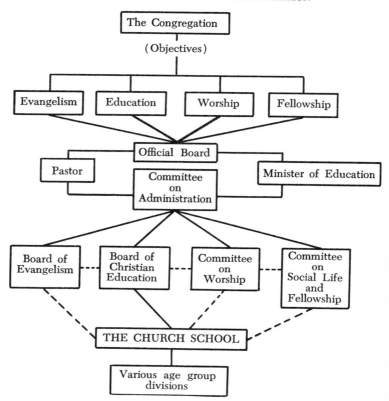

pastor and the official board. His responsibilities are particularly in the field of education, where he gives leadership, advice, and supervision. He works closely with the Board of Christian Education.

The *committee on administration* coordinates the work of the official board. It has particular responsibilities for planning the various agenda of business, budget making, and supervision of buildings and equipment. The purpose of administration is to set the stage for the functioning of the program. This committee, therefore, does not have absolute authority over the various boards and commitees of the official board. It works instead in an executive relationship.

[2]A chart showing how organization and administration in this plan are integrated can be found in Appendix I.

The *board of evangelism* is a subcommittee of the official board with primary responsibility for planning and coordinating the entire program of evangelism and missions for the total church. The *committee on worship* has the same responsibility in that area of emphasis. The *committee on social life and fellowship* plans for the entire church in both its internal and external relationships. The *Board of Christian Education* has the direct responsibility for planning and administering the entire instructional program for the congregation. It directs the work of the *church school,* which includes all in the congregation. Instead of breaking up the instructional responsibilities into several departments, this plan makes the church school the school of the church. Through administration the various divisions and departments are integrated into one school system. This will be seen more clearly when the program for administration is discussed later on.

This plan is in line with the best principles. It is Scriptural by keeping objectives and evangelism in the forefront. It is practical because it keeps the organization functional. It is comprehensive because careful provision is made for a *total* program. It is integrated because the vertical relationships are clear, and objectives make possible unity and correlation. It is simple because lines of responsibility are clearly evident. It allows for flexibility, particularly when the various age group divisions are reached. It is graded by focusing the entire program on meeting the needs of particular age groups.

Proper administration of this plan will overcome the objections of Harner to the official board type of organization. By giving the Board of Christian Education overall authority for the total program of education in the local church, the official board by policy can overcome some of the reticence of auxiliaries of the church to receiving supervision. Instead of thinking of Christian education as one separate task among many in the church, this plan provides clearly for integration in the total church program.

This plan is also adaptable to small churches. The official board will be smaller. The primary adaptation, however, lies in the various age group divisions of the church school.

D. ADMINISTRATION OF CHRISTIAN EDUCATION IN THE LOCAL CHURCH

1. *Adequate Administration Needed.* The operation and management of the program of Christian education is no small task, even in small churches. Most churches have realized that no one individual or even one group can properly take care of this responsibility. Administration by various groups of the varied phases of education, however, leaves the church open to serious overlapping and needless competition. Administration by one unusual leader of great ability violates many sound principles and restricts

the scope of the task as well as the quality to be desired. The Board of Christian Education plan has proved in many ways the best way to operate and manage the program. This plan of administration is revealed below in Chart 9.

CHART 9

THE FUNCTIONAL PLAN FOR ADMINISTRATION[3]

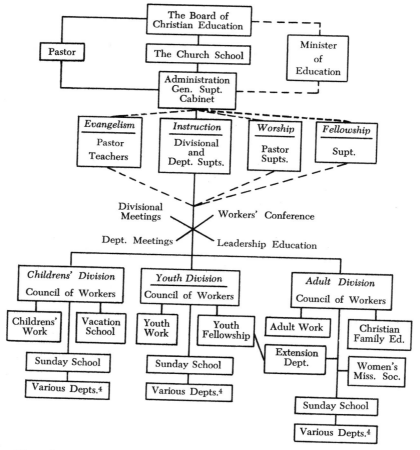

The plan above places the direct responsibility for the church school upon the shoulders of the Board of Christian Education. This board is to see that the church school is the school of the

[3]Chart showing how organization and administration are integrated in this plan is found in Appendix I.
[4]Details on grading found in Chapter 6.

church. Under the supervision of the board, the general superintendent becomes responsible for the administration and the execution of the policies and plans. The pastor and minister of education work as a team with the general superintendent in this great task. Also assisting him is the church school cabinet, composed of the general officers, divisional and departmental officers, pastor, and minister of education (if any). The purpose of this administration is to see that major objectives are achieved.

Each major officer of the program is assigned a primary area of responsibility corresponding with the objectives of Christian education, and they work under the general supervision of the board. The pastor and teachers specialize in educational evangelism. Instruction is directed by divisional and department superintendents. Worship is supervised by pastor and superintendents, as is fellowship. Committees give their assistance. The church is divided into three divisions for the work of Christian education: children, youth, and adults. In each of these divisions the Sunday school becomes the heart of the instructional program. This will keep this organization on a high level of usefulness and will make it possible for it to become the integrating organization in the program of instruction. Around the Sunday school are related the various other schools of instruction in the respective departments, such as vacation church school, etc. The divisions become, therefore, divisions of the church for instructional purposes. All age groups which are engaged in instructional activities of any kind are integrated into one division, thus meeting the demands of the graded principle. The Sunday school is graded into various departments according to the division.

In each division there is a council of workers to coordinate, plan, and administer the work of the division. The council is composed of the divisional superintendent, the various department superintendents of the Sunday school, and the various heads of the other divisions of instruction in the department, such as children's work, youth work, or adult work. The council also will conduct from time to time various divisional and departmental meetings to implement the work of the general program in their respective sections.

At stated intervals the general superintendent will call a "workers' conference" to consider problems and matters of mutual benefit and concern. The pastor and minister of education will lead the program in leadership education and development. This program is larger in scope than teacher training, for it embraces all workers in the program. Both these programs will include the teachers in their meetings and plans. It is also quite possible that special teachers' meetings will be called from time to time in the various divisions.

This plan is adaptable to the *small church*. The Board of Christian Education and the workers' conference can be combined into one group. Divisions can work as departments until the membership increases. Even where there are only two or three workers in the division, one of these workers can serve as both divisional and departmental superintendent. In the Sunday school where the class system of organization is present, one of the teachers can serve as head teacher for the division. In this case, the council of workers could be dispensed with until the church attendance and enrollment increases. Instead of a cabinet, the general superintendent could in this case meet with the head teachers and workers of the various groups. It is apparent that the same principles of administration and organization will direct these efforts in the small church as in the larger ones.

2. *Functional Administration Necessary.* The average book on Christian education in the local church approaches the consideration of the subject topically. The functional approach to administration is concerned with the *tasks* to be done and *who* is to do them. This kind of administration gives guidance to the various officers and workers in the program, giving them a clear picture of their areas of responsibilities and the duties to be performed in them. The functional approach, therefore, places emphasis first on people who serve the Lord and the duties they are to perform. This recognizes the principle of volunteer lay leadership and the need for training. In line with the functional plan of organization and administration pictured above, we are able to set forth the outline of the functional approach to Christian education in the local church as follows:

1. The Work of the Church — purpose, pattern, program
2. The Work of the Board of Christian Education — planning, policy-making, supervision of total program
3. The Work of the Pastor — leadership, leadership education, and evangelism
4. The Work of the Minister of Education — leadership, leadership training, and supervision
5. The Work of the General Superintendent — Administration and supervision
6. The Work of the Department Superintendent — instruction and supervision
7. The Work of the Teacher — instruction and evangelism
8. The Work of the Superintendent of Social Life and Fellowship — social life and fellowship
9. The Work of the Church in Wider Relationships — extension

In the functional plan of administration noted above, it is also possible to break down the general areas of responsibilities into

Work of the Pastor	Work of the Minister of Education	Work of the General Superintendent	Work of the Department Superintendent	Work of the Superintendent of Social Life	Work of the Teacher
Major area: Evangelism and Worship	Major area: Supervision	Major area: Administration	Major area: Supervision	Major area: Fellowship	Major area: Instruction
1. General leadership and helpfulness	1. General leadership	1. Administration	1. Administration	1. Fellowship	1. Preparation
2. Supervision	2. Leadership training	2. Supervision	2. Grading	2. Social Life	2. Information
3. Leadership development and education	3. Supervision	3. Standards	3. Curriculum	3. Recreation	3. Presentation
4. Evangelism	4. Administration	4. Organization	4. Teacher training	4. Relations	4. Extension
5. Building a co-ordinated and well-balanced program	5. Teaching	5. Grading	5. Records	5. Personal preparation	5. Evangelization
6. Administration	6. Shepherding	6. Worship	6. Promotion		6. Spiritual development
7. Personal preparation	7. Promotion	7. Promotion	7. Visitation and evangelism		
	8. Personal preparation	8. Conferences and meetings	8. Special days		
		9. Equipment	9. Fellowship		
		10. Special days	10. Worship		
		11. Finances	11. Expression		
		12. Personnel	12. Personal preparation		
		13. Personal preparation			

The duties in each of these areas of responsibilities are listed in the respective chapters in which these officers are considered. Where the staff is limited, as in a small church for example, then the superintendent and the pastor will be faced with the responsibility of allocating duties to specific persons and sharing in those duties. An illustration of this is supervision. This ordinarily is the work of the Minister or Director of Christian Education. Where this officer is not present, then the pastor and superintendent will have to bear the larger share of the responsibilities in this area.

detailed listings of duties for the *workers* involved in the responsibilities. The manner in which this can be done according to the *objectives* for the program is set forth on page 47.

In the discussion above, emphasis has been laid on function. We have seen that this concept of administration demands the placement of workers and their duties at the forefront of emphasis. It also demands that consideration be given specifically to *how* administration is carried on as well as what is done.

This position seems to be supported by Gable, who has indicated that the word "administer" means "minister," carrying the basic idea of servantship. Along with this he has stressed some very important principles by which all good administrators should operate. They are listed as follows:

1. Administration should operate in harmony with the objectives of the church.
2. Administration must be flexible, yet stable.
3. Administration must be concerned about people.
4. Administration performs a series of functions:
   a. Planning
   b. Organizing
   c. Executing
   d. Supervising
   e. Coordinating
   f. Publicizing
   g. Evaluating[5]

SUGGESTED READING — CHAPTER 1*

Anderson, *Charting the Course*, Chapter 2
Benson, *Techniques of a Working Church*, Parts I - III
Byrne, "The Ministry of Teaching," *Asbury Seminarian* (Winter, 1956), p. 36
Crossland, *How to Build Up Your Church School*, Chapter 1
Cummings, *Christian Education in the Local Church*, Chapter 1
Harner, *The Educational Work of the Church*, Chapters 1, 2, 3
Heim, *Leading a Sunday Church School*, Chapter 5
Hensley, *The Pastor as Educational Director*, Chapter 1
Hoiland, *Planning Christian Education in the Local Church*, Chapter 1
Lobingier, *The Better Church School*, Chapter 1
Munro, *The Pastor and Religious Education*, Chapter 5
Murch, *Christian Education and the Local.Church*, Chapter 11
NCCC, *Organization and Administration of Christian Education in the Local Church*, Chapters 1-3

[5]Lee J. Gable, *Christian Nurture Through the Church* (New York National Council of Churches of Christ in the U.S.A., 1955), pp. 34-38.
* See updated Bibliography at back of book.

Price, *et al, Survey of Religious Education,* Chapter 8
Riggs, *A Successful Sunday School,* Chapter 1
Schisler, *Christian Teaching in the Churches,* Chapter 2
Smart, *The Teaching Ministry of the Church,* Chapter 5
Squires, *Educational Movements of Today,* Chapter 5

THE WORK OF THE BOARD OF CHRISTIAN EDUCATION

OUTLINE FOR CHAPTER 2

(Policy-making and Planning)

A. THE PLACE OF THE BOARD
   1. Title
   2. Function
   3. Importance

B. CONSTITUTION AND ORGANIZATION OF THE BOARD
   1. Constitution
   2. Personnel and Membership
   3. Size
   4. Officers
   5. Organization

C. THE WORK OF THE BOARD
   1. Responsibilities
   2. Duties
   3. Meetings

D. RELATIONSHIPS OF THE BOARD
   1. To the Official Board
   2. To the Workers' Conference
   3. To the Chairman
   4. To the Superintendent
   5. To the Pastor
   6. To the Director

E. THE BOARD IN SMALL CHURCHES
   1. Constitution
   2. Duties
   3. Meetings

2 | THE WORK OF THE BOARD OF CHRISTIAN EDUCATION

(Policy-making and Planning)

A. THE PLACE OF THE BOARD

1. *Title.* A variety of titles are used by various church groups to identify this group of church workers. Some use "Commission on Education"; others use the "Committee on Christian Education." The most common term, perhaps, is the "Local Church Board of Christian Education." That is the title chosen for this consideration.

2. *Function.* In order that the local church may be organized and administered to carry forward most effectively the work of Christian education in its church school and in the congregation at large, the function of the Board of Christian Education is to plan, organize, and administer this work. Perhaps this function can be understood a little more clearly in chart form on page 54.

3. *Importance.* The significance of the board is determined by its strategic place in the total program and by the service which it renders to individual workers. This body is important also because no *one* person can effectively manage all the elements in a total program of Christian education. No *one* person can understand all the needs and interests of all age groups. No *one* person can know the most effective methods of meeting those needs. Furthermore, various viewpoints are needed to avoid overlapping, confusion, neglect, and frustration.

In delicate situations and instances where misfits of leadership exist, a group can handle matters more easily and tactfully. A group will more readily assure the continuity of policies in force when leaders change.

Such a board makes Christian education officially a part of the total program of the church. Wider representation in board personnel develops understanding support, new leadership, and maintains a democratic balance of power. This board can educate the congregation as to the importance of Christian education. It will give its full support to officers and teachers, thereby lifting the morale of all workers. By official appointment or election of officers and teachers, they feel the importance of their positions. The Board of Christian Education provides for Christian education *in* the church, *of* the church, and *by* the church.

53

B. CONSTITUTION AND ORGANIZATION OF THE BOARD

1. *Constitution.* Church policy in some denominations makes provision for the Board of Christian Education. In the local church, particularly where there is no denominational policy to guide them, a board may be created by appointment of the official board or through election of the congregation.

2. *Personnel and Membership.* People who have a vision and particular concern for Christian education should serve on the

CHART 10

The Board of Christian
Education

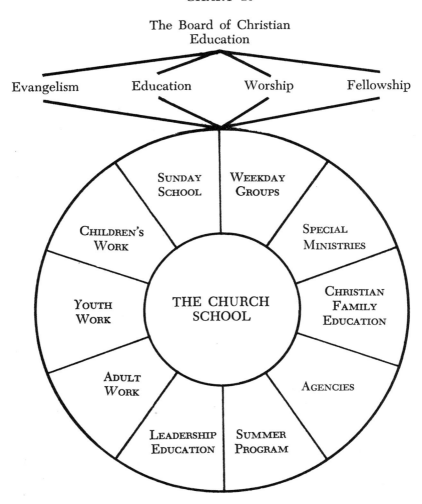

board. Of course where it is possible to secure people with experience and professional training, these should be given preference, provided they are genuinely Christian. The nature of the work of this board requires personnel of a representative character, that is, all age groups of the church and church school should be represented in its membership. At least one person for each of the facets of the church program as represented in Chart 10 should be included in the membership.

Membership on good boards would include at least the following workers:

(1) Pastor
(2) Director of Religious Education, if any
(3) General Superintendent of the Sunday School
(4) Department or Divisional Superintendents
(5) Representative of Women's work
(6) Representative of the Official Board
(7) Representatives of other church agencies
(8) Representative of youth
(9) Members at large
(10) General Secretary of the church school

All members are expected to attend regularly and be cooperative, alert, and energetic. Their vision will motivate long-range planning, and they should keep well-informed on Christian education in general, as well as the denominational program in particular. Members will believe firmly in the power of the Gospel through Christian education to change hearts and lives. In all things they will seek to be a spiritual example for all scholars. They will study their job, the program, and the needs of the congregation.

3. *Size.* Size will vary with the denomination and the local church. The board should be large enough to be representative but not too large to make meetings awkward. The concerns of the children, youth, adults, and the home should be definitely provided for. It is quite possible for one person to represent two or three interests at once. For example, a primary department superintendent may be a parent and bear a burden for missions, thus representing the home, the school, and missions.

It has been suggested that where enrollment reaches 100 to 250, from 5 to 7 members may be sufficient. In medium and larger churches, the situation may call for 12 to 15 members. Membership can be kept small and other leaders and workers invited occasionally to meetings of the board to give counsel and advice. In some instances denominational policy determines exact size.

Terms of office should be for a period of years — two or three — and more in some instances. Terms should be staggered to assure the continuity of the program.

4. *Officers.* A chairman is the first requisite. It has been suggested that this person be a consecrated layman, someone other than the pastor, superintendent, or director. His primary responsibility is to set up various agenda and to preside at meetings. Other officers include a vice-chairman and secretary. The director of religious education and Sunday school superintendent serve as executive officers of the board. The same principles should direct terms of office here as for the membership in general. The general secretary of the church school may serve as secretary of this group.

5. *Organization.* There are two general plans of organization used for sub-dividing responsibility. The first is called the "functional subdivision," where members are assigned to fields or functions, such as leadership education, curriculum, equipment, etc. The second plan is known as "age group division." In this plan members are subdivided for the oversight of age groups, such as children, youth, and adult divisions of the church school. Both plans have their advantages and disadvantages.

The combination plan seems to be the best one. This plan calls for each member of the board to take an age group as a permanent assignment. They also take special fields or functions for limited periods as the needs of the church may require. These may be changed from time to time without interrupting continuous age group study and oversight. The plan takes the following form:

Leadership Development **Worship — Evangelism** **Study — Temperance** **Service — Stewardship** **Missionary Education** **Fellowship — Recreation** **Housing and Equipment** **D.V.B.S. — Weekday School** **Parent-Teacher Organization —** **Home Relations** **Visitation**	**CHILDREN'S WORK** **YOUTH WORK** **ADULT WORK**

Certain committees might be set up on a permanent basis. Some of these might include audio-visual, evangelism, parent education, library, workers' conference, alcohol education, budget, leadership education, curriculum, worship, and stewardship. Special committees of a temporary nature may be appointed as needed.

It might be wise for a new board to operate as a committee of the whole until it gains experience. Committees can then be set up as they become necessary. With regard to the use of committees, the important thing to remember is to use only what is thought best for the church.

C. THE WORK OF THE BOARD

1. *Responsibilities.* According to Chart 10 the primary responsibility of the Board of Christian Education is for the church school, which is the school of the church. Its first duty is to see that the objectives of the church are realized through the school. These we have already seen are evangelism, education, worship, and fellowship. The board should be careful to see that *all* these objectives work in *all areas* of the church school. The process looks something like this:

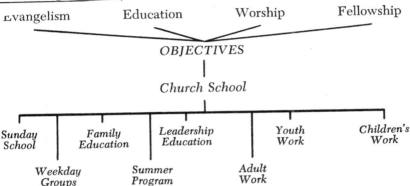

Evangelism   Education   Worship   Fellowship

OBJECTIVES

Church School

Sunday School | Family Education | Leadership Education | Youth Work | Children's Work

Weekday Groups | Summer Program | Adult Work

In carrying out the great program of the church through the church school, the board utilizes certain channels of expression which also are revealed on Chart 10 as the Sunday school, certain weekday groups, Christian family education, summer program, leadership education, adult work, and childrens' work. Under this plan a comprehensive program can be provided. Following the allocation of responsibility as recorded in Chart 10, the listing of various responsibilities of the board is as follows:

I. SUNDAY SCHOOL
    A. Time schedules
        1. This includes Sunday programs
        2. Dates for beginning and ending terms
        3. Dates for special days and periods, etc.
    B. Departments, classes, and divisions
        1. Organization, grouping, and grading
        2. Equipment and facilities
        3. Materials for study, worship, and activities
    C. Literature and supplies
        1. Curriculum materials for teachers and pupils
        2. Library for leaders and pupils
        3. Maps, pictures, audio-visuals of various kinds

    D. Leadership
      1. Selection and enlistment
      2. Training, dedication, and supervision
      3. Recognition
    E. Records
      1. Policies and supervision
      2. Reporting
    F. Evangelism
      1. Outreach
      2. Enrollment and attendance
      3. Personal and group techniques
    G. Finances
      1. Budgeting
      2. Expenditures
    H. Wider relationships
      1. Cooperation with other Christian groups
      2. Home and parent education
      3. Public relations

Under this plan the Sunday school becomes the heart of the instructional program.

  II. WEEKDAY GROUPS

    A. The Vacation Bible School

The responsibilities for this part of the program can be performed best through the appointment of a subcommittee on Vacation Bible School work to plan the year round for the school. Responsibilities of this committee would include vision, promotion, advance preparation to include the type of school, time schedules, place, finances, facilities, materials, leadership, training of workers, transportation, publicity, and a calendar, organization, administration, and follow-up.

    B. Weekday Church School

Here again a special committee of the board is quite useful. Responsibilities would include planning the type of school, promotion and publicity, program, organization, attendance, curriculum, and reports. Where there is participation with other groups, the committee shall have delegated responsibility to work with them,

    C. Other activities with possible weekday possibilities include recreation, scout work, special study classes, training classes, special group meetings, and mission study groups.

 III. CHRISTIAN FAMILY EDUCATION

    A. Cultivation of home members in all age groups
    B. Study groups in marriage and Christian home-making

C. Program for home-church school cooperation
D. Parent education classes
E. Christian literature for the home
F. Observation of special days, such as National Family Week
G. Plan for family activities in the church, such as family nights, family picnics, hobbies, etc.

IV. SUMMER PROGRAM

A. Survey the opportunities
   1. Previous church participation
   2. Opportunities for children, such as vacation church school, story hours, camps, hikes, picnics, junior camps, etc.
   3. Opportunities for youth, such as camps, conferences, institutes, assemblies, projects, etc.
   4. Opportunities for adults, such as family camps, picnics, travel caravan, conventions, etc.
B. Determine the needs to be met in the local church
C. Possible cooperation with other groups and community activities
D. Build the program, give publicity, and report results
E. Correlate with the total program

V. LEADERSHIP EDUCATION

A. Survey the leadership needs
   1. List the positions to be filled; evaluate present program
   2. Study the present staff for improvement
   3. List possible leaders; make a talent survey
B. Plan, promote, and administer a program
   1. Leadership enlistment, selection, recruitment
   2. Set up leadership classes and/or schools
   3. Provide a continuing leadership training class
   4. Regular workers' conferences
   5. A workers' library
   6. Departmental planning conferences
   7. Observation and apprenticeship
   8. Supervision
   9. Institutes, conventions, workshops
   10. Clinics
   11. Laboratory school
   12. Audio-visual resources
   13. Guided reading and correspondence courses
   14. Teacher and worker covenants
   15. Recognition for achievement and constant evaluation

VI. ADULT WORK

    A. Survey of present organizations as to aim, functions, activities and results

    B. Better coordination of the work

    C. Creation and supervision of a young adult fellowship

    D. Plan, promote, and administer a program to include:

        1. Evangelism

        2. Home or Extension Department

        3. Projects

        4. Recreation, social life, and leisure time

        5. Stewardship

        6. Children and youth relationships

        7. Cooperation in community character building projects

        8. Week-night classes

        9. Discussion groups

      10. Men's fellowship and women's missionary groups

      11. Particular attention to single adults

      12. Particular attention to older adults

VII. YOUTH WORK

    A. Survey of present organizations as to aim, functions, activities, and results

    B. Plan, promote, and administer a program to include:

        1. A Sunday evening society or fellowship

        2. Special interest groups, such as music, drama, missions, etc.

        3. Correlation of church school with other activities

        4. Projects

        5. Service training activities, possibly an extension group

        6. Supervised recreation, social life, leisure time activities

        7. Special classes and discussion groups

        8. Christian home instruction

        9. Evangelism

      10. Preparation for adulthood

VIII. CHILDREN'S WORK

    A. Survey of present organizations as to aim, functions, activities, and results

    B. Plan, promote, and administer a program to include:

        1. Provision for nursery, beginner, and primary children during morning worship service

        2. Provision for a junior church service

3. Extra-sessions which might include Bible clubs, choirs, extended Sunday school class periods
4. Scouts, Cubs, Brownies
5. Pastor's classes

2. *Duties.* The responsibilities of the board as outlined in the previous section largely determine what its duties are. On the other hand, because of the fact that there are important matters which overlap in these areas, it is necessary to make a separate listing of duties for the sake of clarity.

There are certain general duties of the board which call for a determination of policies and planning the total program for the church school. In this the board is responsible for directing the total educational program of the congregation, seeing to it that there is comprehensiveness, balance, and quality in all that goes on. More specifically, the duties can be outlined as follows:

1. To organize, manage, and supervise all educational activities in the Sunday school, weekday schools and organizations.
2. To coordinate the work of the various organizations and committees.
3. To see that the total program is properly organized.
4. To study the educational needs of the church.
5. To provide for all necessary meetings of the various committees and organizations in the program.
6. To provide for the proper observance of special days, such as Rally Day, Promotion Day, etc.
7. To see that adequate supervision is made available to all divisions of the church school.
8. To keep the members of the congregation informed on the needs, progress, and program of the church school.
9. To see that special education on the evils of beverage alcohol, race relations, world peace, community service, etc., is given to the congregation.
10. To encourage cooperation in community matters and interdenominational projects.
11. To constantly review the curriculum situation and counsel with workers on materials and methods.
12. To allocate space for departments, classes, and other groups and to study needs for facilities.
13. To provide a library for leadership needs.
14. To set up and administer a program of leadership education.
15. To select and elect officers and teachers for the church school.
16. To provide guidance for youth in Christian vocations and in Christian service.

17. To create throughout the church school both an attitude and a program of evangelism and to cooperate in the total church program of evangelism.
18. To cooperate in the church program of missions, to cultivate the missionary spirit in all divisions, and to provide a definite missionary curriculum for all age groups.
19. To seek to constantly increase enrollment and attendance and also to make careful provision for an absentee follow-up program.
20. To constantly evaluate the total program to determine if needs are being met and standards are being maintained.
21. To plan carefully for a budgetary system of finances in the church school.
22. To insure that all pupils are taught the Christian use of money, promoting the tithe as a minimum of giving.
23. To carefully make provision for definite program of training in Christian service in all divisions of the church school.
24. To provide for a program of Christian family education and careful home-church cooperation, planning also for various family activities in the church program.
25. To assist the pastor and various administrative officers in making vital decisions.
26. To arrange for the keeping of accurate and permanent records and to make them available where needed.
27. To create a program calendar of the year's activities in all divisions of the church school.
28. To arrange for church representation in all phases of Christian education worthy of participation outside the local church.
29. To make careful reports of its work to the official board and see that others make regular reports.
30. To modernize all procedures and techniques as far as possible.
31. To meet regularly for the study and discussion of the educational needs and problems of the congregation.
32. To execute resolutions and policies handed down to it by the official board.
33. To consider and act upon proposed changes in the program.
34. To set up standards and qualifications for the leadership of the church school.
35. To adopt a "Standard of Excellence or Achievement" for the church school.
36. To give particular attention to the work and needs of the Sunday school teacher.

37. To constantly study its own work, duties, and responsibilities.
38. To give careful consideration to the interpretation of music in the church, to the quality of music, to its ministry, and to the training of the pupils in all divisions.
39. To provide opportunities for youth initiative.
40. To inform the people about the denominational program of Christian education, including schools and colleges.

3. *Meetings.* The board meets as often as it is necessary in order to conduct its business. Once a month has been recommended and once a quarter is a minimum. In some situations where the workers' conference is held as a separate meeting, the board will meet either once or twice a quarter and the conference the remaining time.

All meetings should begin on time and members should be notified by the secretary in advance of each session. Meetings should be characterized by fellowship, worship, and information as well as business. As far as possible, details should be left for committees and only general policies decided upon in the group meeting. This can be assured where the chairman carefully makes provision for an agendum of procedures for the meetings. Each agendum might take something of the following form:

Brief devotional
Opening statements by —
    The pastor
    Other ministers
    Chairman
Inspirational address or discussion (may be at end)
Minutes
Reports from —
    Superintendent
    Other officers
    Various committees
Consideration of various recommendations by —
    Officers
    Committees
Program emphases
Local needs
Old business
New business
Adjournment

The agenda will vary from time to time and the chairman may find assistance from his executive committee, the pastor, and superintendent.

Where the board is meeting for the first time, the first thing to do is effect the organization by the election of a chairman, vice-chairman, and secretary. Then set a time for the meetings. Following this a brief survey of the duties of the board can be given by the pastor or some other responsible officer. Finally, determine a plan for studying needs and for supervising the work.

In all instances careful records of the various meetings of the board, along with reports which are made to it, should be compiled and preserved for future reference.

D. RELATIONSHIPS OF THE BOARD

1. *To the Official Board.* The official board is the ruling body of the church. The Board of Christian Education has delegated authority from the official board to conduct the educational affairs of the church school. Regular reports to the official board should be made by this body. The official board, on the other hand, will not usurp the authority of the Board of Christian Education, but will give it freedom to work within its sphere of responsibility.

2. *To the Workers' Conference.* The board has the power to formulate all policies concerning the total program of Christian education in the church. This makes the workers' conference subject to the board. The workers' conference is not a policy-making body. Instead it is composed of all workers in the church school who come together for study, inspiration, discussions, worship, and fellowship. The workers' conference, however, may make recommendations to the board.

3. *To the Chairman.* The chairman of the board is the presiding officer, not an administrator. He is responsible for the various agenda, but should ask the help of the pastor and superintendent. He is the servant of the board.

4. *To the Superintendent.* The church school superintendent is an executive officer of the board. His responsibility is to see to it that the policies and plans of the board are carried out in the Sunday school. He reports regularly to the board about the Sunday school and submits any recommendations and suggestions he deems wise.

5. *To the Pastor.* The pastor is the overseer of the total church program. This makes him responsible to the official board for the church school. He works within the board, not over it. He provides information, inspiration, counsel, and supervision for all that goes on. He is a member *ex officio* of all organizations and committees. The pastor is a leader, not a dictator.

6. *To the Director.* The "director of religious education," or "minister of education," is also an executive officer of the board. His greatest service is given through supervision and leadership training. As such he is a Christian education specialist and his voice should carry great weight in board meetings, but he too will not be

a dictator. He will work closely with the chairman, pastor, and superintendent.

E. THE BOARD IN SMALL CHURCHES

1. *Constitution.* It has been suggested that in small churches the Board of Christian Education and the workers' conference be combined into one group. Both groups will function as one body, with the exception of the election of the workers. In the latter case, the teachers and officers can withdraw from the meeting until this matter has been attended to.

In addition to the members of the Board of Christian Education already suggested in a previous section, the following members should be added in the small church:

All Sunday school teachers and assistants
All church school officers and assistants
All other leaders of other groups

In small churches the board itself may not be larger than three members.

2. *Duties.* The duties in the case of this combined body will be those of both the Board of Christian Education and the workers' conference, with the exception of the election of workers as mentioned immediately above. This plan in no way reflects on the ability of this group to perform the various responsibilities called for.

3. *Meetings.* In general, the procedure for meetings should follow the monthly plan. This is more necessary where the two groups are combined than it would be where they meet separately. All suggestions for conducting the meetings will serve here as well as in the cases mentioned above.

SUGGESTED READINGS — CHAPTER 2*

Byrne, H. W., *My Sunday School Handbook, For the Board of Christian Education,* No. 4

Cummings, Oliver D., *Christian Education in the Local Church,* Chapter 3

Hoiland, Richard, *Planning Christian Education in the Local Church,* Revised Edition, Chapter 1

Kramer, A. H., *A Guide for Boards of Christian Education in Congregations*

Methodist Publishing House, *The Commission on Education and the Workers' Conference*

National Council of Churches of Christ, *The Board of Christian Education in the Local Church*

Vieth, *Improving the Sunday School,* Chapter 2

Vieth, *The Church School,* Chapters 2-6

* See updated Bibliography at back of book.

THE WORK OF THE PASTOR IN
CHRISTIAN EDUCATION

OUTLINE FOR CHAPTER 3
(Leadership, Training, Evangelism)

A. THE PLACE OF THE PASTOR IN CHRISTIAN EDUCATION
  1. His Office in the Church
  2. His Place in Christian Education
  3. His Convictions
  4. His Preparation
  5. His Work

B. GENERAL RESPONSIBILITIES OF THE PASTOR
  1. General Duties
  2. The Pastor's Place in Sunday School
  3. Some Relationships

C. SPECIFIC RESPONSIBILITIES OF THE PASTOR
  1. General Leadership and Helpfulness
  2. Administration
  3. Building the Program
  4. Leadership Development and Education
  5. Supervision
  6. Evangelism and Missions
  7. Summary

3 | THE WORK OF THE PASTOR IN CHRISTIAN EDUCATION

(Leadership, Training, Evangelism)

A. THE PLACE OF THE PASTOR IN CHRISTIAN EDUCATION

1. *His Office in the Church.* The pastor is the overseer of the total church program. In this his duties are many and varied. He should be a preacher of the Gospel, a church administrator, and a shepherd of the flock. No better summary of his office can be found perhaps than that recorded in Ephesians 4:11, 12. Here the minister is referred to in the Greek as a "pastor-teacher." Literally, this means he is a "shepherd-teacher." The true pastor is both a shepherd and a teacher in one person. The pastor must be a teacher. The teacher must be a pastor.

Other references reveal a wide variety of titles by which the preacher was known: minister (Matt. 20:25-28); (I Tim. 4:6), shepherd (John 21:15-17), builder (I Cor. 3:10-15), elder (II John 1:1), father (I Cor. 4:14, 15), overseer (I Tim. 3:1), steward (I Cor. 4:1), and watchman (Heb. 13:17). In the New Testament sense, the pastor is a man who has an inner call from the Holy Spirit and an external call from the church to preach the Gospel. His purpose is to address the minds and hearts of men with Scriptural truths for the salvation and spiritual profit of his hearers. The method which he uses is that of witnessing to God's saving truths, which includes interpreting, expounding, and exhorting; he has a message from God.

In I Timothy 4:11-14, we read of three main public duties of the preacher: (1) to read publicly, followed by an address or a sermon; (2) to teach doctrine; and (3) to exhort the people. The Greek here for "reading" is *anagnosis* which means a public reading, or a reading followed by a public address somewhat similar to a sermon. Teaching or doctrine *(didaskalia)* is an appeal to the mind. Exhortation or preaching is an appeal to the heart. It is to be noted that preaching *and* teaching are part of the pastor's duties.

2. *His Place in Christian Education.* The history of Christian education reveals that ever since apostolic times the pastor has not been too closely associated with the field of Christian education in the local church. Someone has said, "He began to persecute, then to patronize, then to participate, and now pushes and prays

for the Sunday school." Actually, when Robert Raikes started his Sunday school in England, many pastors openly fought his program. It remained for John Wesley to demonstrate in the early Methodist societies that the Sunday school was a place of great ministry for the pastor among the children.

It is reported that Dr. E. Y. Mullins, once president of Southern Baptist Theological Seminary in Louisville, Kentucky, commented on the strategic place of the pastor in Christian education by saying: "A hostile pastor equals a dead Sunday school; an indifferent pastor equals an inefficient Sunday school; an officious pastor equals a chaotic Sunday school, but a cooperating and sympathetic pastor equals an efficient Sunday school."

Today it is widely recognized that the field of Christian education, particularly in the Sunday school, presents the pastor with unprecedented opportunities for pastoral ministry. Recognizing that the scope of his work is so large that he cannot possibly carry out all responsibilities personally, many pastors specialize in this field and find that it broadens their ministry many fold. As a church administrator, there are many duties beyond the power of one man to perform. An efficient and trained staff will provide a well-organized and smoothly operating church.

Recognized by many as the greatest single source and most fruitful field of evangelism, large numbers of pastors are training their staffs and workers to be under-pastors and evangelists. By working through the Sunday school, many contacts are made for evangelism. As a shepherd, pastors are finding that the church school staff produces many under-shepherds who will visit the sick, make new contacts, and follow up old ones. In fact, a place of service is provided for all members.

Thus we may conclude that the pastor holds a central place in the field of Christian education, for it provides the widest possible opportunities for him to carry out his teaching and evangelistic ministry.

3. *His Convictions.* To properly carry out his functions and satisfactorily realize his purposes in this field, the pastor must have definite convictions regarding the work. He must believe thoroughly in Christian education. A vision for the work is required. He must have information. No pastor knows his field if he does not know Christian education. He cannot be a true pastor without carrying out his responsibilities in this area of church work and life.

The pastor must be convinced that he must give time to this work. The National Sunday School Association recommends that the pastor should give fifty percent of his time to the field. This does not mean that he will have to do all the work himself. Instead by training others for the task he will spend his time most profitably and enlarge both *his* ministry and that of his workers. He must be convinced that all phases of the ministry can be covered in this field.

Plenty of preaching material is provided in this field of labor. Thus it covers all phases of Christian ministry — Bible study, doctrine, history, theology, philosophy, literature, illustrations, stories, etc.

The pastor actually needs to be a philosopher of Christian education. He should be able to exercise solid principles of the field, not only for his personal benefit and guidance, but also for the benefit of all the workers so that both an efficient and fruitful ministry can be realized.

If the pastor manifests relative indifference to the work of his church school, someone should quietly suggest some reading which might bring him to a deeper appreciation of its importance. Others might take him to outstanding conferences, workshops, and conventions so that he might be informed and inspired.

4. *His Preparation.* Many pastors have realized after a period of service on the field that they need the skills so necessary for a teaching ministry. The writer has repeatedly had the experience of consecrated pastors relating to him their desires for greater knowledge in the field of Christian education. Many have felt that they were improperly trained for the pastoral work in their school careers.

Academically speaking, a college education resulting in the bachelor's degree is considered a bare minimum for ministers today. If possible, there should be graduate work beyond college. In many denominations the Bachelor of Divinity degree is considered a necessity for entrance. Included in such graduate work should be a proportionate amount of studies in the field of Christian education in the local church. In fact, some might desire to specialize in this field. Where such school training is lacking, ministers will be forced to personal study of the problems which beset them. This can be done through reading and through personal observation of other schools, churches, and methods. Attendance at conventions, workshops, institutes, and conferences have proved greatly beneficial to many ministers.

5. *His Work.* A functional approach to the work of the pastor in Christian education demands that his work in the church be specific as well as general. While it is true that the pastor has general oversight of the total program, it is wise for him to have particular tasks for his personal attention because of their strategic importance in the building of the kingdom and in the development of the local church.

Careful study and analysis of the work of the pastor in Christian education reveals at least six areas of responsibility to which the pastor can give personal and particular attention. In fact, he should become a specialist in all six of these areas.

1. General leadership and helpfulness
2. Administration
3. Building a well-balanced program
4. Leadership education and development
5. Supervision
6. Evangelism and Missions

B. GENERAL RESPONSIBILITIES OF THE PASTOR

1. *General Duties.* The pastor should give general direction and supervision to the total program of the church. He is obligated, therefore, to know Sunday school work. He should attend the Sunday school as regularly as possible. His presence there is an encouragement to the staff. He also finds there many opportunities for study and supervision.

The pastor should work with the Board of Christian Education and the general superintendent in formulating and directing the policies of the school. He may teach a Sunday school class, depending on the size of the church, but looking at the matter as a whole it is best perhaps for him not to teach a class. Some men find it profitable, however, and get a substitute to take the class while visitation and supervision is engaged in. Other men find that it hinders them in carrying out administrative and supervisory responsibilities, not to speak of tiring them considerably for the preaching service.

There are some things that the pastor definitely should not do. He should avoid being general superintendent. This may be necessary in small schools or in a school that is just being started, but he should see that the right person is selected as soon as possible. Pastors should not *run* the Sunday school. If they do, they will likely neglect other things which should be done. There is a multiplicity of pastoral duties, sermons, study, prayer, etc., which demand attention. Pastors cannot do everything. There is also the possibility of usurping the work of some good layman if the pastor "takes over" the Sunday school. Instead, it is much better for the pastor to develop leaders for the various offices — enlisting, training, and directing them instead of "running the show." Time must also be given to overcoming opposition to policies and practices which are good. Too much administration will prohibit this duty.

Harner pointed out that the minister who is his own director has five main functions in the field of Christian education:

1. He must interpret the privilege and task of religious education to the entire congregation

2. He must visualize the congregation's program of religious education as a whole and organize it as a unit
3. He must vitalize the major educational agencies within the congregation
4. He must procure, train, and inspire leaders
5. He must participate directly at necessary and strategic places in the program of religious education[1]

2. *The Pastor's Place in Sunday School.* As pastor of the whole church, he should be the spiritual and inspirational head of the Sunday school. Success will greatly depend on his cooperation. He will stand by the officers and teachers on the staff, assisting, encouraging, correcting, supporting, and equipping them for the task. Successful pastors have found that it pays to give particular attention to the Sunday school because in so doing they build up the church as a whole. Leaders, workers, and members of the church of tomorrow are in the Sunday school today. Such pastors find that a full ministry is provided by the opportunities which are presented in all phases and divisions of Sunday school work. For the pastor to be busily engaged in Sunday school work and development means that he is busily engaged in the work and development of his church. The pastor has an important place in the Sunday school.

It is the pastors duty to see that the work of the Sunday school is done and done well. If the superintendent and workers lag, it is the pastor's solemn responsibility, with all possible tact, kindness, but firmness, to see that good results are obtained. In doing this, the minister does not merely exercise pastoral authority, but rather demonstrates leadership tempered with Christian charity.

3. *Some Relationships.* Besides holding a strategic place in the Sunday school and being responsible for certain general duties, the pastor bears some close relationships to various personnel in the total program. Here lie some of his general responsibilities as he deals with other people in the program.

First is his relationship to the *director of religious education.* The pastor is head of the church and, as such, is head of all Christian education. The director, therefore, is legally under the direct supervision of the pastor and is responsible to the pastor. While this is understood, at the same time there should be definite responsibilities assigned to the director and clearly understood by the pastor. Furthermore the pastor should strongly back the director in all his efforts. The director cannot do his job well without the pastor's full support and cooperation. They should be

[1]Nevin C. Harner, "The Educational Ministry of the Church," in Philip H. Lotz, ed., *Orientation in Religious Education,* copyright 1950 by Pierce and Smith, Chapter 30. Used by permission of Abingdon Press.

friends and work closely together. The pastor will be careful to recognize the achievements of the director. In a very real sense, the director is a "minister of education," assistant to the pastor in charge.

The *general superintendent* is the administrative head of the Sunday school. He should, however, seek the advice and help of the pastor. Pastor and superintendent are friends and should talk things over. They should confer on matters of personnel, and they need to cooperate fully and closely in the whole church program. They should recognize the work as one work. Therefore the pastor should have a Sunday school vision and the superintendent a church vision. The pastor will recognize the achievements of the superintendent. Someone has suggested that the pastor should work *with* the superintendent, not *over* him. Someone else has pictured the relationship in the following manner:

The Superintendent is practical; the pastor is inspirational
The Superintendent is mechanical; the pastor is dynamic
The Superintendent organizes; the pastor creates

In the case of removing the superintendent, it is wise for the pastor to go slowly and work through the Board of Christian Education.

The pastor has a close relationship to *department superintendents*. He can reveal the place of the departments in the life of the school. He can point out that the various department superintendents and associates are assistants and co-laborers with the general superintendent. He can emphasize that the big job of Christian education demands many hands and that the department superintendent helps to concentrate the task.

The pastor will occasionally place materials for worship into the hands of the department superintendents and offer helpful suggestions from time to time. He will assist them in the work of supervision. He will attend departmental meetings and conduct departmental conferences. In such meetings he can be greatly helpful in solving touchy problems and they can cooperate in evangelism and leadership education. In every way possible the pastor will support the department superintendents by prayer, by encouragement, by sympathy, and by giving adequate recognition of their achievements.

We shall now turn to some of the specific responsibilities which the pastor faces.

C. Specific Responsibilities of the Pastor

1. *General Leadership and Helpfulness.* The pastor is often referred to as "general flunky." By this is meant that he should be ready to do a great many things and help everybody. Applied to the program of Christian education, this is certainly true for the

pastor. There are many things which the average pastor can do to help everything and everyone. He is an overseer (Acts 20:28).

One of the first of these opportunities is his chance to *inspire* his staff and congregation. This can be accomplished by keeping the educational work of the church before the official board and congregation. An informed people often are inspired people. In a very real sense, in doing this the pastor can develop "the spirit of Christian education." From the pulpit the pastor can show the meaning of Christian education and its importance for the home and church. Included in his pastoral duties should be calls upon the workers themselves to help, encourage, and inspire them. He might find it convenient on these visits to suggest helpful materials and new ideas to them. The workers need pastoral care sometimes more desperately than the members. By taking his workers to conventions, conferences, institutes, workshops, and area meetings, the pastor evinces an interest in his workers and demonstrates his concern for their success. By suggesting good reading materials, books, clippings from magazines, and the general use of materials and methods, he proves his burden for the problems and welfare of his staff. Through the personal use of bulletin boards, posters, newspapers, and announcements, the pastor reveals his concern for the general dissemination of information on the progress which is being made in the total program of Christian education in his church. All these things provide indications of a good spirit in the pastor's leadership and they serve by way of example to motivate and inspire others to follow in his stead.

Inspiration can be developed through the cultivation of an "inner circle" of Sunday school friends who have the pastor's point of view and training (if it is good). In fact such a group is often imperative if the pastor is to succeed in developing his program. This is particularly true where new ideas are suggested and new steps are in prospect. In developing this group, the pastor should constantly keep before his workers the "bigness" of the job with the challenge and necessity of it. Actually, this amounts to indoctrinating the group. Some might call this "politicking," but if it is kept "sanctified," it is appropriate, particularly where standards and not personal opinion become the guiding factors. Preliminary conferences with the superintendent and various chairmen of the several groups will be greatly helpful in keeping the pastor's point of view in the forefront. By all means, the pastor's motives should be clean and true to the objectives of Christian education. This will demand an education in perennial evangelism and thereby keep first things first.

Inspiration can also be achieved through a deliberate attempt on the part of the pastor to create and maintain "a mind to work."

Diligence and patience in application will soon result in inspiring accomplishments.

As we have seen, the pastoral function includes teaching. A second opportunity of general helpfulness is provided, therefore, through pastoral *instruction*. Inspiration must be followed by information, both of which will lead to intelligent action.

The pastor should challenge his congregation to Christian service and instruct them as a whole in these responsibilities at the morning and evening worship services, at mid-week services, and other available opportunities. Very helpful at this point is the practice of some pastors in preaching on what constitutes "a call" to Christian service, as well as the specific need for physical, mental, and spiritual preparation for the task. He should use every opportunity for creating in parents a sense of need for the program of Christian education. He should keep the principle of gradation ever before his people — graded curriculum, evangelism, materials, equipment, and workers. He should constantly emphasize the necessity of adequate support financially and otherwise for the total program. His instruction will not only take these informal channels but at stated intervals he will conduct classes of various kinds to inform and train his people.

Thus we see that there are many intangibles in this area of leadership and helpfulness. In general, however, it can be said that a pastor who cares, who shares, and who dares is the pastor who can rejoice in the success of his program.

2. *Administration.* Administration refers to management and operation. Someone must be in charge of the program. As pastor, the minister is anxious for the total church to be managed and operated properly. This naturally includes the Sunday school. But he must be careful not to supercede the superintendent in this area of responsibility, for this is the primary duty of that officer. Instead, the pastor will give general oversight and supervision to this phase of the program to see that it is done properly and efficiently. In this, he will be particularly responsible to see that objectives are clearly held before the staff and pupils and that standards are kept high. He will be particularly vigilant in holding the great primary objectives before the entire church school. These we have seen are evangelism, education, worship, and fellowship. The pastor will see that all these phases are effectually promoted and practiced in the church school.

The pastor will encourage the organization of a Board of Christian Education or a "committee on education" to help plan and coordinate the program. He should see that there is a general superintendent to serve as an executive officer of this board and as an assistant to the pastor in carrying out the educational function of the church. He should encourage the creation and maintenance of the departments in the work of the church school, with department superintendents to assist the general superintendent and to administer the work of the various departments.

He should see that overlapping and neglect in certain areas of the work are overcome. He will recognize the three divisions of the work — children, youth, and adult — and see that they are integrated in the total program.

The pastor should be alert in making provisions for the various schools in a good program, such as daily vacation Bible school, school of evangelism, school of missions, and school of leadership training.

Along with the board and in close cooperation with the superintendent, the pastor will be responsible to see that proper and adequate buildings and equipment are provided. All pastors should know the importance of good facilities. They should study their building, both while it is empty and while it is being used, to see that it is used to optimum efficiency. Where it is evident, such study will include the possibility of a new building or the improvement of the present facilities. In all of these matters the pastor's helpful suggestions will be of great assistance to the superintendent.

The proper administration of the church school demands team work. In this the pastor, the superintendent, and the director of religious education form the team. Actually, the superintendent and director are co-workers with the pastor in the important task of helping the Board of Christian Education establish policies and build the total program of the church school. These three should confer frequently and regularly on all matters pertaining to the educational program. Although they are mutually concerned with the total program, yet each will be given specific responsibilities. In general, the pastor will be concerned primarily with evangelism and leadership, the superintendent with administration, and the director with supervision and training.

It is important also that team work be accomplished among the workers. A practical approach to this is the use of a manual of procedure in which clear job descriptions are recorded and duties listed. Vieth gives an illustration of such a manual by suggesting that the following items be included in it:

Purpose: To make the work of officers and teachers easier through having a definite way of doing things.

Item 1: Hours of church school sessions

Item 2: Pupils: ages, enrollment procedure, attendance standards, discipline

Item 3: Use of facilities

Item 4: Organization of the church school, terms of office, etc.

Item 5:   Duties of officers and teachers

Item 6:   Supplies[2]

3. *Building the Program.* The objectives of Christian education demand a balanced and well-rounded program of Christian education. As an administrator, the pastor should take particular pains to see that the church school has this kind of program. In so doing, he will have a stronger church program because the program of the church school is actually the program of the church.

By virtue of his position, the pastor should lead in the development of a coordinated and well-balanced program. In the development of the program, however, the pastor should avoid "pet programs" and promote all the organizations. This demands a *critical analysis* of the denominational program with a careful *adaptation* to the local church situation.

The pastor should remember that, on the one hand, "set" programs lead to ritualism and the danger of spiritual poverty, but on the other hand no plans often lead to the danger of "stereotyping the Holy Spirit." The Spirit can lead for a year as well as for one day. It should be noted further that the Holy Spirit can help such a program to be flexible, though planned. In the light of these facts, the pastor should help the board and all others concerned to wisely, carefully, and prayerfully develop a calendar of activities for the entire year.

The following is an example of the type of activities which can possibly go into a calendar for the local church school. Leaders, of course, will not want to adopt all the suggestions for the annual calendar as listed below, but the list will serve as a guide in the selection of activities to be included.

October

1. Rally Day
2. Missionary Day
3. Columbus Day
4. World Temperance Sunday
5. Halloween
6. United Nations Day
7. Laymen's Day
8. National Bible Week
9. World-wide Communion Sunday
10. Good month to emphasize an enlargement program
11. Promote December items

November

1. Armistice Day
2. Thanksgiving Day
3. Missionary Sunday
4. Decision Day
5. All Saints Day
6. Good month to emphasize Bible study
7. Promote Christmas plans
8. Plan for workers' training class
9. Or weekly training class
10. Monthly workers' conference

[2]Paul H. Vieth, *The Church School* (Philadelphia: Christian Education Press, 1957), p. 67. Used by permission.

12. Promote Thanksgiving plans
13. Check on Sunday School for the past year
14. Sunday school year begins
15. Monthly workers' conference

11. Census
12. Father-Son Banquet

December

1. Universal Bible Sunday
2. Christmas Day
3. Missionary Sunday
4. Promote training plans
5. Monthly workers' conference

January

1. Epiphany Sunday
2. Missionary Sunday
3. Universal Week of Prayer
4. New Year's Day
5. Monthly workers' conference
6. Youth Week

February

1. World Day of Prayer
2. Boy Scout Sunday
3. Lincoln's Birthday
4. Washington's Birthday
5. Valentine's Day
6. National Freedom Day
7. National Crime Prevention Week
8. Plan Easter activities
9. Missionary Sunday
10. National Smile Week
11. Monthly workers' conference
12. Promote March plans

March

1. Palm Sunday
2. Missionary Sunday
3. Plan a loyalty campaign to follow up Easter
4. Monthly workers' conference
5. School of missions
6. Promote April plans
7. Plan for May
8. Mother's Day plans

April

1. Easter Sunday
2. Arbor Day
3. National Baby Week
4. Loyalty Campaign
5. Plan for D.V.B.S.
6. Childrens' Day plans
7. Father's Day plans
8. Graduates
9. Good Friday
10. Missionary Sunday
11. Monthly workers' conference

May

1. May Day
2. National Family Week
3. I Am an American Day
4. National Day of Prayer
5. Pentecost Sunday
6. Memorial Day
7. Promote D.V.B.S.
8. Promote summer camps
9. Missionary Sunday
10. Mother's Day
11. Mother and Daughter Banquet
12. Monthly workers' conference

June

1. Flag Day
2. Childrens' Day
3. D.V.B.S.
4. Father's Day
5. Decision Sunday
6. Promote youth camps
7. Missionary Sunday
8. Monthly workers' conference

July

1. Independence Day
2. Missionary Sunday
3. Plans for new year
4. Plans to get vacationers
5. Monthly workers' conference
6. Summer leadership classes
7. Sunday school picnic

August

1. Friendship Day
2. Homecoming Sunday
3. Missionary Sunday
4. Plan for Promotion Day
5. Plan for Installation Day
6. Plan for Rally Day
7. Plan for enlargement
8. Get vacationers back
9. Monthly workers' conference
10. Summer leadership training classes

September

1. Labor Day
2. Missionary Sunday
3. Robert Raikes' Birthday (Sept. 14)
4. Religious Education Week
5. Promotion Day
6. Installation Day
7. Plan for Rally Day
8. Plan for enlargement
9. Monthly workers' conference
10 Start attendance crusade
11. Workers' retreat to plan for new year's work

It is further suggested that a theme for each month be adopted. Such a theme will prove to be the guiding factor in setting the pace of the promotional emphasis for that particular month. An example of this type of planning is provided by Crossland's book on *How to Build Up Your Church School* (Nashville: Abingdon Press, 1948), pp. 132-140. A year's program can be laid out if your workers will plan to give time to a retreat in the fall of each year during which the program is definitely planned (see Appendix II for an example).

Several factors enter into the planning for the annual program. A curriculum chart which shows the subject matter being used for the current year is quite helpful in selecting themes for the various periods. In this way activities can be integrated and correlated with the classwork for the period. Such charts often list month by month the subjects of study of each of the organizations of the church.

A denominational calendar is quite helpful in planning. Church school plans should be correlated with as many denominational emphases as possible during the year. Particularly is this true of special days being observed throughout the denomination. It is also wise to compile a list of your local church groups with their plans so that conflicts and overlaps can be avoided. The wise pastor will also provide the planning committee with his pulpit plans for the year. All these items are quite helpful and useful in creating an integrated and correlated program for the entire church school.

The planning committee is faced with the problem of determining a pattern of action for the year. This, of course, is done best through the selection of monthly themes. Someone has suggested the following pattern for use in constructing the year's calendar, not so much as a formal plan but as a framework of planning. The plan calls for three periods of emphasis as follows:

Period one —   Easter to Autumn
                Theme: "Revitalizing the Church"
Period Two —   Autumn to New Year
                Theme: "Rallying the Forces of the Church"
Period Three — New Year to Easter
                Theme: "Winning People to Christ"

In Period One an examination of the activities and organizations of the church will be made to affect any possible changes and improvements. It will be a period of planning and follow-up. Problems of attendance, the quality of worship, and standards will be emphasized. Summer plans also will be included in this period.

Period Two will be concerned with the presentation of plans to the whole church. Preparation for visitation evangelism will be made. Training conferences of all kinds will be conducted.

Period Three gives complete emphasis to evangelism. All methods of evangelism decided upon will be used, driving toward an Easter goal.

Besides being concerned with plans and patterns for action, the planning committee should be acquainted with the techniques of program planning. The following suggestion may prove helpful to some committee in planning its year's calendar:

Column 1 — List the events of the past year. Consult your bulletin.

Column 2 — Provide a list of events and prospects in the denominational calendar and general church year.

Column 3 — Create a list of local church events and plans, such as Rally Day, leadership training, evangelism, stewardship, missions, etc.

Column 1	Column 2	Column 3
Program last year	Denominational and church year	Local church plans

After studying the three columns, make a synthesis and correlate the plans into one master calendar. September should find the plan ready to operate. It has been suggested that a few areas have been neglected in some programs, such as church music and Christian culture, including concerts, book reviews, plays, and dramas.

The whole process for the master calendar would probably look something like this:

CHART 11

The Master Calendar

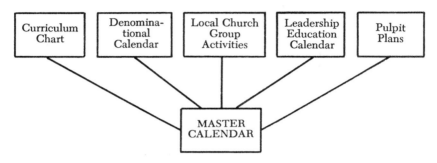

The plan above is suggested for use by some central planning group or committee, particularly the Board of Christian Education. The method, however, is also adaptable to the individual units of the program, such as Sunday school, youth groups, etc. In fact, the master calendar for the entire program can be created more easily if the individual units of the program would prepare their calendars in advance.

4. *Leadership Development and Education.* This area provides the pastor with perhaps his greatest opportunities. The development of leaders will multiply his ministry many fold and result in greater fruit for the kingdom. In this area there are general responsibilities in addition to those which concern the building of a specific program of leadership training.

It is reputed that Walt Whitman said: "Produce great persons; the rest follows." This is certainly true in church leadership. Good people filled with the Spirit provide a rich source of leadership potential for development. One of the first general responsibilities of the pastor, therefore, is to see that all teachers and workers have a genuine Christian experience and evangelical theology. Where these are missing, the statement of Jesus applies: "If the blind lead the blind, both shall fall into the ditch" (Matt. 15:14).

The pastor should be constantly on the lookout for prospective teachers and workers who might become leaders. This is a major concern. Skill in leadership selection is one of the greatest assets the pastor may have. This skill should be exercised not only for the church school but also in the selection and training of church officers, such as elders, deacons, stewards, and others.

The pastor needs to be constantly alert to all possible service opportunities. There is a wide variety of categories in the average church and church school which call for the service of many people. Some of these include teaching, reaching the people, winning the lost, training other workers, music, social life, keeping records, social service, and many full-time callings in the church program at large.

Recognizing the tremendous opportunities presented through training the membership, the pastor should not, if he has the time, be averse to becoming director or superintendent of a leadership training department. In this department there will be training sessions of a variety for adults who can be taught perhaps in a continuous leadership training class which meets during the Sunday school hour. Possibly the same kind of class might be used for prospective adult workers in the larger churches, or week-night classes can be organized. There certainly will be many opportunities for in-service training situations for those already in the program.

The best way, however, for the pastor to realize the largest fruit in leadership development and training is through a formal program of leadership education. Here the responsibilities of the pastor are shared largely by the Board of Christian Education, the general superintendent of the church school, and the director of religious education. This brings us to consideration of some of the specific things a pastor can do in this regard.

In building the program of leadership education in the local church, there are specific objectives which need to be set up. Some of these objectives include:

1. To see what we need leaders for, where they can serve, and why
2. To discover the right kind of leaders
3. To enlist leaders and stress a divine call to service
4. To train leaders, both initially and through a continuous program of growth
5. To insure a continuous resupply of leaders

The first logical step to take in building a program is to make an analysis of the situation in the local church. This will perhaps cover first an evaluation of the present agencies involved in the program, such as workers' conferences, clinics, leadership classes and schools, institutes, supervision, observation, etc. Some kind of an evaluation schedule will prove helpful in making this analysis and in checking the effectiveness of the various agencies. Appendix III, No. 1 is a sample of this kind of evaluation schedule. What are the results of the work of the teachers? A self-rating scale will prove beneficial at this point. This too is illustrated in Appendix III, Nos. 2 and 3. What are the results in the hearts and lives of the pupils? Their classwork? Upon the basis of these representative findings it is possible for the planning group to set up goals for the program as well as to discover what positions need to be filled and the type of personality and training necessary to fill them. Greatly helpful to responsible leaders at this point is the use of a "standard" for a workers' training program. Harner has some good suggestions in this regard. The standard which he developed can be examined in Appendix III, No. 4.

Some of the specific steps to be taken in building a good program of leadership education are:

1. Determine the leaders needed
2. Locate the leaders
3. Enlist the leaders
4. Train the leaders

In *determining* the leaders needed, the appointment of a special committee to list all possible jobs and duties which need to be performed in the work of the church and church school is beneficial. Form No. 5 in Appendix III shows the results of the work of one committee of this kind. Such a list could be presented to the Board of Christian Education to serve as a guide in putting people to work for the Lord. It will also give some indication regarding the types of personality needed.

In *locating* the leaders, the first step is to pray. "Pray ye the Lord of the harvest, that he will send forth labourers into his harvest" (Matt. 9:38). Prayer and faith together with a formal and thorough program of leadership training will revolutionize the program in the average church. In addition to these things, a leadership census or survey will prove helpful. The purpose of this census would be to develop a list of all the talents and interests of the members of the congregation which might in any way be used in the work of the church program. Several illustrations of these talent surveys are provided in Appendix III, Nos. 6-9.

The suggestion has been made that a special Sunday be set aside for work of this kind, with the pastor preaching perhaps on the "Stewardship of Time and Talents" or some similar subject. The sermon could be followed by having the members fill out the census blanks. Those not present could be contacted later until the membership has been covered thoroughly. It should be made clear, however, that the mere signing of the census blank does not automatically secure a place of service in the church, but instead it provides an indication of the interests and willingness of the signer. Such a list should be kept up-to-date as new members are received.

Besides the talent survey, every other available opportunity for discovering prospective workers should be used. These opportunities might include borrowing talent from other groups, part-time workers who have special talents, and careful personal surveys of adult classes and groups together with the young people.

After prospective leaders are located, the next step concerns recruitment and *enlistment*. Here again it has been found that the appointment of a special committee facilitates this work. A "committee on personnel" appointed by the board will have the responsibility of receiving the list of leaders needed and the results of any leadership and talent surveys which have been made. The first duty to be performed by this committee will be to set up a philosophy of selection, enlistment, and approach. Perhaps one of the first things to be done by the committee is to confer with representatives of all groups to evaluate all possible prospects which might be found in those groups. Another suggestion is to make the matter of selection and recruitment of chief concern at some special workers' conference where plans can be crystallized.

The personnel committee will work out a pattern of approach in contacting the prospective leaders by visitation. A minimum of two people, more in some situations, will call on the prospects for a personal interview. Enlistment of leaders should not be attempted in a public meeting. Careful decisions should be made as to who will do this calling. The pastor and superintendent have formed many successful teams in many churches. In other instances the general superintendent and department superintendents have been successful. Still others have used the superintendent and/or members of some adult classes.

Some churches have found an "Annual Member Enlistment Sunday" useful. This special day is preceded by careful preparation, by finding leaders and getting them signed up. All signers should be assured that a period of training will be provided for them at some time during the immediate church year. On this occasion the pastor preaches on some phases of Christian service. The week following, the committee does the calling necessary. The best time for this program seems to be in the fall in connection with "Christian Education Week."

High spiritual standards should direct the committee in its initial plans for selection. Wherever possible certain professional standards should be used in evaluating possible prospects for places of leadership. Some churches have been bulwarked for this emphasis by planning for an annual volunteer "life-service" appeal to the youth of the church. The visitors should proceed in this program with great faith and confidence in the leadership of the Holy Spirit, who is the great Motivator of the Lord of the Harvests to send forth laborers into His harvest.

After much prayer and careful consideration, the committee picks the person who seems best qualified for the position and makes an appointment for an interview. The enlistment approach should be made on the highest possible level. It should be one of high challenge. Actually, the places of service are places of ministry. This should be pointed out. Such places of service will require the sacrifice of time, energy, and personal desires. Serving Christ is not easy, but the committee should encourage each prospect with the assurance that there will be definite support and careful periods of training provided for him. No worker should ever be enlisted without being given assurance that much will be expected of him and training provided. Make it clear that attendance, promptness, keeping records, attendance at workers' conferences, calling in homes, etc., will be expected of all workers. There should be definite explanation of all duties and responsibilities involved in the position. Weldon Crossland has a suggested sales talk for use by committees in enlistment procedures. See his *How to Build Up Your Church School*, pp. 44-46.

The committee should capitalize on the deeper urges of life which produce action. Some of these motives include:

1. Gratitude to God for the blessings He has bestowed
2. Love for Christ and the desire to share this love
3. Interest in and love for children, who are so easily molded
4. Love for young people who stand at life's crossroads
5. A burden for perplexed adults who need guidance and encouragement
6. The merited approval of those who admire and respect Christian workers (not the best, but useful with some)
7. A sense of partnership in a great enterprise
8. Desire to maintain and develop the great institutions of the home and the church
9. The joy of soul winning
10. The smile of God's approval

The committee should also plan for the offering of many incentives during the period of enlistment emphasis. Some plans might call for:

1. Frequent presentations and challenges from the pulpit of the need and importance of God's call and service
2. Dedication services and special appeals for consecration
3. Exaltation of the dignity of the ministry of teaching
4. Development and use of a "Leader's Covenant" (See Appendix III, Number 12)
5. Expression of appreciation for service rendered both privately and publicly
6. Use of every possible promotional device to inform the people

7. Provision of surroundings, tools, and equipment which make the work pleasant and satisfying
8. Provision of selected and promising leaders with special training privileges
9. Making of appeals through the use of Scripture, poetry, prayer, stories, and pictures
10. Use of personal testimonies of successful and fruitful leaders

Some other ways to stimulate interest might include round table discussions of needs and prospects, challenging speakers, reports by delegates to conventions, demonstrations, exhibits, and the observance of a special Leadership Education Day.

Enlistment should be followed by *training* and education. No program is complete without choosing carefully the methods and training procedures of a comprehensive program of leadership education. Immediate training plans for the new prospective leaders should be made. Do not start out new prospects without giving them some help. This can be done in a variety of ways, including guided reading on age group and teaching methods, personal interviews with older teachers and superintendents, special classes over short periods of time, observation and apprenticeship, and summer leadership and laboratory schools.

The Board of Christian Education will help to determine the policies to be carried out in a formal long-range program of leadership education. The various agencies of training will be canvassed and those which most adequately fit the local situation will be chosen. There is a wide range of agencies at the disposal of wide-awake churches today which include:

1. Leadership classes and schools — local, denominational, interdenominational
2. In-service training for those already in the service, including supervision and coaching
3. A continuing leadership class, conducted each Sunday much as a Sunday school class is operated
4. Observation of others on the job
5. Workers' conferences composed of all workers who come together at stated periods for inspiration, study and training
6. Departmental planning conference and right use of literature
7. Apprenticeship
8. Supervision
9. Guided reading through a leadership library, periodicals, and leadership guides
10. Sunday school institutes
11. Local church clinics

12. Laboratory schools
13. Teacher rotation
14. Visits from professional workers
15. Correspondence courses
16. Workshops and conventions
17. One-day demonstration school for teachers[3]

Many churches are finding it inconvenient to set up a leadership training program by themselves, so they combine with sister churches and denominations in cooperative leadership schools. Here professional skills and ideas can be pooled to the great advantage of all concerned. This is particularly true of small churches. A typical program might include:

6:00 p.m.   Supper or light lunch
6:45 p.m.   Class period
7:50 p.m.   Intermission, demonstration, or coffee break
8:00 p.m.   Class period
9:00 p.m.   Dismissal

The major sources for curriculum materials are supplied by the following:

1. Protestant Standard Leadership Training Curriculum, product of over 40 denominations in cooperation with the National Council of Churches
2. The Evangelical Teacher Training Association, an interdenominational and evangelical group with headquarters in Chicago
3. The leadership training manuals of the Southern Baptists, Assemblies of God, and the publications of Standard Press and Judson Press are widely used
4. Local denominational materials

All these plans can be made practical and workable through the careful planning and the creation of a calendar of leadership activities. Here the month by month program for the local church is plotted out in detail. See Appendix III, No. 10 for an illustration. It is wise for small churches and churches new at the job not to try too much at first. Move slowly into your new program of education for service. Develop a gradual, long-range program.

Adequate recognition of the place and service of the church school staff is not complete until personnel are presented before the church and consecrated to their tasks. This is accomplished in many places through the use of an annual installation service. The entire staff is brought before the congregation, dedicated to their tasks, given a charge by the pastor, and laid upon the hearts

[3]Used by the Presbyterian Church, U.S.A. See Herman J. Sweet, "They Learn to Teach by Watching." *International Journal of Religious Education* (October 1956), p. 21.

of the congregation for prayer, support, cooperation, and encouragement. Reference to Appendix III, No. 11 will provide the reader with a sample order of service for an installation program. In connection with this service, some churches recognize the workers who have completed study courses in preparation for their work. Others use an annual banquet for all church workers, at which time recognitions of achievement and expressions of appreciation are given.

Leaders may be motivated to take training for the Lord's service through the following suggestions:

1. Have key leaders sold on the need for it
2. Distribute promotional material on such training
3. Have the board pass a policy in which training is required
4. Visit other churches which are successful; get testimonies
5. Have the pastor preach on the subject
6. Use self-rating scales; give tests and discuss the results
7. Use audio-visual aids to promote the cause
8. Pray much about it

5. *Supervision.* While supervision is primarily the particular work of the director of religious education, the pastor and other officers must assume their share of the burden and to take heavy duties in this regard where there is no director in the program. Where administration places stress upon organization, operation, and management, supervision emphasizes improvement. As "overseer" of the entire program the pastor should constantly stress the need for quality and improvement.

Supervisors work a great deal with people. In this regard, the pastor is forced to work with people as they *are*, rather than what he wants them to be, constantly striving, of course, to bring them to his ideal. Here the pastor is faced with a twofold obligation. First, he must get his workers to see the *need* for improvements. People expect the pastor to be acquainted with programs, standards, and methods. If he is, he can be greatly helpful in leading his workers to higher levels of achievement.

The pastor should be willing to compromise on matters of method to get his staff to adopt better ones. It is not wise to try to revolutionize the program all at once. Modification and adaptation are best for a while. Then too there are the traditions which have already been set up. Many pastors have had difficulty because they failed to recognize the accomplishments and habits of the past. In all these efforts toward improvement, the pastor should be a friendly helper, not a "snooping spy."

The work of supervision demands that certain emphases take precedence over others. The pastor should remember that pupils are more important than programs. Strategic phases of the program as a whole and where greatest efforts should be concentrated lie in the cradle roll, nursery, and adolescent departments. Adult education, too, should have its share of attention, for this is often a greatly neglected area.

Working with officers and teachers demands *mutual* planning and sharing of ideas. Here it is the responsibility of the pastor to work *within* his group, but not over it. In fact, good supervision has been characterized as "intimate sharing in burden-bearing." Where it is recognized that there are joint responsibilities, it should also be noted that there needs to be definite accountability. Many staffs suffer from lack of reporting techniques by which evaluations can be made and progress charted.

Important in the work of the supervisor is the setting up of spiritual objectives and adequate standards of procedure. He is concerned also with discovering unused talent, in-service training, the elimination of undesirables, and the use of correct methods. In all this work the supervisor will constantly make evaluations, discover weaknesses, and suggest remedies. The tremendous scope of this work leads the average pastor to insist on the placing of a director of religious education on the staff.

Perhaps the place of largest emphasis in supervision directly concerns the teaching-learning process. Supervisors can do a tremendous amount of good in encouraging, inspiring, and assisting teachers with their classes. Procedures include sitting down with these workers, sympathetically analyzing their difficulties, and working with them toward solution. Techniques include pre-class planning, class observations, and post-class conferences. Where the pastor cannot do this kind of work, perhaps his wife or some consecrated public school teacher or other professional worker can be used. Where a director is present, of course such work is his immediate responsibility.

An adequate and comprehensive program of supervision will be designed to cover the following areas in the program:
1. Building morale
2. Improving workers
3. Improving human relations
4. Working together
5. Personnel administration
6. Improving the curriculum
7. Improving class instruction
8. Improving worship
9. Improving service training and activities
10. Improving social and recreational activities
11. Improvement through tests and measurements
12. Constant self-evaluation

6. *Evangelism and Missions.* Evangelism is the supreme work of the church, and this makes it likewise the primary work of the

church school. The pastor's particular duty is to see that evangelism has its proper place in the program and that good practices are observed.

Certain general duties call for the pastor to instruct the teachers and workers in evangelistic techniques, visit to carry out the responsibilities of an evangelist, and train others to do the same. Where "decision days" are practiced in the local church, the pastor is expected to be the supervisor and director of all activities engaged in on that day. Where preparation for church membership is stressed, the pastor should be the teacher of the church membership class.

The pastor should be alert to the fact that evangelism in the church school will vitalize the entire staff and program and infuse it with a spirit which nothing else can impart. Where the evangelist spirit and practice is evident, growth is the natural result.

Many pastors have found the Sunday school to be their chief evangelistic agency. Studies have revealed this organization to be the feeder of the church. In fact, the Sunday school program is designed to be an informal soul winning agency. The very nature of the Sunday school is to reach, teach, and win the people. Barnett has listed ten major reasons why the Sunday school should be used as the chief evangelistic agency in the church.

1. It has the Bible as its textbook
2. It has soul winners in its work
3. It has the lost in its membership
4. It has the influence of the combined workers on its staff
5. It prepares hearts to receive the gospel message
6. It has graded lessons
7. It has graded buildings
8. It has graded pupils
9. Its record shows that this is true
10. The relation of conversions to gains in the school shows this place[4]

In the light of these pertinent facts, the pastor should make evangelism the heart of the church school work. This can be done in a large number of ways. First, he can provide a good example in the practice and techniques of personal work and soul winning. This is accomplished through the manifestation of a burden for souls and the actual demonstration of soul winning procedures. He can guide the teachers and workers in their own efforts, often saving them from the practice of improper techniques. In fact, it should be understood that they are partners in this great task. The pastor should keep himself in constant readiness for the teach-

[4] J. N. Barnett, *The Place of the Sunday School in Evangelism* (Nashville, Tenn.: The Sunday School Board of the Southern Baptist Convention, 1945), pp. 29-40.

ers' call for assistance. He can encourage the workers in their efforts and will often deal personally with the pupils on the spot. In the church at large, the pastor can do much good by preaching to the congregation on evangelism. He can be invited to speak to classes and departments, giving invitations under the leadership of the Spirit. The pastor can give his time to conduct classes of training for visitation campaigns and soul winning efforts. He can pray much for and with the workers. Plans and policies will be greatly affected by the attitude of the pastor. Perhaps one of his greatest services can be rendered in cooperation with the superintendent and others in the selection of officers and teachers who will be evangelistic in spirit and practice.

The program of evangelism in the church school should not be left to chance, but instead there should be careful annual planning. The pastor must not hesitate to assume a major role in this planning. He should be a co-worker with the various superintendents, teachers, and parents in this most important work.

Of great assistance to the pastor in planning the work is the appointment of a special committee on evangelism for the church school. Personnel might include the pastor, superintendents, and representatives of teachers and departments. In small churches all the teachers might serve on the committee. The organization of this committee may vary, but the primary responsibilities are clearly outlined in Chart 12 as follows:

CHART 12

RESPONSIBILITIES OF THE COMMITTEE ON EVANGELISM

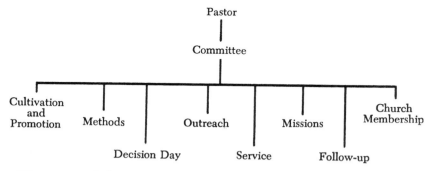

The responsibilities as outlined above concern the entire church program, including the church school. Primary duties of the committee would include:

1. Development of the spirit of evangelism in the church
2. Planning of the year's program of evangelism in the school

3. Distribution of literature on evangelism
4. Creation and maintenance of a record system which shows names, addresses, conversion, church membership, service record
5. Use of letters and forms to teachers, pupils, and parents
6. Promotion of the spiritual life of the school
7. Promotion of seasons and spirit of prayer
8. Guide in leadership training in evangelism, particularly teachers
9. Where used, to help the pastor prepare for "decision day"
10. Make plans for the use of special days, such as Easter, Children's Day, Rally Day, etc.
11. Promotion of spiritual life in the home
12. Assistance in soul winning methods
13. Promotion of visitation campaigns, census taking, etc.
14. Develop prayer lists for unconverted
15. Instruction classes in church membership and Christian life
16. Plans for cooperation in community efforts of evangelism

The observance of decision day gives the entire church school a chance to participate in the program of evangelism and personal soul winning. The primary advantage of this day is that it gives pupils a chance to express outwardly their relationship to Jesus Christ. This day, however, should not be merely an occasion of counting heads. The danger of working with children with mass methods of evangelism is that they might respond in "sheep" fashion, merely following the leader who "happens to go forward." Instead, there should be careful and prayerful preparation made for this day.

Some church schools use Palm Sunday as a favorable time for the day. Others would use some day in January or February in order to give time for a follow-up class of instruction led by the pastor in preparing converts for Christian living and church membership.

Careful advance preparation needs to be made for decision day. This would include special seasons of prayer and particular attention given to the regular program to provide an evangelistic atmosphere. Every possible effort should be made to bring the pupils to Christ before the actual day arrives. Then the day can be used for testimony.

The program for the day should be in the hands of the pastor. Songs, prayers, lessons, activities, etc., should all be planned to reach a spiritual climax for the day. Special prayer meetings should be conducted to invoke the power and presence of the Holy Spirit on that occasion. Special speakers may be used, but the pastor's influence is considered of greatest value at this time. Particular efforts on the day can be made in the various departments to bring pupils to a decision for Christ. At the appointed time a general assembly can be conducted where reports can be made and praise offered to God. Follow-up of decision day would include instruction in Christian living, church membership classes, assignments to places of service, and development of devotional life.

While most workers in Christian education are appreciative of methods of evangelism, many realize that fruit in soul winning in the church school depends to a larger extent upon the spirit and atmosphere of the school. Where the Holy Spirit is honored and obeyed, there is a good chance of having this atmosphere. The development of this "spirit" is largely the product of the work of the pastor and church school leaders. Each and every one of these workers must know experimentally what it is to be born again and to "walk in the Spirit." Joy, peace, humility, and cooperation, with a burden and love for souls, will certainly go far in producing this spirit. The atmosphere will be characterized also by reverence, law, order, and decency. The spiritual life of the school depends also on the spiritual condition of the pupils. Leaders should stress therefore the importance of regular attendance, Bible reading, prayer, service, and soul winning. Occasional opening programs will help in this regard. Such a school will be honored with much fruit.

The program of evangelism is not complete without working for outreach and enlargement. "Go ye into all the world." One of the most effective ways to evangelize is to reach people and get them into the church school. The Sunday school forces stand organized. Everyone should be put to work to reach others. Advance preparation, however, is essential. Added space and more workers are necessary. Workers need to be trained to visit and follow-up. On the whole, contests are to be avoided in this work. Steps for this kind of emphasis are so well known that large discussion is unnecessary.

1. Prepare the space and the workers
2. Build a prospect file
   a. Through a church family census
   b. Through a community census
3. Visit the prospects
   a. Training and prayer
   b. Regular visitation periods by classes, departments, and teams
   c. Reports
   d. Follow-up
   e. Extension work of all kinds
4. Assimilation

Evangelism, in its comprehensive meaning, includes conversion and regeneration, growth, training, and Christian service. This kind of evangelism does not end with decision day. It demands that everyone be put to work extending the kingdom. People are saved to serve. This service includes opportunities at home, "in Judea and Samaria," such as social service, temperance, youth work, etc. Sunday school officers should plan definite service programs which fall into these avenues.

Every church school should be a missionary school; every teacher should bear a missionary message. The missionary outreach naturally follows the missionary outlook. Every Sunday school needs some direct tie with a mission land. This leads naturally to the observation that evangelism is not complete without a program of missionary education.

The pastor is in charge of missions in his church because this is a phase of the program of evangelism. He should develop the spirit of missions in his congregation. This can be done through preaching and bearing a burden for the cause. He can select missionary hymns and express his love and concern for the whole world in his prayers. He can agitate for a strong missions program in the church. By keeping the mission field before the people, much can be done toward building the program. A good spirit of missions often leads to a good program of missions. Missionary education is an integral part of evangelism in particular and Christian education in general.

It is suggested that the pastor have a subcommittee of some kind to assist him in the development of the missionary program in the church and church school. This committee may be a part of the Board of Christian Education or an independent one. The best plan, however, is to make missions a distinct part of the evangelistic responsibilities as revealed by Chart 12. In very small churches often the entire responsibility rests upon an individual. In any event, the members of this committee should have a missionary burden and vision and be able to interpret it to others.

Missions should have a large part in the Sunday school program. In fact one may well question whether it is possible to have genuine Christian education anywhere without missionary education. Missionary needs can be stressed in the lessons taught, prayers uttered, and songs used. Many schools use one Sunday a month for missionary emphasis and receiving of an offering. The "missions committee," headed by the pastor, should include Sunday school workers by all means, perhaps representatives of each department. Where possible, a special room should be provided for the use of this committee where materials, literature of all kinds, pictures, charts, maps, curios, and a library can be provided. The primary responsibilities of the committee include the following:

1. Short talks on missions
2. Posters placed in strategic places
3. Distribution of literature
4. Subscriptions to missionary periodicals
5. Guide in planning missionary worship programs
6. Urge teachers to stress missions in classes
7. Show audio-visual aids of all kinds on missions
8. Help to organize mission study classes
9. Supervise the grading of missionary education
10. Plan and conduct an annual "School of Missions"
11. Direct correspondence with missionaries and fields
12. Secure missionary speakers
13. Direct all missionary projects of the church
14. Plan work a year in advance
15. Coordinate the various missionary efforts in the different departments
16. Stress the importance of prayer and giving to missions
17. Guide in the choice of special days which stress missions
18. Assemble and make available program material
19. Urge cooperation in missionary projects and education
20. Keep church informed on the denominational program

Lobingier has pointed out some principles by which it is possible to include missionary education in the program of the church school.

1. We must try in every possible way to keep it from being regarded as an "extra."
2. We cannot have a satisfactory program of missionary education unless the leaders are themselves missionary personalities who, in their own viewpoint and practice, reflect the spirit they are trying to develop.
3. In choosing curriculum materials let missionary education be one of the criteria (but by no means the only one) by which you will make your selection.
4. Know and use the interdenominational missionary education materials of the Friendship Press.
5. Some of the best missionary education is achieved through reading well-chosen books.
6. Personal contact with nationals of other countries or with missionaries at home on furlough is an important part of the church school program of missionary education.
7. Correspondence also has real value.
8. Visual aids have as important a place in missionary education as in other phases of Christian education.
9. Service projects not only help the persons or the causes served; they are of equal value to the participants themselves.

10. The whole question of the church school's financial policy is related to missionary education.
11. Utilize the opportunity offered by summer schools, camps, and conferences.
12. Always keep in mind the principle of gradation[5].

7. *Summary.* The minister has a strategic place in the local church program of Christian education. As the minister goes, so goes the program. What has been said above only touches the surface of some of the possibilities of a wide-awake and aggressive minister of the Gospel of Jesus Christ. Perhaps a good way to close this discussion would be to summarize in outline form some of the possibilities which the minister has in strategic areas of his church program to see that Christian education is adequate, comprehensive, and fruitful.

Pulpit Possibilities

1. Stress the importance of Christian education
2. Inform the people, promote and advertise the program
3. Preach to meet the needs of the people
4. Demonstrate the proper use of the Bible and correct interpretation
5. Promote Christian family life
6. Stress the importance of prayer and strong devotional life
7. Preach great doctrines
8. Apply the principles of the Gospel to everyday life
9. Train the people in the art of worship
10. Cultivate strong financial support

Work with Children

1. Get acquainted with them, be their pastor, their friend; talk to them; play with them
2. Be sure a vacation church school is provided and take part in it
3. See that they are provided with adequate and attractive facilities
4. Give assistance to parents and teachers who work with them
5. Set a good example for them in life and ministry
6. See that good curriculum materials, and recreational equipment are provided for them
7. Train them in worship
8. Visit their classes
9. Promote week-day religious education

Work with Youth

1. Be their friendly counselor
2. Show an interest in their school and social life
3. Stand by them in time of trouble

Work with Adults

1. Provide leadership education
2. Guide them in Christian service

[5]List from John L. Lobingier, *The Better Church School* (Boston: The Pilgrim Press, 1952), Chapter 5, pp. 62-70. Used by permission.

4. Use them in the church program, in choirs, as ushers, etc.
5. Attend their classes and youth evening meetings
6. Help them with the Bible
7. Give them vocational guidance
8. Challenge them to Christian service
9. Guide them in church projects
10. Give them leadership education and training
11. Preach to them at home, in church, at Commencement and Baccalaureate occasions
12. Promote camps and conferences for youth

3. Point out social responsibilities and relationships
4. Guide them in Bible study and interpretation
5. Instruct them in Christian ethics
6. Give them wholesome social life and recreation
7. Challenge them with a world-wide vision for missions
8. Lead them to greater love and appreciation for the church
9. Set up a Christian family education program for them
10. Give particular attention to young adults
11. Provide special study courses, church projects, and Christian literature

By no means does the above list exhaust the possibilities. Instructional opportunities are provided by the needs of church committees, choirs, special study groups, standing committees, community contacts, and talent surveys. In all these things the pastor should have at least an acquaintance with what is going on and in some cases actually enter directly into educational provisions planned to meet these needs.

SUGGESTED READING — CHAPTER 3*

Barnette, *A Church Using Its Sunday School*, Chapter 5
————————, *The Place of the Sunday School in Evangelism*
Benson, *Ideas for Sunday School Growth*
————————, *Planning Church School Workers' Conferences*
Board of Education, *A Program of Leader Development*, Revised Edition, Presbyterian Church, U.S., 1953
Brown, *Plans for Sunday School Evangelism*
Byrne, *My Sunday School Handbook, for the Pastor*, No. 3
Crossland, *Better Leaders for Your Church*
————————, *How to Build Up Your Church School*, Chapter 3
Eaken, *Missions in the Sunday School*
ETTA, *A Guide for Sunday School Evangelism*
Flake, *Sunday School Officers and Their Work*, Chapter 2

* See updated Bibliography at back of book.

Forsyth, *The Ministry and Christian Nurture,* Chapters 1, 2, 10
Foster, *How a Small Church Can Have Good Christian Education,*
  Chapters 4, 5
Frost, *The School of the Church,* Chapter 8
Gable, *Christian Nurture Through the Church,* Chapters 4-6, 11
Gwynn, *Leadership Education in the Local Church*
Harner, *Missionary Education in Your Church,* Revised Edition
————————, *The Educational Work of the Church,* Chapter 8
Hensley, *The Pastor as Education Director*
Hixson, *Missions in the Sunday School*
Knowles, *How to Develop Better Leaders*
Lawrence, *My Message to Sunday School Workers,* Chapters 12-14,
  19, 25
Leavell, *The Successful Sunday School at Work,* Chapter 3
Lindhorst, *The Minister Teaches Religion*
Lobingier, *The Better Church School,* Chapter 5
Lotz, *Orientation in Religious Education,* Chapters 30-31
Mason, *Abiding Values in Christian Education,* Chapter 6
McKibben, *Guiding Workers in Christian Education*
Mead, *Modern Methods in Sunday School Work,* Chapters 28, 29
Milhouse, *Enlisting and Developing Church Leaders*
Munro, *The Pastor and Religious Education*
Murch, *Christian Education of the Local Church,* Chapter 20, 33
Person, *The Minister in Christian Education*
Robbins, *Winning the Children*
Smith, *The Pastor at Work in Christian Education*
Trumbull, *Yale Lectures on the Sunday School,* Chapters 7, 9, 10

THE WORK OF THE DIRECTOR OF
CHRISTIAN EDUCATION

OUTLINE FOR CHAPTER 4

(Supervision and Leadership)

A. THE PLACE OF THE DIRECTOR
1. In the Past
2. In the Present
3. In the Future

B. THE NEED FOR A DIRECTOR
1. To perform the Christian Mission
2. To assist the Pastor
3. To aid the Lay Workers

C. THE QUALIFICATIONS FOR A DIRECTOR
1. Personal Qualifications
2. Professional Qualifications

D. THE DUTIES OF A DIRECTOR
1. General Leadership
2. Leadership Training
3. Administration
4. Teaching
5. Shepherding the workers
6. Promotion
7. Supervision

E. THE RELATIONSHIPS OF A DIRECTOR
1. To God
2. To the Congregation
3. To the Pastor and Superintendent
4. To the Board of Christian Education
5. To the Staff

F. THE SELECTION OF A DIRECTOR
1. First Steps
2. Interview
3. Arrangements
4. Finances
5. Arrival
6. Rewards

4 | THE WORK OF THE DIRECTOR OF CHRISTIAN EDUCATION

(Supervision and Leadership)

A. THE PLACE OF THE DIRECTOR

1. *In the Past.* Most everyone is willing to admit the superiority of Jesus Christ as Teacher. Jesus knew Christian education as no other. He knew His subject, He knew how to proclaim the message successfully, and He knew how to get others to live it and carry it to a lost world. His methods have motivated countless efforts since His day. He was a Director of Christian education. Following closely upon Jesus was the apostle Paul, an educational evangelist. He too was a director. He was a master teacher who taught others to teach. Aside from teachers and ministers, the world did not see a director of Christian education, as we know one today, until the twentieth century.

No one knows the exact origin of the office of director. It is believed that it sprang from the necessity of offering assistance to both the pastor and the general superintendent. Because of the rapid development of the teaching ministry and program of the church, vast changes made extreme increase in leadership necessary. Several denominations began to hire educational specialists to give supervision to the work, and this gradually worked down to the local church level.

2. *In the present.* With the increase of interest in various Christian schools to provide training for this type of ministry, along with the awakening of the local church to the need for it, the *director* of Christian education enjoys greater status today than ever before.

As never before churches are recognizing the need for giving assistance to pastors in the development of the teaching ministry of the church. It is also recognized that teachers and officers need the training and supervision which this specialist can provide. Society is demanding a higher quality of service than ever before.

The present tendency is to raise the status of this office from a "directorate" to a ministry. The term "director of Christian education" is now used to describe a professional worker with training beyond the college degree. People without much preparation are called "associates" or "assistants in Christian education." A

103

popular term for this group is "educational assistant." "Minister of education" is reserved for those who bear ministerial credentials and work in the field of Christian education. Denominations are beginning to list important standards for preparation, selection, and use of directors.

Present practice in many places is to hire a combination worker to help with more than one phase of the program. Thus we find directors serving also as youth workers and ministers of music. Young people in increasing numbers are preparing for these positions.

3. *In the Future.* This worker is destined to remain with us and play a larger part in the local church program. As church and church school enrollments increase, the program will demand close study, supervision, and more leadership. The leadership of the church will need and demand more help as the church faces its educational ministry. The complexity of this ministry calls for professional guidance and particular preparation and consecration. Young people in increasing numbers will be attracted to this ministry.

B. THE NEED FOR A DIRECTOR

1. *To Perform the Christian Mission.* The ministry of Jesus Christ and the church demand the best that men can give to it. The Great Commission is a teaching commission. Instruction is a vital part of the kingdom. The church is made up of varied channels of ministry and reaches all ages. To such a ministry the director can give himself with the confidence that he is performing a genuine service to God and to his fellowmen.

2. *To Assist the Pastor.* In a previous chapter we have seen that the objectives of the church are four-fold: evangelism, education, worship, and fellowship. Each of these phases actually demands a specialist in order to achieve greatest results. The average pastor today, however, is expected to supply the necessary results in all these areas. But no man can expect to be equally effective in every area. The program of the successful church today is beyond the power of one man to control. He simply does not have the time, energy, or knowledge to do all the necessary work. Even in small churches an adequate program demands pastoral assistance of some kind. On the other hand, even where directors are present to assist the pastor, all pastors should keep in close touch with the educational program of the church.

Harold C. Mason has listed six good reasons why the average and large church needs a director.

1. The high standards in public education demand of the church school a better trained personnel.

2. The call of the world is so demanding of time and interest

in this complex age that the church must counteract it with a wholesome, spiritual, well-filled Christian program.

3. The pastor needs the help of a specialist in the field of Christian education.

4. Christian education as an agency in evangelism is very important in terms of promotion, curriculum, organization, administration, instruction, and demands more time and attention than the hard-pressed pastor can give it.

5. The duties of the director in the smaller church may include the duties of the church secretary, the parish visitor, and the leader of music.

6. The employment of a trained pastor and a director provides sufficient professional leadership in education to train and maintain an adequate volunteer staff of workers.[1]

3. *To Aid the Lay Workers.* As long as the principle of volunteer lay leadership and service is maintained, assistance is demanded. One of the grave needs in the church today is to educate and train the members for Christian service and to improve the quality of that service. The crying need for integrating, correlating, and coordinating these workers is without argument. This is where the pastor's work needs supplementing by that which a director can supply. Where the program of the church makes room for leadership education, development, and supervision, the quality and quantity of Christian service rendered by the consecrated lay people of the church steadily improves and increases. In fact, a great deal of the success to which any director can point is attributed to his behind-the-scenes work with lay leaders. Most of his contacts will be personal rather than public.

C. THE QUALIFICATIONS OF A DIRECTOR

1. *Personal Qualifications.* The demands of the better churches and standards set in the schools make possible higher qualifications for directors. Personal qualifications are linked with professional training and experience in good directors.

Standing highest among the personal traits demanded is *spirituality.* A ministry must be performed by a minister. This demands conversion and regeneration as the minimum essential. He should be filled with the Spirit and strive earnestly to "walk in the Spirit." Only those who know the way can lead others in it. Following closely on this is the conviction of a *definite call* of God to do this work. Only in this way can spiritual preparation be deepened for this important work. Other desirable qualities are many and include the following:

[1]Harold C. Mason, *Abiding Values in Christian Education* (Westwood, N. J.: Fleming H. Revell, 1955), pp. 150, 151.

1. Love for people, particularly children and youth
2. Unselfishness
3. Humility
4. Self-control
5. Emotional maturity
6. Patience
7. Obedience
8. Cooperativeness
9. Growth in grace
10. Good health
11. Neat appearance and cleanliness
12. Studious
13. Vision
14. Leadership ability
15. Special talents, if possible
16. Sincerity
17. Attractive personality
18. Sense of humor
19. Diligence
20. Common sense

2. *Professional Qualifications.* Professional ability concerns aptness and training for the work. The educational ministry demands specialized knowledge and skills. The bachelors degree from a college of merit and spiritual standards is basic today. Advanced work beyond college is preferable. Directors need to know educational philosophy, psychology, and principles of teaching, not to speak of a thorough acquaintance with the Bible. Ministers of education will want to add seminary training to their experience. In some schools the master's degree in religious education can be combined with the work for the Bachelor of Divinity.

Beyond these academic requirements there should be continued growth and development. Refresher courses, conferences, reading, observation, and other similar opportunities will afford him this training. Of particular significance is the need for being constantly alert to the need for supervision and new developments. An interchange of ideas with other directors proves beneficial and motivating.

D. THE DUTIES OF A DIRECTOR

1. *General Leadership.* As a member of the staff the director has leadership responsibilities. He is a leader of leaders. He should know the nature and principles of leadership. He must demonstrate by life and service what it means to be a Christian leader. In this, his responsibility is no less than that of the pastor. While it is recognized that the work of directors varies from church to church as the local situation demands, yet as a leader there are

definite areas of responsibility in which the director is expected
to excell. They are:
1. General leadership and helpfulness
2. Leadership training
3. Administration
4. Teaching
5. Shepherding the workers
6. Promotion
7. Supervision

The director is expected to work closely with the pastor and
superintendent. They should work as a team. All three should
demonstrate good Christian leadership. The scope of such leadership depends on how active the pastor and superintendent are and
the extent to which the staff is active. As soon as leadership becomes available, the director may well turn his personal attention
to areas where such leadership is lacking. In any event, like the
pastor, the director should have contact with all ages and workers.

2. *Leadership Training.* Directors can be greatly helpful to
pastors and superintendents in the education and development of
lay leaders. He can conduct leadership classes and supervise the
in-service training of staff members. He is valuable in giving particular attention to new and young workers. He may be particularly
useful in the enlistment of new workers. He can keep the training
materials and methods up-to-date. The pastor may even allow
him to conduct classes in church membership. In fact, the director
can be a key leader in helping the pastor and Board of Christian
Education develop a sound year-round program of leadership
education. The details of this program were discussed in the
previous chapter on "The Work of the Pastor in Christian
Education."

3. *Administration.* The director is an administrator because
he is concerned with total operation, procedures, and management.
In this, however, he is not to usurp the place of the superintendent
in the Sunday school.

Along with the superintendent the director is interested in the
efficient functioning of each organization in the church school. He
is concerned too with keeping able and efficient leaders supplied
for these organizations. Often he proves helpful in filling vacancies.

Some details needing particular attention in this area are:
making clear to workers what their duties are, record maintenance,
enrollment and classification procedures, ordering and distribution
of supplies, and follow-up of absentees. Other responsibilities
include checking space and equipment, size and organization of
classes, schedules of meetings, and curriculum details, to mention
only a few. One word of warning is in order here. Directors should

not specialize in this area. Train leaders to do this and give attention to leadership development and supervision.

Many opportunities are provided to cooperate with denominational, interdenominational, community, and world-wide agencies. Good administration keeps well informed and keeps pace with developments outside the local church. Directors may show their knowledge and skills as time permits.

Program building and the creation of an annual calendar of activities is highly important and necessary. A well-planned, carefully balanced, and comprehensive program is one of the administrator's greatest responsibilities.

4. *Teaching.* Good directors cannot avoid teaching responsibilities of one kind or another. Primarily, however, the director is a teacher of teachers. In this he should be thoroughly familiar with psychology and principles of teaching. This duty overlaps with that of supervision in many instances.

Teaching responsibilities for directors lie largely in the realm of leadership training. At times they may be called upon to teach particular units of study, to demonstrate teaching techniques, and to hold teachers' meetings. Occasionally directors are called upon to teach classes, but as soon as leaders can be found and trained, the director should move on to the work of observation, evaluation, and supervision. One instance — the vacation church school — may prove to be an exception. In the main, however, directors should be thought of as resource persons who are free to give advice and help at any time. Some directors may feel that they make a distinctive contribution by improving the quality and content of Bible teaching.

5. *Shepherding.* A good director is a shepherd of his staff of workers just as the pastor is the shepherd of his congregation. Here is a function that the two can mutually share. A great deal of good can be accomplished by the director who calls in the homes and who counsels with groups and individuals. In these instances he finds opportunities not only for witnessing and soul winning, but also for interpreting the program of Christian education to the people and the workers. He can be particularly helpful in developing better home-church school relationships. Many opportunities for counseling workers can be obtained as well in the home. A director who knows the people and contacts the field is in a better position to guide the ministry of the church school.

Parents need assistance with home problems, young people need guidance, and workers need encouragement and inspiration. In all these matters and many more, directors find opportunities to be good shepherds.

Some directors make it a practice to select prospects for soul winning opportunities. They are evangelists and desire to be used of the Lord in this fashion. Furthermore, close contact with teachers requires directors to shepherd them in soul winning activities.

6. *Promotion.* Promotion concerns enlargement and growth. Extension is the work of the Great Commission in action. Reaching people with the Gospel is our most important work. In this the director needs to be acquainted with techniques of census taking, enlargement, and visitation.

Interpretation of the program to the public is important also. In this the director is of valuable assistance to the superintendent. Promotional techniques will be discussed more fully in a chapter to come. Suffice to say, a committee on publicity to help the director and superintendent is helpful.

An extension department will promote enlargement by reaching groups outside the walls and membership of the church. This department also provides many service opportunities for adults and young people.

7. *Supervision.* At the heart of supervision lies improvement. The administrator gives himself to organization and management, whereas the supervisor strives for better quality. It is here that a director can make unique contributions to the program and staff. It is here that he can be a specialist. Here he can give his efforts to increase the effectiveness of the educative process, striving for highest and best results, to improve the teaching-learning situation.

Good supervision places emphasis on *positive* results. It is not spying nor "snooper-vision," as some choose to call it. Neither is it mere fault-finding or "casting a genial influence." It should also be noted that good supervision is definitely not diplomatic manipulation of a staff to gain the personal ends of the supervision.

The *functions* of good supervision are clearly drawn today. Some of the most common ones include the following:

1. To keep the objectives of Christian education before the staff and the school.
2. To develop standards of procedure for guidance in and evaluation of the program.
3. To assist in the development of a comprehensive and well-balanced curriculum by which the objectives are realized.
4. To work *within* the staff, not over it.
5. To encourage leadership and develop skill in human relations.
6. To direct group processes.
7. To develop skill in personnel administration.
8. To diagnose difficulties, tracing inefficiency and poor results.
9. To prescribe remedies which will help to realize better results.
10. To develop and use the skills of evaluation and testing.

It is evident that such functions will keep the director close to the students, staff, and program. His greatest contributions many times will come through working with people. It is obvious also that he must know all the educational essentials of a good program and staff before good supervision can take place.

To many staff members, the term "supervision" brings a shudder and they think of an inspector or inquisitor of some kind. To overcome this, a program of supervision should be supported by the Board of Christian Education. The position of the director as supervisor must be clearly understood. Instead of an inspector, he will be a helper, an adviser, and friend. Ideally, supervision is a cooperative enterprise between the director, workers, and pupils. Everyone becomes a learner. Teacher and workers thus have some one with whom they can intimately talk over the problems encountered in the work. The director will develop and encourage initiative, self-reliance, intelligent independence, and the assumption of responsibility on the part of all workers. The experience and wisdom of older workers will be used to greatest advantage. Helpful also at this point is making sure that everyone is personally acquainted with what is being attempted, that all have "common" understanding of the task. Such understanding will include objectives, methods, materials, activities, strengths, and weaknesses. Everyone puts his shoulder to the wheel to realize a better and bigger program. In the light of these facts, therefore, a well-organized plan of supervision will manifest certain well-defined features, such as:

1. Clearly defined objectives
2. Changes made on the basis of objective evaluation
3. Procedures will include:
   a. Getting the facts
   b. Passing judgment on them *with the staff*
   c. Making plans for revision
4. Development of techniques and devices for carrying out plans such as personal conferences, rating scales, tests, etc.

In getting started with such a program the director may find some of the following suggestions helpful.

1. Be humble, friendly, and willing to learn
2. Let the staff know that the program and progress belongs to them
3. Do not hesitate to ask the assistance of the staff, particularly the more experienced workers
4. Impress on the group the need for cooperation and teamwork
5. Judge past efforts as sparingly as possible
6. Create a spirit of fellowship, sympathy, and sharing — "This is *our* school"

7. Do not make drastic changes at first
8. Start with problems of *the staff*. Ask workers to list such problems
9. Form discussion groups to study the needed improvements
10. Assure the staff that all workers are welcome to the director's help and attention
11. Discuss evidences of needed changes in open conference
12. Start with minor problems at first
13. Be careful about chance remarks
14. Set a good example of promptness, hard work, and thoroughness
15. Remain spiritual and friendly on the job

Space prohibits a full discussion on the problems of supervision. The subject requires a separate volume. For the sake of completion, however, the following list reveals the remarkable scope of the work of a good supervisor and areas where the director is desperately needed in many instances to help solve problems and raise the quality of work.

I. BUILDING MORALE
   A. How can the quality of staff morale be determined?
   B. What do workers desire as "job satisfactions"?
   C. What can be done to build morale and provide job satisfactions?

II. LEADERSHIP IMPROVEMENT
   A. What is the significance of leadership improvement?
   B. What are the bases for the improvement of the workers?
   C. What methods for improvement of the workers can we use?
   D. How can people be encouraged to assume responsibility?
   E. How can workers be assisted in executing responsibility?
   F. What conditions discourage the assumption of responsibility?
   G. How can creativeness be increased?
   H. How can "lazy" workers be helped?
   I. How can "colorless" workers be helped?
   J. How can "older" workers be helped?
   K. How can workers who disagree be helped?

III. HUMAN RELATIONS
   A. How can staff harmony be promoted?
   B. How can conflict and friction be avoided?
   C. How can staff conflicts be overcome?

IV. WORKING TOGETHER
   A. How can the power of a group be released?
   B. How can a group operate to release its full power?

C. How can staff meetings be improved?

D. How can the work of the group be coordinated?

V. PERSONNEL ADMINISTRATION

A. How should workers be selected and enlisted?

B. How can new workers be helped?

C. How can growth be encouraged?

D. How can reassignments be made?

E. How can staff needs be met?

F. How can the staff be trained?

G. How can incapable workers be dismissed?

VI. THE CURRICULUM

A. What is the curriculum?

B. What part does good supervision play in developing an enlarged and increased understanding of the curriculum for all workers?

C. How can curriculum materials and activities be evaluated?

D. How can curriculum difficulties be located and solved?

E. How can rooms and equipment be utilized best to help achieve curriculum objectives?

VII. CLASS INSTRUCTION

A. How can teaching procedures be studied?

B. How can teachers be helped to understand the nature of teaching?

C. What are the best methods to use?

D. What are the techniques of observation, visitation, and counseling to be used with the teachers?

E. What observation devices are available?

VIII. WORSHIP

A. How can a clear understanding of the true nature of worship be achieved?

B. How can worship programs be improved?

C. How can worship difficulties and defects be discovered?

D. How can leaders be trained in worship?

E. How can the group evaluate worship?

IX. SERVICE TRAINING

A. What are the objectives of service training and activity?

B. How can the present program be evaluated and improved?

C. How can community contacts be made?

X. SOCIAL AND RECREATIONAL ACTIVITY

A. What part do these play in the curriculum?

B. What are the objectives of social life and recreation?

C. How can the program be measured and improved?

XI. MEASUREMENT
    A. What are the purposes of testing?
    B. What types of tests and measurements can be used?
    C. How can teachers evaluate their work?
    D. How can all self-evaluation be encouraged?
    E. How can group-evaluation be achieved?
    F. How can the total program be evaluated?
    G. Are our records effective?

In addition to a general grasp of the whole field of supervision, the director should be acquainted with particular techniques and devices which will prove helpful to him in his work and to the staff. Just as the Sunday school teacher approaches his class on Sunday, so the director should think of his staff as a class. He should be vitally interested in their spiritual experience, their problems, needs, and progress. To arrive at this information requires close knowledge of the actual situations in which the staff works. One of the best techniques in good supervision in this regard is that of observation and helpful visitation.

There arises the problem of overcoming the fears, resentment, distrust, and misunderstanding of the staff when they realize that they will be observed. This can be overcome in part through the establishment of a policy by the Board of Christian education. The best way, however, is to approach the staff with deep sympathy and understanding. The director, as supervisor, is a helping teacher and staff member. He is not there to criticize but to assist, to give constructive assistance in the actual situation. This may require a long period of time for some workers. Leaders should do everything possible to help create the right attitude toward constructive criticism.

The personal conference seems to be the most helpful device at the disposal of the director for this work. The purpose of such a conference is to provide for specific and detailed attention to individual problems of the workers. The procedure involves a threefold process which leads to a possible climax or solution to the problem under consideration:
    1. Preparing for the conference
    2. Conducting the conference
    3. Conserving the results of the conference

Preparation for the conference is largely the responsibility of the director himself. He will need certain vital information about the worker to be interviewed. Some have found that a personnel blank of some kind which is kept on file will provide the director with basic information which might prove helpful to him in the approach to an understanding of the worker and his problem. A sample of this kind of blank is provided in Appendix IV, No. 1. In addition to this, the director will need to collect materials on the problem to be discussed. Further material may be collected when he actually observes the situation or the problem involved.

Further preparation should be made in advance of the conference itself. In fact, if possible, the director should work out a plan of procedure. The plan might include such items as probable reactions to proposed criticism or new ideas, plans to make the most of these reactions, or careful suggestions for improvement and solution of the proposed problem. No director should enter this kind of conference "cold." Workers should be encouraged to submit problems in advance in order to make this kind of preparation on the part of the director possible.

In the second phase, that of *conducting* the conference, the director should seek first to set up a friendly atmosphere. Make the conference personal by dealing with personal qualities of the worker, his skills and faults. It should also be impersonal, in that personal feelings on the part of the director and worker are subservient to the interests of securing improvement in the work. Criticisms should be both constructive and remedial, favorable and unfavorable.

While defects will be carefully noted, the director should be as generous as possible with favorable comments. By all means he should seek to develop the teacher and worker for general leadership.

The third phase is *conservation*. The director should keep a good record of results. In some instances, important conclusions should be made available to groups. Whatever changes are proposed, the director should give definite assistance in carrying them out. He should keep a careful check on progress of any activities involved from changes suggested. During the conference itself, the director will find it helpful to keep a record of problems at large which might be suggested or discovered and which might serve as points of discussion in group conference which are to come.

The procedure outlined above is a general approach to the problem of counseling workers. Perhaps the most fruitful place where this kind of work can be carried on is with the teachers. The improvement of class instruction is one of the most practical results of a director's work. Here he is concerned not so much with materials as with the improvement of teaching procedures and techniques. This requires actual study of the conditions prevalent in the classroom itself. His job is to locate teaching difficulties and observe what procedures are used. He should evaluate results and attempt to measure pupil reaction and growth. He will need skill in applying corrective measures in a wide variety of problems.

One of the first responsibilities in the improvement of learning and teaching is to help the teacher to understand the nature of teaching. This will involve a knowledge of what instruction is, the methods to be employed, and the outcomes to be expected.

The personal conference, as outlined above, seems to be the most helpful device available to the director. The purpose of such a conference is to help the teacher with specific and detailed problems involved in the teaching-learning process. The general procedure will be to diagnose the problem, secure the facts, and prescribe the remedy. Particular techniques involved would include observation of teaching procedures, possibly with the use of guides or check lists, and a follow-up conference.

Preparation should be made by the director in approaching the problem. He should acquaint himself with materials, methods, possible reactions of the teacher and pupil, and possible solutions. It is important also that the proper attitude be present between the director and teacher. The director should visit a class only upon the invitation of the teacher. He should point out that they are co-laborers in the task and that he is there to help, not to criticize. They will cooperate in whatever improvement is to be realized. New teachers should expect to be helped in this way at an early period of their experience.

For some, it seems best for the classroom visit to be unannounced, but in general the recommendation is in favor of a *pre-teaching conference* with the teacher. In this conference, both director and teacher should clearly understand the purposes involved and the part that each will be expected to play. Mutual planning for the class session to come might be the best way to conduct this conference. The director can help the teacher think through the class procedures and techniques. Perhaps a lesson plan could be employed to accomplish this. They may choose to deal with any phase of teaching itself, or with materials and activities. They might talk about the appropriate method for this lesson. They can try to anticipate difficulties which might arise and attempt to work out solutions in advance. They could talk about problem cases or formulate standards for the class. This and a multiplicity of other considerations might possibly consume their attention.

The pre-teaching conference is followed by the *visit to the classroom* while the class is in session. If advance planning in the pre-teaching conference has been thorough, the visit should result in maximum effectiveness. An earnest desire on the part of the teacher for success will help him to overcome his reticence to be observed and visited. Where it is absolutely impossible for the director to make a visit of this kind, he can resort to the pre-teaching and post-teaching conferences. In some cases, an observation window makes it possible for the observer to remain outside and unseen by the class.

The director, who is perhaps well-known by the group, can plan to arrive early and be in the classroom before the class begins. In children's classes it might be less noticeable for him to participate in the activities with the teacher and pupils. In older classes he might desire to make his entrance as unobtrusive as possible, even remaining in the background. The important thing for him to remember is that he has come to observe what is going on. Whether he can do that more through participation or not may be a debatable question. This problem should be talked over with the teacher in advance planning. No doubt the individual situation will dictate the best procedure.

The director may wish to take notes during his visit. Again, he will have to decide whether such notes will be taken during participation and recorded mentally, or whether writing shall be done during the class. Perhaps this will be determined largely by the purpose of his visit. If, for example, he wishes to visit for purposes of general, overall observation, he might wish to use a device for general observation. A sample of this kind of device can be examined in Appendix IV, No. 2. If there are particular problems to be observed, then a particular kind of check list might prove helpful. For example, he might want to observe the use of questions and the questioning method on the part of the teacher. Or he might be interested in what part directed discussion and problem-solving have in the lesson development. Other areas for analysis might include storytelling, memory work, dramatization, and a whole host of other methods. Samples of check lists suitable for this kind of observation can be found by consulting Frank M. McKibben, *Improving Religious Education Through Supervision* (Nashville, Tenn.: Abingdon-Cokesbury Press, 1931). Another device is called the "activity analysis," where a record of all observable activity is kept by taking notes and later discussing the results. Some directors have found tape recorders useful in this work. Whatever method of observation is used to record what takes place in the class, three steps are involved in the process:

1. Get the facts through personal observation
2. Analyze and interpret the facts
3. Outline remedial and corrective measures

A most important point for the director to remember in doing his observation is not to forget the *pupils*. What are their attitudes? Do they give attention? Are they interested in the lesson? Are they comfortable? Then he can turn his attention to external factors. It is also well for him to remember that the teacher is the key to the whole situation.

The third step in the observation process concerns the *follow-up conference*. To be most effective, this too needs to be a personal conference. After a period of time has elapsed, the director and teacher should talk over the results of the class. About the middle of the week is a good time. Evaluation should be made as objective as possible. It has been suggested that the positive approach is much better to open the conference. A question like "What pleased you most?" will serve to call attention to the good results first. The director might ask the teacher what he himself would suggest for improvement, or he might ask what changes he has to suggest. "What materials do you need?" "How can I help further?" Whatever is done, the whole matter should be a cooperative venture to work out corrective measures. Perhaps the director can suggest some reading which bears on the problems revealed. He might point out the advantages of visiting more experienced and successful teachers. It may be necessary to modify the physical conditions, lighting, or ventilation in some way. Perhaps a change of method or more variety of method would prove helpful. It may be that the teacher needs to make a self-evaluation. If so, a check list or self-rating scale, such as illustrated in Appendix III, might prove beneficial.

The director should ever bear in mind that supervision is a continuous process. One or even two such visits to the classroom may not prove sufficient for some cases. Every available opportunity for encouragement, growth, and improvement should be used. One last suggestion may prove of value to the director. Where it is not possible to arrange personal follow-up conferences with the various workers after a period of analysis or observation, some kind of written report may be given to the workers by the director. The report should cover both positive and negative reactions of the director, as well as a personal note of appreciation and sympathy. An illustration of this procedure is included in Appendix IV, No 3.

A final area of the director's supervisory work is that of *evaluation*. He needs to be thoroughly familiar with the various types of tests and measurements and alert to whatever signs of progress and growth are evident. The total program should be watched constantly and he naturally should work with the pastor and superintendents in evaluating results in this area. The use of standards will be of great assistance in this regard, The director might like to use some kind of check list or rating scale to obtain data for the total program. Appendix IV, No. 4 shows a sample of this kind of thing. He will be desirous too of helping teachers to develop the spirit of experimentation and measurement of results. In this work he can encourage the use of rating scales, check lists, and certain standardized tests. He can assist them in the creation of knowledge tests of the objective type for classroom use. Above all, however, the director will see that the objectives of testing in religious education are realized. He will stress that the center of focus in an evaluation program is the improvement of the learning situation for the pupils. Various methods of accomplishing these things include outside speakers who challenge and instruct, pupil reactions, emphasis on constant improvement, student-teacher planning and measurement, cooperative efforts in the creation of check lists, and group judgment on group progress. More attention will be given to tests for use in the classroom in a later chapter.

E. THE RELATIONSHIPS OF A DIRECTOR

1. *To God.* As any other Christian worker, the director should know God through personal experience. He must grow in grace and in the knowledge of God, and walk in the power of the Spirit. Only in this way will he realize the greatest fruit in divine service. The cultivation of spiritual life through daily Bible reading and prayer is more important for this leader than for many others. Through submission to the direction of the Spirit, he can direct others most effectively.

2. *To the congregation.* The director is responsible to the congregation just as the pastor is. In order for him to minister most effectively therefore, he should think of the local congregation as his sheep. He should love them and make himself available to them as friend, counselor, leader, and teacher, In turn, the congregation should receive the director as a minister, make him feel at home, and place themselves at his disposal. Every effort should be made to avoid making him a "glorified office boy" or errand boy. A good suggestion is for the pastor to present the director to the congregation and fully explain all relationships involved, appealing for mutual understanding and cooperation.

The denominational program is ordinarily carried out in the local church. The director should cooperate in this as far as possible. This can be done through giving assistance to the various organizations of the church.

In some instances the director is a member of the church council or official board. In such cases he renders valuable assistance in total program planning and building.

3. *To the Pastor and Sunday School Superintendent.* Ideally, these leaders should work as a team. Careful division of responsibilities needs to be worked out so that overlapping of duties can be avoided. The pastor will maintain overseer-ship of the total program, with the other two definitely responsible to him. All of them are responsible for working closely with the Board of Christian Education. The best statement perhaps on the division of responsibilities can be found in the pamphlet, "The Minister, the Director of Christian Education, and the Sunday School Superintendent — A Team" (see reading list). Each of these officers should clearly understand his relationship to the other.

4. *To the Board of Christian Education.* The board is responsible for total planning, program building, and policy-making

in the field of Christian education. The director, therefore, will have a very close relationship to the board and must feel his responsibility to it. As an executive officer of the board, the director will see that the policies and plans of the board are interpreted and practiced throughout the church school. He will assist the board in all of its work wherever possible, and in many instances will be the primary source of information for the board. Naturally he will be expected to report periodically to the board as to his own work and conditions within the school. As a resource person the services of the director to the board cannot be overestimated.

5. *To the Staff.* The director will have a close relationship to the staff. In fact, he will shepherd and instruct them, This will take place in groups and personal conferences. Again, as a resource person the director can be of great benefit to the staff. Through coordination of efforts, keeping morale high and spiritual, conducting meetings, and keeping the staff working effectively, the director will prove immeasureably valuable in increasing the fruits of the entire program. By meeting with committees, organizations, and groups, the director can supply consultation services, program ideas, materials and methods, all of which make for a more interesting and instructive program.

F. THE SELECTION OF A DIRECTOR

1. *First Steps.* The very first step which a church should take is to determine whether it needs a director of Christian education or not. At the first indication of a sense of need, perhaps a committee can be appointed to survey the situation. The survey should determine whether or not another worker can fit into the program, the type of worker which is needed, the age groups which sense the need of greater assistance, and the attitude of the pastor and superintendent. In some instances pastors are completely averse to the hiring of an educational worker because they feel sufficient for the task. The size of the congregation will prove to be a factor worth considering also. Small churches might possibly consider the worth of a part-time director. In other situations it might prove beneficial for two or three churches to combine and call a director, to be paid through cooperative effort. In other situations, a combination worker might be needed, although it should be pointed out that combination workers often lose their effectiveness if they have too many responsibilities to take care of.

It is debatable whether men or women are best suited for the task of a director. A church will have to determine what it wants. Women are often considered better workers with children and provide the pastor with less unwholesome competition. On the other hand, the present trend is toward "ministers of education" who will specialize in educational work and even work with children.

The survey should also bring out clearly the relationships of a director, his duties, and responsibilities. A director from a nearby church might prove helpful in realizing these purposes.

By all means the congregation should be prepared for this worker. They, too, need to know his relationships, duties, and responsibilities. They need to be convinced of his place in the program and of the benefits of his work in their midst. After all they have to finance the program! Then too, they should be sold on his coming so that they will give him their full support and cooperation.

The first contact with a prospective worker should be clear on the need and place of such a worker in the local church, on duties, needs, working conditions, and financial arrangements. In fact, a full statement of Christian educational philosophy along with the various details of hiring might prove extremely beneficial and influential to a prospective director.

Qualified directors are few in number and the sources are limited. Much encouragement, however, can be found in the fact that schools are beginning to prepare youth for this type of ministry. Among the sources to which a pastor or church can turn for these workers are denominational placement boards, advice and counsel of neighboring pastors and directors, colleges, and seminaries. Many churches have resorted to the device of picking a person in the local church who has promise and ability and giving him special training. Many pastors' wives have fitted into situations like this. Others have found former public school teachers or supervisors who had the qualifications and character to give part-time help. Still others have used part-time paid directors in cooperation with other churches.

2. *Interview.* Following the initial contact and when interest has been expressed, the prospective director should be invited to the local church for an interview. This gives those involved a mutual opportunity to look things over personally and come to a greater and more satisfactory understanding. The visit should take several days, with all expenses paid by the church. During his stay, the prospect can exchange educational views with the church and talk over the local philosophy of Christian education. As far as possible a clear picture of duties, responsibilities, and schedule should be given the worker. It is not necessary for a visit of this kind to place either the church or the worker under any obligation. It may be that the worker would not be suitable for the local situation or it may be that he himself feels that he could not fit into the situation.

Following a period of time during which both parties give more consideration and a great deal of prayer to the matter, if the board, the pastor, and the ruling body of the church feel that the candidate has the qualifications, personality, and ability to fit into the situation, then the pastor can be instructed to write the worker, giving a formal statement of duties, salary, term, and other arrangements which might prove mutually agreeable.

3. *Arrangements.* If the prospective director accepts the position, the local church should set about immediately to make adequate provision for his coming. Arrangements will include such matters as office space, equipment, supplies, secretarial help, and living quarters. The latter might prove to be a big factor in salary arrangements. In addition, the church should prepare its spirit to receive the new worker, to make him happy and satisfied, and to help him feel at home.

4. *Finances.* Financial resources should be adequate to cover salary, supplies, equipment, curriculum materials, etc. This calls for careful budgeting. The salary should be in line with commensurate professional assistance in other churches. It should allow for living accommodations and be comparable to that of the pastor. Vernon Kraft found in his survey that salaries ranged from $2400.00 to $6400.00 per year, with an average of $4,000.00[2].

5. *Arrival of the Director.* When the new director arrives, everything humanly possible should be done to make him feel at home. It is customary for many directors to begin their work at the beginning of the Sunday school year or the fiscal year of the church. For many, this comes the latter part of September or the first week of October. Other churches find it more convenient for the director to start earlier during the planning period of the church when the total program for the coming church year is taking shape. The advantage of this is obvious.

A personal welcome for the director and his family should be planned by the church. The importance of this worker and that which he represents can be brought home to the congregation through a special service of installation and dedication planned for that purpose. Here the pastor can introduce the worker to the congregation, allow him to preach to the group, and then formally induct him into the work of the church. Often churches follow this with a reception of some kind, giving members an opportunity to get personally acquainted with the director and his family.

Too much should not be expected of the new worker upon his arrival. Time should be given for him to get acquainted with the program and the staff and to organize his work for the new year. Perhaps an extended period of experimentation will be necessary before any real progress can be seen.

6. *Rewards.* Most of the rewards for this kind of work are intangible. As a ministry, the worker should not expect "fleshly"

[2]Vernon Kraft, *The Local Church Director of Christian Education* (Chicago: Moody Press, 1957), p. 49.

remuneration, although he can expect some of this. If he is paid a comparable salary to the other professional and skilled workers in the church, he need not worry about this. Then, too, in this time when the church is stressing the importance of a multiple ministry for the local church, the average director can expect tenure and security in his work, particularly in the kind of church which can afford to hire him in the first place.

Intangible rewards are more satisfactory, and there are many. There is the satisfaction of a ministry of the Gospel, of training others to minister. There is the opportunity for personal, intellectual, and cultural enrichment and growth. There are the many opportunities for Christian fellowship and study and the knowledge that one is yoked with other great workers in the greatest cause on earth. Above all, there will be the thrill of seeing souls saved and growing up into all things in Christ Jesus and the infinite satisfaction of knowing that one is in the center of God's will. These, along with the thrills which come of helping others get results in the service of the Master, should serve to motivate our continued love and loyalty and the giving of our best in the service of God through the Church.

<h3 style="text-align:center">SUGGESTED READING — CHAPTER 4*</h3>

Benson, "Why An Educational Director?" (pamphlet, *Moody Monthly*)
Cope, *Efficiency in the Sunday School*, Chapter 4
  Religious Education in the Church, Chapter 21
Cummings, *Christian Education in the Local Church*, Chapter 4
Edge, *Does God Want You as a Minister of Education?*
Harper, *The Minister of Education*
Hensley, *The Pastor as Educational Director*, Chapter 8
Kraft, *The Director of Christian Education in the Local Church*
Lawrance, *My Messages to Sunday School Workers*, Chapter 11
Lotz, *Orientation in Religious Education*, Chapter 30
Mason, *Abiding Values in Christian Education*, Chapter 18
McComb, Louise, D.C.E., *A Challenging Career in Christian Education.*
Miller, *Education for Christian Living*, Chapter 21
  The Pastor and Religious Education, Chapter 7
Munro, H. C., *The Director of Religious Education*
Myers, *Teaching Religion*, Chapter 11 and 12
NCCC, "The Minister, the Director of Christian Education and the Sunday School Superintendent — A Team" (a pamphlet)
  The Orientation and Administration of Christian Education in the Local Church, Chapter 7.
Prugh, *The Parish Director of Christian Education*
Vieth, *The Church and Christian Education*, Chapter 6
  Improving Your Sunday School, Chapter 4

* See updated Bibliography at back of book.

THE WORK OF THE GENERAL SUPERINTENDENT

OUTLINE FOR CHAPTER 5

(Administration and Supervision)

A. THE OFFICE OF THE GENERAL SUPERINTENDENT
   1. Place in the Church and Sunday School
   2. Qualifications
   3. Election
   4. Relationships
   5. Responsibilities

B. THE FUNCTIONS OF THE GENERAL SUPERINTENDENT
   1. Organization
   2. Administration
   3. Supervision

C. THE RESPONSIBILITIES OF THE GENERAL SUPERINTENDENT
   1. Standards
   2. Conferences and Meetings
   3. Finances
   4. Buildings and Equipment
   5. Promotion and Publicity
   6. Atmosphere and Spirituality
   7. Extension
   8. Special Days and Worship
   9. Personal Preparation

D. THE SPECIFIC DUTIES OF THE GENERAL SUPERINTENDENT
   1. Sunday Duties
   2. Other Duties

E. THE ASSISTANTS OF THE GENERAL SUPERINTENDENT
   1. The Associate Superintendent
   2. Departmental and Divisional Superintendents
   3. The General Secretary and Treasurer
   4. Other Officers

5 | THE WORK OF THE GENERAL SUPERINTENDENT

(Administration and Supervision)

A. The Office of the General Superintendent

1. *Place in the Church and Sunday School.* The Sunday school superintendent holds a strategic and important place in the church program. He is considered an honored member of the church, should be elected by the church, and takes his place as a church officer. This will make him the official head of the Sunday school, a co-worker with the pastor in seeing that the educational function of the church is realized.

A proper conception of this office will be of great assistance in securing a qualified person to fill it as well as a motive to accept the position. It will also motivate the right kind of response on the part of the staff toward the work of the superintendent.

The office of superintendent is described as one which has certain *sacred* trusts and responsibilities. It is to be expected, therefore, that every possible effort should be made to carry out this ministry and bear heavy responsibility. Such responsibility demands authority, but it is authority of leadership, not dictatorship. Unlimited opportunities come to the superintendent who, in cooperation with the pastor, finds people who need God, wins them to Christ, and then puts them to work in the service of the King. Faithfulness in his task will bring many rewards as he shares in every victory in every class and department.

Dr. Clate Risley, General Secretary of the National Sunday School Association, has given a fine summary of the position which the superintendent holds in the church:

A *privileged layman.* His is the greatest task any layman can have.

A *leader.* He is the leader of the Sunday school. The test of a good leader is not so much what he can do himself as what he can inspire others to do.

An *executive.* He executes directives of the Board of Christian Education.

A *director.* What the director is to the band, the superintendent is to the Sunday school. Harmony or discord are largely the result of his administration.

An organizer. An organizer more than anything else sees the various parts of the whole.

An administrator. The prefix "ad" relates to giving direction; the word "minister" means servant: an administrator therefore directs servants or those serving.

A supervisor. To do a good job of supervising one must have SUPER vision, seeing more and farther than others.

A business manager. He manages the affairs of the biggest business in all the world — God's business, the Sunday school.

A servant. He is a servant or minister of the church, chosen directly or indirectly by the church, responsible to the church.

A promoter. He takes initiative in pushing the total Sunday school program.

An advisor. He is an advisor to department superintendents and other officers.

A trainer. The success of the task depends upon trained workers. The superintendent is interested in a good training program.

A talent scout. He is always on the lookout for workers of every kind.

A salesman. The Sunday school needs salesmen. The superintendent is head salesman, selling the Sunday school to the whole church and community.

A teacher. He is a teacher of teachers, showing the way.

A worker. No lazy man need consider the task. It takes time and energy.[1]

2. *Qualifications.* A place of such magnitude and responsibility as pictured above demands a person who is well qualified. While big business has taught us many things about organization and systematization, in the final analysis success has depended primarily on people. The same is true in the church school. Neither the constitution, nor the by-laws, nor organization, no matter how good, can insure success. The success of the Sunday school depends largely upon the superintendent. The first great requisite for a successful Sunday school is that the right man be chosen for the job of superintendent. The following qualifications picture the ideal superintendent. Secure a man who can come as close as possible to these qualities.

[1]Clate A. Risley, "Sunday School Superintendents," in NSSA Sunday School Convention Workshop Outlines, Vol. VII (Chicago: National Sunday School Association), p. 55.

Spiritual Qualities
1. Christian character, not dress or personality
2. A divine call to his work
3. Clean moral life
4. Strong faith
5. A Bible student
6. Uses time in God's service
7. A liberal giver
8. A man of prayer
9. One with compassion for the lost

Mental Qualities
1. A student of the Word
2. A student of human nature
3. A student of Sunday school administration
4. A student of the principles of teaching
5. A student of materials, buildings, and equipment

Professional Qualities
1. A good organizer
2. An efficient administrator
3. An effective supervisor
4. Aggressiveness
5. Imagination
6. Resourcefulness
7. A willing counselor
8. One who keeps up-to-date

Leadership Qualities
1. Vision
2. Enthusiasm
3. Executive ability
4. Aggressiveness
5. Perseverance
6. Tactfulness
7. Helpfulness
8. Patience
9. Cheerfulness
10. Progressiveness
11. Sympathy
12. Understanding

Personality Factors
1. Even-tempered
2. Pleasant manner
3. Pleasant appearance
4. Friendly
5. Genuine love for people
6. Punctual

7. Loyal
8. Dependable
9. Courteous
10. Unselfish

3. *Election.* Who should be superintendent? The director? An old man? A woman? A young man? Paid directors eliminate valuable lay contributions as well as emphasizing the educational phase of Sunday school work at the expense of administration and other phases. Older men, even who have passed the dead line of fifty, are often fresh, wise in counsel, vigorous, versatile, and as enthusiastic as middle-aged men. Young men are often rejected because "a prophet is not without honor save in his own country." Fearing that promotion may develop vanity, some churches hesitate to put them in office even though they have the desirable qualifications and would welcome opportunity for service. A woman is rarely a Sunday school superintendent. If men are unavailable, however, a sensible Christian woman with tact to govern and knowledge to teach might effectively fill the office.

Election of the Sunday school superintendent is usually done according to the church constitution. Frequently it is for a term of one year, for two reasons. (1) If several qualified men are available, an opportunity for service for all is made possible. (2) If the candidate proves to be a misfit, a one-year term facilitates his inconspicuous removal from office. In the event that no constitution exists or that it only vaguely or inadequately covers Sunday school officer elections, the following considerations should be taken into account.

Teachers doing voluntarily the heaviest part of the work and understanding the demands and difficulties of the case should have a voice in the selection of the superintendent. Since the superintendent leads and directs and has a right to demand cooperation, he should be the man of their choice.

The pastor too should have a voice in selecting the superintendent. Since he is commissioned to "feed the flock" and ordained to "teach," he is responsible for doctrines taught in the church. Sunday school teachers are his assistants. He is also liable for false teaching and heresies that might creep into his church. Inasmuch as the superintendent influences the appointing of teachers, determining subject matter and method of instruction, it seems reasonable that the pastor and superintendent work as a team in effecting the tone and tempo of the church. They should be able to pull together.

Officers or the governing board of the church should also have a voice in the election of the superintendent since matters affecting the order of discipline of the church are involved in the Sunday school. The superintendent can quietly either depreciate or exalt the teachers' and pupils' estimation of the church; thus church officers have an interest. If the board cannot approve the teachers' and pastor's choice, another mutually agreeable candidate should be sought.

Whatever method is used, the term of office should be long enough to give the superintendent a chance to succeed and develop his program. This can be done, even when the one-year term is required, by re-election.

4. *Relationships.* The superintendent should be a member of the church in good active standing. In some cases he might be a member of the ruling body of the church, depending on the framework of organization. In any event, he should be responsible to the church, either directly or through the Board of Christian Education.

He has a close relationship to the *pastor.* They are co-laborers. Their cooperation is imperative, and success is often measured by the extent of their collaboration. Where friction is present, failure is almost certain until there is a change of office. They should pray and plan together, promoting the interests of both.

The superintendent is generally a member *ex officio* of the *Board of Christian Education* and is an executive officer of the board. In this his responsibility is to carry out the policies and directives of the board in the Sunday school. At all times he is responsible to the board for his efforts and for a progress report. He is to keep the board informed of what is going on and what the needs of the school are from time to time.

The superintendent is expected to carry a burden for his *staff.* He will pray for them and assist them in every way possible. This he will do through advice and consultations. He will see that they are provided with adequate facilities, materials, and equipment wherever possible. He will seek their counsel and utilize their ideas in the management and supervision of the school. He will meet regularly with leaders for prayer, business, and planning and will coordinate the work of the whole group.

Where a *director of religious education* is present, the superintendent will work closely with him as he supervises the various members of the staff, particularly the teachers. In fact, it might prove helpful for them to allocate certain types of supervisory work to each other.

A good superintendent will not overlook the *pupils.* He will love them, encourage them, and know them by name. At times he will control them with firmness but always with love. He protects them from bad influences from both teachers and fellow students.

Successful superintendents know the importance of good home-church school relationships. They seek the counsel of *parents* and work them into the program wherever possible. He will use parent-teacher conferences as a means by which to get better acquainted with parents and to deepen Christian fellowship. Occasional reports and letters to parents will keep them informed on school progress.

5. *Responsibilities.* The functional concept of church school administration, as discussed in Chapter 1, demands that specific responsibilities be delegated to each of the major officers. While it is true that the superintendent is expected to be "general flunky" in most situations, it is necessary for him to be specifically trained for certain areas of work to be most effective. While the two areas of administration and supervision are assigned to the superintendent, there are detailed responsibilities and duties which are required of him.

The functions of the superintendent are clear and obligatory and shall be discussed in the following order in the section which follows:

1. Organization
2. Administration
3. Supervision

In carrying out these functions the superintendent's work will cut across a number of specific areas of responsibility, among which are:

1. Standards
2. Conferences and meetings
3. Finances
4. Buildings and equipment
5. Promotion and publicity
6. Atmosphere and spirituality
7. Extension
8. Special days and worship
9. Personnel preparation

There will also be specific duties to carry out at certain periods of time, such as:

1. Duties on Sunday
2. Other duties — weekly, monthly, annually

The above plan is practical where the organization has made provision for the use of department superintendents. The plan is clear because specific areas of responsibility have been assigned to the superintendent. Where department superintendents are absent, or where they are derelict in their performance, it becomes the obligation of the superintendent to assume other responsibilities, such as:

1. Curriculum (in departments)
2. Grading
3. Worship and expression
4. Accomplishments
5. Departmental promotion
6. Teacher training
7. Records
8. Home relations
9. Special days (in departments)
10. Methods
11. Measurement
12. Evangelism (in classes)

B. THE FUNCTIONS OF THE GENERAL SUPERINTENDENT

1. *Organization.* In organization the superintendent is concerned with the division of the work and the workers. The organization of the total program has been discussed quite thoroughly in Chapter 1, but it is the responsibility of the superintendent to see things as a whole and particularly how the church school fits into the total program. He will be careful to see that the Sunday school becomes the heart of the instructional program of the church and that the three main divisions — children, youth, and adults — are maintained. In these divisions will be found the framework upon which the organization hangs and they will include departments. As far as personnel, space, and resources will allow, he will maintain the departmental system as follows:

1. Cradle Roll
2. Nursery
3. Beginner or Kindergarten
4. Primary
5. Junior
6. Junior High (Intermediate)
7. Senior High
8. Young People
9. Adults
10. Home or Extension

Organization also calls for the management of the staff of workers, giving them assignments, materials, and equipment. It calls for the promotion of the work in the church and to the public. It calls for adequate financial support. A good administrator will not try to accomplish all this work alone. Instead, he will carefully organize his workers to accomplish the desired goals.

It is not necessary at this point to list the various officers and workers on the staff. The functional concept demands that this be done in the "setting" of each worker. For example, the work of the treasurer will be under the general supervision of the superintendent and will be discussed, therefore, in the section on responsibilities which follows. Others will be discussed in the closing section of the chapter.

It is helpful to note at this point that the superintendent has two classes of workers to organize: (1) administrators and (2) educators. Administrators consist of the superintendent and all general officers who have the responsibility of organizing and operating the church school. In some instances they will also assist in securing the educational workers. They are vitally concerned as well with the promotion and extension of the school. It is evident therefore that such workers should possess executive and business abilities.

The educational workers are concerned primarily with the teaching-learning process. Thus they are concerned with the curriculum and all departmental and classroom situations. Teachers are included.

In the selection of these workers, the superintendent will work with the pastor and/or director. Selection and training were discussed fully in Chapter 3 on the work of the pastor.

2. *Administration.* The concept of the superintendent as an administrator broadens his work rather than limiting it. In the past he was concerned primarily with "opening Sunday school." Now with the advent of the departmental system, the superintendent is not merely responsible for one service, but several of them in the departments. Instead of leading one small segment of the program, he now leads various groups and their leaders.

Administration refers to management and operation. The policies and directives from the Board of Education and various planning commissions must be carried out in the school. The machinery of the school must be put into operation. Many practical matters demand the superintendent's attention, such as enrollment, records, equipment, supplies, attendance, curriculum, schedules, etc. Although he may delegate many of these duties to others, he is still responsible for them. This is where executive ability is of great value to the superintendent.

Some of the marks of good administration are:
1. Vision
2. Growth
3. Integration with church program
4. Stability in handling staff personnel and problems
5. Skillful evaluation of ability
6. Patience
7. Perseverance
8. Clear purposes and objectives
9. Friendship without familiarity
10. Confidence
11. Alertness for new ideas
12. Efficiency
13. Prayer
14. Spirituality

Good administration is concerned with the total program; therefore the total program should be carefully planned annually for as much as a year in advance. Every effort should be put forth to maintain the highest possible standards in the program and organizations.

Co-ordination of efforts and plans are necessary for good administration. The activities of the various groups and departments need to be co-ordinated so that an overall unified program is developed. Communicating the information to the proper source for clearance is essential.

Promotion provides a basis for getting the program before the church and the public. Every known method — spoken, written, visual — should be used by the administrator in accomplishing this goal.

Financial matters, regarding both support and disbursement of funds, need to be handled with carefulness and efficiency. The stewardship of money will be a great concern to the superintendent.

The program of worship will receive particular attention by the superintendent. In those situations where there is the assembly type of worship, he will be expected to lead directly in the act and practice of worship. Besides leading the worship service itself, the superintendent will make provisions for training in worship, dealing with such matters as the nature and purpose of worship, schedules, and instructional periods.

Of great assistance to the superintendent in carrying out his responsibilities in organization and administration is the "committee on administration of the church school." Some call it the "cabinet" or "Sunday school committee." Chart 9 in Chapter 1 shows the relation of this committee to the Board of Christian Education above it and the divisions of the church school below it. Chart 13 on page 134 reveals the provision for this committee as it is abstracted from the general plan of organization. Here one can see the functions of administration a little more clearly.

The committee on administration is composed of the general superintendent — who is chairman — the pastor, the director, the superintendents of the various instructional divisions and the general officers, including the secretary and treasurer. In small churches the divisional superintendents will likely be the same as department superintendents, but in large churches it is quite possible that only the divisional superintendents will be present on the committee to represent the instructional departments.

The purpose of this committee is to facilitate the work of the superintendent in administration. This body, therefore, is not a policy-making group; instead it is a business body. Its objectives are the objectives of Christian education. The functional concept demands that there be a primary committee for each one of the ob-

jectives. It shall be expected, therefore, that the objectives of
evangelism, education, worship, and fellowship will be represented
by standing committees as revealed in Chart 13 below. In addition to the work of the committees, the administrative responsibili-

CHART 13
THE COMMITTEE ON ADMINISTRATION FOR THE CHURCH SCHOOL
(Cabinet)

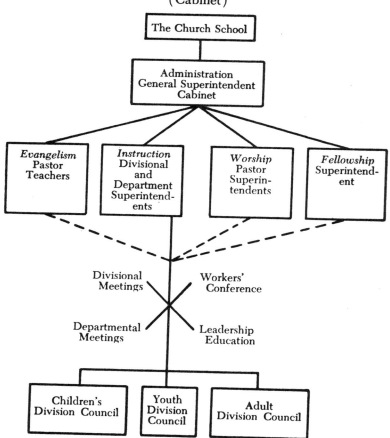

ties of this group will include the functioning of the various divisional and departmental meetings of the church school, the workers'
conference, and leadership education. While it is true that certain
of these functions are under the direct supervision of administrative officers (for example, evangelism and the pastor), yet the
work of the committee on administration is to assist these various

officers in the planning and execution of their responsibilities. The committee, therefore, will serve as a clearing house for all problems and directives. It will also serve as a means of checking the progress which has been made. It will make sure that the functions of administration, organization, and supervision are adequately accomplished. Meetings should be planned monthly with procedures controlled by usual parliamentary methods.

At the divisional level there is a "council of workers," whose responsibility it is to plan and administrate the work of the division. The Sunday school with its various instructional departments forms the core of the instructional program. The committee on administration will make provision for regular meetings of these councils and receive reports of their work. It will consider all general matters of business which concern these departments, such as finances, promotion, space, supplies, etc.

This plan is quite adaptable to the small church. No matter how small the staff may be in such churches, there will be a general officer of some kind to represent a division of work. In the various divisions of the church school perhaps one teacher could serve in the double capacity of, for example, teacher-superintendent. This is also true in the various Sunday school departments.

The operation of the Sunday schedule is the responsibility of the general superintendent. He is assisted in planning by the committee on administration or cabinet. More about this is considered in the last section of this chapter.

3. *Supervision.* Improvement and efficiency is at the heart of supervision. There must be constant and continuous improvement in both quantity and quality. The superintendent should be concerned that the Sunday school be the best possible school. In this work he will collaborate with the pastor and director of religious education. All these individuals, as well as department superintendents, are concerned with the problems of supervision. While it is true that the director is primarily concerned with this area, yet the superintendent cannot possibly escape some responsibility in this regard. This is particularly true where there is no director on the staff. Then the primary responsibility will rest upon the superintendent and the department workers.

In doing the work of supervision, the superintendent is not actually employed in the work of the officers and teachers himself. Instead, he is assisting them in reaching a higher level of accomplishment and in measurement of results. Here again, as pointed out earlier, the greater part of this work will be done with the teachers in improving the quality of class instruction and learning. Included in the expected outcomes of this kind of work will be the inculcation of new ideas, the development of newer and better attitudes toward work, the lifting of morale, adoption of new materials and methods, evaluation of results, workers conferences, better records, etc.

This kind of work calls naturally for a great many conferences with the teachers and officers. Personal conferences give the superintendent an opportunity to face actual situations and give practical assistance. He may choose to call in outside workers and consultants to assist him in this work occasionally. Where he does not feel that he has the skill for observation, the superintendent may supervise "at a distance" through the departmental officers and workers who are in intimate contact with the classroom situation. Of course, where there is a director on the staff, the superintendent will confer with him and refer workers to this officer for direct assistance. It is wise, however, for the superintendent even in a situation of this kind to do some of the work of supervision himself. It will be a matter of planning with the director what areas of emphasis and need should be attended to.

Heim reported the results of a survey on advising a novice on supervising techniques in church school improvement as follows:

1. Proceed slowly in making changes
2. Win confidence in proposed changes
3. Work cooperatively in making changes
4. Study the situation by careful analysis
5. Select a point of attack
6. Plan in detail
7. Secure support of everybody concerned
8. Complete the enterprise[2]

C. THE RESPONSIBILITIES OF THE GENERAL SUPERINTENDENT

1.   *Standards*

Nature and Purpose. The functional concept of administration stresses objectives and workers rather than topics in planning. The primary responsibility of the superintendent, therefore, is to keep standards ever before him and the staff. Without clearly defined standards, the superintendent has no sound basis for procedure, operation, or analysis. The adoption of a set of Sunday school standards will greatly facilitate the work of the whole staff.

Traditionally, a standard has served as a basis of comparison, a means of measurement. In early days men used the handbreadth, the foot, and the cubit. Now we use standardized measures and weights.

God has used standards. His Word validates the use of a standard. Christ is the measure of a perfect man (Eph. 4:13). Paul compared churches and givers.

[2]Ralph D. Heim, *Leading a Sunday Church School* (Philadelphia: The Muhlenberg Press, 1950), Chapter 3. The points quoted above are paragraph headings.

A standard is nothing more than an instrument, a plan of work. Thus, it has been observed, "a Sunday school standard is an established rule in measuring, guiding and judging the Sunday school in its organization, administration, curriculum, leadership, methods of operation and spirituality."

How do you know you have a good school? What does your school need or lack? A standard will help you answer these questions. The program of the early church, as carried out by the apostles, was united and moved toward a common objective. They had a plan of work. The Sunday school needs this kind of incentive to do better work. A well-developed standard will give it just such an incentive in workable features and attainable goals.

Arthur Flake, says:

"A good Sunday school is not an accident. It must be built. In order to build a good Sunday school three things are necessary:

(1) The essentials of a good Sunday school must be known.

(2) The plans for building a good Sunday school must be understood.

(3) The specifications for building a good Sunday school faithfully followed."[3]

The ideal Sunday school standard sets forth clearly the essentials of a good school, and the plans for building such a school. Such a standard, however, must not be considered as an end in itself, but rather a means to an end.

The adoption and successful use of a standard will do several things for a Sunday school:

1. It will motivate better work
2. It will provide an ideal for which to strive
3. It will keep the program properly balanced
4. It will provide unity for operation
5. It will provide a basis for evaluation

The Superintendent and Standards. The superintendent needs to work with the pastor, director, and Board of Christian Education — in fact, the whole staff — in setting up standards for the entire church school. No more important task than this can be engaged in. Where interest is lacking among other officers and leaders, then the superintendent should take the lead in introducing the matter to the staff.

Where the superintendent is fortunate enough to be a member of a denomination which has a national standard, it will be relatively easy to adopt the standard. In such cases, the central govern-

[3]Arthur Flake, *Building a Standard Sunday School* (Nashville, Tenn.: The Sunday School Board of the Southern Baptist Convention, 1950), p. 12.

ing body of the group should make available at check-time a report form for each school on which their standing with respect to the standard is ascertained. Individual schools adopting the standard should make an annual evaluation under their own initiative, seeking to raise the total score from year to year. The final test is the extent to which the standard leads pupils to live the Christian life and staff members to become better leaders (see Appendix V).

An award system of some kind is used in many churches in connection with the recognition of accomplishments by the standard. An illustration of this is the system used by the Assemblies of God. Recognition for both individual persons and individual churches should be provided for. "Gold Crown Schools" and "Silver Crown Schools'" help to place one in the corresponding category decided upon.

It has been suggested that a standard can be applied at any time of the year. Some have found, however, that it is preferable to start at the opening of one of the quarters of the Sunday school year. Perhaps the ideal time is at the beginning of the school year, the first Sunday in October.

The first step toward introducing the standard is a thorough study of the requirements of the various features of the standard by the pastor and superintendent. When the leaders thoroughly understand the standard, then gather the rest of the staff and explain thoroughly and fully the purpose and value of the standard with its various features. Enlist the interest and aid of the workers and pupils in order to assure full cooperation in carrying out the plan. Hang a copy of the standard on the wall. The ideal standard, if followed implicitly, will bring out in leaders, officers, teachers, and pupils qualities which will get results. This cannot be accomplished, however, unless everyone concerned is convinced of the values involved. Actually, the conclusion of the matter is a willingness on the part of the staff to put into the program the necessary amount of time, effort, and consecration, regardless of the cost, and be satisfied with nothing less than absolute thoroughness in every detail. After all, the Christian ministry is the greatest work in the world and it demands our absolute best.

As soon as possible after a standard has been adopted for the school as a whole, each department and class should adopt one for their respective areas of responsibility, all of which are integrated with the group standard. An illustration of this is the system of standards used by the Southern Baptist Convention.

2. Conferences and Meetings

Pattern. Sunday school standards demand a unified and well-organized school. A school which is unified in purpose and organization and enthusiastic in administration and activities inspires both workers and pupils. It is the work of the superintendent to strive to this end. He cannot, however, accomplish this alone. Group meetings of various kinds are essential in meeting the goals, and cooperation and coordination of effort is necessary to realize efficiency.

The various features of the church school program call for a variety of group conferences. A comprehensive administrative framework calls for meetings concerned primarily with business, others with instruction, some for fellowship, still others for counsel, and all for fellowship. A good superintendent will work out a pattern for meetings by which all these functions are provided for and through which good results are obtained.

Three patterns are practiced at large in church schools today: (1) the weekly system, which provides one evening each week for the school, (2) the bi-weekly system, providing for two meetings per month, and (3) the monthly plan. The plans outlined below are illustrative.

Weekly Pattern
(One evening per week)

1st Thursday — committee on administration, or executive conference

2nd Thursday — workers' conference (general conference)

3rd Thursday — Divisional and/or departmental conferences

4th Thursday — Board of Christian Education and class meetings

Bi-Weekly Pattern
(Two evenings per month)

1st Thursday — committee on administration, or executive conference, and Board of Christian Education

3rd Thursday — workers conference, or general conference, and divisional and/or departmental conferences

Monthly Pattern
(One evening per month)

1st month in Quarter — Board of Christian Education, and class meetings

2nd month in quarter — workers' conference, and departmental meetings

3rd month in quarter — committee on administration

The advantage of the weekly pattern is that one full evening a week provides adequate time for planning and discussion. The workers' conference can have a general session for instruction and inspiration, followed by a leadership training class of some kind. The bi-weekly pattern is comprehensive but calls for longer periods of time. The monthly pattern is similar to the bi-weekly except that meetings do not occur as often. It is often used in small and country churches. The superintendent and committee on administration will be faced with adopting one of these patterns for effective work.

Where none of these patterns can be used, the superintendent is faced with calling meetings whenever possible. This situation, however, does not have to exist even in small churches. Where it does exist and where there is no Board of Christian Education, then by all means the superintendent should call a monthly meeting of his committee on administration to conduct business, and then attempt to have a separate training period some time during the year. This haphazard plan is definitely in practice but not recommended. A *minimum* pattern calls for:

1. A Board of Christian Education
2. A Committee on Administration
3. A Workers' Conference

The Committee on Administration. This committee is an executive one. It is concerned primarily with business routine, but it is also a channel of coordination and operation. The work of this committee was discussed at length in the preceding section. Suffice to say, the superintendent will look to this committee, composed of general officers and departmental leaders, to see that the objectives are realized on the one hand and that there is smooth operation on the other. Some schools prefer to use the term "Sunday school council" (see Chart 13).

Some of the responsibilities besides business with which this committee is concerned include outlining the program for the workers' conference, organization of plans and policies to be submitted to the Board of Christian Education, and recommendations. An agendum might look like the following:

Devotions
Minutes
Correspondence
Committee reports
Unfinished business
Reports of officers and superintendents
New business
Prayer

An executive committee — composed of general superintendent as chairman, the pastor and/or director of Christian education, and general secretary — may meet during the interim to prepare various agenda for the meetings and to take care of interim business. A report of their activities should be expected at the regular meeting of the committee.

Divisional and Departmental Meetings. The church school is organized into three divisions, no matter how large or small a church may be: (1) children's division, from birth through 11 years;

(2) youth division, ages 12 through 24; and (3) adult division, ages over 24. A good superintendent will recognize the value of calling separate meetings for these divisions. In medium and large churches these divisions will have departments within them. In such cases department meetings will be necessary. In small churches, however, one meeting may well suffice for both division and department.

Each division needs a superintendent and a council of workers to assist him. In large churches Sunday school department superintendents will be on this council along with workers in other church groups, such as MYF counselors, vacation church school director, etc. At stated intervals meetings should be called to facilitate the business of the divisions, make plans, and train workers. Departmental meetings will be concerned primarily with problems and needs within each department of the Sunday school. More will be said about these meetings in Chapter 6 on "the work of the department superintendent."

The General Superintendent will try to be present at these meetings as much as time will allow. He will remind the workers of their responsibilities and give assistance to them whenever and wherever possible. In small churches he will find many opportunities to give a great deal of time and attention to these meetings, but he should never usurp the position of the divisional or departmental superintendent.

Class Meetings. The values of organized classes in Sunday school are widely known. They are useful particularly in youth and adult divisions and older classes in the children's division. Among other purposes, organized classes make it possible for social and expressional activities to be carried out. Opportunities for service can be made realities. In the adult division, however, the general superintendent should be alert to any tendencies toward "independence." On the other hand, he can be greatly helpful to teachers and classes by suggesting projects and service activities. They can be particularly helpful in visitation, soul winning, and extension work. In fact, the wise pastor and superintendent know that no great Sunday school or church can be built unless they give strong and systematic support to organized classes. Special days and seasons provide these classes with unusual opportunities to demonstrate their worth and effectiveness.

Teachers' Meetings. In the past many superintendents performed invaluable services to workers and teachers in teachers' meetings. Such periods were given to instruction, inspiration, prayer, fellowship, and counsel. They were useful in days when uniform lessons were used throughout the entire school. Graded lessons and departmental organization have made changes, to the extent that teachers' meetings are no longer possible in many schools.

Where this type of conference is still conducted, time should be given to this responsibility alone. These meetings are not times for debating issues or theology, nor are they merely lecture periods. Instead, they are times for lesson study and teaching teachers what and how to teach; definite opportunities for asking questions and raising problems should be allowed. Occasionally, longer meetings may be conducted to consider larger questions, such as the library, music, and organization.

The best person available should lead a teachers' meeting. This may be the superintendent or the pastor. If the superintendent is not doing too well, help him, meet with him, and train him for the job.

The Workers' Conference. It is not possible for the business and responsibilities of the average church school to be cared for in one meeting per month. This is particularly true in small churches because the tendency is to consider one meeting adequate. When one considers, however, the multiplicity of curriculum and teaching problems, finances, not to speak of hundreds of administrative problems, one meeting cannot possibly take care of things.

The workers' conference is designed to overcome this difficulty. This meeting is simply a conference of all the workers to solve problems and make plans which result in improvement. Where the Board of Christian Education is concerned with policy making and total program planning and the committee on administration or Sunday school council with business and operation, the workers' conference is devoted to instruction, inspiration, planning, training, and problem solving. Next to the prayer meeting the superintendent will find this conference of perhaps greatest benefit to him.

In a small church it is often wise for the church Board of Christian Education and the workers' conference to serve as one body, except in the election of officers and teachers, in which case the board itself will act.

A workers' conference serves two main purposes: (1) It provides opportunity for the dissemination of information, and (2) It provides a clearing house for all sorts of problems and propositions. Other purposes include counsel, inspiration, instruction, fellowship, enthusiasm, and dedication. An overall function of the conference is leadership education; it provides "on the job" training. These training enterprises center in the life experiences of teachers, in their own teaching experience. An efficient superintendent who studies his school will find plenty of problems suitable for study and discussion at the workers' conference. Some of the more strategic areas in which problems arise include new workers, records, standards, classroom problems, and curriculum.

Membership in the workers' conference should consist of all workers and officers with definite church school responsibilities. Variations will be made in the membership list depending upon the size of the school and denominational policies. As a part of the teacher's covenant or appointment to a class, it should be stated that attendance is expected at the workers' conference.

The success or failure of a conference depends largely on the amount of preliminary planning. Since workers' meetings are so vital, it is well to arrange a well-planned program that has been initiated a year or, at least, six months in advance. The Board of Christian Education is responsible for the appointment of a group to plan the year's program of workers' conferences. This group might be the board itself, a committee from the board, or groups outside the board.

The most important fact to remember in planning is the use of a theme. Perhaps the denomination has a yearly theme which can be followed, and then monthly themes worked out which contribute toward the development of the year's theme. During the conference, remember that no worker's opinion is too humble for consideration. Some kind of short, interesting features might be inserted to break the monotony of the workers' conference. Perhaps a ten minute drill, designed to aid the teacher along the line of pedagogy, Bible history, geography, or a short paper read on some practical aspect of church school work, would be good.

Many schools have conferences on a ten month schedule. One effective way of securing attendance is through a supper, followed by a program which ends by 9:00 P.M. The supper has the advantages of fellowship, and is often the only opportunity for workers to get acquainted with one another. At this time they can also have common worship. Constant effort must be employed to secure regular attendance. If one worker is absent, it will impair the progress of the whole church school.

How long should the conference last? No more than ninety minutes, unless a workers' supper is included. The best time for starting and closing will differ from group to group. The important rules are to begin and stop on time and keep the program moving smoothly.

The primary feature of the month should be varied. Variety is one of the key elements to the success of a workers' conference. A good rule is to plan a different type for each month of the year. Types of conferences are: speaker, panel, debate, group discussion, clinic, forum, symposium, report of meetings, report of visits, reviews, demonstration, workshop, exhibits, business reports, special problems, content coaching, covenant and planning.

Four kinds of conferences might be held: general, departmental, organizational, and parental. It is evident that the size of the school and the nature of the problem will have a bearing on the kind of conference to be held. An attempt should always be made to reach conclusions at each conference. General meetings might be held for inspiration, matters of common interest, fun and fellowship. Departmental meetings would be for a study of current church school lessons, etc. The combined meetings would consider some topic or problem followed by specialized consideration of it on the part of representatives from different age groups.

The themes might possibly be arranged on a calendar as follows:

DATE	Aug.	Sept.	Oct.	Nov.	Dec.	Etc.
WHAT?	Retreat Rally Day	Grading	Worship	Etc.		
WHO?	Officers Workers	Mr. Jones	Mrs. Smith			
WHEN?	28th Camp	7th	8th	etc.		
How?	Dis-cussion	Panel	Demon-stration	etc.		
COM?			Christ-mas			
DEVOTIONS						

The topic chosen for each month should express variety. These topics will arise naturally from the work of the school. They will be matters of importance to all. A constant study of the church school needs by the superintendent will reveal more problems than can be considered. Themes may be arranged in the form of a calendar. Possible year-round themes are: home and church school in cooperation; stewardship, evangelism, indoctrination, teacher training and growth. Or these themes might be adopted on a seasonal basis. Possible monthly themes might be as follows:

January .....study Personal evangelism; pupil prayer lists
February ....Temperance; home calling
March ......Evangelism; plan for next quarter
April ......D.V.B.S.; special days
May ....Summer interest; camps; summer attendance
June ....Home-church cooperation
July ....Equipment; stewardship emphasis in school, class, and personal life
August .....Rally day; picnics; book reviews

September ... Grading the church for teaching
October ..... Worship; elements, aids; curriculum
November ... Teacher: qualifications, improvement, teachers use check-up chart
December ... Emphasis on coming year's goals; expansion and extension.

3. Finances

Financial Motivation. Every Sunday school superintendent who endeavors to build a successful Sunday school must instigate a sound financial program. He must stimulate his people not only to pay their tithes but to give God an offering which is over and above the tithe. He must instill in his people motives for giving.

Every Sunday school has a financial need. Some schools have programs that supply the finances for those needs in a respectable and Christlike manner, while others find themselves in a state of financial embarrassment all the time. Some schools are unable to meet their needs because they have no financial program. This usually indicates a state of spiritual starvation in the school.

Some Sunday schools have an inadequate financial program or a partial program. Some denominational objectives are fostered by the few participating members. Then as the needs arise and current expenses go into arrears, the pastor and superintendent urge the members to give until it hurts. Under such conditions, it hurts to give anything!

A good financial program will keep the school financially sound. It should educate and enlist in scriptural giving every man, woman, and child who regularly attends the church and school. This will keep the school free from debt for current expenses and missions. The objective of a good financial program is to get every member to contribute to the Sunday school regulary his tithe and also an offering. The local merchants with their "pay as you go" plan have proven that we can pay a lot of money if we pay it a little at a time.

Financial Education. Probably the most important item in a program of finance is the provision made for educating boys and girls in the Christian use of money; they need instruction in stewardship, tithing, and systematic giving.

Christian stewardship is not a matter of what we can do for God; it is rather a matter of what God can do with us and through us. Boys and girls must be taught God's ownership of their possessions, and yet His wonderful partnership which He entrusts to His children — the privilege and responsibility of a wise expenditure of His capital. Children and young people especially need to be reminded that providence has a large part in production, and that personal acquisition is far more dependent upon God and society than the efforts of the individual.

Boys and girls need instruction in tithing. The practice of tithing can be developed in childhood and become a fixed habit in later life. It has been said, "Bring up a child to give pennies, and when he is old he will not depart from it." Tithing is a habit which needs to be learned in youth.

Not only does the principle of stewardship and tithing need to be taught, but it needs to find expression in systematic giving. The New Testament plan as set forth by Paul is, "Upon the first day of the week, let every one lay by him in store as God has prospered him" (I Cor. 16:2). Even when Sunday school pupils cannot be brought to tithe their income, they can at least be urged to make a systematic offering. The weekly envelope in conjunction with the Six Point Record System will give an excellent opportunity to put this instruction into practice.

Financial Administration. Good financial administration is the answer for every Sunday school with financial problems. A real Sunday school cannot exist without money. This is clearly a church obligation. It has been estimated that not more than one-half of all church members contribute to the current expenses and that only one-fourth of all members contribute to missions. Is it any wonder that 200,000 churches in America expend two to three million dollars each year for interest on borrowed money? Good financial administration could end all this.

Every school should have a treasurer. In small schools the office may be combined with that of secretary. Among his many duties would be helping to prepare the financial budget, bank and expend the monies, and make periodic reports. Some schools put him in charge of financial education. In larger churches it might be desirable to have a financial committee for the purpose of preparing the financial program and considering ways and means of putting it into effect. The treasurer would be chairman of this committee. Some churches use a financial secretary who keeps records of all contributions, receives monies, and deposits them. Where this custom is followed, the treasurer receives monies and disburses funds. Whatever system is used, careful provisions for auditing the books and records should be made. A quarterly report is especially helpful.

Every school should have a financial budget; it may be in conjunction with the church budget or it may be separate. A budget is a prepared financial statement showing the probable income and expenditures for the ensuing year. The budget should be prepared by the treasurer or the financial committee and recommended by the teachers and officers for adoption at the opening of the Sunday school year. The budget should be approved by the committee on administration or board of christian education and adopted by the official board of the church. It should be divided into three parts: the current expenses, expansion, and missions.

The current expenses include such items as housing, promotions, salaries, office materials, advertisements, etc., as administration expenses. Educational costs cover Sunday school literature, Bibles, books, object lessons, etc. Social expenditures include conferences, socials, annual picnics, etc. The expansion section of the budget should set aside funds for the new building or renovation or expansion of the old one. Additional equipment both for repairing or replacement will be needed. The missions section of the budget provides monies for missions; it should expand proportionately with the rest of the budget.

Having prepared a budget, the next step is to plan for the income. Pledges are desirable for adults, but are not advocated for Sunday school scholars. The act of seeking advanced pledges turns the offerings into collections and the fixing of the amount in advance detracts from the gift's educational value; character is established by free choices. Besides, all children could not pledge the same amount and this would lead to emotional frustration. Children should be encouraged to bring love gifts to God every Sunday during the regular offering. The custom of dispensing with class "collections" and receiving offerings as a part of the worship service has much to commend it. Where the class system is used, dignify the habit of giving rather than the amount. Avoid rivalry in giving.

Special offerings can be taken periodically for the building fund and missions, but this should be at regular times, not just when the need is pressing. Avoid high pressure appeals for candy and picnics. Other sources of finance for the school may come from the church budget, class projects, or gifts from generous individuals.

The superintendent is obligated to inform his school about financial needs and *causes*. This can be done through a *periodic* statement which includes also a statement of disbursements. An informed school will give more.

Dignity should characterize the custom of receiving offerings. As a part of the worship service, the offering is dignified. In reporting the amounts given, Marion Lawrance suggested that the record show the number who omitted giving on a particular Sunday.

"A good Sunday school costs something; and it ought to be worth all that it costs."

4. *Buildings and Equipment*

Responsibility. In the average church the trustees generally have the oversight of property. Where proper attention to church school needs are lacking on their part, the pastor and superintendent should call to their attention the various needs present in the program. At least annually the superintendent, along with the teachers, trustees and even the pastor, should inspect the rooms and departments of the school building. Such matters as light, heat, ventilation, color, size of furniture, cabinet space, visual aids, etc., need to be considered. All these things have teaching significance and have psychological as well as spiritual implications. Plans for improvement and expansion may be guided by the best which good theory demands.

While it is true that good teachers can often succeed without tools, it is also true that they can do a *better* job with good conditions and effective tools. Proper equipment stimulates confidence and inspires to greater efforts. It attracts pupils to the classroom. With little effort the average school can improve its teaching-learning conditions. The result will be larger numbers, better discipline, and spiritual fruit.

Superintendents need to know ideal building conditions and standards. Such knowledge is obviously helpful in planning new school structures, but it is also necessary in improving and remodeling old ones. Small changes made gradually will bring the superintendent to his ideal.

Principles. Certain principles are present to direct the erection of new buildings and the improvement of old ones. Every effort should be exerted to practice the following principles and standards:

1. Present and future needs of pupils and workers should guide planning and improvement
2. An annual survey of buildings and equipment will make analysis possible
3. A comprehensive program calls for provision for worship, instruction, social life, and administration
4. Housing, equipment and supplies must follow the graded principle
5. Activities in the curriculum demand larger classrooms, flexible equipment, and a wide variety of supplies
6. Quality and beauty should approximate the prevailing standards for community homes
7. Equipment should be sturdy and permanent, but comfortable and suitable
8. Economy in construction and use is essential today
9. Both building and equipment should be adaptable for use and expansion and must be functional
10. All building should be to the glory of God

The average superintendent must "sell" his people on these principles. Trips to neighboring churches may show them what is being done. Parents can be informed of needs and invited to see them. The church can provide an adequate budget. To do this the superintendent must constantly study the building and needs.

Housing. In the past the Uniform Lesson system gave birth to the "Akron plan," which called for a semi-circular building with partitioned classrooms facing the platform. The present-day emphasis on grading and departments calls for separate classrooms, departments, and even sanctuaries. The departmental plan has been considered more economical and better adapted to worship, study, expression, and social life.

A good school building demands certain provisions. Offices and rooms are needed for management and operation. Comfort demands rest rooms, storage space, and cloak-rooms. Instruction calls for classrooms and assembly spaces for study, expression, and training. Worship demands beauty, quietness, space, and quality. Fellowship calls for recreation, a kitchen, and possibly a playground. Even in small churches this pattern should be a guiding factor.

In addition to the above factors, however, is that of present-day trends. Among these are the increasing use of audio-visual aids, the integration of church and Sunday schools into a seven-day program, demands for church libraries, and activities in the curriculum which require more space and equipment. Most recently, however, are the suggestions which came out of the 1954 meeting of the Chicago Conference on Christian Education and Church Building. The results of this meeting are recorded in the recent publication of the National Council of the Churches of Christ and authored by C. Harry Atkinson, *Building and Equipping for Christian Education*[4] (Readers may refer to the reference in the reading list at the end of this chapter). Some of their analysis shows trends toward teaching larger groups. This calls for larger classrooms because activities are being stressed. Activities in turn demand more flexibility in the use of rooms, the wider utilization of movable partitions, and larger storage space. All these trends show that more freedom is being extended to pupils. It is believed that less formality leads to more variety and better interest. Multiple use of both space and equipment is to be noted. In some larger churches two Sunday school sessions are used and a through-the-week program is observed. All these changes have been motivated by "changing patterns of modern life" and the desire to meet human needs. The tendency today, therefore, seems to be away from the traditional departmental assembly plan back to the single classroom plan where worship becomes a part of the dynamic teaching process. Until this plan has been proved, many evangelicals will hesitate to accept it, although some may prove to be interested in the other trends. On the other hand, this trend is certainly

[4]Revised. See also Mildred C. Widber and S. T. Ritenour, *Focus: Building for Christian Education* (Philadelphia: Pilgrim Press, 1969).

closer to the apostolic plan and interlocutory methods of the early church which called for small catechetical group meetings and pupil participation. In a recent survey of new churches, Virgil E. Foster indicated some present day trends as follows:

> As it plans a new building or the modernization of an old one, a church must take into account all of the responsibilities it needs to face. It must make provision for the increasing number of older people; for the children's and young people's club groups during the week; for choirs and Sunday-evening youth fellowship groups; for couples' clubs, women's meetings, and many others.[5]

He then goes on to point out certain questions which each church needs to face in developing a master plan:

> Will there be multiple sessions of the church school and more than one church worship service?
>
> Should the church plan to expand its church school session to one and a half hours or two hours?
>
> How much of a club program, such as Scouting, is needed?
>
> How many youth fellowships will there be on Sunday evening, and will they meet simultaneously?
>
> Will they need a kitchenette, power for audio-visuals, and recreation facilities?
>
> What choirs will there be, and what shall be their relation to the church school and youth program?
>
> Are there to be adult and young adult programs on Sunday morning? How many?
>
> How will the church school rooms be used during the week? Will the women's groups use them?
>
> Will there be a weekday nursery and kindergarten?
>
> What is the real purpose of each program in terms of what is to happen to persons?[6]

Much study has been given to space needs. Tendency toward larger classes increases the need for more space. Space needs vary from 25 to 30 square feet per pupil for pre-school pupils to 6 to 10 square feet in older departments. Of course, the small church has to use whatever space is available. The trend is away from basements too. Avoid basements when possible. Someone said, "A basement Sunday school room is a debasement to the Sunday school idea."

Decoration is important. Harsh colors should be avoided. Dark rooms may need light colors to reflect more light. Bright

---

[5]Virgil E. Foster, "Plan for the Whole Program," *International Journal of Religious Education* (Feb. 1960), p. 4. This whole issue is devoted to recent trends and principles of building and equipping for Christian education in the local church.
[6]*Ibid.*

rooms need quiet colors. Walls, woodwork and floor coverings should blend with other colors and the activities involved.

More will be said about space needs in the chapter which follows.

Equipment and Supplies. Superintendents should insist on equipment of high quality, particularly in the children's division. Deep impressions on children and parents are made by good equipment. This goes for both large and small churches. It is reprehensible for any church school to use "cast-off" equipment and materials, even though Grandma did use a chair for forty years and then donate it to the Sunday school!

Another important principle is that of grading. Equipment and materials should be adapted to the age groups. It is a sad picture to see small children sitting on chairs designed for adults.

Space prohibits the discussion of the details needed in each classroom and department at this point. Superintendents may refer to the next chapter and to the master bibliography in the back of this book for recommended sources where proper information is available. General needs, however, call for such items as blackboards, bulletin boards, chairs, desks, cabinets, coat racks, curtains, shades and drapes, floor coverings, maps, charts, office equipment, pictures, audio-visual equipment, public address system, signal system, tables, screens, toys, cribs, and many other items too numerous to mention.

All workers should be urged to take good care of everything, maintaining order, cleanliness, and supply. Reverence needs to be developed in this regard. All that has been said here applies also to supplies. Quality, grading, quarterly, conservation, and economy are all demanded in handling supplies.

Audio-visual equipment to be purchased first includes a filmstrip projector and screen. A combination projector will show 2 x 2 slides. Motion picture equipment should come last.

The Small Church. It is quite possible that this discussion should have begun with the small church, because the great majority of schools are found in churches below 300 enrollment. All that has been said, however, about quality and high ideals is just as applicable here as elsewhere. In fact due to the intimate situation in small churches these matters assume perhaps greater importance. In some respects it is also easier to achieve beauty, order, and essential unity in small churches.

In the *one-room* church, where the building is used for worship and Sunday school sessions, the superintendent must make careful adjustments in both space and equipment. Flexible seating makes possible the shifting of equipment. A folding chair of high quality and durability is recommended. Pews cannot be easily moved, but where they exist they should be confined to the center of the room. Corners and sides can be filled with chairs and screens. In cases where pews are present, they may be reversed and used as benches. Backs can be used for display. The piano can be turned around and the back used. Corners can be used for storage. Drop leaves can be placed on walls in corners and on the back of pews.

Screens and curtains can be used to separate groups. Screens can serve also as blackboards and bulletin boards. One side can be used for hanging boards on it, thus providing double purpose equipment. The space in front between the first pew and pulpit can be used for a class by reversing the first pew. One class can sit in the choir or another behind the piano. It might be possible to relocate classes to give a better balance in the use of space. Nearby buildings and homes might provide additional possibilities. Where the weather permits, classes can meet outside under a shade tree.

The *two- or three-room* church has fewer problems of space. Where such rooms are available, the small children can be removed from the sanctuary. Where a basement is available, of course, arrangements can be made for classes there, but avoid this if possible. Keep the small children, however, upstairs. Basements also serve for fellowship occasions, but the trend today is definitely away from basements.

Multiple sessions solve space problems in some churches. This is also done in larger churches to avoid new construction. This plan calls for members to live relatively close to the church. In the case where a church has a basement or two or three rooms, the following plan might work:

9:00 - 9:50 a.m.   Primaries and juniors
10:00 - 10:50 a.m.   Junior high, youth, and adults
11:00 - 12:00 noon   Pre-school and morning worship

Variations to this plan are as follows:

9:00 - 9:45   Church school (1) youth, (2) adults without children, (3) parents with children in youth groups

10:00 - 11:00   Church worship service and extended session for children

11:15 - 12:00   Church school for (1) children, and (2) parents of children

There are other variations of this plan.

Improvements. An annual survey of facilities guided by the superintendent will keep needs before the staff. Where this is not done, the important thing for the superintendent to do is to make a first effort. Where needs are discovered, then a program of improvement can be laid out and responsibility delegated to see that action is taken. Factors to be considered in such improvements would include the number of people in the constituency, how those in attendance are grouped and graded, the actual space conditions and equipment, and possible adjustments to be made.

Some of the strategic areas where improvements can be made without a great deal of expenditure include keeping floors, walls, rest rooms, windows, rugs, and furniture clean. The application of soap and cleaning fluids can make a vast difference, not to speak of new paint. Good order for supplies and materials provide an atmosphere of confidence. Surplus literature, supplies, and accessories can be placed in proper storage and thus save time, space, and money. Careful checks on ventilation and heating may well prove invaluable in keeping attendance up and absenteeism down, not to speak of decreasing the chances of spreading disease. Since there is a direct correlation between physical posture and mental alertness, good chairs and desks, even though they cost more, will be less costly in the long run. It does not take a great deal to make your own equipment in this regard. The matter of light, color, and sound are important enough to ask for outside assistance in ascertaining whether the school has proper conditions or not. Since music is so important in church work, the best equipment possible should be secured and kept in good condition.

Where facilities are lacking, or in the case of a small church with limited finances, a superintendent might suggest some "do it yourself" projects to effect some improvements. Where volunteer workers are carefully organized and supervised, much good can be accomplished. Such work must be carefully planned in advance as to materials, storage, personnel, cost, etc., to meet actual needs. Items should be constructed of quality materials as far as possible. Possibilities include coat racks, seating, tables, screens, partitions, files, supply cabinets, maps, charts, records, black boards, bulletin boards, worship equipment, and many other items. The best source perhaps for guidance in this kind of work is *How to Make Church School Equipment* by Thelma Adair and Elizabeth McCort.

New Building. New buildings are a church responsibility but the superintendent in such cases should be interested in the educational unit. For many years we have been told that new buildings should be carefully planned from the inside out. Function should not be sacrificed for beauty, but careful procedure will make both efficiency and beauty possible. All buildings should be planned with the total program in mind. Furthermore, they should be located and erected with the needs of the constituency in mind. As far as the church school is concerned, twice the floor space presently used will make future expansion in enrollment possible.

Following a decision to build, the congregation must solidly back the project. A special building committee should be appointed to plan and direct the campaign. Various sub-committees will be needed to care for details of building, equipment, and finances. This committee will seek the counsel of specialists in planning church facilities. A professional consultant will give assistance in planning, in determining needs, and in forecasting the future. He will help prepare the way for the architect. Such assistance is often available through denominational workers and literature.

Every effort should be exerted to erect buildings or remodel them to meet quality standards, making them beautiful, practical, durable, economical, and educational. Floor plans should be designed to meet the needs of all age groups which are to be found in the building. Plans should include provisions for audio-visual equipment in each classroom. Keep the ideal in the forefront and consider trends.

Choose the best architect possible, one who knows church objectives and has kept abreast of educational trends and practices. Competence should be expected but a good personality enables him to work well with responsible committees. In the financial campaign the members need to be inspired, informed, organized, and enlisted in a schedule of payments which they can handle. Don't forget to include future expansion in the master plan. Construct the building so as to allow for changes in room size and form. Refer to open room suggestions in chapter 7.

5. *Promotion and Publicity*

Principles. The value of advertising and publicity is unquestioned. In recent years advertising media and techniques have passed the tests of ethical demands. The church must not ignore the possibilities in presenting the Gospel through the media of publicity and of reaching the unreached with the message through these means.

The term "promotion" refers to the advancement of a person, cause, or organization. It refers to both publicity and advertising and may be applied to people within the church ranks as well as to those outside. "Publicity" concerns the free attention which is given to the public, while "advertising" generally concerns payment for announcements to the public.

The responsibility for promotion and publicity lies with the pastor and board of the church. Actually the pastor, the director, and general superintendent should work as a team in carrying out the various responsibilities involved. The superintendent could be personally and particularly concerned with the planning and procedures involved in the church school itself. Many churches provide a special publicity committee to plan and carry forward a comprehensive program of promotion and publicity. In such cases, the committee may be directly responsible to the church ruling body or to the Sunday school council or Christian education committee. Periodic reports to such committees should be made. Personnel of this group might well include someone who has had newspaper and/or radio experience.

In small churches the general superintendent may find it possible to do this work without too much trouble, but in medium size and larger churches a director of publicity with a committee is imperative. Such a director must be supplied with announcements, plans, programs, and statistics by the various superintendents and secretaries. Perhaps each department can have a reporter to handle promotion within the department and work with the director. It is possible that these reporters could work with the director in forming a publicity committee.

All efforts in this field should be directed by the best principles of promotion and advertising and certainly should be in keeping with the Christian spirit and practice. Since there are certain types of advertising not suitable for religious purposes, only those methods should be used which are adaptable to interpreting the mission of the church, which are consistent with the basic program of the church, and which help to achieve spiritual objectives.

Your aims are important, so bear in mind that your efforts should be directed toward the following:

1. To arouse the membership
2. To arrest the attention of visitors and the community
3. To attract heedless people
4. To preach and teach the Gospel through various media

Your goals are important also. In setting them, one must be realistic and gear the program to the possibilities involved. Goals should also be set in the light of the number of workers available. Don't forget the amount of room space available and be sure to consider your ability to absorb new members in the light of the population of the town.

A definite program of promotion and publicity should be planned for the year. The best way to do this is to gear the program to special monthly events involved in the church and Sunday school calendar.

Types of Publicity. Two main areas of publicity and advertising are possible in Christian circles: (1) publicity which is intra-church, and (2) that which is extra-church. Intra-church methods refer to any advertising which is conducted within the church and from the church. Various channels of publicity include (1) the spoken word, covering such methods as conversation, telephone, interview, announcements, and radio; (2) the printed word, including letters, leaflets, booklets, brochures, church bulletins, year books, newspapers, and magazines; (3) graphic visual methods, covering photographs, charts, diagrams, maps, cartoons, posters, billboards, exhibits, films, and television; and (4) special events, including special days, weeks, anniversaries, and dinners.

Publicity within the church includes such media as:

Bulletins	Announcements
Printed order of service	Exhibits and posters
Telephone committee	Letter writing
Pastoral contacts	Enclosures
Reports and records	Church yearbook and directory
Church paper	Pulpit ministry
Questionnaires	Sermon excerpts
Church calendar	Pictures
Movies	Slides and filmstrips

Publicity media to be employed *outside* the church includes:

Pictures	Handbills and dodgers
Outdoor advertising	Window cards
Personal letters	Local newspapers
Church advertising	Radio and television
Denominational papers	Feature meetings
Conventions	Conferences
Posters	Tracts
Visitation	Signs and banners
P.A. system	Telephone

Space does not allow a full discussion of the above methods. Good books which prove helpful are Brodie, *Keeping Your Church in the News,* and Henry, *Successful Church Publicity.*

We have attempted to show the importance and different methods of promoting the Sunday school in the eyes of the community, and we believe that all these methods are good and will work. It should be pointed out, however, that methods in themselves will not build a great school. There is no substitute for prayer and a reliance on the power of the Holy Spirit. A school that is on fire for God, active, and always on the go will be its own best advertisement. There is no more profitable and encouraging work today than among the youth of our land. Use every method that has been suggested and invent more of your own. Harness this to the power of the Spirit and you will have a Sunday school that will be the marvel of the community.

6. *Atmosphere and Spirituality*

Atmosphere. There is much that a superintendent can do to create the proper "spirit" in the staff and the student body of the Sunday school. Through the manifestation of Christ-likeness and the spirit of joy, he can do much to keep an optimistic and energetic atmosphere in the school. He can motivate everyone to strive to be at his best in the service of the Lord. He can express appreciation for sincere efforts in such service. He can inform the people of the program and thus engage them in fruitful and intelligent cooperation. He can challenge everyone to build the kingdom with all possible haste. He can leave the impression that this is "our" school. The "our" spirit will enable both staff and students to feel that they "belong" to the school, that they have a part to play in its success and welfare.

One of the greatest contributions the superintendent can make is to cultivate the spirit and practice of cooperation. Definitely there is much difference between "operation" and "cooperation." It is possible to have the former without the latter, but certainly not at optimum capacity. The superintendent can do much to break down the spirit of independence which often characterizes workers and departments. He will constantly keep before the staff and pupils the necessity of working in close harmony and relations to help the school as a whole. He will seek to develop universal understanding and mutual helpfulness. In order to achieve this condition, the superintendent should give careful and prayerful attention to his own spirit, constantly manifesting friendship, kindness, and consideration for all concerned.

Atmosphere in the whole school can also be developed through the program which is operated and planned at a high level. This will help to draw the public. High standards and efficient operation attract people.

Social life plays a large part in the creation of the right kind of atmosphere. Much enthusiasm and harmony can be generated through well-planned and spiritually directed social programs from time to time. Although this responsibility may well be that of a specialist, the superintendent can do much toward engendering the spirit of love, appreciation, and mutual concern in social situations. Some superintendents entertain the staff annually at some kind of banquet occasion to recognize achievements and express appreciation.

Where the custom of general assemblies is practiced, the superintendent can do much to build up enthusiasm and support in the school. Careful planning will be characterized by variety, reports, awards, recognition, and perhaps special features from time to time. Thus he is able to deepen school loyalties and cultivate unity of spirit.

Three good rules, if they are observed, will help to provide the right kind of atmosphere. Let everything be done as *quietly* as possible, let everything be done *on time,* and let everything and everyone be *in the proper place.* Thus time will be saved, interruptions avoided, and noise reduced to a minimum.

Spirituality. Where the success of secular schools is measured largely by the fruitfulness of faculty and growth in knowledge, size, and efficiency, the Sunday school must constantly strive for spiritual growth and efficiency. Without this the Sunday school loses its real purpose for existence. There must be divine life in the school.

The superintendent can do much to help develop the spiritual life of the school. He can constantly keep before the staff and workers the absolute necessity of being born of the Spirit and walking in the Spirit. He can provide opportunities for testimony and constantly keep evangelism in the foreground. Where the Holy Spirit is honored in life and practice, the pupils will be deeply affected and there will be a genuine manifestation of Christian love for God, His Word and will, and for our fellowmen.

The use of an installation service is greatly helpful in keeping spiritual life and objectives before the staff and congregation. General assemblies and special days may be used for times of testimony, praise, and reports of victories in hearts and lives. Much has already been said regarding the procedures of evangelism in a previous chapter.

The superintendent will also find many opportunities to press home the importance of church attendance and worship. He can express appreciation for the pastor and the ministry of the church. He can stress the great importance of missions and the work of God's servants around the world. Other suggestions include:

1. Possible use of a unified service
2. Constant announcements in assemblies
3. Periodic check on pupils who do attend
4. Recognition of those who attend
5. Personal conferences with officers and teachers
6. Personal work by officers and teachers
7. Good example on part of all workers
8. Use of the Four or Six Point Record System
9. Enlisting the cooperation of the parents
10. Banner to class with largest attendance
11. Special section occasionally for children in church
12. Occasional specialties in the church service for children and youth
13. Special music in church sponsored by Sunday school
14. Reports in Sunday school of preacher's text
15. Indoctrination of the school on the importance of church

The argument that children cannot understand the sermon is weak. The same can be said of adults. The benefit of church going is not dependent entirely on the sermon, but also on personal association and fellowship, the atmosphere produced by prayer, music and architecture, not to speak of the pastor. Children from eight or nine years of age should be in the church service.

7. *Extension*

Responsibility. In a previous chapter on the work of the pastor, it was pointed out that extension is a part of evangelistic responsibilities and that the pastor should be the key leader. Superintendents, however, should be alert to the application of evangelistic principles and methods in the church school and should be anxious to work with the pastor in carrying out this great responsibility in the total program.

The workers also should be imbued with the spirit and practice of evangelism. In fact the graded principle demands definite allocation of evangelistic responsibilities to the leaders. For example, junior workers should be specifically burdened for junior pupils and prospects. In this narrowing of responsibility, greater efficiency is achieved in reaching those to whom the workers are particularly responsible.

Methods. A variety of methods for extension can be used in church schools. Of particularly usefulness, however, are methods employed in the establishment of branch Sunday schools, an extension department, visitation and absentee follow-up, and missions.

The steps included in extension are well known and need no extended comment. They follow somewhat the following pattern:

I. Preparation
    A. Vision — compassion — prayer
    B. Information
        1. Check church rolls
        2. Take a census
II. Action
    A. Provide additional space
    B. Provide additional workers
    C. Visitation
    D. Classification
    E. Identification
    F. Evangelization

The superintendent needs to be acquainted with the wealth of literature now available on this subject.

8. *Special Days and Worship*

Special Days. The term "special days" has reference to occasions which the average person celebrates because they have a peculiar significance in his life.

To the Sunday school is delegated the responsibility for the proper understanding and celebration of most special emphases. There is no more fitting institution available for tying all ages into the church program. The children gain a better understanding of historical provisions, and parents and visitors are attracted to the school. Excellent prospect lists are thus secured. Then too, cooperative enterprises engage the enthusiasm and loyalty which builds better Christians. Besides these, but not least, is the fact that evangelism, via the unusual, is improved.

While all these benefits are sought, they should not be alone the primary motive for observing special days; the Sunday school is avowedly a teaching agency. No program, unless it be evangelism, should be permitted to hinder the planned preparation of the individual teachers. Each class can give the proper emphasis upon the occasion and should supplement the group program, so the relative importance of an instance determines the extent to which class activity may be set aside. Too frequently a non-planning and inconsiderate superintendent will cancel class activity to favor some innovation or to honor a visitor. The consideration that all age groups cannot be appealed to on the same basis should be another check to over-compounding assemblages. A child of five will not give undivided attention to a speaker for more than a few minutes, while the more disciplined adult will become impatient with repetitious engagements of simple observances which are geared to the understanding of children. In addition, more comprehensive and practiced presentations are required than convenience will generally allow for a mixed group.

Reasonable consideration thus dictates that commemoration of the proper special days must be well planned and scheduled. Departmental provision will generally be found most practical. The educational board should schedule the program ahead sufficiently for proper preparation. Usually a year's plans should be known ahead, for as soon as one presentation has been completed it is time to begin its subsequent anniversary.

In preparation for the fete, the challenge should go first to the teachers. Only after loyal cooperation and enthusiasm of the staff has been aroused can a successful program be launched. The teacher will then endeavor to enfuse the scholars with the same ardor. When the whole school is actively behind the program, supplemental suggestions will be fostered and accepted. Unanimity first will reduce the tendency to discordant hindrances and will overcome unforeseen circumstances.

Since the whole purpose of the celebration is aimed toward an educational aspect, it is important that even the practice periods should be informational. Costuming, wording, background, etc., should all give the participants better appreciation of other days and climes. They should challenge them to studious examination of modern-day problems.

A side issue to be avoided in signalizing any service is that of negating any Christian principles. Too frequently after a Christmas program, which has emphasized love, there is heard complaint that "Junior" did not carry this or that outstanding part. Children, who are taught that it is more blessed to give than to receive, are disappointed with receiving less than some other person. Another consideration that is sometimes misconstrued is that advertising campaigns degenerate into mere door to door mendacity.

The administration of special days should be in charge of a "special days committee." Days to be observed should be marked on a special days calendar. This committee should keep a file of accessible programs, including literature, a list of programs already used, scrapbook of ideas, etc. They can provide assistance to workers, discover and use new talent, advertise, enlist the interest of parents, and keep objectives in mind. This committee will work closely, of course, with the superintendents in planning the observances of special days.

Promotion Day. The year can be considered as ending or beginning with the promotion day. Since installation of officers is an accompanying practice, we will consider it first. It is the best opportunity for promoting the Christian education program. The whole year has been put into the students and fair recognition needs to be given to those who have completed the assignment. It is the one Sunday school-wide program and because of its inclusiveness, it needs to be minutely planned. Every person should know where he will fit in and yet be interested in the rest of the service. Attention can be held by varying the program from year to year and by retaining announcements until the last. The presence of God needs to be realized to engender enthusiastic approach into another year's work. The interest of the occasion may be heightened by bringing in a prominent speaker. Send out invitations so that there is one hundred percent attendance. The day is often classed as a rally in that many visitors are expected. Paramount to advancing the Sunday school, the teachers should have a prominent part in the program. Some intimation of the successes of the past year and plans for the new year should be announced. Opportunity for ingenuity is presented by the desire for decoration. The season is such that many flowers can be used. It is worthy of the greatest effort of the year.

An effective procedure which is employed by many Sunday schools is to have the classes sit in groups and, beginning with the oldest group to be transferred, have them shift locations. Certificates of completion can be awarded. Before each department receives its diplomas, it is often best for the teacher to explain what has been done, and in carrying out the program the names should be called out so that everyone is introduced. Departmental numbers may be attached to the program and the pastor should have opportunity to present a challenge. In some schools the department superintendent gives a short talk on next year's course of study.

As part of the service, new officers and teachers should stand at the front of the church during an installation proceeding. This gives them a feeling of sacred duty and poses the congregation behind them. A pledge of faithfulness may be quoted to confirm their responsibility.

Decision Day. The business of the Sunday school is to evangelize. Decision day provides a great opportunity to evangelize children through four aspects. First, it is here that a large number of non-believers are congregated. A poll of Sunday schools in the South a few years ago disclosed that three-fourths of the juniors and more than half of the intermediates made no profession of Christ, while only a little less than half of the youth group made any claim. Second, the membership of the Sunday school receives the basic teaching necessary to grasping salvation truths. The Holy Spirit works through the Word. Third, the Sunday school group presents the age which is most susceptible to gospel truth. They are not hardened by sin, so profound faith in the Bible and their teachers facilitates their being won. Finally, it is in the Sunday school that the soul winners of the church are in most evidence. The individual contact arouses the spirit of prayer, concern for souls, and study for methods and truths leading to harvest.

While every day should be decision day, there are several advantages to conducting a special program with evangelistic emphasis at least three or four times a year. It contacts unreached individuals in the form of visitors. Extensive effort and prayer to improve the quest cannot fail to attract guests and win such as would be led. The uniqueness of being something different will catch the attention of others. Testimonies and instructions before new faces will direct the thoughts of some toward Christ. Then too, the separated occasion affords the pastor marvelous opportunity to reach attenuated hearts.

The effort to tie children into the church should be a continuous activity. Eighty-five percent of church membership comes from the Sunday school, but less than twenty percent of the Sunday school finds its way into the church program. The statement of confession before a combined group is a step toward joining the church. Usually Easter is set aside for that purpose. It could more appropriately be entitled "enlistment day," "announcement day," "Testimony day," or some other related term. The announcement involves the church in sustaining the individual's profession. Opportunity for him to train and fulfil a responsibility is the felicitous position in which the church is placed. When prayer goes into and follows the decision day program, much can result. The superintendent should not wait until the day arrives to strive for "decisions." Indeed personal work should be done *before* that day, particularly among children. Prayer groups should be formed at least one month in advance. The pastor, teachers, and parents should work together for the salvation of the children.

Missionary Day. Decision leads into ministering, and ministering is approached by two avenues — home and foreign missions. Again, missions cannot be successfully relegated to one day a year. It is the continuous responsibility of every Christian. The only purpose of the existence of the church is missions. However, special occasions can be aligned with missions, and a planned program will emphasize certain days to sustain interest. Visiting missionaries prefer the combined program to economize on their time. United projects add incentive because of the greater apparent results. Twenty dollars' worth of produce appeals more than the twenty cents a Sunday that some beginners' class might contribute to a cause.

A novel program that has netted much interest is the "Summer Christmas Tree." Giving at that time offers the convenience of sending a present to the field for distribution on their Christmas. It also spreads the Christmas spirit over a greater period of time. The program can be varied from the tree-centered emphasis, more conveniently reducing a misapplication of the meaning.

Hearing from foreign fields redoubles the appeal to children. As children of their own age write, they understand the customs and become more tolerant in their home relations. Platform exercises center the interest of a greater group of people and the educational features of participation abet the child's training. For the greatest interest a focused program should be adopted. One field should be emphasized for such a period as shall acquaint the most people with the conditions of that area.

In considering missions, the home field should not be forgotten. There are opportunities for vacationers to visit these fields and report back. Local opportunities for mission work and prayer should also be surveyed. A planned program with an active committee will find sufficient material here to engage every available opportunity for presentation. Interracial work, jail openings, orphanages, old people's homes — all come under the category for study. Bulletin boards should keep the members acquainted with activities between programs, and prayer for the fields should be a part of every class session.

Children's Day. This day is primarily an exhibition day of the children's work. It comes at the time of year when interest is at its highest and achievement most apparent. The program of the church is brought before the public and, properly planned, engages every faculty that can be fostered. Since drama is favored in the public schools, there is no reason why it cannot be given a Christian turn. However, care must be taken not to make the program a mere entertainment. In all cases it may not be advisable to set aside a full period for the demonstration. The adult opening exercise can be a sufficient notice of talents and learning. The revelation ties the parents together. as they behold other parents' children working with their own.

The children's day program demands long advanced preparation. If the students know that their work is going to be exhibited, they will be more careful to have it completed from the beginning. Presentation of Bible characters and customs require protracted evaluations. The extensive range of imagination and ingenuity should provide an unlimited list of profitable productions. Too much attention cannot be given to originality.

Sunday school picnic. The annual picnic is an outstanding event in most Sunday schools. Again it might better be reserved to departmental observing. At any rate, care must be taken that it is promotional and not just a desultory activity. Every moment should be planned and disciplined lest any clique wanders off and the cooperative spirit be lost. Sharing of responsibility improves discipline in this matter. Good picnics do not just happen. Committees to organize work, play, and worship are necessary. Transportation creates a problem. Usually some distant curio stirs the greatest interest. Athletic contests vitalize the program. Trophies in preference to prizes should be issued. The worship program will be freer, but the outdoors aspect of most picnics has great educative value. As the students develop mentally, their social contacts must widen. Social activity in the form of the picnic allows the first expression of any Sunday school engagement. While the social cannot be the only end, developing this sector of the individual's life is significant to an adjusted society.

Lesser Days. The holidays, rally programs, and worship emphases of most other occasions can be treated more efficiently in the departmental exercises. Christmas and Easter may perhaps merit the added recognition of a program period aside from the Sunday school hour, but more and more the institutional treatment of these is being discontinued. Partiality and the accompanying evils of the compound program are avoided. Individual departmental attention usually begets more favorable celebration. Even Christmas parties or related fellowships can be directed along more conducive lines of worship.

Special emphases to temperance, prayer, songs, etc., and the church calendar can provide a wholesome program for the year's departmental opening exercises. Observance of national or denominational birthdays can challenge character and patriotism. Bringing in Bible characters is helpful. Relationships of a practical nature can be fostered by visitation, challenges, home worship engagements, and miscellaneous attractive presentations. Nearly every denomination has a suggestive outline of memorializations with helps that favor an alert Sunday school board.

Christian Education Week. This special emphasis embraces the use of several special days in one period of time. Many churches use the last Sunday in September to the first Sunday in October for Christian education week. Of course other times may be chosen by individual churches. The primary purpose is to highlight the importance and total program of Christian education in the local church. Some of the stated purposes of such an observation have been given as follows:

1. To give evidence of the basic oneness of the Christian fellowship
2. To emphasize joint responsibility of the church, home, and community for Christian education
3. To create a climate favorable to the support and the strengthening of Christian education in the home, the church, and the community (public relations)
4. To give opportunity for the local church to —
   a. Analyze and evaluate its present program of Christian education
   b. Plan for the future
5. To foster a renewal of commitment to the learning-teaching task of the church
6. To make significant use of rally day, wherever it is observed as a part of Christian education week.

A day-by-day suggestion for the observance of this week is suggested below:

Sunday — Rally and Promotion Day
Monday — Workers' Conference or Leaders' Night (banquet)
Tuesday — Family-at-Home Day
Wednesday — Family-at-Church Day (prayer meeting, etc.)
Thursday — Community for Christ Day
Friday — Youth Day
Saturday — Personal Meditation Day or Visitation Day
Sunday — World Communion Day and Installation Service

Worship. Worship is the particular responsibility of the pastor, as previously pointed out. This area, however, is so important and includes so many that the pastor would be wise to use a committee to assist him. This is particularly true in the church school. Where the general assembly type of worship service is used, as in the case of many smaller church schools, the general superintendent in most cases has charge. Even in larger schools, where the departmental system of worship is used, the superintendent can give supervisory assistance. Because the present-day trend is toward the departmental type of worship service in the church school, a full discussion of this problem will be reserved for the chapter on the work of the departmental superintendent.

9. Personal Preparation

In order to best think of others and work with others, the superintendent must think of himself. To carry out his functions, duties, and responsibilities demands time and effort in personal preparation. It is a matter of consecration *plus* preparation. He must have the information to direct his efforts. This means prayer, counsel, and study. Some of the major items of concern to which the superintendent can give special study are:

1. The Bible — content and doctrine
2. Methods — officers and teachers
3. Sunday school administration
4. Sunday school finance
5. Parliamentary law
6. Duties of all the workers
7. Sunday school facilities
8. Sunday school standards
9. Promotional methods
10. Human nature
11. Principles of teaching
12. The denominational program

This kind of preparation can be secured among other ways through reading, observation, attendance at conferences and conventions, and visiting successful schools.

D. SPECIFIC DUTIES OF THE GENERAL SUPERINTENDENT

1. *Sunday Duties.* The duties of the superintendent on Sunday can be organized into four general areas of responsibility:

1. Pre-session duties
2. The worship period
3. The class period
4. Closing assembly (where used)

"On time" for the superintendent means that he should arrive in the building at least thirty minutes *before* the opening bell. This gives him time to adequately prepare himself, the staff, and the atmosphere for the school session of the day. This period should not be used for social and business purposes. Occasionally it may be used for a *short* prayer period. Most profitably the period can be used for some of the following purposes:

Time to get acquainted
Time to check staff and equipment

Time to encourage workers
Time for workers to get ready
Time for coordinating activities
Time for well-planned pre-session activities

School opens with a worship period. This is true whether or not the general assembly system is used. If the superintendent does not lead worship himself, he should supervise the use of the departmental system of worship and give assistance wherever possible.

Where the general assembly system is used, every possible effort should be made to create a family type of worship atmosphere. Ushers should be placed at the door to assist people and stop late-comers or to enforce whatever rules are agreed upon. The school should be opened with an agreed upon signal by the superintendent promptly at the appointed time. Chords from the piano are recommended. Such signals should be given as quietly as possible and never repeated. This period should be carefully planned ahead of time and should be characterized by variety, fellowship, and depth of spirituality. The details of this period will be dealt with in the chapter which follows. Where there is no closing assembly period, some time should be given here to promote Sunday school attendance, church service attendance, visitation, and recognitions. Announcements should be kept to a minimum.

The lesson period lasts from 30 to 40 minutes in the average Sunday school. During this time the superintendent can do much which administration and supervision demands. He can remain at the office to greet visitors and see that the general officers are carrying out their duties properly. Later on he may choose to visit classes and departments. By all means he will be available for any problems which arise and especially to deal with discipline problems. Pupils should not be allowed to leave classes without permission from the teachers nor should they be allowed to leave school without reporting to the superintendent or general secretary.

Where schools use closing assembly periods, the superintendent will be in charge. The time can be used for a variety of purposes but make the period as short as possible. The lesson can be pressed home to the school by lifting up outstanding points of the lesson or through the use of short questions. Not more than five minutes should be used for this. Make all announcements brief. Recognize visitors briefly but do not call on them to speak to the school. Dismiss the school promptly at the appointed time, driving home the importance of church attendance if the worship service of the church follows the school session.

2. *Other Duties.* The work of the superintendent demands a great deal of time and effort through the week, during the month in fact, all the year. Some of the most common of these duties can be listed as follows:

Weekly Duties	*Monthly Duties*	*Annual Duties*
1. Prepare Sunday program	1. Preside at worker's conferences	1. Attend the NSSA convention
2. Study the lesson	2. Consult with the department workers	2. Help pastor plan annual dedication service for the workers
3. Be acquainted with all lessons	3. Attend Sunday school conferences and conventions	3. Attend training classes
4. Visit workers and pupils as time allows	4. Conduct cabinet meetings	4. Send an annual letter of thanks to the staff
5. Attend prayer meeting	5. Plan for special days	5. Help plan the annual workers' banquet
6. Occasional social gatherings	6. Keep a date book and calendar of activities	6. Survey building and equipment needs
7. Study names of pupils	7. Keep eye on monthly attendance trends	7. Read books on Sunday school work
8. Greet and write pupils	8. Help plan parent-teacher programs	8. Plan annual award picnic
9. Check on absentee workers.	9. Meditate on school — compare, analyze, and evaluate	9. Help plan daily vacation Bible school
10. Watch for new workers	10. Keep a memo book for suggestions, records and appointments	10. Plan annual Sunday school calendar
11. Watch attendance	11. Attend Board of Christian Education	11. Make an annual report to the church
12. Obtain report from the general secretary and treasurer	12. Check on progress toward standards	12. Help with annual census when used
13. See that pastor gets proper announcements	13. Glance over the lesson materials	13. Evaluate total program
14. See that building, equipment and supplies are prepared for each Sunday	14. Keep up with church calendar	14. Revise standards
15. See that pupils' and officers' needs are met	15. Check record system	
16. See that teachers' needs are met		
17. Promote interests of the school between Sundays		
18. Show appreciation for the work of the staff		
19. Supervision of census		
20. Soul winning		

A good superintendent will plan ahead through the week. A small notebook is useful to keep notes and jot down suggestions that come to him. Names, addresses, telephone numbers of all workers should also be kept in this book.

Good planning calls for at least one full evening per week, even two, to have time to:

1. Examine last Sunday's reports and records
2. Note classes and departments which deserve recognition
3. Notice classes and departments which lag in attendance and offering
4. Study reports of officers, departments, and classes
5. Prepare reports for boards and conferences
6. Telephone or write teachers and officers who were ill; also get out notices to other individuals and groups
7. Plan agendum for monthly workers' conference
8. Plan recommendations to Board of Christian Education
9. Read periodicals, leaflets, and books on Christian education
10. Study his work or take courses
11. Have conferences with pastor and general officers
12. See that special days are observed

E. Assistants to the General Superintendent

1. *The Associate Superintendent.* This officer is more than a mere assistant, more than an emergency person. Possessing all the qualifications of the superintendent, this worker fills a most important place in the Sunday school. The general superintendent should call on him not only to substitiute in his absence but to fulfill definite duties and assume specific responsibilities. The Methodists give this worker the responsibility of membership promotion, cultivation, and follow-up. The superintendent will have frequent sessions with his associate workers for prayer, planning, and cooperation. The problems of organization, administration, and supervision are too great for one man to perform; therefore this officer should be assigned specific duties each Sunday and through the week. Common duties have included providing substitute workers, assignment of new pupils, assisting the general superintendent, supervision of pupils and workers, assisting in discipline, and welcoming.

The number of associate superintendents is determined by the size of the school, the needs of the general superintendent, and the arrangement of the building or buildings. Separate entrances and scattered departments often demand several workers of this kind. In large schools divisional superintendents are virtually associate superintendents. Possibilities for this worker are almost unlimited, as shown by the following list:

Superintendent of social life	Superintendent of adult division
Superintendent of attendance	Superintendent of equipment
Superintendent of education	Superintendent of youth division
Superintendent of evangelism	Superintendent of publicity
Superintendent of missions	Superintendent of stewardship

Superintendent of finances   Superintendent of spiritual life
Superintendent of activities   Superintendent of community work
Superintendent of children's division

In small schools several of these responsibilities can be handled by one officer.

2. *Departmental and Divisional Superintendents.* In larger schools departmental and divisional superintendents are necessary. Departmental superintendents will be discussed fully in the next chapter.

As the enrollment of a school increases and classes multiply, departments will have corresponding growth. This means that several departments often make up a Sunday school division. Three divisions comprise the work of every Sunday school, no matter what size — children (from birth through 12); youth (ages 13 through 24); and adult (over 24). Even in small schools three teachers can be appointed to assume divisional responsibilities. Thus the superintendent along with these three comprise an executive committee or committee on administration.

Beside possessing Christian character, these workers should specialize in the work of their respective divisions, understand and love the pupils, and be able administrators and supervisors under the control of the general superintendent.

The duties of department superintendents will be dealt with in detail in the chapter which follows. In a larger church school perhaps divisional superintendents will work in the three divisions mentioned above. Some of their duties include:

1. Give general assistance to the general superintendent, sometimes comprising an executive council of the church school.
2. Act as chairman of the divisional council of workers, including departmental superintendents of the Sunday school and other workers in the division.
3. See that an adequate staff of workers is maintained in the division.
4. See that divisional workers are trained.
5. See that best possible provision is made for space, equipment, and materials.
6. Confer with divisional workers.
7. Observe the best principles of organization in the division.
8. Plan for interdepartmental activities.
9. Promote interdepartmental social life and fellowship.
10. Constantly search for prospective workers.
11. Seek greater understanding of the principle of grading in the division.

12. Plan the recommendations and reports to the Board of Christian Education.
13. Consider ways of executing board policies in the division.
14. Represent the division on the Board of Christian Education.
15. Keep accurate records of the division.
16. Constantly seek self-improvement.
17. Specialize in supervision.
18. Cooperate with other general officers.

3. *The General Secretary and Treasurer.* Perhaps the general superintendent's most practical assistant is the general secretary. Records and the record system are so important that one of the most efficient people in the whole church should take this responsibility. Accuracy, neatness, honesty, and efficiency are primary qualifications in addition to spiritual fitness. Bookkeepers and clerks are good sources from which to draw. Special training in addition to experience will be necessary.

Some of the most common duties include:

Compile statistics	Supervise collection of records
Keep record system	Explain record system to pupils
Train class secretaries	Explain record system to workers
Train department secretaries	Send announcements to homes
Report to the school	Send announcements to pastor
Assist all workers	Help with publicity and promotion
Provide duplicate cards	Help select other secretaries
Order literature	Help with pupil classification
Make periodic summaries	Keep records for promotion day
Work with treasurer	Take care of storing literature
Keep birthday records	Keep a history of the school
Correspondence	Check school supplies

At least thirty days in advance the secretary should order the lesson materials. The order is made up through the cooperation of the secretary and departmental workers. After being checked by the General Superintendent, the order is sent in. No "standing orders" should be allowed.

The record system is the primary responsibility of this worker. The details of the record system will be considered in the next chapter.

Every secretary needs certain tools, including: a desk with drawers, filing cabinet, enrollment records, a general record, book for compiling statistics, an announcement board, special day cards, and report blanks. Where he has the duties of treasurer, he will need all necessary equipment for that position. Refer to the previous discussion on finances for the treasurer's duties.

Possible assistants might include a corresponding secretary, birthday secretary, enrollment secretary or registrar, statistical secretary and recording secretary. Size will help determine the need.

Not the least of the secretary's responsibilities is that of keeping a record of meetings. This is particularly true of the committee on administration or cabinet business meetings; reports and minutes should be kept.

4. *Other Officers.* Additional officers may be added according to the size and requirements of the school. These may include a chorister or director of music, pianist, ushers, registrar, and librarian. Music and the library will be considered later.

Because the church school embraces more than the Sunday school, other leaders will be needed for various collateral activities in the program. In the children's division there will be a director of the vacation church school and director of children's work. The latter's work concerns children's mission groups, Bible clubs, and perhaps scout work. In the youth division there will be clubs, scout work, and youth fellowship workers. The present tendency, however, is to use the same leaders for Sunday morning and evening groups in youth work. In the adult division one might find leaders of fellowship groups, missions groups, young adult groups, men's groups, etc. The superintendent may not contact these directly, but through the divisional councils he will be able to integrate the work of the whole church school. At least the Board of Christian Education can see that this is done.

As the church school grows larger, there may be need for workers for specialized tasks, such as alcohol education, stewardship, counseling, community service, missions, finances, visitation, family education, etc.

SUGGESTED READING CHAPTER 5*

Adair, *How to Make Church School Equipment*
Arnold, *Special Programs for the Sunday School*
Atkinson, *Building and Equipping for Christian Education*
Benson, C., *The Sunday School in Action*, Chapters 11, 12, 13, 14, 15
Benson, E. G., *Planning Church School Workers' Conferences*
Breck, *Special Day Programs and Selections*
Campbell, *The Superintendent Wants to Know*
Conover, *The Church School and Parish House Building*
Crossland, *How to Build Up Your Church School*, Chapter 7 and 8
Flake, *Building a Standard Sunday School*
      Sunday School Officers and Their Work
      The True Functions of a Sunday School, Chapter 9

*On supervision, refer to the chapters on pastor and director. Also refer to updated Bibliography at back of book.

Foster, *How a Small Church Can Have Good Christian Education,*
Chapters 1-5, 8-13
Heim, *Leading a Sunday Church School,* Chapters 14, 15, 17
Herrick, *Outstanding Days*
Jones, *The Church School Superintendent*
Lawrance, *My Message to Sunday School Workers,* Chapters 19,
21, 23
Lobingier, *The Better Church School,* Chapters 8, 10
McMichael, *The New Superintendent*
Murch, *Christian Education and the Local Church,* Chapters 34, 35
Riggs, *A Successful Sunday School,* Chapters 4, 6
Ross and McRae, *The Superintendent Faces His Task*
Vieth, *Improving Your Sunday School,* Chapters 1, 5, 8, 9
Vincent, *The Modern Sunday School,* Chapter 5
Wallin, *Keys for the Sunday School Superintendent and Officers*

THE WORK OF THE DEPARTMENT SUPERINTENDENT

OUTLINE FOR CHAPTER 6

(Education and Evangelism)

A. THE OFFICE OF DEPARTMENT SUPERINTENDENT
   1. The Departmental Concept
   2. Qualifications
   3. Election
   4. Relationships
   5. Responsibilities

B. THE FUNCTIONS OF THE DEPARTMENT SUPERINTENDENT
   1. Organization
   2. Administration
   3. Supervision
   4. Duties

C. THE RESPONSIBILITIES OF THE DEPARTMENT SUPERINTENDENT
   1. Grading and Grouping
   2. Worship
   3. Evangelism and Attendance
   4. Records
   5. Curriculum
   6. Program

6 | THE WORK OF THE DEPARTMENTAL SUPERINTENDENT

(Education and Evangelism)

A. THE OFFICE OF DEPARTMENTAL SUPERINTENDENT

1. *The Departmental Concept.* The office of department superintendent was first used in larger Sunday schools in the early part of the present century. As a school became too large for the general superintendent to manage well, the children and youth divisions were often placed in charge of department superintendents who acted virtually as assistant superintendents. By World War I superintendents over all departments became popular. Since that time there has been almost universal acceptance of the principle that department superintendents are needed in all departments, regardless of the size of the school.

Two primary concerns focus attention on the importance of and need for department superintendents. First, the scope and comprehensiveness of the modern church school, and even the Sunday school, demands that the general superintendent be given assistance. There is a definite area of responsibility for an office between the general superintendent and the teacher. Someone is also needed to provide the teacher with the atmosphere for mental and spiritual instruction. In fact, the correct functioning of this office can change a school from a conglomeration of classes to a unified school of instruction, where every class is a contribution to the total school. The proper filling of this office relieves the general superintendent of many duties so he may become skilled in the administration of the school. The teacher may also give far more attention to the needs of class members. Every age can have each program and all activities geared to its level.

Second, the department is increasingly being recognized as the central unit of the school. In the department is where the teaching-learning process actually takes place. It is here that the Gospel is applied directly to hearts and lives. Two primary purposes are revealed therefore: (1) to win souls, and (2) to increase educational effectiveness.

The relation of the department superintendent to his own department is analogous to that which the general superintendent has to the total school. This actually means that each department is virtually a little school in itself, although not independent from the

177

rest. This means therefore that the function of the department superintendent must include some administration and supervision. However, the primary function of this officer is educational. One of his major concerns is to assist the teachers in achieving the goals of instruction and evangelism. In this he will naturally see the importance as well of full cooperation with the general officers as they work toward improvement and enlargement.

Many *advantages* for departmental organization can be listed, among which are the following:

1. Adaptation of exercises and teaching methods and materials to the mental, physical, social, and spiritual capacities of pupils.
2. The association of pupils of the same general age and similar mental development.
3. Specialization of teachers and workers in departmental skills and problems.
4. The fostering of a strong departmental spirit.
5. Closer association of parents through social and other departmental meetings.
6. Specific allocation of evangelistic responsibilities to workers and pupils.

2. *Qualifications.* A departmental superintendent needs two primary qualifications in addition to Christian character — the ability to lead and the ability to follow. He leads his own department and follows the general superintendent. By virtue of occupying a mediating position, the ability to cooperate should be high on the list. Also of great importance are the qualities which fit this officer for specialization with a certain age level.

Spiritual qualifications are much the same as those listed for the general superintendent in the previous chapter. In addition to these it is important for the person involved to feel called of the Holy Spirit to work with his particular age group.

Since this officer is primarily an educational worker, academic qualifications are important too. Wherever possible, specific training and experience should be required. The ability to study is useful as well. It will be necessary for this officer to study departmental manuals, pupil psychology, and curriculum materials in order to become a specialist in his department.

Executive ability is helpful to this officer. He will be faced with the responsibility of administering the department. This means assuming the chairmanship of business meetings and conducting departmental conferences of various kinds. He will also be expected to work closely with the general superintendent in the selection and placement of workers within the department. It is generally conceded that women, particularly young married women, are most suitable to superintend the various children's departments and that men are useful in the other departments. This is based on their experience as mothers or association with children. This should not, however, preclude the possibility of using well-qualified men for these positions. Many schools use mature young men of leadership ability and strong personality to work with youth and children.

3. *Election.* There are in many Sunday schools no set rules for the election of department superintendents. Usually they are elected annually by the Board of Christian Education upon the nomination of the general superintendent and with the approval of the minister. In some cases they are appointed by the general superintendent with the approval of the minister or director of religious education. It seems certain they should never be elected either by the department or the school at large, for here little consideration can be given to their qualifications for the task. For the best operation, the teachers of the department should be given a choice or a chance to approve the department superintendent. However, it is a grave mistake to have a department superintendent appoint the officers and teachers who serve in his department. In a small school where the number of workers limit the organization, one of the teachers of a department may be the superintendent. It should be only a temporary situation, however, and should be remedied as the number of available workers increases. Only an exceptional person is capable of being a teacher and a department superintendent at the same time, and even then the work and effectiveness in both fields is limited. Often the growth of a school is stunted by the lack of proper organization at this point. When it is necessary for a teacher to act in this capacity, some of the duties of the office must be delegated to the other teachers and helpers in the department.

4. *Relationships.* A department superintendent is not an independent worker. Instead, above him he is obligated to work in close cooperation with the general superintendent and other general officers of the school. He must constantly recognize that his department is *one* part of the whole school and the church. He will be receptive to suggestions from the pastor and director of religious education. He will cooperate with all those officers in the program of leadership training and development. He will represent the various boards to his department staff in the presentation of policies and operation of the program.

Below him are the teachers and department officers. He will be a leader and an inspiring example. He will organize and supervise. He will represent their needs and best interests to the general officers and boards of the church school.

This officer is responsible to the general superintendent for the administration of general school policies within his department. He will also cooperate with other department superintendents and maintain a spirit of mutual interest and unity of purpose. Where a director of religious education is present, he will work closely with this officer in the educational and leadership training phases of the program. In the latter case, particular attention will be given to the teaching-learning process.

5. *Responsibilities.* The functional concept of administration demands that certain educational functions and responsibilities be definitely assigned to this officer. All his efforts should be directed toward enabling the teachers to carry out the functions and objectives in education and evangelism through their particular departments.

The primary responsibilities which must be borne by this officer include:

1. Functions — organization, administration, supervision
2. Grading and grouping
3. Worship
4. Evangelism and attendance
5. Records
6. Curriculum
7. Program

B. The Functions of the Department Superintendent

1. *Organization.* Like the general superintendent and pastor, the department superintendent is concerned with organization. He carries out this function, however, in a different manner from the other two. At one and the same time he must be conscious of two concerns: (1) the integration of his department with other departments and the organizational structure above them, and (2) the framework of his own department within. This means that the department superintendent will be concerned with classes, space, facilities, and a staff of department workers.

Of primary importance in the department organization is the selection of suitable workers for the department. Such workers must be trained for their positions and supervised on the job. Although some personnel will vary from department to department, the following list includes workers common to almost all departments:

1. Associate Department Superintendent
2. Pianist
3. Chorister
4. Department Secretary
5. Department Librarian
6. Teachers and Assistants
7. Associates

All of these workers must assume shares of general responsibility for the welfare of the department but they should also be carefully trained for specific duties. Some of those duties are revealed by the following lists:

Associate Department Superintendent

1. Give general assistance to the department superintendent
2. Be prepared to teach in the department
3. Often help in other groups outside the Sunday school, such as DVBS
4. May serve as counselor
5. Be present 10 or 15 minutes before opening bell
6. May be responsible for the signal system for the department
7. May lead workers in visitation
8. Protect department from interruption
9. Take care of visitors and late comers
10. May be responsible for department growth
11. May be responsible for absentees
12. Promote teacher training
13. Promote home cooperation
14. Study and know pupils
15. Attend workers' meeting
16. May serve as librarian
17. Check on workers' attendance at department meetings
18. Help arrange the assembly room
19. Train vice presidents of organized classes

Department Secretary

1. Responsible for department records
2. Make out reports which require record information
3. Check attendance in nursery and beginner departments
4. Submit needs for supplies and materials to the general secretary
5. May be responsible for the signal system in the department
6. Train other workers in the use of the records, particularly class secretaries
7. Secures and keeps department enrollment
8. Supply information for workers and teachers at department meetings
9. Classify pupils
10. Mark records of children in beginner department
11. Teach all department workers how to use the record system
12. Keep department minutes

Pianist

1. Be present 10 or 15 minutes before opening bell
2. Often plays softly during pre-session period
3. Sometimes is a main pre-session attraction
4. May gear music to lessons on theme of the day
5. Play simply in Children's division
6. May serve as associate teacher during class period
7. May assist the other workers during class period
8. Plays appropriately for different occasions
9. May promote stewardship and missions in the department
10. Should memorize frequently used songs and choruses

Chorister

1. Help plan music for the opening worship session
2. Lead singing whenever needed
3. Must not show off
4. May assist other workers during the class period
5. May serve as associate teacher
6. Collect music from all sources useful for the department
7. Keep department instruments in tune
8. Help classes learn new songs
9. Train pupils in music skills
10. Maintain cheerful spirit in the department
11. Stress the messages in music
12. May be responsible for fellowship and service activities in the department
13. Greet pupils and newcomers

Teachers

1. Find and enlist pupils in regular attendance
2. Learn to know the pupils
3. Visit pupils
4. Pray for pupils
5. Study other good teachers
6. Organize classes in Junior and older groups
7. Keep evangelism central

8. Improve methods
9. Study the work of teaching
10. Thoroughly prepare lessons
11. Survey needs and abilities of pupils
12. Maintain close home contacts
13. Contact absentees
14. Organize older classes
14. May train class chairman of social life in organized classes
15. Take care of song books

Librarian

1. See that study materials and story papers are distributed to the classes
2. Place all materials before the class period begins
3. Is custodian of materials and equipment for the department
4. Store all excess materials and supplies
5. File pictures and materials for the department
6. File all audio-visual aids and equipment for the department
7. Check out any projection equipment from church library
8. Promote good reading
9. Study reading needs, habits, and interests of pupils

Associates

1. Serve as general helpers wherever needed in the department
2. Be subject to department officers and teachers

Substitute Teachers

1. Have lesson materials at hand
2. Attend workers' meetings
3. Be available for teaching
4. Study the work of teaching
5. Cooperate with regular teacher
6. Often visit the class
7. Help in visitation

The duties of the department superintendent are listed in a later section of this chapter on the administrative responsibilities of this officer.

In addition to a staff of workers, organizational responsibilities include space, facilities, and all other environmental factors which directly affect the teaching-learning process. The department superintendent must learn to operate and control all these factors so that objectives can be reached.

The following chart reveals in outline form some of these responsibilities. Each department superintendent should study long and carefully the requirements in these areas.

2. *Administration.* As an administrator the department superintendent studies the work of the department and builds a comprehensive, well-balanced program. He sees that all workers perform at optimum efficiency. He is careful to see that all workers are clear on their responsibilities and duties. He checks to see that such duties are actually performed.

In addition to the operation of the total program of the department in cooperation with other departments, the administration of the department itself on Sunday is an important obligation of the department superintendent. This work is generally divided into three periods: (1) pre-session, (2) session, and (3) post-session. Pre-session responsibilities include such matters as seeing that all possible preparation has been made by officers and teachers for the session to follow. A quick survey can be made of the building and equipment to see that everything has been properly arranged, that supplies and materials are at hand and that records are in order. It is important also to see that all early comers are properly welcomed and that visitors are made to feel at home. All department officers can be briefed on their duties and last minute plans made for the opening worship period where this is used. Some groups choose to use part of the pre-session period for prayer. Teachers at least should be in their rooms with their pupils for pre-session activities.

The session includes the opening worship and/or the class period. Where worship is employed, the department superintendent or someone designated by him will lead. This will be fully discussed in a section on worship to follow. Following the assembly period, classes should convene as early as possible. During the class period superintendents should do everything possible to keep disturbances and distractions to a minimum. Time may also be spent in observing the teachers and classes in action. This will provide data for supervisory purposes. Care should be taken that department officers operate during this time without interfering with the classes. This is particularly true of the department secretary who receives the class records.

The post-session period provides the department superintendent and other department officers with opportunities to urge pupils to attend preaching services, particularly where morning church worship follows the Sunday school hour. In fact, these workers should set a good example in their own attendance at such services.

Some department superintendents find it helpful to lay out a general pattern of responsibility for department officers such as that which follows:

Officer	Primary Responsibility	Secondary Responsibility
Department Superintendent	Evangelism, administration, and supervision	Train class presidents
Associate Superintendent	Growth, follow-up, and teacher training	Train class vice presidents
Department Secretary	Records, supplies, and materials	Train class secretaries Promote stewardship and missions
Pianist	Music	Promote fellowship and service activities
Chorister	Singing	
Librarian	Department library custodian, audio-visual aids	Promote good reading Promote home-church relations
Teachers	Evangelism and instruction	

Such a plan gets away from the idea of "assistants" in the department. Instead, each one should feel that he has a primary job to do for the Lord. Where the department enrollment remains small, only one associate superintendent will be necessary, but where the department grows to as many as ten classes, another associate may be necessary. In such cases the department superintendent needs to divide responsibilities clearly for both associates. For example, one associate could be in charge of membership cultivation and

CHART 14

DEPARTMENTAL SPACE, EQUIPMENT AND MATERIALS

Item	NURSERY	BEGINNER	PRIMARY	JUNIOR	JR. HIGH	SR. HIGH	ADULTS
Space per pupil	25-35 sq. feet	25-35 sq. ft.	20-30 sq. ft.	20-30 sq. ft.	15-18 sq. ft.	10-12 sq. ft.	8-10 sq. ft.
Number	8-15	20-25	25-35	20-30	10-15	20-25	Varies
Toilets	10" high	10" high	14" high	16" high	adult	adult	STANDARD EQUIPMENT
Basins	24" high	24" high	28" high	30" high	adult	adult	
Hangers	30"-36" high	42" high	40"-48" high	48"-54" high	adult	adult	
Cabinets	open	open	open and closed	open and closed	adult	adult	
Tack Boards	25"-27"	28"-30"	Eye-level	Eye-level	----	----	
Chairs	Cribs Chairs 6"-8" high	8"-10" high	12"-14" high	14"-16" high	16"-18" high	17"-18" high	
Tables	16"-18" high 24" x 36" wide	18"-20" high 28" x 48" wide	24" high 30" x 48" or 54"	26" high 30" x 48" or 54"	26"-28" high	28"-30" high	
Other Material and Equipment	Graded literature Bible Books Pictures	Graded literature Bible Books Pictures	Graded literature Bibles Paper Pencils	Graded literature Bibles Paper Pencils	Graded literature Bibles Paper Pencils	Recommended Literature Tables for study and discussion Bibles Pictures	

Large	Large blocks	Crayons	Record player	Maps	Audio-visual aids
Crayons	2x4x8	Paste	Song books	Bulletin board	Books
Puzzles	2x4x12	Scissors	Books	Blackboard	Piano
House-keeping toys	Floor toys	Song books	Crayons	Chalkboard	Turn-over Charts
Rug	House keeping toys	Pictures	Paste	Maps (Wall)	Globe
Large blocks	Offering container	Books	Scissors	Song books	Maps
2x4x8	Song books	Plants	Offering container	Pictures	Portable blackboard
2x4x12	Puzzles	Nature materials	Wastebasket	Audio-visual aids	Bulletin board
Floor toys	Wooden animals	Waste-basket	Plants	Easels	Lecterns
Ball	Easels	Clock	Nature materials	Youth library	Cabinets
Song book	Waste-basket	Easels	Movable blackboard	Piano	Recreation equipment
Offering container	Storage space for supplies	Audio-visual aids	Chalkboard	Record player	Dictionaries
Waste-basket	Large crayons	Song charts	Easels	Research materials	Reference books
Clock	Plants	Globe	Bible dictionary	Offering container	Concordance
Plants	Paper	Offering container	Bible maps	Storage space	Library
Easels	Scissors	Blackboards	Globe	Recreation equipment	Song books
Wooden animals	Piano	Chalkboard	Reference books	Turn-over charts	Offering container
Storage space for toys	Clock	Bulletin board	Dictionary		
Piano		Storage space	Translations		
Music supplies		Piano	Bible picture books		
Play pens		Sand Table	Bulletin board		
Beds			Concordance		
Aquarium			Storage space		
			Audio-visual aids		
			Piano		

visitation, while the other could assist the department superintendent with the Sunday program.

Not the least of the department superintendent's administrative tasks is that of planning and conducting various department meetings and conferences. At least once a month all workers of each department need to meet for consultation and joint planning. The time of such meetings can be worked out in cooperation with the general superintendent. The work of each department is so important and so complex that it requires close collaboration on the part of all workers in the department. Such meetings also contribute greatly to the individual development of the workers. Problems can be solved and misunderstandings ironed out in these meetings. Necessary business can also be transacted. Some schools use this time for study and discussion of Sunday school lessons. Other uses might include preview sessions, aims, or visitation. In addition to study, efficiency, and discussion, these meetings afford opportunities for fellowship.

The time for department meetings often falls just after a general session of the workers' conference for the whole school, or it may meet before or after other church meetings. Many find it convenient to meet in this way to reduce the number of trips to the church. For obvious reasons, Sunday is not considered a good time.

The department superintendent is responsible for the agenda of these meetings. This does not mean, however, that he has to conduct all meetings. Instead, he may find it wise to delegate this to the associate department superintendent occasionally. Other schools use the planning committee procedure with either one of the superintendents as chairman. All department workers will serve as members of this committee from time to time. In any event, planning should cover at least a year, with enough flexibility allowed for emergencies and discussion of unforeseen problems. As far as possible the plans should center around the practical problems of the department workers. Do not allow the meetings to become routine. Careful planning will preclude this result.

The agenda for a good department meeting will include at least the following elements:

Devotions	Discussion
Prayer	Planning
Reports	Study and Training

Reports should be presented in written form for the records. Visitation, telephone calls, use of the mail, souls saved, enrollment, etc., are illustrations of reports. Plans, problems, and activities of the various classes can be surveyed. New workers can be counseled. Plans for special days can be laid. Worship programs may be planned. An example of an agenda used in one situation follows:

SAMPLE AGENDA FOR DEPARTMENT MEETING

1. Open meeting with prayer; emphasize any special requests from teachers and pupils
2. Have department secretary call roll and read minutes
3. Reports of committees
4. Report all sick and absentee pupils
5. Report all visits and contacts in interest of pupils
6. Discussion of class matters and problems, class by class
7. Discussion of what can be done about the
   (1) new pupils   (4) rooms
   (2) literature   (5) discipline
   (3) equipment   (6) record system, etc.
8. Be sure that workers know their duties
9. Discuss teacher training and evangelism
10. Set up the worship assembly programs
11. Discuss methods of teaching
12. Discuss the lessons for the month and how to use them
13. Discuss plans for organized visitation or the observance of a Visitation Day
14. Make provisions for recreation, etc.

3. *Supervision.* It was previously observed that *improvement* is stressed in the concept of supervision. Each department superintendent will want his workers to improve the quality of their work. The best work, however, centers in constantly improving the teaching-learning process. Of course where a director of religious education is on the staff, department superintendents can call upon him to guide this work. Where none is present, the department superintendent must fill the gap. A sound knowledge of the principles of teaching and the psychology of learning are greatly helpful to the supervisor at this point.

Important in the work of supervision is the matter of constantly keeping spiritual and academic objectives before the teachers and department workers. As far as possible the work needs to be kept at the highest level of efficiency and practice. This calls for constant evaluation to identify problems and weaknesses and outline specific remedies. Personal counseling with teachers has made large contributions toward improving the quality of their work. Here the department superintendent is urged to use the conference method of counseling. This was discussed in detail in Chapter 4 on the work of the director of Christian education.

In addition to the problems of the teacher, the department superintendent is also interested in general conditions which prevail among the workers. His constant concern is for the spiritual condition of the workers and the atmosphere in which they work. He will strive always to get rid of any elements of sin, jealousy, or selfishness which strike at the deeper life of the workers. Here much prayer will be demanded.

Where problems arise, the department superintendent should not hesitate to go to the general superintendent and pastor for assistance. It may be that a tactful counseling session or a visit into the home of the workers will lead to a peaceful and satisfactory solution of personal problems among members of the staff.

Tests and measurements are important in supervision. Where a director of Christian education is on the staff, the department superintendent can consult with him about department standards. Good supervision calls for keeping objectives at the forefront. This will provide some basis for evaluation of the department program. If possible, secure a department standard and compare it with the status quo. Constant observation and checking also provides bases for improvement. Outside professional workers can often supply needed help in this area. Of course, the superintendent should constantly be interested in what is happening in the classroom. Various tests and measurements will be more fully discussed in the chapter which follows on the work of the teacher.

4. *Duties.* Department superintendents have a multitude of duties. For convenience sake they are listed as follows:

A. In preparing for the academic year (planning the work)
   1. See that the necessary teachers and workers are secured.
   2. See that the teachers and workers understand their duties.
   3. See that a program of teacher-training is set up through the monthly meetings, special reading assignments and on-the-job experience.
   4. See that a system of visitation is established.
   5. See that an adequate record system is established.
   6. See that the curriculum is in order.
   7. See that adequate facilities and equipment are available
   8. Plan the assembly exercises for the year, and other expressional activities.
   9. Plan class and age group goal for the year.
   10. Compare notes with the general superintendent and with the Sunday school council.

B. In pursuing the academic year (working the plan)
   1. See that the program is carried out.
   2. See that pupils are welcomed, enrolled, and properly graded.
   3. See that an evangelistic emphasis is maintained (visit by pastor).
   4. Be ready to fill vacancies when necessary.

5. Visit (early in the class period) and study the need of the classes, standing ready to give help where needed.
6. Refrain from "snoopervision" and fault-finding (sit in rear).
7. Give honest recognition (through proper installation, promotion) and inspire enthusiasm.
8. Keep teachers in touch with best materials, methods, and books.
9. Be ready to give practical suggestions for improvement.
10. Require of secretary accurate records of attendance and punctuality.
11. Require of teachers a definite lesson plan.
12. All class activities approved.
13. Conduct monthly department conferences.
14. Attend all workers' conferences and councils.
15. Present needs of department to church officials.
16. Distribution of helpful literature on Sunday school work.
17. Direct plans for home cooperation.
18. Cooperate with the general superintendent and pastor.
19. Study and know needs, abilities, and interests of pupils.
20. Share in visitation.
21. Study class rolls as to size.
22. Encourage classes to organize (junior and above).
23. Start new classes.
24. Maintain organization of the department.
25. Keep the department properly graded.

C. General duties
1. Direct getting and holding people in the department.
2. See that the department has adequate equipment.
3. Maintain regular conferences of teachers and officers.
4. Promote a standard of education.
5. See that the officers of the department do their jobs and know their duties.
6. Set up standards for the department.
7. Attend church services, including prayer meetings.
8. Make after-services contacts for the department.
9. Keep in touch with the registrar and absentee workers.
10. Attend all district and denominational meetings possible.
11. Make an annual report to the board.
12. Oversee and promote department growth.
13. Help place new members and visitors.
14. Assist pastor and general superintendent in selecting and enlisting workers.
15. Urge workers and pupils to attend church.

D. Sunday duties
  1. Be present early.
  2. Superintend platform exercises when your department has charge (or meets separately). Keep the program varied and interesting.
  3. During the class period:
     (a.) Be sure the staff is on hand; fill vacancies.
     (b.) Help place new members and visitors.
     (c.) Be ready to teach or help where needed.
     (d.) Visit and study the needs of the classes.
     (e.) Supervise the work of the department secretaries:
        (1) Instruct the class and department secretaries.
        (2) Know how to use the class record books.
        (3) See that class reports get to the general secretary.
        (4) See that new pupils are registered and assigned.
        (5) See that absentees are reported to the registrar or general secretary.

E. Monthly duties.
  1. Attend the meetings of the Board of Christian Education and/or the Sunday school council.
  2. Prepare for departmental meetings with workers.
  3. See that all teachers and workers in the department attend the general and departmental meetings of which they are a part.
  4. Call on the absentees and sick of the department.
  5. Assign calls to others; have a visitation day.

C. RESPONSIBILITIES OF THE DEPARTMENT SUPERINTENDENT

1. *Grading and Grouping*

Definition and Purposes. Simply stated, grading is the grouping of pupils of similar ages, needs, and characteristics into departments and classes in the church school teaching situation. This problem is not new, but the departmental system of school organization is now an established principle in sound church school administration. Experience has taught us that learning gospel truths most effectively means a division of pupils into departments and setting up graded classes, so that each pupil may receive Christian truth in the best possible way.

The primary purpose of grading is to meet the needs of the student body on the level of understanding, needs, and interests at each stage of pupil development. The great objective, of course, is to bring pupils to Christlikeness of character and activity in His service.

Pattern. The pattern for this principle lies in the Word of God. There God is pictured as one who has graded the universe — stars, planets, and suns move according to a variety of designs and levels of placement. He assigned the Israelites definite positions for marching, working, fighting, and camping. Jesus fed the hungry multitudes by courses.

God has graded people. Children, youth, and adults are markedly different. God has planned it that way. Grading is a part of our being. Nothing is more apparent than the differences between children, youth, and adults — in size, mental capacity, and spiritual discernment. Psychologists have made detailed studies of this principle. Chart 15 shows some results of their studies.

Thus, grading is not too difficult when we follow God's design. The various periods of human development are ordained of God, and all we have to do is recognize the scientific classification that He has made. We do this by recognizing the three divisions — children, youth, and adult — and dividing the divisions into departments and classes. In this way we cooperate wisely with God's plan; we can discover how He made life and what are its characteristics, needs, and capacities at each stage of development. "There is a spiritual work to be accomplished at each period of life that can never be done so well as then."

All this leads to the inevitable conclusion that grading affects all that goes on in the school. In many respects, therefore, this is one of the most important factors to be considered by superintendents. Because grading is most clearly seen at the classroom level, educational workers are most concerned with it. All department superintendents will see that the principle is fully practiced and that the following outcomes be anticipated:

1. Graded pupils
2. Graded lessons
3. Graded teachers
4. Graded quarters
5. Graded equipment
6. Graded control
7. Graded evangelism
8. Graded worship

Advantages. The following list reveals the many values and advantages of grading in the church school:

A. To the students
   1. Fellowship with students of own age and interests
   2. Participation in learning situations with other students on the same level of understanding and accomplishment
   3. A program is provided to meet individual needs

CHART 15
PSYCHOLOGY AND CHURCH SCHOOL GRADING

GRADING (Psychological Development)

	Childhood — Growth				Adolescence — Development			Adulthood — Maturity		
Period	EARLY	MIDDLE	MIDDLE	LATER	EARLY	MIDDLE	LATER	EARLY	MIDDLE	LATER
Name	Infancy	Kindergarten	Primary	Junior	Intermediates	Seniors	Young People	Adult	Adult	Adult
Ages	B-3	4 - 5	6 - 7 - 8	9 - 10 - 11	12 - 13 - 14	15 - 16 - 17	18 - 24	25 - 40	41 - 70	over 70
Key Word	Detection	Reception	Action	Exertion	Transition	Aspiration	Verification	Application	Production	Meditation
Characteristics	Discovers World, Places, Things, Self, People, Rapid Growth, Sensuous, Regular Prayer	Questions, Movement, Trusting, Credulous	Restless, Activity, Adventure, Expression, Curious, Reverance	Great Energy, Memory, Clanish, Worshipper	Rapid Change, Critical, Emotional, Faith over Reason, Instability, Cliquishness	Achievement, Idealism, Independence, Radical, Extreme Doubting, Great Problems, Age of Decisions	Maturity, Reason, Judgment, Many Choices, Vocation, Marriage, College, Evaluation, Earnestness	Maturity, Age of Action, The Worker, Life Career, Life Philosopher, Religion Applied	Maturity, Settled In Vocation, Practical Faith In Man, Faith in God Deepened or Rejected	Senility, Dependence, Reminiscence, Hope, Faith or Fear

Church School Grading (GRADING)

Division	Name	Ages	Grade / Department	Aim
Children's Division	Cradle Roll (at Home) / Nursery (at Church)	Ages: B-3	Preschool	Motivation
Children's Division	Beginner	Ages 4-5	Preschool	Direction
Children's Division	Primary	Ages 6-7-8	Grade 1-2-3	Regulation
Children's Division	Junior	Ages 9-10-11	Grade 4-5-6	Stimulation
Youth Division	Jr. High	Ages 12-13-14	Grade 7-8-9	Association
Youth Division	Seniors	Ages 15-16-17	Grade 10-11-12	Preparation
Youth Division	Young People	Ages 18-24	College	Exortation
Adult Division	Young Adults	Ages 25-40		Administration
Adult Division	Middle Adults	Ages 41-70		Cooperation
Adult Division	Older Adults	Ages over 70		Veneration

    4. A challenge to make progress is presented to each one
    5. Contact is made with many workers at various levels
    6. Stewardship is stimulated
    7. Happily located pupils are contented pupils
    8. Promotion stimulates pupil interest and achievement
B. To the teachers, officers, and workers
    1. Greater and wider opportunities for Christian service are made available to everyone
    2. Specialization is provided for in training
    3. Definite needs and interests are pin-pointed
    4. Specific administrative procedures can be applied to meet particular problems clearly revealed
    5. Bible study is geared to pupil understanding, needs, and interests
    6. Consistency in the use of curriculum materials
    7. Evaluation of progress made is more clearly seen
    8. Materials, facilities, and equipment can be intelligently applied to the needs of the classes
    9. Teachers can become specialists in a certain grade level
   10. Teachers can become proficient in applying truth to particular age levels through an understanding of the psychological characteristics of those levels
   11. Records can be more adequately kept and more intelligently interpreted.
   12. Responsibilities of workers are pin-pointed to specific age levels, thus obligating them to reach pupils of a particular group with the Gospel
   13. Close supervision of all workers
   14. Individual workers and teachers are made responsible for winning each lost pupil to Christ
   15. Visitation is stimulated
   16. More accurate information is made available
   17. Results of evangelism are conserved better

Basis and Space. A first step is to determine what basis will be used for grouping pupils. This has been a source of great controversy among Christian educators. Some use scholastic attainment, some grade according to various ideas of congeniality, and some even according to social relationships. Still others try to use a combination of methods. While the age basis is probably the most practical basis to use, one must consider the whole pupil in classification. There is such a thing as physical age, social age, mental age, and even spiritual age. The most popular basis perhaps at this time is to consider progress made in the public school grades, particularly in the children and youth divisions. It should be remembered, on the other hand, that other factors sometimes largely affect pupil classification. Workers should use common sense in placing pupils but not lose sight of considering such factors as retardedness, brilliance, and size. Particular care should be exercised in dealing with pupils in junior and senior high groups where social, physical, and emotional factors are sharp. Rules need to be very flexible for these groups. Rather than shove them out of school, put them in somewhere in an effort to hold them. Of course, when pupils are out of the public school, the age basis is probably the best procedure to follow. Older young people and adults each have similar problems and needs which can be met in classes for their particular age.

Space and number of workers are also important factors in grading, particularly at the beginning of a grading effort in the school. The problem of enough teachers and officers can be solved by a good leadership education program in advance of expansion needs. Space problems can be solved through a re-study of the use of the present space, remodeling, or the erection of a new building. Several denominations have made studies of their constituencies to find out what space situation trends were present in their midst. The following is a comparative study of some representative findings:

The above figures are only general averages. A great many variations were noted according to geographical areas. It should

		Southern Baptist [*]	Nazarene [**]	Presbyterian U.S.A. [***]	Disciples of Christ [***]	Methodists [***]
DEPARTMENTS	AGES	SPACE	SPACE	SPACE	SPACE	SPACE
Nursery	B-3	4-7%	4%	6-8%	4%	6-8%
Beginner	4-5	5-6%	8%	12-17%	8%	8%
Primary	6-8	9-10%	12%	18-25%	12%	12%
Junior	9-11	13%	12%	15-21%	12%	12%
Junior High	12-14	13%	12%	12-16%	10½%	11%
Senior High	15-17	13-15%	11%	10-13%	9½%	10%
Young People	18-24	13-15%	19%	....	40%	5%
Adult	over 24	40-60%	22%	27%	40%	35%

* Harrell, W. A. *Planning Better Church Buildings*, p. 45.
** Harper, Albert F., *The Nazarene Sunday School*, p. 42.
*** Atkinson, C. Harry, *Building and Equipping for Christian Education*, p. 26.

not be assumed that such figures can be used in all situations, because each church will have to consider its own peculiar needs in the light of the local situation.

Bearing in mind that the above figures are only approximate, the average of the figures listed in the chart will give a church only an approximate basis for planning. With this in mind, perhaps the following chart will illustrate the type of thinking demanded in meeting space problems in relation to classification:

CHART 16

APPROXIMATE SPACE NEEDS FOR THE CHURCH SCHOOL

DEPARTMENTS	AGES	PERCENTAGE OF SPACE (Average)	ATTENDANCE BELOW 100		ATTENDANCE 100-150		ATTENDANCE 150-300		ATTENDANCE 300-600	
			No. of Depts.	No. of Class	No. of Depts.	No. of Class	No. of Depts.	No. of Class	No. of Depts.	No. of Class
Nursery	B-3	6-8	1	1	1	1	1	2	1	3
Beginner	4-5	9-12	1	1	1	2	1	2-3	1-2	3-6
Primary	6-8	12-14	1	1	1	2-3	1	3-4	1-2	4-9
Junior	9-11	12-14	1	1	1	2-3	1	3-4	1-2	4-9
Jr. High	12-14	11-14	1	1	1	2-3	1	3-4	1-2	4-9
Seniors	15-17	12-14	1	1	1	2-3	1	3-4	1-2	4-9
Young People	18-24	20-25	1	2	1	2	1	2-3	1-2	3-6
Adults	Over 24	35-40	1	2	1	3	1	3-5	1-3	4-8

Grouping. Individual denominations largely determine for themselves the pattern of grouping and organization for their local churches. In a very real sense, however, each local church should study carefully its own peculiar local situation and plan accordingly. To guide such planning it is helpful to study traditional ways of grouping. The patterns commonly accepted thus far include three divisions divided into departments and classes as follows:

TRADITIONAL DEPARTMENTS

Children's Division
    Nursery Department — Ages B - 3   Pre-school
    Beginner Department — Ages 4-5 Pre-school
    Primary Department — Ages 6-8   Grades 1-3
    Junior Department — Ages 9-11   Grades 4-6

Youth Division
    Junior High Department — Ages 12-14   Grades 7-9
    Senior High Department — Ages 15-17   Grades 10-12
    Young People's Department — Ages 18-24   College Age

CHART 17

PROGRESSIVE GUIDE FOR GRADING AND ENLARGEMENT

No. of classes or depts.

5 — Cradle Roll | Pre-school Nursery B - 5 yrs. | Grades 1-6 6 - 11 yrs | Grades 7-12 12 - 17 or 18 yrs. | Y.P. - Adult All over 18

6 — Cradle Roll | Pre-school Nursery B - 5 yrs. | Grades 1-3 Primary 6 - 8 yrs. | Grades 4-6 Junior 9 - 11 yrs. | Grades 7-12 Youth 12 - 17 or 18 yrs. | Y.P. - Adult All over 18

7 — Cradle Roll | Pre-school Nursery B - 5 yrs. | Grades 1-3 Primary 6 - 8 yrs. | Grades 4-6 Junior 9 - 11 yrs. | Grades 7-9 Jr. High 12 - 14 yrs. | Grades 10-12 Sr. High 15 - 17, 18 yrs. | Y.P. - Adult All over 18

9 — Cradle Roll B - 3 yrs. | Nursery B - 3 yrs. | Beginners 4 - 5 yrs. | Primary Grades 1 - 3 6 - 8 yrs. | Junior Grades 4-6 9 - 11 yrs. | Jr. High Grades 7-9 12 - 14 yrs. | Sr. High Grades 10-12 15 - 17, 18 yrs. | Young People College 18 - 24 yrs. | Adult All over 24 yrs.

11 — Cradle Roll B - 3 yrs. | Nursery B - 3 yrs. | Beginners 4 - 6 yrs. | Primary Grades 1-3 6 - 8 yrs. | Junior Grades 4-6 9 - 11 yrs. | Jr. High Grades 7-8 12 - 14 yrs. | Seniors Grades 10-12 15 - 17, 18 yrs. | Y. People College Age 18-24 yrs. | Young Adult 24 - 40 yrs. | Mid. Adult 41 - 65 yrs. | Older Adults over 65

Adult Division

> Young Adult Department — Ages 25 to about 40
> Middle Adult Department — Ages 41 to about 70
> Older Adult Department — Ages over 70

The above grouping concerns those pupils who use the facilities of the church school. Two other groupings are necessary to take care of pupils who cannot use the facilities:

1. The Cradle Roll
2. The Extension or Home Department

The cradle roll is perhaps the most important department in the church school. It works at both ends of the school at the same time. It enrolls the new babies until they become members of the nursery department and also works with the parents. It thus becomes a feeder for the church school. Actually, this work falls within the responsibility of the children's division.

The extension department ministers to the shut-ins and to the shut-outs — those who are confined to homes because of illness or other reasons and those who cannot attend services because of circumstances or work responsibilities. Other possibilities include a ministry to the unfortunates of the community.

In addition to space and classification problems is the problem of a pattern of growth. In starting a new Sunday school, only a few departments and classes are needed. All schools should keep the ideal pattern of the departmental plan in mind from the very beginning. In small schools the whole division may act as a department, with one teacher assuming the duties of a departmental superintendent. Multiplication is accomplished through division into departments and classes. Chart 17 is suggestive of a general pattern of growth toward the goal of a closely graded ideal departmental system.

From this chart it is seen that all the departments need not be organized at first. As the school multiplies, more divisions can be made. Pre-school children are divided naturally from children who are in school. High school youth are separated from elementary school children, and a separate youth department is justified on the basis of peculiar needs and intimate relationships at this age. The drop-out problem also stresses the importance of closer and graded supervision. Some schools may also find it feasible to have separate classes for boys and girls among older juniors and junior highs. Because of the intimate nature of spiritual instruction and certain adolescent difficulties, this procedure is needed in Sunday school work.

Below are three patterns of suggested adaptations for the small, medium, and large churches.

PATTERN 1

THE SMALL CHURCH — PLAN 1

Cradle Roll — B-3 (at home)
Pre-school — Ages 3 to 5 or 6 (at school)
Primary-Junior — Ages 6-11, Grades 1-6
Youth — Ages 12-17 or 18, Grades 7-12
Young People-Adults — Ages over 18

THE SMALL CHURCH — PLAN 2

Cradle Roll — B-3 (at home)
Pre-school — Ages 3-5 or 6 (at school)
Primary — Ages 6-8, Grades 1-3
Junior — Ages 9-11, Grades 4-6
Youth — Ages 12-17, or 18, Grades 7-12
Young People-Adults — Ages over 18

THE SMALL CHURCH — PLAN 3

Cradle Roll — B-3 (at home)
Pre-school — Ages 3-5 or 6 (at school)
Primary — Ages 6-8, Grades 1-3
Junior — Ages 9-11, Grades 4-6
Junior High — Ages 12-14, Grades 7-9
Senior High — Ages 15-17, or 18, Grades 10-12
Young People-Adults — Ages over 18

PATTERN 2

THE MEDIUM CHURCH — PLAN 1

Cradle Roll — B-3 (at home)
Nursery — B-3 (at school)
Beginners — Ages 4-5 or 6, Preschool
Primary — Ages 6-8, Grades 1-3
Junior — Ages 9-11, Grades 4-6
Junior High — Ages 12-14, Grades 7-9
Senior High — Ages 15-17, or 18, Grades 10-12
Young People — Ages 18-24, College Age
Adults — Ages over 24

THE MEDIUM CHURCH — PLAN 2

Cradle Roll — B-3 (at home)
Nursery — B-3 (at school)
   or
Nursery — under 3 and 3 (at school)
Beginners — Ages 4-5, Preschool
Primary — Ages 6-8, Grades 1-3
Junior — Ages 9-11, Grades 4-6
Junior High — Ages 12-14, Grades 7-9

Senior High — Ages 15-17, or 18, Grades 10-12
Young People — Ages 18-24, College Age
Young Adults — Ages 24-40
Adults — Ages 40-65 or 70 or adult, over 40
Older Adults — Ages over 65 or 70 or adult, over 40

PATTERN 3

THE LARGE CHURCH — PLAN 1

Cradle Roll — B-2 (At home)
Nursery — Age 2 (at school)
Nursery — Age 3 (at school)
Beginners — Ages 4-5 or 6, Preschool
Primary — Ages 6-7, Grades, 1-2
Primary-Junior — Ages 8-9, Grades 3-4
Junior — Ages 10-11, Grades, 5-6
Junior High — Ages 12-14, Grades 7-9
Senior High — Ages 15-17, or 18, Grades 10-12
Young People — Ages 18-24, College Age
Young Adults — Ages 25-40
Adults — Ages 40-65
Older Adults — Ages over 65

THE LARGE CHURCH — PLAN 2

Separate room or rooms for each class or grade.

The *two-grade plan* is becoming increasingly popular now even among smaller church schools, particularly in the children's division. The psychology of individual differences demands a recognition of the great differences which exists between children of an age span of three years. This plan, therefore, calls for a primary class or department consisting of two grades, a primary-junior group, and a junior group. The plan looks like this:

Primary Class or Dept.
Grades 1 — 2
Ages 6 — 7
Primary-Junior Class or Dept.
Grades 3 — 4
Ages 8 — 9
Junior Class or Dept.
Grades 5 — 6
Ages 10 — 11

The same plan can be extended further into the youth division just as well. Where used, however, it is obvious that special curriculum materials will be needed. When attendance does not exceed 25 pupils in each group, three rooms are sufficient for this plan.

In the *group-graded plan* three grades can be combined in one group, provided attendance does not exceed 25 pupils. A separate room for each group will be needed.

Three-grade departments demand a room for each separate grade. One room should be larger than the other two to permit group worship. Attendance in this plan needs to be limited to about 15 pupils per grade in the children's division.

In the *single-grade* plan, each grade will have a separate room. In the children's division attendance should be kept around 15 with a maximum of 25 in the children's division. Where used, worship very likely is conducted in the class rooms.

Grading Adults. The basis for grading children and youth is quite clear, but it is more difficult with adults because there are no neat dividing lines for them. In the past the custom usually has been to organize young married people into classes and then let them move into older groups as the years go by. With the present emphasis on adult education in the secular world, attention has been focused on the possibilities of adult learning. Rather than grading adults according to interest groups, it is now stressed that there are periods of adult development just as clearly drawn as in other stages of personality development. Graded adults place men and women of approximately the same age, interests, and needs together. This makes for better attendance, closer fellowship, and easier instruction. Ralph E. Longshore has listed a number of obvious advantages in grading adults when he expressed the Southern Baptist feeling about this problem: Why Grade Adults?

1. To reach more adults
2. To start more classes
3. To distribute prospects better
4. To provide better teaching
5. To put new teachers to work
6. To win more people to Christ
7. To develop Christians
8. To build fellowship
9. To assure better attendance
10. To assure a church centered program[1]

To accomplish grading among adults will require a great deal of patience, prayer, and education. Once the workers are sold on it, the classes must be made to see the immediate advantages. Every effort should be made to convince them of the greater benefits involved. Articles on good results can be posted; special speakers can share their good experiences; visits to successful schools can be made; committees can study carefully the problems involved.

[1]Ralph E. Longshore, "Why Grade Adults?" *Sunday School Builder* (March 1956), p. 50

By keeping everyone informed and giving irrefutable demonstrations of values involved, adults can be graded. A simple age basis plus annual promotion will suffice to keep the plan in operation.

Promotion and Classification. Once a school has been graded properly, it can be kept that way by (1) the use of systematic promotion, (2) the keeping of good records, and (3) proper classification of new members.

Promotion day is an annual occasion usually observed the last Sunday in September.

New members should be assigned to their proper age groups as early as possible. Long probationary periods are not wise. Where exceptions to the age-grade basis of classification are to be made, the Sunday school board or cabinet should help workers decide each individual case. Some kind of rule is necessary to guide the promotion of pupils. For example, those who are in the first grade at public school and who passed the sixth birthday, or will pass the sixth birthday within three months after promotion day, may be advanced to the primary class. Some schools use a special classification superintendent or registrar to assist with these matters.

Departmentalization. A school should move to the ideal pattern of full departmentalization as soon as conditions permit. Schools below an enrollment of 100 meeting in one to three rooms could not expect to reach the ideal until further space is provided. Other schools of 150 enrollment and over may have a partial system, particularly in the children's division. The best schools will be fully departmentalized. No matter what size the school may be, it should be properly graded, even where the class system of organization is used.

As soon as there are two or more classes in any one age group, you have the basis for beginning departmentalization. One of the teachers of these classes or someone else can be appointed head teacher or superintendent and plan periodic departmental meetings. Another procedure for small schools below 100 enrollment is to form a department of each division until the enrollment justifies further divisions. Progress toward full departmentalization will be gradual as growth takes place but the ideal should constantly guide in adjusting to the increase.

Traditionally, the decision to organize additional classes has rested upon the size of the classes. In the children and youth divisions the ideal class size has been held to 8-10 for many years, although at present there is a tendency to move to larger classes, particularly where there are skillful teachers in charge.

Size of departments is a debatable matter. Here again the situation depends on number of workers and the ability of the workers. In the average church school, however, it has been suggested that divisions into more departments should be made when the enrollment exceeds the figures listed below:

For Nursery — 20 pupils
For Beginners — 25-30 pupils
For Primaries and Juniors — 35-50 pupils
For Youth — 50-75 pupils
For Adults — 75-100 pupils

In churches where a desire is expressed to move toward departmentalization, this decision should come from the Board of Christian Education or similar group. Teachers and officers should have a chance to study the whole plan before action is actually taken. Transition should be made slowly and gradually so that there will be complete cooperation and understanding. Promotion day has been recommended as a good time to begin.

The decision to departmentalize will rest largely on two primary factors: facilities and personnel. A good building designed to meet the needs of the various age groups is imperative for a departmentalized school. Naturally, more workers are demanded in this kind of school. Advance preparation should be made in each church *before* departmentalization is attempted.

2. Worship

Nature of Worship. The department superintendent has direct responsibility for developing worshipful attitudes and directing worship activities. These things involve good leadership, skillful and reverent conducting of services, and the development of a program of worship training. Leading pupils and workers into God's presence is a most important task. The principles of worship which he employs can be applied to both departmental and general assembly types of worship.

Dictionaries define worship as "adoration, veneration, reverence given to Deity." In church school work worship is realizing the presence of God and practicing His presence. The will, feelings, motives, purposes, and acts of the individual are brought into harmony with the will of God through worship. Sincere effort is made to have communion and fellowship with God in genuine worship. Wherever worship is given "in spirit and in truth," the following elements must be present:

1. Adoration
2. Praise
3. Thanksgiving
4. Truth of message
5. Offering
6. Confession and penitence
7. Humility and dependence

8. Sincerity
9. Prayer
10. Atmosphere — room and attitudes

Purposes of Worship. The superintendent has a twofold purpose in the development of a program of worship in his department: (1) to provide for the *act* of worship, and (2) to provide training *for* worship. The act of worship is both objective and subjective, the former being something given to God and the latter something which takes place within the individual. Training for worship involves practice in the act of worship as well as the creation of certain concepts, attitudes, appreciations, and aptitudes for public church worship and services. Through all this it is hoped that the general objectives of Christian education will be realized.

Paulsen has listed the functions of worship as follows:

1. To assist in developing awareness of the existence of God as an objective reality, and to begin to do it with the little child.
2. To help develop those inner drives and compulsions which send us out to live in the daily round of experience in home, school, leisure and world of work, the Christian attitudes and principles taught in the classroom.
3. To make provision for the element of decision, commitment, even conversion when that is the basic need.
4. To help persons appropriate spiritual resources for living.
5. To prepare the young ultimately to take their place as permanent and as worshipping members of the adult congregation[2].

The Place of Worship. The above discussion reveals the vast importance of worship in the church school. It has an important place among all ages. "Opening exercises," therefore, are greatly inadequate either in the "act" of worship or in training for worship. Without being stilted or too formal, worship should be true worship in the opening sessions of the church school whether used in general assembly or departments. The singing of a song or two, followed by a short prayer, announcements, and dismissal to classes is certainly not a worship service.

Schools which employ skillful techniques in planning and conducting real worship services have found them of immeasureable value in preparing pupils for the instructional program to follow and as attractive and profitable promotional devices. Good opening sessions of worship result in punctuality and greater interest.

In nursery and beginner departments there will likely be no formal worship service. Instead, worship will be spontaneous, free,

---

[2]Irwin G. Paulsen, *The Church School and Worship* (New York: The Macmillan Co., 1940), Chapter 2.

and informal, an integrated part of the class activities in which there will be frequent expressions of praise and thanksgiving to God.

In the primary department spontaneous worship will continue, but there should be planned services also. If possible, the children may participate in planning them. All worship materials and orders of service need to be simple for this group. Silence may be employed occasionally. Adult and theological language should be avoided. Stress God as Creator, Author, a loving, providing, protecting Father, the Source of help and Lord of life with a plan for all.

Above the primary department the superintendent can plan for a rather permanently formal type of worship program to which we shall now turn our attention.

The Program of Worship. A comprehensive program of worship in the church school will be closely integrated with the total program of worship in the church. This means that the pastor will be directly concerned with worship wherever it takes place in the program and he should be contacted by superintendents for assistance and counsel in developing and conducting worship programs in the school. The pastor will also be helpful in evaluating the program and in taking part at times.

Possibly of greatest help is a "worship committee" for the church school and/or departments to assist the superintendents in planning and conducting various types of worship activities. This committee will be responsible for clear-cut purposes of opening services, the content of such services, orders of worship, materials for use in the programs, the environment for worship, worship training, and the relation of church school and congregational worship.

The trend today, even in evangelical schools, is away from the traditional "opening exercise," the purpose of which was to "prepare the way" for the lesson to follow. Under this plan about all that was accomplished was to provide a "pep session" for the Sunday school. In the light of the fact that many who attend Sunday school never go to congregational worship services, it is extremely important that opening sessions in Sunday school be real worship experiences and give training for the right kind of worship. This brings into focus the matter of what are the purposes of opening services in the church school. The following list might suggest some:

1. Not as a buffer for late comers, but to create a spiritual atmosphere for beginning Sunday school.
2. To offer all in the Sunday school the privilege of worship.
3. To impress visitors with the Sunday school program of worship.

4. To unify the Sunday school program for the day.
5. To produce an appetite for the Bible lesson period.
6. To provide background for lessons; prepare receptive hearts.
7. To train workers, leaders, and pupils in worship.
8. To give additional instruction in the Word beyond that found in the lesson.
9. To provide evangelistic opportunities.
10. To supply opportunities for graded worship.

The content of the worship service concerns the Christian message. In order to get this message across best, the worship committee and superintendent should choose a theme for the day, one that is specific and positive and which has ethical bearing and a real challenge in it. Such a theme may be chosen in a variety of ways. One way is to freely choose a theme (that is, originate one) — such as prayer or the love of God — and build the worship service around it. A second way is to use a series of themes on one subject. For example, Jesus the Friend — of sinners, of children, of all races, etc. A third way is to correlate the worship theme with that of the department lesson for the day. For example, if the lesson theme is "What Prayer Does," the worship theme might be correlated with it by using the theme, "How God Talks to Us Today." The advantage of this last method is quite evident, particularly where group graded materials are being used in the department.

To make this kind of planning most effective, the worship committee needs to create a calendar of themes with the services built around them for as much as six months to a year in advance. Where the desire is to correlate with the lessons being taught, the committee should secure a curriculum chart to get information on future lessons coming up during the year. A wide variety of themes may be chosen from an almost inexhaustible source of ideas from the following suggestive areas of curriculum emphases:

1. Doctrine
2. Skits
3. Object lessons
4. Stories
5. Art
6. Songs
7. Honor class
8. Honor department
9. Special days
10. Christian biography
11. Practical problems
12. Evangelism and soul winning
13. Missions
14. Devotional
15. Catechism
16. Memory verses
17. Special subjects
18. Testimonies
19. Church history
20. Audio-visuals

By planning well in advance, a group of workers can think of many original ideas to use in opening sessions which will be of mutual benefit and interest to the various departments in the church school.

There are no set procedures in developing and using a form or order of service. Those conducting the service may use their own discretion in this matter, being careful however to evaluate their plans to see if all elements of genuine worship are present. Two samples of a general assembly order of service are provided below:

Order No. 1

Music
Call to worship
Prayer (unison or leader)
Scripture reading (may be responsive; be on theme)
Story or talk (develop theme)
Hymn
Prayer (dedicatory in nature)
Benediction

Order No. 2

Prelude
Ascriptions of praise
Hymn
Call to prayer
Prayer
Response after prayer (by all)
Material on theme (develop through a variety of means)
Hymn
Moments of dedication (silence, prayer, music, or altar call)
Benediction (Choral or instrumental)

The question often arises, "Shall the same order of service be used repeatedly?" If the school is new at this kind of worship, it might be wise to use the same order of service for a period of time for training purposes, then change to a second or third order, but be sure to vary the contents of them. If the school is used to this kind of order of service, then frequent changes and great flexibility will be necessary.

Where this kind of service is well-planned and well-executed, a period of 15 to 20 minutes may be used, but not over 20 minutes. In no case should teaching time be usurped by the opening sessions.

Materials for worship can be drawn from a wide variety of sources, including books of prayer, prepared services, worship program books, anthologies, story books, devotional books, periodicals, newspapers, biography, and scrapbooks. These materials should be chosen and adapted according to the demands of the graded principle. During the service they will take a wide variety of forms according to the following list:

Instrumental music	Litanies	Talks
Hymns	Doxologies	Stories
Prayers	Gloria	Drama
Calls to worship	Choral responses	Readings
Ascriptions of praise	Offering prayers	Silence
Sentences of invitation	Creeds	Benedictions
Responsive readings	Anthems	Pictures
Devotional readings	Affirmations of faith	Introduction to hymns

Every possible effort should be made to create a good environment for worship, one characterized by beauty, cleanliness, and order. Some schools use a worship center with appropriate symbols and arrangement.

Worship services should start promptly. A hand signal, the chords of a chosen hymn, or the superintendent standing quietly may prove sufficient to begin with. The service should move quietly and reverently through its climax to a conclusion. Every possible distraction should be eliminated and good order insisted upon. Latecomers can be withheld until the service is over.

Worship Training. The disposition and capacity for worship are not accidental. Planned training will lead to good leaders and worshipers. Leaders should be taught how to conduct group worship. This can be done through observation, coaching, and study. Workers' conferences may be used to study the improvement of the total worship program.

Pupils may be trained for a few minutes each Sunday. One method is to use about 10 minutes before the worship period. Another way is to occasionally use a full 20 or 30 minutes. A third method may result in a combination of the first two mentioned. A suggested schedule may look like this:

(1) Coaching, drilling, announcements — ten minutes

(2) Worship period — ten-twelve minutes

(3) Lesson period — thirty-forty minutes

Some training emphases will include developing an appreciation and understanding of sacred music through hymn study. Great recordings are useful for this. Training in the use of the ritual will include prayers, creeds, glorias, responses, benedictions, etc. They need to be interpreted and memorized. Drill in unison speaking and in posture may also be engaged in. A system of posture should be agreed upon, such as stand for praise, sit for instruction, kneel or bow for prayer. Other elements of instruction might include training in religious art and symbolism as used or in the significance of worship. The pastor should play a large part in providing this kind of instruction.

Special efforts should be made to get pupils into the church worship services. Constant urging, together with good examples on the part of all workers, will go far toward eliciting good response. Create and maintain a strong departmental loyalty in attending church. Secure the cooperation of parents. Train pupils to look for special help in such services.

Worship in the Small Church School. It is more difficult to plan and conduct worship in the small school, particularly the one-room school. All the principles of worship previously mentioned would certainly apply in small churches. The primary differences would lie in planning and conducting worship programs in a small setting. The family type worship has been suggested for small churches many times. This means more participation on the part of everyone than is ordinarily expected in larger churches. In fact, many small churches use some type of round-robin system wherein classes take turns in presenting worship programs for the whole group. Where this is not used and where a general assembly type is not desired, then it becomes imperative for the general superintendent to plan for a staggering of the schedule to make provision for various groups to use a worship period. Of course where there are two or three rooms, one room can be used by various groups at planned intervals for worship purposes. In a one-room school, some classes can proceed with classwork behind screens or temporary partitions of some kind, while the rest of the school unites in worship at the front of the building near the pulpit.

In the family type worship which draws all classes into one room, a round-robin system of conducting programs will recognize age group needs and interests in one service. The following schedule is suggestive of possibilities:

1st Sunday — Children's leaders plan worship for children
2nd Sunday — Youth leaders and youth plan worship for youth
3rd Sunday — reserved for adults
4th Sunday — missionary service with special offering
5th Sunday — special feature or dramatization

Foster has suggested some simple but important principles to be kept in mind when planning worship of a family style in a one-room church school:

1. The service should be of the family type
2. There must be careful advance preparation
3. The service must be planned with children in mind
4. There must be cooperation by all age groups of the school
5. Children and young people must share in the leadership
6. The service must be beautiful and dignified
7. Only the best materials and songs should be used
8. The central idea or theme should be visualized[3]

The Combined Service. Many feel that the benediction following the Sunday school lesson is an invitation for everyone to go home. To overcome this, some use the combined service. The

[3]Virgil E. Foster, *How a Small Church Can Have Good Christian Education* (New York: Harper & Brothers, 1956), p. 20.

values of this service are many. Greater church attendance is obvious of course. The pastor is brought into vital support of the Sunday school. The people feel that the Sunday school is in the church and that the church was at Sunday school. It is evident also that this plan will save time and avoid duplication. It will provide an opportunity to give real worship experiences to those who miss them under the old Sunday school plan. Quite often the sermon will prepare the way for the lesson period (when this follows). Many schools have found that finances increase and noise and confusion decrease. Of course, there are disadvantages too. It is different and such newness often lacks attractiveness to some people. It shortens the total time people are under church influence on Sunday. To some this plan will prove an inconvenience.

No set pattern has been laid for the order of service. Some schools open with the class period first; others prefer to have the sermon first. Two suggested orders of service follow:

No. I
9:30 A.M. — Quiet Music
Call to Worship
Invocation
Hymn
Scripture
Prayer
Special Music
Announcements
Offering
Hymn (Small children may go to classes)
9:55 A.M. — Sermon
10:25 A.M. — Music (instrumental or vocal)
10:30 A.M. — Classes
11:15 A.M. — Dismissal from classes or closing department assemblies or a closing general assembly, with dismissal at 11:30 A.M.

No. II
9:30 A.M. — Opening Department sessions
9:45 A.M. — Classes
10:30 A.M. — Assemble for worship
Call to worship
Invocation
Music
Scripture
Prayer
Special Music
Offering
11:00 A.M. — Sermon
11:30 A.M. — Dismissal

The above plans can be varied to meet local needs and interests. It is probably wise to give some particular attention to 100 per cent classes and pupils. The report of the secretary should be made to "live" during the general assembly period.

The introduction of this plan will require much tact and patience until people can get adjusted to it. Workers will have to be patient in moving classes and departments to the sanctuary. Superintendents and pastor will be forced to observe strict punctuality in conducting the services. Space will have to be reserved for various groups.

3. Evangelism and Attendance

Departmental Concept. A great deal about evangelism has already been said in previous chapters (on the pastor and superintendent). As practiced in the department, evangelism is broadly conceived to include the functions of:

1. Soul-winning
2. Attendance and enrollment
3. Enlargement and outreach
4. Missions

Soul winning and missions were discussed quite fully in Chapter 3 on the work of the pastor. Suffice to say here that the department superintendent and teachers need to work closely with the pastor and general superintendent in seeing that soul winning at home and abroad is emphasized, studied, and practiced in the department. Practical training in evangelism is provided in the department through strong emphasis on matters of enrollment, attendance, enlargement, and outreach.

Enrollment. The best way to increase attendance is to secure and increase enrollments. Enrollment is important because it gives the pupil a sense of belonging, gives workers and teachers definite responsibility in evangelism, and results in larger classes. Active enrollment includes all who have agreed to become members of the classes, including the nursery class and cradle roll. The latter are especially important because of the prospects of including parents. Some schools also include the home department, extension department, and branch Sunday schools in active enrollment.

Sources and techniques of enrollment to include pupils are gleaned from the following list:

1. Survey the community by house-to-house canvass
2. Create class responsibility lists
3. Check church families not attending school
4. Use all possible weekday activities
5. Investigate contacts through public schools
6. Use individual pupils to contact others
7. Pay particular attention to visitors
8. Use every available means to advertise
9. Review old records periodically
10. Conduct a regular visitation program

Some schools appoint a registrar or enrollment secretary to direct enrollment procedures and to see that class and department records are kept. Others provide a membership card or certificate to new members.

Everyone should work at the job of keeping members enrolled. Some system for carefully checking the removal of members from class rolls should be adopted. Some schools use a "drop slip" to show reasons for dropping a name from the roll. Pupils should be dropped only when one or more of the following reasons are given:

1. Death
2. Moving out of town
3. When they ask to be removed
4. When they join some other Sunday school

All workers and pupils need to be enrollment conscious. Increases in enrollment should be recognized in assemblies, departments, and classes. Goals should be set and definite plans made to reach them.

Extension Department. Enrollment, attendance, and evangelism needs to be extended to groups outside the Sunday school. The extension department is that part of the Sunday school which is organized to take the Sunday school to all people who are permanently or temporarily unable to attend Sunday school themselves. According to Acts 5:42, the early church preached and taught in every house. It is not only Scriptural but it offers opportunities to win souls and serve others outside the walls of the church. There are almost unlimited benefits to be derived from an extension department.

The aged, the shut-ins, people confined to institutions such as county homes, jails, etc., families living in rural districts out of reach of the church, under-privileged families, persons employed on Sunday such as nurses, firemen, policemen, trainmen, and expectant mothers and children in homes who are not able to attend — these and more offer many opportunities to extend the ministry of the Sunday school.

After a careful community study, the Board of Christian Education should appoint one of the best and most spiritual workers as superintendent of this department. A secretary and a spiritual, sacrificial teacher who will visit will be required. This is hard work and requires a great deal of skill and consecration.

Attendance, Punctuality, and Visitation. Good attendance depends on how pupil conscious the workers and class members are. A real interest in and a concern and burden for pupils is the secret of it all. In addition, a program of real quality is attractive. The maintenance of deep spirituality will draw many people to the church school. A strong visitation program will bear fruit if the visitors are persistent in their efforts and Christ-like in spirit. An attendance goal provides incentive and something concrete for which to strive.

The department superintendent should keep the importance of regular attendance before children, parents, and workers. He will constantly stress to the teachers the harm of irregular attendance. The general superintendent can stress regular attendance in assemblies. Teachers can promote it in the classroom.

Very important to attendance is the follow-up of absentees. This stops leaks before they begin. Careful records of absentees should be kept each Sunday and some kind of system of visitation used to follow them up. Do not be satisfied with simply sending a "miss you" card. Actually, it is considered lazy to let Uncle Sam do the visiting for you. Of course, a card is better than nothing, but a personal visit or a telephone call is much better. Persistent absenteeism should lead workers to a careful study of the reasons involved.

A warm-hearted atmosphere of friendliness, cheerfulness, and fellowship will be sufficient to keep many, but this should never be taken for granted. A deliberate effort on the part of everyone to be friendly and neighborly, with a genuine manifestation of concern, will go a long way toward increasing attendance.

Every department should plan regular and/or special days for visitation. Like Jesus, Sunday schools should "seek the lost." Every class should develop a prospect list, even the small children. Beginners are capable of inviting children of their own age to Sunday school. Who knows but what simple visitations by children will lead to great adult personal workers of tomorrow! Such periods as "Round-up Week" or "Visitation Week" drive home the importance of contacting others for Christ.

Punctuality is important too. The time is so short at most that the loss of ten or fifteen minutes becomes serious. Interesting, spiritual, and well-planned opening sessions will draw late-comers earlier next time. Pre-session periods which are well-planned and efficiently conducted will also draw many pupils to the church on time. Where a school faces the punctuality problem, here again is revealed the necessity of careful study and analysis. Set a goal of 70-80-90 per cent on time and strive to attain it. Of course where this is done, it becomes particularly important for all workers to set a good example by being on time. All superintendents should start programs precisely at their appointed times and close at the right times.

In some instances, schools have closed doors to latecomers until a convenient time for them to enter. In other cases they are ushered in at stated intervals but kept in certain seats or rooms.

The use of prizes in motivating attendance is discouraged.

If not carefully used, they lead to pride, jealousy, and selfishness. The spirit of true Christianity is giving, not getting. Mild use of awards and competition, however, may prove stimulating, but even these should not be overstressed. Awards should be conferred as an evidence of the providence and goodness of God. The best competition, after all, is to compete with one's own record.

Other helpful suggestions for increasing attendance include: planning and working an attendance crusade, studying reasons for attendance and non-attendance, using all available channels of publicity, parent cooperation, public recognition of new members, and genuine Christian fellowship.

4. Records

Importance. Good records provide the church school with a register of the membership, activities, history, and accomplishments of the school. They provide accurate information for judging trends, achievements, and progress. The value of good records, therefore, is unquestioned. Of course, it is possible to have a school and many records, but an effective school is largely dependent on an adequate record system and the efficient use of such records.

Generally speaking, records are used to preserve and render usable certain types of information about the pupils and the school. They help to reach objectives and provide an incentive for improvement. More specifically, records are Scriptural. The Word abounds with instances where God required good records. God Himself is a Keeper of records. This is because He is interested in individuals. The primary importance, therefore, of good records in any church school lies in what they contribute toward the discovery, salvation, development, and progress of the pupils. The school exists for the pupils. The success of the school will depend, therefore, on what it does for pupils. These benefits cannot be measured without a good record system.

Values. We have seen in a general way the importance of good church records. Perhaps, however, a formal listing of their values will prove helpful. Good records will accomplish the following:

1. They will challenge the entire school
2. They provide a complete register on pupils and leaders
3. They provide a basis for evaluation and measurement
4. They reveal strengths and weaknesses
5. They make efficient operation possible
6. They provide up-to-date statistics for classes, departments, and the total school
7. They provide a list of prospective new pupils
8. They encourage attendance and membership

9. They help teachers with their teaching problems, giving indications of spiritual condition, attendance, study habits, etc.
10. They teach pupils Christian character-building habits such as reverence, faithfulness, and responsibility
11. They can be used to guide in curriculum planning
12. They furnish the key to budgetary matters
13. They furnish information in ordering supplies
14. They are essential in planning the promotion of the pupils
15. They move people
16. They help the general and departmental superintendents get a clear picture of constituency and progress

Principles. Good practice is the result of operating upon the basis of sound principles. This is no less true in the case of good records. Following is a list of good principles which contribute to the efficient operation of a record system:

1. *Simplicity* — all workers must understand how to operate the system
2. *Current* — kept up-to-date
3. *System* — continuity in spite of the overturn of workers
4. *Cumulative* — records of past, present, and future form a complete picture
5. *Economy* — inexpensive blanks, forms, and books
6. *Permanence* — books and files to preserve the records and materials
7. *Skill* — trained and faithful general secretary, department and class secretaries
8. *Participation* — all personnel must take part for greatest effectiveness
9. *Uniformity* — the same throughout the whole school, with few adjustments
10. *Spiritual* — carefully used, evaluations made from them, all to challenge the school, departments, and classes to be more like Christ and serve Him faithfully

Types. There are many record systems. Almost every denomination has one of its own. Naturally each group feels that it must use the kinds of records which meet particular needs. The following classifications reveal the possibilities of various types of records.

In general, records and reports of a church school fall into four categories:

1. Record and report of the whole school
2. Record and report of each department
3. Record and report of each class
4. Record and report of each pupil and visitor

More specifically, records can be classified in greater detail into the following list:

The Classification of Sunday School Records

A. Individual Records
   1. Enrollment data
      Name; date of birth; address; telephone; Christian; grade in public school; church membership; parents' names; church relationship; occupation; type of home; last Sunday school attended
   2. Performance
      On time; prepared lessons; offerings; attending church; bringing Bible
   3. Cumulative
      All basic information in items 1 and 2, plus a case history of each pupil, is handed on from class to class as pupil is promoted. A record of teachers' observations and experiences with the pupil
B. Class records
   1. Enrollment fluctuations; attendance fluctuations; new members; offerings; follow-up program; grade of class; weekly, monthly, quarterly, yearly; quality of work as indicated by the six point system; group projects and achievements
C. Departmental records
   1. Enrollment fluctuations; attendance fluctuations; offerings; new members; follow-up program; departmental activities; minutes of the workers' conference; grade of department on six point system basis: weekly, monthly, quarterly and yearly; file of worship programs; promotion day records
D. Whole school records
   1. Enrollment fluctuations; attendance fluctuations; offerings; grade according to six-point system; comparisons with previous years; follow-up program; minutes of workers' conferences; activities of whole school (picnics, special programs, surveys); workers' training certificates; number joining church through the Sunday school
E. Staff records
   1. Qualifications
      General education
      Special training
      Experience
      Teacher's covenant
   2. Performance
      Attendance and punctuality; attendance of workers' conferences; visitation of students and follow-up; progress in self-improvement by reading, training, etc.;

response to supervision; other leadership activities; church attendance.

F. Surveys
   1. Survey of congregation to discover new workers
   2. Checkup of progress toward standards or goals
   3. Survey of the community for prospects
   4. Program for calendar year

G. Business records
   These records are to keep data on transactions of the organization. The minutes and files of correspondence should be kept.

H. Curriculum records
   1. Preserve the story of the Sunday school program.
   2. List units undertaken with copies of procedures and evaluations.

I. Financial records
   Indicate financial achievements, status, needs, and limitations of the school. Such things as the check books, order books, files of canceled checks, cash and budget account blanks, and reports of various treasurers are included.

J. Personality records
   1. They are a guide in the planning of a program
   2. Result from personality tests or rating charts
   3. Show experiences of vocational and recreational interests

K. Prospect records
   These records are for the expansion of the Sunday school. May be secured from a community census, by the pastor or other workers, or from Sunday school pupils.

L. Registration records or blanks
   Gather information upon the entrance of the pupil and assign him temporarily until a class record is made

M. Reports to parents — Summary of data kept may mention attendance, attitude, achievement, punctuality.

N. Withdrawal or removal records
   Disclosing some of the obvious failures of the school

O. Reports to the church
   1. Local
   2. Denomination

P. Absentee records
   1. Forms and reports
   2. Visitation system
   3. Visitation records
   4. Report records to teachers and officers
   5. Cards, letters, telephone calls
   6. Notices to teacher for absentee report

Q. History
    1. Of class, departments, groups
    2. Of entire school
R. Visitors
    Information should go to teacher, department secretary, and Sunday school office
S. Family file
    Prospect list; useful in calling; one card per family, listing all members
T. Comparative records
    1. For classes
    2. For departments
    3. For whole school
U. Visual records
    1. Graphs on Sunday school attendance
    2. Maps, graphs, charts on community areas unreached

Operation. The operation of a good record system demands three phases of activity: (1) administering the records, (2) giving reports from the records, and (3) filing records and reports.

The responsibility for administering records lies with the general superintendent for the school as a whole and with the various department superintendents who supervise the work of the classes. An integrated and well-organized system of records demands close cooperation. The discussion of records was placed in the category of the responsibilities of the department superintendent because any record system starts with the pupils who make up the classes located in the various departments. Then too, the success of the record system depends directly on how well the teachers and department workers do their jobs.

The first step in administering records is to determine what type of record system is needed for the school. In spite of the multiplicity of systems, they fall into two general types: (1) the simplified system and (2) the advanced system. The simplified system involves counting and recording attendances and offerings. Some systems also include a report of those staying for church, a report of the weather, and various comparative statistics of former years. The class record book provides a record of desired facts and data on individual pupils, such as name, address, phone, birthday, spirituality, etc. Some include data on absentees, visitations, converts, new members, visitors, chapters read in the Bible, etc. The Sunday school secretary's book can be used for both the department and the whole school. Pages are provided to record the attendances and offerings of classes and departments. Other pages record attendance of workers at conferences, a record of training of workers, and personal data on the workers. Still others record comparative data on the work of former years.

An example of the advanced system of records is the Four and Six Point Record System. This system has become very popular and enjoys wide use at the present time. More will be said about it in a later section of this chapter.

Small schools will find that it is probably wise to start out with some form of a simplified system, but as growth proceeds the school should move to an advanced system as early as possible because of the obvious advantages of such a system.

In any system of records, operation will depend upon the system contained in the records. Of course the steps involved in the operation of any particular record system depends upon the type of records adopted, and naturally such steps will vary. In the main, however, a good record system, small or large, will provide record materials, such as forms, cards, etc., which make provision for the following steps:

1. Classification (grading and grouping)
   a. Visitor's classification slip
   b. Prospect slip (when needed)
   c. Some schools use visitor's welcome card
2. Enrollment
   a. Class and department assignment
   b. Promotion record on back
   c. In advanced system, record of pupil progress, grades
3. Individual record card
   a. Record of attendance for at least three years
   b. Used to record grades for Six Point Record System also
   c. Used in the classroom
4. Class record book
   a. Names transferred from enrollment cards
   b. Used in both simple and advanced systems
   c. Includes visitor record and prospect list
5. For Six Point System
   a. Individual report envelope — grade and offering
   b. Weekly class report
   c. Department report
6. General report
   a. Record book for the general secretary
   b. Names, addresses of all workers
   c. Total records for each class and department
   d. Monthly, quarterly, and annual summaries
7. Absentee record
   a. Date of absence
   b. Visitation record — reason for absence, results

8. Pupil's personal record
   a. Record of attendance
   b. Report card to parents

In addition to the above record materials, some schools use what is called a "cumulative record" of the individual pupil. Each teacher keeps a notebook in which the basic information on every pupil in the class is kept. In addition to this information, the teacher records personal observations and experiences with his pupils and at promotion time passes this information along to the next teacher. The value of this kind of record to the teachers is obvious.

Keeping all such records properly demands centralization of control. In the business world, bookkeeping systems are centralized under a head bookkeeper or in an accounting department. The wisdom of this is evident. In a church school the same pattern should be followed. Records should be centralized in the general secretary's office where officers and teachers may secure full information on the work of any member, class, department, and the entire school. This, of course, demands an efficient corps of secretaries.

The duties of the general secretary were mentioned previously (Chapter 5). For the sake of completion, it is sufficient to point out here that the general secretary is in charge of all records. He oversees the use of all records, including class books, enrollment and classification records, class and departmental reports. He supervises the making of all reports — weekly, monthly, quarterly, annual — and orders all literature after consultation with various departmental and class secretaries and superintendents. Not the least of his duties is the training of the whole Sunday school staff in taking accurate records. This he may do through an annual class for instruction, through monthly conferences on records and through frequent instruction of class officers.

In small schools the general secretary can probably handle all matters concerning records, but in medium size schools and large schools additional secretaries are needed. The following list shows some of the possible workers with their general duties:

Department Secretary

1. Arrives half hour early to ready department records and materials
2. Welcomes and registers visitors
3. Keeps membership file current
4. Furnishes department superintendent with any helpful information from records
5. Checks class records, particularly noting absentees
6. Trains class secretaries
7. Maintains prospect list

Absentee Secretary

1. Checks rolls for absentees
2. Contacts homes of absentees

3. Checks on visitors
4. Leads visitation of absentees and visitors
5. Maintains a family file

Attendance Secretary

1. Tabulates attendance rolls of total school
2. Checks rolls
3. Prepares new rolls for teachers and general secretary

Membership Secretary

1. Keeps membership roll current
2. Prepares membership cards for department and general files
3. Orders and distributes materials and supplies

Routine marking of records in the class should take the least possible time. Roll calling is unnecessary when a class secretary or assistant is properly instructed to mark the class records.

Registrar (For Larger Schools)

1. Records the records of individual pupils
2. Keeps enrollment cards and file current
3. Keeps list of teachers
4. Prepares monthly report of each pupil for parents
5. Follows up absentees
6. Records and averages monthly grades (Six Point System)
7. Issues promotion certificates and diplomas
8. Keeps materials and supplies on hand
9. Assists general secretary
10. Makes out permanent record cards
11. Sees that class record books are used properly
12. Plans promotion day programs
13. Cooperates in extension program
14. Informs self on grading and curriculum

Efficient operation of a good record system also demands provision for the making of reports. This is in keeping with the principle that "responsibility demands accountability": Every worker should be accountable to someone and required to make a report. To make this possible, forms for gathering, compiling, and summarizing information on the actual work accomplished in church school sessions should be provided. The officers need to have the means of looking at the work of the whole school by departments, by classes, and by individual workers and members.

Teachers and department superintendents should make written reports to their superiors on such matters as lessons taught, attendance increases, visits made, souls saved, telephone calls, cards and letters sent out, etc. The general superintendent should make at least an annual report to the Board of Christian Education and/or the church board. All boards and committees should report to higher administrative groups in the organization. In the final analysis, the congregation needs an annual report of all church and church school programs.

Since records tell what the school has done, is doing, and should be doing, the general secretary's report is most important. The time is past when this report is given verbally to the church school assembly. Such a method is not only time consuming but monotonous and uninteresting, generally given in a perfunctory manner. Instead, the general secretary's report should be made to "live." This can be done through visualizing his reports. This can be accomplished by using an attendance and offering record board or a blackboard. It can be done in church bulletins, by graphs at workers' conferences, and by occasional opening session programs on records. Special opportunities for close study of records can be given at business meetings where the implications of class, department, and school reports on enrollment, visitors, offerings, etc., can be studied. Following is a list of some possible implications:

1. Number of latecomers can be indicative of the quality of opening services
2. Number of withdrawals, whether permanent or temporary, can tell a story
3. Records of pupil's work over a period of years may help to determine his qualification for leadership
4. Strengths and weaknesses are revealed
5. Trends in attendance may reveal growth or a static condition over several years
6. Averages for classes and departments can be compared in the present and with past records. A 75 per cent portion of enrollment in attendance is considered a healthy school.
7. Checks can be made on whether goals have been achieved or not.
8. Recognition of outstanding accomplishments of pupils, classes, and departments

Two outstanding systems have been created to assist in this kind of reporting. One is the "Sunday School Traffic Light" geared to the Six Point Record System and designed to build attendance, increase interest, and improve quality. The second one is "The Good Shepherd Six Point Plan" for church enlargement, designed to bring in new recruits and solve the absentee problem. The former can be ordered from the National Sunday School Association, Chicago, Illinois. The latter is owned and sold by H. B. Peter, Adrian, Michigan.

A filing system is necessary for good records. At least four files are useful: (1) prospects, (2) absentees, (3) permanent enrollment, and (4) staff and faculty personnel information and leadership training records. Fireproof steel files should be used for permanent records. Shelf space is needed for books and bulky materials. A central registration and placement desk or counter is also quite helpful.

In some advanced systems the individual record cards are also filed. In this case a 4 x 6 filing case can be left in a department or classroom. The permanent enrollment file should be stored by classes or departments in alphabetical order. Some schools also divide these cards into active and inactive sections. This work can be done by secretaries during the week. A few schools have found it wise to keep an accurate account of all material equipment on file. Periodic checks on such things as books, chairs, etc, will reveal any wasteful habits and needs for replacements and repair.

All superintendents should watch average attendance figures. A good average shows that the school is healthy. A low average may indicate bad weather, sickness, dissatisfaction of some kind, or a bad follow-up system. Whatever the cause, remedies must be prescribed. Other evaluations can be made by studying the problems of tardiness and withdrawals. Where over 15 per cent of the pupils are tardy, a school has a serious problem. A good follow-up system will reduce absences and withdrawals.

The Six Point Record System. The Six Point Record System, as worked out by the Southern Baptist Convention, is perhaps the best illustration of an advanced record system. There are several variations of this plan developed on a more simple basis by other groups, such as American Baptists, Assemblies of God, Gospel Light Press, Scripture Press, National Fellowship of Brethren, and others. The six points are based on Scripture in the following manner:

1. Attendance (Ps. 122:1)   4. Offering (I Cor. 16:2; Prov. 3:9)
2. On Time (Jer. 48:10 ASV) 5. Prepared Lesson (Ps. 119:11)
3. Bible Brought (Eph. 6:17) 6. Church Attendance (Heb. 10:25)

From this one can see that the system is so named because it sets out six well-defined duties for class members to perform and provides a means for securing and tabulating information on how they qualify on these points at each session of the school. The charts below show how the points are distributed on which the members are graded and the values placed on each.

Attendance 20
On Time 10
Bible Brought 10
Offering 10
Prepared Lesson 30
Church Attendance 20

TOTAL 100

The system has been adapted so that pupils of the younger age groups can meet the requirements made of them. The primary pupils are graded on only four points, as follows:

Attendance	40
On Time	20
Offering	10
Memory Verse	30

TOTAL	100

The nursery class and beginner pupils are marked on only two points:

Attendance	60
On Time	40

TOTAL	100

All officers and teachers are graded on all six points, regardless of the department in which they work. All credits are based on actual attendance.

5. *Curriculum*

Background. In early English Sunday schools the curriculum was rather secular. In addition to reading, writing, morals and manners, and spelling, the catechism was used to get across Bible teachings. In America the early schools followed the English pattern, but religious rather than secular aims were dominant. In this the catechism played a large part up until 1815.

From about 1815 to 1840 came the Period of Bible Emphasis. The decline of religion at the end of the eighteenth century, the rise of the spirit of democracy, the advance of public education, the Wesleyan revival with its consequent spiritual awakening in the first part of the nineteenth century were forces which contributed to making the Bible dominant in the curriculum during this period. In 1816, the American Bible Society was founded and Bibles became cheaper and more widely available. Although the movement was away from the doctrinal content of the catechism, the memory method was substituted, overstressing the importance of memorizing long Bible passages. The Question Book was created to deal directly with Biblical content rather than doctrine. In this book some of the first attempts to systematize Bible study and grade the content were made. This gave rise to wide use of Bible questions.

The period of 1840 to 1872 is known as the Babel Period. This period was characterized by great confusion in the use of curriculum materials. The American Sunday School Union suggested dates for certain lessons. The Moravian practice of a verse a day was advocated. Various denominations began to write their own lesson materials. Some groups were beginning to stress the importance of pupil needs and the need for graded lesson materials.

Marked changes came in 1872 when the reaction against the Babel Period came to a head during the International Sunday School Convention, at which time the first committee on Uniform Lessons was appointed. This system was widely adopted because it seemed to secure Bible study and unity for the curriculum. Between 1872 and 1914 no radical changes were made.

However, during the period of 1890 to 1900 much opposition arose to the Uniform Lesson plan and strong advocates for graded lessons arose. Various individuals and some denominational groups began to experiment with graded lessons. At the Louisville Convention of 1908, the Lesson Committee was directed to prepare International Graded Lessons. By 1914 the series was ready. At this time the International Lesson Committee was reorganized to include representatives from the denominations. Pressures from these led to a modification of the Uniform Lessons and by 1918 the series became known as the International Improved Uniform Lessons. Grading, however, still did not dominate curriculum theory at this time. In 1920, Luther Weigle led a group which surveyed the use and value of Uniform Lessons. Although these lessons were retained, the group-graded and closely graded lessons were also adopted. A new lesson series was published called the International Sunday School Lessons, Group Graded Series and it was also recommended that the closely graded lessons be continued.

Other battles raged over curriculum theory and materials. One was the battle over extra-biblical materials. Although the Bible was dominant, pressure from outstanding editors led to the inclusion of such things as missionary stories.

The rise of liberal theology markedly affected both curriculum theory and materials. John Dewey's experience-centered theories led to a marked social emphasis in curriculum materials. In 1917, the Religious Education Association advocated the Dewey formula for Sunday school lessons. Major denominations began to adopt this pattern.

The orthodox denominations reacted by returning to a Bible-centered curriculum of Uniform Lessons. In 1933 the All-Bible-Graded Series was offered by Moody Bible Institute for orthodox groups. Since that time until the present there has been a marked cleavage between orthodox and liberal groups. Curriculum materials have reached somewhat of a modern "Babel period" because of the vast variety of materials now available, but we are now beginning to witness a mild return to Bible-centered and Gospel-centered materials.

Theory and Principles of the Curriculum. The word "curriculum" is derived from the Latin word meaning "a place of running; a race.course." A course of study, therefore, is a line of progress through a series of subjects. In its broadest meaning, the curriculum includes all activities and experiences which are initiated or utilized by the church and school for the accomplishment of the aims of Christian education. A more narrow meaning, but commonly held, refers to the curriculum as areas or fields of subject matter organized into learning areas. Both meanings are used in church school circles but best theory seems to demand that classes, worship, hymns, prayers, lesson materials, etc., all be included within the framework of the curriculum. A Christian curriculum is such when the authority of Christ and the realization of His authority in our lives is the justification for all educational activity. All subject matter will be recognized as a revelation of His truth; all activities will be motivated by His life and will and Spirit. Whether conceived in broad or narrow terms, a Christian curriculum centers in Christ. It is the medium employed by the school to achieve the ends of Christian education. The curriculum is given design by the course of study. Basic facts and principles of child development set the stage for curriculum design. All this is guided by the Word of God.

The whole-person-in-life doing the will of God is the object of the Christian curriculum. The personal goal is Christlikeness. The curriculum, therefore, may be thought of as guided experience. Properly, it includes evangelism, instruction, worship, fellowship, and service.

Several major concepts of the nature and purpose of learning areas or subject matter fields have been advocated:

1. The knowledge concept
2. The disciplinary concept
3. The social concept
4. The creative concept

In the knowledge concept, factual material is organized for mastery. Subject matter is graded on a quantitative basis from level to level. One's education is measured in terms of the amount of information he has stored up during the years.

The disciplinary concept stresses the importance of the learner's mental powers. "Faculty psychology" is at the basis of this view, which states that the mind has certain faculties which are exercised or developed by the mastery of certain subject matter. *What* is learned is not as important as *how* it is learned.

The social concept stresses the needs of the individual as he functions in the social structure. These needs guide the selection of curriculum materials. Modern industry in the framework of democracy provides the pattern for curriculum construction. Problem solving becomes the method. Information is meaningless apart from the social structure.

The creative concept emphasizes the psychological nature of the individual. Man has a creative capacity and the development of this power is the goal of education. Learning activities must motivate this power. Self-expression, self-appraisal, self-activity, and motivation are the key concepts. The curriculum consists of activities which are adjusted constantly to pupil needs.

The Christian recognizes that the above theories have elements of truth, but all of them lack basic elements. All fail to reckon with *all* individual resources and needs, for man is a spiritual being. The social and creative concepts fail to recognize a pre-existent order of truth to be understood and also completely ignore the great tragedy of sin in human history. No need is expressed for redemption outside of man himself. Furthermore, all these views regard man from the standpoint of humanism or rationalism. The Christian looks to a transcendant God for his curriculum theory.

The Christian concept of curriculum theory is known as the bi-polar theory. The key is the revealed will of God. Divine revelation forms the basis for knowing purposes and objectives by which authority is guided. These principles lead to the development of the Christian curriculum as revealed in chart form as follows:

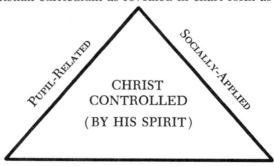

BIBLE-INTEGRATED

In addition to basic principles which form the foundation of this theory, the Christian recognizes the broad basis of the curriculum which demands the inclusion of the "setting" for learning or framework for teaching. This he calls the structure of Christian education. The history of education reveals that education in every age has had an inner structure, a coherent power to hold it together. For the Greeks it was loyalty and eloquence; for the Hebrews it was knowledge of the law and obedience; in the Middle Ages it was knowledge and discipline. For the Christian, this structure is characterized by:

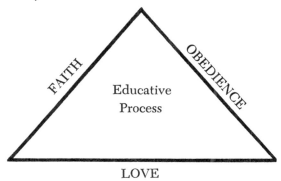

The above theory places Christ at the center of the curriculum. Dr. James D. Murch commented on this principle by saying:

"When we give Christ His proper authority in curriculum there will be no loss of emphasis upon the Scriptures, for He insisted that 'They are they that testify of me'; the church will not be relegated to a place of minor importance, for it is 'the body of Christ' purchased by His own precious blood; the pupil will not be neglected, for Christ came to give man life and give it 'more abundantly.' When the pupil accepts the control of Christ, his attitudes, habits, conduct, relationships and ideals will be immeasureably enriched.[4]

Such a discussion calls our attention to the fact that there are many principles which underlie good curriculum theory. The following list is suggestive:

1. The curriculum should be Christ-controlled through His Spirit

2. The curriculum should be Bible-integrated; the Bible is the textbook

3. The curriculum should be pupil-related, graded to the needs of the pupil and psychological laws applied

4. The curriculum should be socially-applied, providing suggestions and opportunities for practicing the Gospel and recognizing the obligations of the Church to the community, to society as a whole, and to the home

5. The curriculum should seek to develop personality in its fullest — physically, mentally, socially, spiritually

6. The curriculum should be unified in purpose, content, and scope

[4]James D. Murch, *Christian Education and the Local Church* (Cincinnati: Standard Publishing Company, 1943), 151.

7. The curriculum should be comprehensive, including subject matter, skills, the total Christian heritage, and all ages
8. The curriculum should be evangelistic, seeking to bring all ages to a knowledge of Jesus Christ as Saviour and Lord
9. The curriculum should build the church of tomorrow, evoking convictions, service, and leadership
10. The curriculum should be missionary, appealing to all ages, all groups, and all nations
11. The curriculum should be flexible, making room for changes in scope, content, and methods
12. The curriculum will provide for balance, giving adequate time for comprehensive treatment
13. The curriculum should be well-organized so that sequence will provide for themes, seasonal interests, units of study and cumulative learnings.
14. The curriculum should provide attractive and practical materials of high quality

Factors in Curriculum Construction. The curriculum for Christian education is a result of the combination of several integrated factors. In fact the curriculum may be viewed from the angle called the "educative process." The whole curriculum is focused on instruction which involves both teaching and learning. This is a manifold process. The task of the Christian teacher is to be aware of this many-sided task and to develop skill in the manipulation of its several facets. In this whole process the teacher works with the Spirit of God in integrating these varied factors to focus them on the learner in an attempt to realize the great goals of Christian teaching. The pattern appears somewhat as follows:

1. Purposes and objectives provide guide lines for initiating and culminating the educative process
2. The teacher stands before the student as the oracle of God with the truth of God
3. The focus of the educative process is the pupil
4. The structure of Christian education provides the atmosphere in which the whole process takes place. This structure is provided by Christian love, faith, and obedience.
5. The curriculum provides the truth-content by which the revelation of God is organized and presented to the student. Herein we find justification for course content with all truth assuming importance to the extent to which it is revelatory of God. The pattern by which this is accomplished is fourfold: (1) evangelism, (2) instruction, (3) worship, and (4) fellowship.
6. The methods provide the mediums of communication through which the curriculum content reaches its desti-

nation. Such methods must be spiritual, varied, graded, unified, integrated, comprehensive, flexible, personal, social, and Biblical. They should be integrated with the principles of teaching and learning.

To the evangelical, the will of God is the highest expression of values. In Christian education, purposes, and objectives represent those values. As a co-worker with God, the Christian teacher is directed by objectives found in the Word of God, whereas secular educators discover theirs through social analysis. Generally speaking, educational goals provide direction for the educative process. More specifically, goals provide motivation, guide lines for the selection of materials and methods, the basis for evaluation, and most of all the means whereby integration and correlation of the Christian curriculum is made possible. The true aim of Christian education is redemptive. The purpose of education is to restore the image of God in man through Christ, which leads to Christ-like character and conduct. Integration can be attained only in this way. Subject matter, then, becomes a means to this end.

As a Christian educator, the Christian teacher has a twofold function. First, as a Christian he is expected to be a witness; he is to reveal God in Christlike living and service. As an educator he is an oracle of God (I Peter 4:10-11). As such he is God's mouthpiece. As such, he is also expected to operate properly as a witness. This brings in the importance of methodology as the teacher operates in relation to God-given pedagogical principles. This will be dealt with later. Let it suffice to point out here that the teacher should see that the classroom climate be characterized by Christian love, faith, and obedience.

All these matters involve the place of the pupil. In Christian education, God — not man — is central. God is the end, not the pupil. To be like God is the great goal strived for. The result is, therefore, that the student becomes the *focus* of the educative process, but not the end. The entire educative process is directed toward the student but becomes a means to an end in bringing him to Christlikeness.

Teaching and learning processes are vital factors in the curriculum. However, our primary emphasis at this point is subject matter, so we will reserve a discussion of these factors until a later chapter.

The structure in which the curriculum operates is most important. Important in this element are divine or spiritual factors. There are supernatural agencies at the disposal of the Christian teacher which make his job one of cooperation with God. These agencies include the person and work of the Holy Spirit (who is the Spirit of Truth), the power of the Word of God (which is the sword of the Spirit), the capacities of the regenerated self to learn, the impact of the Christian personality of the teacher, and what we might call the "structure of Christian education," which embraces atmosphere. The Holy Spirit is present to convict, to guide, to enlighten, and to impress the student as well as to guide and empower the teacher. The Word of God has spiritual power, as evidenced by the words of Jesus: "The words that I speak unto you, they are spirit and they are life" (John 6:63). Love forms the coherent motivation which directs redeemed man's heart and life. Faith opens the way to true knowledge and understanding because the more frequently one dwells upon an object by faith, the more he feels its power. Obedience is the surrender of love and faith.

Besides Christian structure, there are certain external factors which directly affect the teaching-learning process and which must be controlled by the teacher. These factors include the attitude of the teacher toward the pupil and his work, the subject, the lesson presentation, and class spirit, size, and facilities. As far as possible, all these things should be kept at optimum efficiency.

The final factor to be considered in the curriculum is subject matter. To this we now turn our attention in the following section.

Subject Matter and Materials. The Christian curriculum begins properly with the Bible, the Word of God. This is true when conceiving of the curriculum broadly as comprehending all that goes on in the school situation, or more narrowly in terms of factual materials for subject matter. The Word of God provides both content and principles by which all subject matter content is evaluated and used.

While it is recognized that there are a number of channels through which the truth of God can reach the human heart, the primary process now is through the written revelation of God contained in the Holy Scriptures. The Bible, therefore, becomes the center in the subject matter curriculum. It contains the record of God's truth as inspired by God's Spirit and revealing God's Person, His Son, and His dealings with man. As such, it is also the basis by which all other channels of truth are judged, used, and evaluated. All other subjects and truth are to be related to the Bible. It becomes the integrating and correlating factor in the subject matter curriculum. Through the Bible the interrelatedness of all subjects and truth take their rise in Bible study, draw from the Bible their materials wherever possible, and return to the Bible with their contributions of fact, interpretation, and practical application.

Where secular educators rely on natural interpretation and human reasoning to realize meanings from study content, the Christian teacher exercises supernatural interpretation. Essentially, this becomes a reinterpretation of God's revelation.

Operating upon the basis that there are both cultural and

spiritual products in the curriculum, the Christian educator can proceed in his interpretation of the specific subject matter in a twofold way. First, he will try to discover the *factual* knowledge provided for him by the subject under consideration and how it is organized for study. Second, he will apply the principles of super-natural interpretation to these facts in order (1) to discover God and His attributes, and (2) to reveal the implications of these dis-coveries both personally and socially. This process reveals the spiritual knowledge within the facts. .

This evangelical position is in marked contrast to the modern practice among some who take a *functional* view of the place of the Bible in the curriculum. This position is clearly revealed by Ralph Heim in his *Leading a Sunday Church School*, Chapter 10. Advo-cates of this view utilize the Bible "as a resource to show the direc-tion for and give support to the on-going Christian faith-life of per-sons and groups" (p. 174). Bible materials are used as illustrations of Christian character and activity. The Bible is used as *one* source in solving personal and social problems. While it is admitted that this view demands that the Bible become an element of *control* in Christian character and conduct, it is weak in that it relegates the power of the Word and of the Spirit to the background. Actu-ally, the true position demands that both elements be included, but with primary emphasis upon the former.

We now turn our attention to the various types of curriculum materials. Major types include uniform lessons, closely graded lessons, departmental lessons, graded elective materials, weekday materials, and daily vacation Bible school materials.

It might be argued that in order to meet the demands of an ideal curriculum it would be necessary for each church to publish its own lesson materials and hence to maintain a full-time worker whose only work would be to analyze the pupils, choose the work, prepare material for the help of the pupils and for the teacher, and then publish it in such a way as to get it into their hands. In part this is true. There is no one published curriculum for Sunday school use that will meet all these qualifications which have been set up, especially in the field of student need since each Sunday school has a somewhat different requirement in that realm; nevertheless, it is possible to approximate the ideal in any local situation.

Each publisher of Sunday school materials maintains a staff of persons trained in curriculum building and application. Each will have a somewhat different idea of what the curriculum should be and how it should be applied. Those responsible for choosing the curriculum for the particular school should study the entire or-ganization and purpose of each curriculum and then make the de-cision as to which of the planned curricula best fits the local situa-tion and comes closest to the ideal for the particular school in mind.

Nowhere should it be advised to adopt materials of different types in the different classes or departments in the school, except perhaps in the adult and young adult classes. The curriculum for the school up through high school age should be planned and not just thrown together, as is often the case.

If the school adopts the material of one publisher throughout, it will achieve the same end as if it had hired a curriculum director for its own local situation, but will not have to bear the cost of such. Mixing materials would, for instance, train the children for three years in one direction and then switch them over to another material and train them toward some other goal, perhaps even using another doctrinal basis while doing so. The result will not be a well-balanced spiritual education at all, and it could be harmful.

The following situation occurred in one church. An influential teacher was of one theological persuasion and the pastor was of another doctrine entirely. The result was that the children of high school age especially, were completely confused, uninterested in church, irregular in attendance, and had adopted an "I don't care" attitude in their moral as well as in their spiritual lives. This type of difficulty could arise from conflicting curricula as well as from conflicting personalities.

Uniform lessons are basically content-centered, are very prevalent, and have been so for almost 100 years in this country. They are based upon the principle of uniformity. Many students in the school on a given Sunday are given the same text to study. The adults may approach the text from a different angle or with a different method than the juniors, and the primaries may approach it from an entirely different direction again, but it is still the same text.

It has some advantages, especially in a small school. All members of a given family will be studying the same text at the same time, and the text can be used in family devotions during the preceding week if desired. This type of material is also easier on the superintendent in planning his worship service because he can plan it around the text of the day and thus add a bit more to the inculcation of that text in the students' minds.

The primary disadvantage is in the younger departments of the Sunday school. Texts which would be fine for the adults often have absolutely no interest whatever to the younger students. Topical studies which are vital to the high school groups are unsuited to the primary groups. This problem alone has been sufficient to remove the uniform lessons from most of the larger schools and many of the smaller ones.

The closely graded lessons are based upon the same principles as the public school curriculum and have found much favor. Each year there is a different curriculum. Those who are eight years old will all be studying the same thing in the school and the next year when the new class of eight year old students comes up, they will study exactly the same thing that the preceding class studied.

That this system has advantages over the Uniform Lessons is rather obvious. The lessons can be so chosen as to meet most satisfactorily the needs of the age group involved, and taking the entire course could give the student a comprehensive view of the entire Bible and of Christian doctrine. It would be difficult for a small school to adopt it, however, and since by far the majority of Sunday schools are in the bracket below 150 students and since the supply of teachers is almost always limited, this type of curriculum has the organizational problem as its main drawback.

Departmental lessons, sometimes known as "group graded" lessons, help to alleviate the difficulty raised by the closely graded lessons while retaining most of the advantages of that system. In this system each department follows a curriculum cycle, usually three years in length. All students in the department are studying the same lesson at one time, and though all students do not get the cycle in the same order, they all get the same material. For instance one student might get the three courses (one year each) in the ABC order, while the student following him by one year would get the series in BCA order and the next year's students would have the course in CAB order, after which time they would be graduated into the next class and the next department where they would enter into another cycle of courses. It is not possible to select the material to meet the needs of the particular age group nearly as well in a system such as this because of the wider age range of the group, but the difficulty is not especially serious in most cases. If the school is large enough to have simultaneous opening exercises, each department could have its worship as a unit and the lesson could be used as the central theme of the worship service, thus retaining one of the advantages of the uniform lessons.

Most publishers of Sunday school materials also publish individual courses graded for the various Sunday school groups. It is possible for a Sunday school to use this type of materials, but it requires active discrimination and organization on the part of the officers of the Sunday school to do this, and it is usually not advisable. These materials are most commonly used among older youth and adults.

Weekday materials are used to supplement the work of the Sunday school. They are used in weekday religious classes, leadership training courses, mission study groups, and special classes in church history, comparative religions, Christian citizenship, and a multiplicity of other areas.

Vacation Bible school materials are used to cover areas of Bible study, memory work, missionary stories, worship, handwork, etc. These materials are generally used in a summer program or late spring. Youth fellowship materials cover the same general area for youth.

A curriculum has been correctly defined as "all that the pupil does under the guidance and with the help of his leaders," though it is usually thought of primarily as the lesson and lesson materials of the church school. While these do play the primary part, there are collateral activities which are also important in developing the child along desired lines. Music, drama, art, visual aids, and handwork all add to the effectiveness of teaching.

These collateral activities should not be included just at the discretion of the teacher or the pupil but should be planned ahead to supplement the learning activities of the school. They should be under the jurisdiction of the curriculum committee just as much as the selection of the Sunday school materials should be. Those directly affected, such as the social chairman of the affected groups, should be brought in, their recommendations obtained, and their suggestions followed as much as possible, but the primary thing is that the *entire* curriculum be planned.

The same principle holds true with the other organizations of the church which have any educational function about them, such as the youth fellowships, women's missionary guilds, men's brotherhoods, or other such activities. There should definitely be a correlation between these groups in the field of curriculum. This can be done on the higher level without sacrificing any of the independence of the group in question. For example the youth fellowship advisor, president, and worship chairman should meet with the Board of Christian Education or whatever board has the responsibility of the curriculum and draw up their yearly plans. The youth fellowship could then be laid out in conjunction with the yearly plan for the Sunday school in order to complement the subject matter being covered and to provide for a more thorough coverage of each subject.

Music. The educational values of music are unquestioned. For centuries music has been used of God in the church to accomplish His purposes. Music is God-ordained. It is the universal language of the human soul. It is the natural speech of the Christ-filled heart and is the medium through which the soul reaches out to God.

The purpose of music is to express praise, prayer, and gratitude to God, to promote the spirit of devotion and worship, to teach and preserve divine truth, and to unify and point the unsaved to God.

Music should be carefully selected for use in the program of Christian education. Some songs can be chosen for their teaching values, for many teach Bible and doctrinal truths, faith, worship, and love. Other songs have literary value and are useful in the development of proper concepts about the Trinity. Of course, such music often has a musical value by dignifying the truths they represent. It goes without saying that the leadership should be carefully selected and specifically trained for this important part of the program. The quality should be maintained at the highest possible level and all music adapted to the age level at which it is used. This demands a practice of the graded principle.

One can point out many places for music in the program of Christian education. It can be used to summarize or conclude other activities (perhaps after a lesson has been taught or discussion held); it can help prepare children for further learning activities by introducing new ideas and words; it provides variety or a change of activity in conversation or discussion; it motivates and inspires correct conduct and provides a medium through which each child may participate and feel a definite part of the church school. Through united group singing children come to feel a real part of the group. This does more to create spiritual receptibility than many other experiences of mind or body. Of course, worship is the most dynamic opportunity for using music.

Music leaders need to appreciate and exemplify in their leadership the real value and appreciation of the finest type of music, because they are responsible for the character and quality of all the music used in the church school. For this reason the leader who is selected should have a good musical background and some specific training if possible.

In addition to knowing music and being able to conduct with skill, music leaders should also understand the musical limitations and abilities of the particular age group with which they work as to range, comprehension of words, rhythm, harmony of music, etc. Instead of doing most of the singing, leaders should inspire children to sing, more by personality than by action.

The music director of the church school is usually an appointed position. It is extremely important that the director have a thorough understanding of the music program of both the church school and the church in general in order that harmony of selection, use, and quality-concept be achieved. Some of the more specific duties of the music leader in the church school may include the following:

1. Direct singing as to tempo and volume
2. Make sure both words and meaning of songs are understood.
3. Teach new songs in the light of the situation
4. Use a wide variety of types of music
5. Repeat many songs for children
6. Guard the voices of small children from injury

7. Watch for special talent among youth
8. Work with department superintendents in planning worship services and music training periods

The pianist is also an important musician. He may either be a real asset or a decided hindrance, according to the way he meets the best standards set. The best musicians should not be used among the adults necessarily. For many reasons, children demand the best. Excessive use of embellishments, fancy chords, and runs are discouraged when playing for little children, because the simple melody is obscured and the practice is unworthy of the purpose for which the music is intended. The piano itself has an influence upon children. For this reason, the best instrument possible should be secured and kept in tune. Personal promptness and cooperation on the part of the accompanist is always desirable.

High standards should be maintained in the selection of music for the church school. Catchy rhymes and attractive jingles should not form the basis of such selection. As mentioned above, music can be chosen because it has teaching, literary, or musical values.

The matter of grading church music to each particular department and age group is of great value and importance. The subject is wide and there are many details which could be discussed, but it will suffice for our purpose to list merely a few suggestions for using music in the church school.

For Beginners and Primaries

1. Use songs teaching right concepts of God
2. Use songs presenting stories of Jesus' life
3. Use songs of love, tender care of Heavenly Father
4. Use songs of nature
5. High standard "action" choruses can be valuable

For Juniors

1. Use songs of love and emotion, helpfulness and service
2. Use songs of salvation, stewardship, and prayer
3. Repeat many songs

For Junior High or Intermediates

1. Use songs of security, confidence, and trust
2. Use songs of salvation and guidance
3. Use songs of hymnology and those which express theology
4. Avoid wide-range songs

For Young People

1. Use songs of aspiration and victory, consecration and dedication
2. Use songs of comradeship, friendship, and joy
3. Use songs of service, vision, and missions
4. Use songs of decision, invitation, and repentance
5. Teach them the great hymns of the church
6. Avoid childish songs

For Young Adults

1. Use songs of life experiences and daily living
2. Use songs of fellowship, encouragement, assurance, and faith
3. For home builders use songs of life and service

For Older Adults

1. Use songs of assurance and comfort for the storms of life
2. Use songs of hope and heaven for the future
3. Use songs of rest, peace, and quietness for those who are inactive

Memory Work. During the early days of Sunday school work, memorization was quite popular, particularly during the period when the catechism was widely used. Then followed a period when memory work was suppressed in both theory and practice. Today, however, there is a tendency to return to its use but to avoid its rote memory characteristics of other days. The best kind of Christian education will certainly make room for memorizing choice passages, at the same time making sure that there is meaning and understanding present. Lobingier has pointed out that if memory work is to be meaningful and effective, it must be based upon certain conditions:

1. The passage selected must be suitable for the age of those who are learning them
2. The length of any passage that is chosen must be scrutinized in the light of the age and experience of those who are to learn it
3. Memorization has value only if it is "with understanding"
4. A chapter or a verse must be learned in the right way
5. It is wise to make frequent use of the memorized material
6. The best memory program has a close relationship to the pupil's other activities
7. The church school needs a policy regulating what translation of the Bible it will use
8. A church may adopt its own "Memory Curriculum" with definitely chosen Scripture passages, and with suitable hymns and prayers for each grade or department[5]

Within each department it is expected that teachers will take the lead in memory work, particularly in connection with their lessons and activities. In the case where a set program of memory work has been adopted by the church school and particularly in some of the larger schools it might be best to put a special superintendent of memory work in charge of the program.

[5]John L. Lobingier, *The Better Church School* (Boston: Pilgrim Press, 1952), paragraph quotation, pp. 49-51. Used by permission.

Following are suggestions for use with various age groups:

1. Nursery — Bible words and thoughts
2. Beginners — short, simple Bible verses
3. Primary — selected verses and passages on great Bible truths and Christian duties
4. Junior — hymns, verses, passages, chapters, Bible books
5. Junior High — Scripture and hymns, perhaps catechism
6. Senior High — College — Adult — choice of verses, chapters, etc. Perhaps a memory course such as the Navigator's

Audio-visuals. Audio-visual education techniques have become established procedures in all good education. It is now an established fact that these tools enable people to learn more rapidly and permanently through the eye and ear. They are commonly divided into two general categories: non-projected (covering such tools as blackboards, charts, graphs, maps, posters, etc.) and projected (including slides, filmstrips, and motion pictures). Audio aids include recordings, both on tape and record, and the use of recorders, playbacks, radio, etc.

While it is true that most good curriculum materials provide suggestions for securing and using audio-visuals correlated with the lessons materials, it still pertains that teachers and workers need a great deal of assistance in the use of these materials. Selection and correlation therefore needs to be done in the local situation. This calls for a committee of some kind in the local church to do this work. Department superintendents should call on this committee for special study and assistance in the use of materials and equipment.

Usually the committee in charge of audio-visuals is a subcommittee of the Board of Christian Education, and it will have at least the following duties:

1. Responsibility for planning and use of audio-visuals
2. Providing necessary equipment and materials
3. Supervising an audio-visual library
4. Training operators of equipment
5. Submitting an annual budget
6. Interpretation of the meaning and use of audio-visuals
7. Making suggestions to workers on materials available

Stewardship and Service. Stewardship, service, and missions are generally included in the curriculum materials. Thus the laymen in the church come into contact with instruction in these areas. Particular attention, however, needs to be given to the leaders and workers, and this can be done in the leadership training courses which are taught.

Stewardship refers to the giving of time, talents, money, and self to Christian service. Regular and systematic giving, therefore, should be stressed and opportunities for the giving of money provided through some kind of weekly contribution system. In many churches the treasurer of the church or Sunday school is put in charge of stewardship education. He should see that a program of this kind is sponsored in the various departments. Particular emphasis needs to be given to the matter of living a consecrated Christian life which finds channels of service and usefulness. Each local church should study the service possibilities at home and abroad and make a definite effort to use all members directly in some kind of project through which they can express their service. Gospel teams, social work, home missions, extension work, and the ministry to the unfortunates in the community will provide many opportunities for the individual to serve. Of course many channels of service are provided right in the local church.

Superintendents and Curriculum. Regardless of the type of curriculum adopted, one thing to remember is that 90 per cent of curriculum is the teacher. Regardless of the excellence of the curriculum, a poor teacher will turn out a poor product in a poorly educated student. And, conversely, a good teacher can be successful with a poor curriculum. However, a good teacher can be better, and a staff of good teachers can be excellent, if they are united by a good curriculum.

For the average Sunday school the departmental lesson is probably the one to be preferred if a good one is available which will match up with the needs of the students in question. It is often the case that the adults will follow the uniform lesson while the rest of the school will follow a graded series.

Most denominations furnish graded or uniform materials, and some of them furnish both types. This is, of course, highly desirable since the doctrines presented will be harmonious with the emphasis of the church, and the various church days which are emphasized by that denomination can be incorporated in the curriculum.

The entire subject is one of great complexity, and no final answer can ever be given which will fit all schools for all time. The most that can be done is to consider the basic principles and the materials and helps available and, prayerfully considering the training and salvation of those for whom the school is responsible, obtain the best possible curriculum and stick to it.

Superintendents, both general and departmental, can be greatly helpful to teachers and department workers in the selection and use of curriculum materials.

Individual teachers, classes, and departments may share in the selection of materials but approval of their selections should be given by a Board of Christian Education or a committee on curriculum. Selections should be made on the basis of Scriptural principles, age group needs, the total church program, and the long-range plans of the publisher. Other factors to consider include cost, denominational emphasis, size of school and classes, pupil backgrounds, past experience of workers, time available for class with classroom space and equipment, and teaching methods.

Some of the principles involved in selection include:

1. Are materials in harmony with the Bible?
2. Are materials in harmony with objectives?
3. Are materials graded to meet pupil needs?
4. Are materials practical for teacher use?
5. Are materials attractive and of high quality?
6. Are materials adaptable to the local situation?
7. Are extra-biblical materials true to the Bible?
8. Are materials provided for expressional activities which are in line with the will of God revealed in the Bible?
9. Are materials in harmony with good educational principles?
10. Are materials comprehensive, rich, and spiritual enough in content?

Where shall we get curriculum materials? Four ways are commonly used in many schools today.

1. Individual teachers are allowed to choose materials from almost any source
2. Some schools create and publish their own materials
3. Others use some form of denominational materials or modification, or some form of independent materials
4. Others choose from a variety of sources

The first practice should be condemned. The second practice is too difficult for the average church school. The fourth practice destroys integration and results in a hodge-podge curriculum design. The third practice seems to be most widely used. When schools are dissatisfied with their denominational materials because of lack of quality or doctrinal content, they generally turn to some independent publisher in an attempt to get useful materials. Great care should be given by leaders in both planning and evaluation of materials selected by this system.

In addition to providing assistance in selecting and evaluating materials, superintendents can supervise the handling and use of such materials in the classroom. They can help teachers in the teaching situation and assist secretaries in ordering, distributing, and storing materials. These officers can be quite helpful in making suggestions toward the improvement of curriculum procedures. Among such suggestions might be the following:

1. Consult denominational agencies about curriculum problems

2. Study the use of the Bible in classes, departments, in the home, and for personal use
3. Study the use of collateral activities, such as music, art, dramatics, projects, etc.
4. Make use of audio-visual aids in the program
5. Explore the possibilities of expanded sessions for children and youth
6. Study the place and use of facilities and equipment in the program, particularly how they affect teaching and learning
7. Create and use a good library

A *Suggested Curriculum Theory*. A good curriculum theory must have an integrating factor or an organizing principle. Among Christian educators the battle over this has waged furiously at times and has centered around two problems: (1) the relation of the learner to the Christian faith and heritage, particularly contained in the Bible, and (2) relation of the learner to life itself, both individually and socially. There are dangers and advantages in both these positions. Undoubtedly the real truth lies in a synthesis of these opposing views, *provided the synthesis is in harmony with the principles of Scripture.* It is also clear that such a synthesis must be comprehensive so that it includes meeting the needs of the individual, a Christian view of society, God's will in all these things, the church, and in general a statement of world view.

Among evangelicals the tendency has been to emphasize primarily the Christian experience and Christian heritage side of the problem, although many are certainly making desperate efforts to be educationally sound as well. The tremendous problems concerned in a Christ-controlled and Bible-centered approach are well-known, particularly the problems of gradation of Bible content. Consequently, it has been felt by many that certain parts of the Bible are unsuited for certain age groups. In addition to these problems, one notices particularly that by far the large majority among the laity of the church really do not know their Bibles after their learning experiences in the various systems now being used. For a long time the writer has felt that evangelicals should do some rethinking of the whole problem of curriculum theory. The following is submitted, not as a panacea, but as a suggestion for further study.

There is a beautiful story running from Genesis to Revelation, from the first creation to the new creation. It is the chronological story of God's plan of redemption. This story provides the integrating factor and organizing principle. In chart form the theory looks like the illustration on page 242 below.

From this view it can be seen that *divine truth* parallels the *divine story*. Divine truth with consequent applications to the hearts and lives of the pupil follows a progressive pattern which can be adapted by way of the graded principle to the pupil. In this way the Bible student can hang events, personalities, localities, and truths onto the story as it progresses through the Scriptures. As the child matures, divine truth can be studied in more detail in keeping with this comprehension and understanding. For example, beginners can start with the Creation story in Genesis and take big jumps through the entire Scriptures, stopping for applications of truth at those places most acceptable to his experience, yet following the chronological order of the Bible story. Primaries will take "shorter jumps," juniors still shorter, on up the maturity scale to adults who ultimately will be making book studies of the Scriptures.

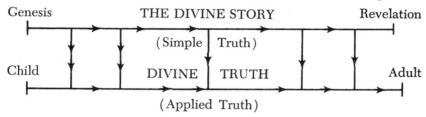

This theory is based on the confidence that the Word and Spirit of God are adequate for all age groups, that God has made man's spirit receptive to His truth at all age levels, that it will comprehend the whole gamut of curriculum demands, including the individual, the home, the church, the social order, and all channels through which the school can express itself. We have yet to see someone rise to a challenge of this kind.

6. Program

Administration. It is the responsibility of the department superintendent to see that all the important factors which go into his particular department be coordinated into an efficiently functioning unit. This means that he will constantly check with the general superintendent to see that his department is fitting into the general church school situation. He will also check often to see that his department is working smoothly in connection with other departments.

One of the most important factors in a department program is well-defined objectives. Constant check on workers and teachers is necessary to see that purposes and objectives are being carried out. This is particularly true for the work being done in the classroom. All department objectives should be closely integrated and correlated with the objectives of Christian education in general and the church school in particular.

One of the most helpful devices to be employed by department superintendents in seeing that a department is properly administered and that the program is fulfilling the highest expectations is that of a department calendar of activities. Here department activities and responsibilities are charted month by month, planned in advance, and carried through with precision. Of course, such a calendar needs to be integrated with that of the church school in general.

Sunday Program. The typical department will provide for a pre-session period, departmental assembly, used particularly for group worship, and various class groups. Typical activities engaged in — in addition to the lessons — will include storytelling, dramatization, games, memory work, music, map-making, and social life.

Wider Relationships. The work of a department is not complete with the Sunday program. There will be through-the-week activities, summer activities, and special activities such as Bible clubs, vacation Bible schools, etc. All this work should be integrated with the Sunday church school program. More will be said about this in Chapter 9.

7. *The Department Superintendent and the Open Room*

For the development and employment of the concepts involved in open room procedures and techniques of teaching, the reader is referred to section D in chapter 7.

SUGGESTED READING — CHAPTER 6*

Allen and Bryan, *Primary Superintendent's Manual*
Allen and Rice, *Junior Superintendent's Manual*
Althoff, *The Church Library Manual*
Atkinson, *Building and Equipping for Christian Education,* Chapters 7-13
Benson, Clarence, *The Sunday School in Action,* Chapter 3, 8
Benson, E. G., *Ideas for Sunday School Growth*
         Planning Church School Workers' Conferences
Byrd and Lee, *Intermediate Superintendent's Manual*
Crossland, *How to Build Up Your Church School,* Chapters 4, 7
DeBlois and Gorham, *Christian Religious Education,* Chapter 8
Fant, *All About the Sunday School,* Chapters 2-4, 12-21
Flake, *Building a Standard Sunday School,* Chapter 4
Foster, *How a Small Church Can Have Good Christian Education,* Chapters 1-5, 8, 10, 11, 12
Gage, *Increasing Church School Attendance*
Harper, *The Nazarene Sunday School,* Chapter 3

* Refer to updated Bibliography at back of book.

Heim, *Leading a Sunday Church School,* Chapters 9, 10, 12
Hurst, *Operation Sunday School,* Chapter 5
Lebar, *Children in the Bible School,* Chapters 13, 15
Lobingier, *The Better Church School,* Chapter 4
Lotz, *Orientation in Religious Education,* Chapter 8
Martin and Moerner, *Worship in the Sunday School,* rev. ed.
Miller, *Education for Christian Living,* Chapter 16
Murch, *Christian Education and the Local Church,* Chapters 14, 24
National Council of Churches, *A Guide for Curriculum in Christian Education*
Noland, *The Six Point Record System and Its Use*
Paulsen, *Church School and Worship*
Person, *An Introduction to Christian Education,* Chapters 4, 5, 10
Peirce and Honderick, *Going With the Gospel* (whole book)
Rice, *The Department Supervisor*
Schisler, *Christian Teaching in the Churches,* Chapter 8
Sisemore, *The Ministry of Visitation*
Smith, *The Pastor at Work in Christian Education,* Chapter 5
Taylor, *Religious Education: A Comprehensive Survey,* Chapter 10-14, 16-19, 23, 25, 29
The Sunday School "Form Folio" (Cowan Publications, Los Angeles)
Tovey, *Music Leadership in Christian Education*
Vieth, *The Church and Christian Education,* Chapter 4
——————, *The Church School,* Chapters 4-14

THE WORK OF THE TEACHER IN
CHRISTIAN EDUCATION

OUTLINE FOR CHAPTER 7

(Instruction and Evangelism)

A. THE TEACHER AND HIS WORK
  1. Importance of the Work
  2. The Nature of the Work
  3. The Function of the Teacher

B. THE TEACHER AND HIS KNOWLEDGE
  1. Of the Lord
  2. Of Sunday School Work
  3. Of the Bible
  4. Of Subjects Related to the Bible
  5. Of the Pupil
  6. Of the Laws of Teaching

C. THE TEACHER AND THE LAWS OF TEACHING
  1. The Law of the Teacher
  2. The Law of the Pupil
  3. The Law of the Language
  4. The Law of the Lesson
  5. The Law of the Teaching Process
  6. The Law of the Learning Process
  7. The Law of Review and Application

D. THE TEACHER AND CREATIVE METHODS
  1. Current Trends
  2. New Developments in Learning Theory
  3. Teaching Methods and Creativity

E. THE TEACHER AND HIS DUTIES
  1. In General
  2. On Sunday
  3. During the Month
  4. The Organized Class
  5. Maintaining Discipline

7 | THE WORK OF THE TEACHER IN CHRISTIAN EDUCATION

(Instruction and Evangelism)

A. THE TEACHER AND HIS WORK

1. *Importance of the Work.* Teaching is important because it is a *sacred ministry.* Teachers are under-pastors. They are shepherds of their classes. In many instances the teacher can get closer to the individual class members than any other person in the church school, including the pastor. Whereas the pastor's task is to shepherd the entire flock, the teacher's task is confined to a small group — his class.

As a *Christian* the teacher's first duty is to get right with God, to have a clear, definite Christian experience, to be converted. Without the new birth it is extremely difficult and almost impossible to do the work of a Christian teacher. Beyond regeneration the teacher should live a consecrated and Spirit-filled life. He should have an earnest purpose to save souls and use the means of grace, such as prayer, almsgiving, attending church, prayer meetings, and observing quiet periods for personal devotions. In addition to exercising self-denial, the teacher's greatest job perhaps is prayer. "This kind cometh not out but by prayer and fasting."

Good teachers will be thorough-going *church members.* They will be intelligent church members, acquainted with both the history and polity of the church, not to speak of its doctrine. They will support the church through gifts of money and labor and will seek to influence others to support it as well, both at home and abroad.

As a *Bible student* the teacher will take time for study. He will learn to think for himself and will seek constantly to embody the truth which he studies.

As a *teacher* he will learn to perform his duties as efficiently as possible. This he will do by observing successful teachers at work, by practicing the best principles, and by reading good books on teaching.

As a *pastor* the teacher will provide an example that is safe to follow. His life and conduct will be above reproach. He will be a faithful friend and shepherd of his flock. He will seek constantly to be like Jesus Christ.

Yes, teaching is important. Jesus was called the Master Teacher. The Jews and early Christian church gave great promi-

247

nence to this office. According to Ephesians 4:11, 12, teaching is really a divine calling. The evangelist founds the church; the pastor shepherds the church; the teacher edifies and builds the church. Christian teachers and Christian teaching are needed desperately today to help build the kingdom of God among men.

2. *The Nature of the Work.* What is teaching? Christian teaching is not religious teaching. One distinctive of Christian teaching is found in Jesus Christ. The high privilege of the Christian teacher is to present Christ to men as the Saviour of the world and to be used as an instrument in His hands in the development of Christ-like character in his pupils.

The word "teach," we are told, is derived from the Anglo-Saxon *taecean,* which means "to show how to do." From this one infers very simply that teaching is helping the pupil to learn. Christian teaching, however, is concerned with Christian specifics. We want our pupils to learn *about* Jesus Christ and to *know* Him. This means that the learner must, through the help of the Holy Spirit, come to a realization of his need for Jesus as personal Saviour. This places regeneration at the very heart of the teaching-learning process. Beyond this there is character development, leading the learner to a life of daily witness, growth in grace, and service, constantly striving toward the Christlike ideal of the perfect man (Ephesians 4:13).

Specific terms have been used to describe the art of teaching. Among them we find the following:

1. Teaching is helping
2. Teaching is awakening
3. Teaching is imparting
4. Teaching is inspiring
5. Teaching is correcting
6. Teaching is sharing
7. Teaching is guiding

One looks at this list and says to himself, "Jesus the Master Teacher did all these things." Jesus taught His disciples by helping them to pray. He taught when He made the woman at the well aware of her deepest need. He imparted knowledge to Nicodemus about the new birth. He inspired simple fishermen to catch men. He corrected the false impressions of the disciples regarding His Messiahship. He shared His time, His skill, and His knowledge over and over again. He guided His followers into the way of life. All true teachers will do these things, and by so doing they will teach and men will learn.

Christian teaching, therefore, is a ministry; it is an art which demands time and careful preparation. It is a science which embodies basic principles. It demands the best that we can give it.

If teachers are willing to pay the price in mastering teaching principles and in making preparation, they will succeed.

Sunday school teacher, what is your concept of your task? Do you think in terms of teaching a "dinky little Sunday school class down at the church"? Do you think in terms of teaching *lessons* only? Or do you think of your task as a sacred ministry, a high and holy privilege? Remember this — every sincere teacher is not alone in His task! The blessed Holy Spirit is with us. He will use us if we give Him a chance, if we work in close harmony with Him, if we are filled with His presence!

Someone has said that "the curriculum is 90 per cent teacher." This being true, every Christian teacher needs to redouble his efforts to be true to his Lord, to prepare for his task, and to strive for results. This means again that teachers who are genuinely Christian will not teach simply because they were asked or because no one else will take the job, but they will teach because they feel the call of God upon them, the urgency of the task, a passion for souls, and because they see the grand reward of souls saved and built up in the faith.

It should be noted, in looking at the great task of Christian education as a whole, that we need several things to accomplish our purposes:

1. The Man
2. The Message
3. The Motive
4. The Method

In offering himself, the Christian teacher provides the man. He has the message in the Word. He has many methods by which he can get this message out to a lost world. But he must be motivated for the task. He must feel like Paul the apostle — "The love of Christ constraineth me." He must feel like Jesus when He looked at the multitudes. He saw them as sheep without a shepherd. He was moved with compassion for them. Without this essential motivation for the task, teachers will not be fruitful in the service of the Master.

3. *The Function of the Teacher.* The Sunday school teacher is a *Christian* educator. This provides us with the clue as to his function. As a Christian the function of the teacher is to reveal God. As such, he is a witness both by life and lip. In life, he witnesses through giving a living demonstration of Christ-likeness. Through lip, he gives expression to the truth concerning the nature of God and the truth of God.

As an educator, the Christian teacher functions in accordance with the mandate of God to teach and in accord with the educational and pedagogical principles contained in the whole educative process. In this regard, the teacher becomes an oracle of God

(I Peter 4:10, 11). This makes him God's mouthpiece. With Jesus he says, "My teaching is not mine but His that sent me . . . . He that speaketh from himself seeketh his own glory" (John 7:16, 18).

Perhaps the apostle Paul expressed it in another way when he said, "Study to show thyself approved unto God; a workman that needeth not to be ashamed, rightly dividing the word of truth" (II Timothy 2:15). Here we see that the function of the teacher is to deliberately concentrate on doing three things: (1) being approved of God, (2) being an efficient workman who is unashamed with his efforts, and (3) handling aright God's truth as recorded in the Bible. In other words, the Sunday school teacher should function as a witness, a worker, and a winner. He witnesses for his Lord by life and lip; he works as hard as it is possible for him to do; and he so handles the Word of God that it wins its way into hearts and lives, resulting in their salvation and service.

Still another way of looking at this matter is suggested for us in the subtitle of this chapter. The teacher is directly responsible for instruction and evangelism. Instruction concerns the handling of the Word in the classroom situation and evangelism is the art of soul winning, for it is in the classroom where you would expect these two matters to be handled most effectively. In other words, the Sunday school teacher needs to be a specialist in the art of teaching and soul winning. Sunday school superintendents must bear this in mind and use administrative techniques to protect this most important ministry of the teacher.

This matter will be given further consideration in a section to come on the laws of teaching.

B. THE TEACHER AND HIS KNOWLEDGE

1. *Of the Lord.* The Sunday school teacher must know many things to be a successful teacher. First and foremost is his knowledge of the Lord. This involves first-hand, experimental knowledge of Jesus Christ as personal Saviour. Without this knowledge, the work of the Sunday school teacher degenerates into that of a mere academician. Jesus said that if the blind lead the blind, both shall fall into the ditch.

This kind of knowledge demands both spiritual qualification and spiritual preparation. The former is obtained through regeneration. The latter is obtained through communion and fellowship with the Lord. This is accomplished by means of prayer, Bible study, devotion, using the means of grace, and daily witness through which the teacher grows in grace. Beyond this lies the Spirit-filled life. A close walk with God is demanded of the teacher. He must "walk in the things of the Spirit." He must manifest the fruit of the Spirit. This likewise is experiential knowledge obtained through complete consecration and the baptism of the

Holy Spirit. No knowledge, therefore, is greater than spiritual knowledge.

2. *Of Sunday School Work.* The work of Sunday school teaching demands a great volume of knowledge and a high quality of efficiency. All this demands specific preparation. Given a high level of spiritual quality among workers, plus a high standard of training, the Sunday school will prosper with the blessing of God.

Since Sunday school teaching is a ministry, it demands the best we can give it, "workmen who need not be ashamed." Teachers must be Spirit-filled, but the Holy Spirit will not honor ignorance. An appreciation for the office of the teacher leads to an appreciation for the need of preparation for the task. The Lord can use teachers, but He can use *trained* teachers *better.*

The list which follows reveals the important areas in which a teacher is expected to have some acquaintance and mastery:

1. A knowledge of the Bible — our textbook
2. A knowledge of related subjects, such as Bible geography, history, archaeology
3. A knowledge of the pupil
4. A knowledge of teaching techniques
5. A knowledge of Sunday school administration
6. A knowledge of how to study

Such training should be provided by the church. If not, the teacher can read good books, take correspondence courses, attend conferences and conventions, and observe others at work. Of course, if it is possible, some special training at a good college or seminary is preferred. The fact that each teacher is a member of a staff of workers also reveals the importance of his training. He needs to know how to work with other teachers and officers and to appreciate the problems of administration and supervision. In all this he will become more sympathetic and cooperate more effectively.

3. *Of the Bible.* The Bible is the textbook of the Sunday school. Knowledge of the Bible, therefore, demands academic knowledge as well as spiritual knowledge. This kind of knowledge can be obtained in two general ways: (1) by devotional study and (2) through the preparation of specific lessons. All teachers should read the Bible devotionally for their own spiritual life, but it will require specific preparation beyond this to master Bible content. Where it is possible, training in some good Bible college is recommended.

On the part of the individual, books *about* the Bible may be read. In this way facts of the Bible — such as books, authors, outlines, etc. — may be obtained. This study, however, should be supplemented by reading books *on* the Bible, such as commentaries, concordances, etc. The Bible itself, on the other hand, has no substitute. It should be read over and over again — as a whole, by individual books, for topics, doctrines, biographies, events, and practical wisdom. Even in the preparation of specific Sunday school lessons, the Bible itself should be read *first*. Next to spiritual knowledge, nothing is more important than Biblical knowledge for the Sunday school teacher.

4. *Of Subjects Related to the Bible.* Knowledge *about* the Bible which supplements knowledge *of* the Bible itself is valuable for the Sunday school teacher. A thorough knowledge of the Bible demands an acquaintance with the people and lands of the Bible, their customs, history, folklore, art, music, etc. In fact, exact Bible knowledge often depends on an acquaintance with these things.

This means that books on Bible history, Bible geography, Bible archaeology, and Bible customs should find their place in the personal library of the Sunday school teacher. Knowledge of these things often "throw light" on Bible subject matter. They also provide a wealth of background material for studying and teaching Sunday school lessons, not to speak of the many interesting and life-like illustrative materials they provide.

5. *Of the Pupil.* Sunday school teachers not only teach lessons, they teach pupils. In fact the lessons are virtually meaningless apart from the pupils. The message is *for* the pupils. This means, therefore, that it is imperative for the teacher to know his pupils. Such knowledge will enable him to properly present the message and the work together with the Holy Spirit in bringing the pupil to Christ-likeness of character and conduct.

It is important for the teacher to know his pupils because each one is an individual with peculiar needs of his own. The magnitude of the task in reaching the spiritual man within also demands a knowledge of the person being dealt with. There are many hindrances and these must be overcome in reaching the soul for Christ. Some of the important things in addition to pupil psychology that a teacher should know about include:

1. An acquaintance with home environment
2. An acquaintance with work environment
3. A knowledge of both the wisdom and the ignorance of the pupil
4. An acquaintance with pupil vocabulary
5. Knowledge of friends, interests, needs, and associates of each pupil
6. Some knowledge of family background

There are a variety of ways by which this kind of knowledge can be acquired by the teacher. He can study his pupils directly by observing them, spending time with them, playing with them, and visiting them at home and at work. Further information can be secured through reading psychology books and Sunday school manuals on pupil characteristics. A special study of the conditions which influence your pupils can be made. Indirect methods for studying pupils include enquiring of others — such as parents, friends, employees, and former teachers — regarding general information about pupils. The public school teachers are often willing to share information with Sunday school teachers. Good fiction often throws light on human nature. Stories in newspapers, magazines, and religious papers supplement this knowledge. Last but not least is retrospection. By recalling one's own personal experiences, teachers can understand the needs and interests of their own pupils.

The next problem is how to record this information for practical use. Some teachers rely on charts of psychological characteristics of age groups. Others hand out questionnaires and gather pertinent information for use in study and teaching. Still others use a notebook in which the names of individual pupils are registered. Some even include a small photograph. At least one page is used to record basic information, including name, address, family, age, birthday, telephone, occupation, church membership, etc. Some teachers also carefully record such things as number of visits to the pupil's home, letters, cards, calls, etc. Others record as much objective information as possible, including such things as observations about home life, community surroundings, school life, work life, companionships, special interests and abilities, temperament and disposition, moral and spiritual difficulties, knowledge of the Bible and religious things, and relationship to Christ and the church. Of course, this kind of information demands constant observation and diligent recording. It would be a good thing for teachers to keep a cumulative record in this form and pass it along from class to class as the pupil advances through the years. A sample questionnaire blank is provided below to illustrate the importance of gathering information about pupils.

A Pupil Questionnaire and Information Blank

Name
Address
Telephone Number
Birthday
Are you a Christian?   Church member?
What distance do you live from the church?
How do you get to Sunday school?
What groups are you a member of?
Do you give a tenth (tithe) of your money to the Lord?
What point on the Sunday school record is hardest for you?

In what ways do you think the Sunday school or your class
  could be made better?
What type of reading do you like best?
Name one or two favorite books.
Do you like music?   What kinds?
Do you study music?   If so, what?
Grade at school?   Which school?
What subjects do you like best?
To what clubs or organizations do you belong?
How much leisure time do you have each day and how do you
  spend it?
Do you do any kind of work for which you are paid? What?
What do you expect to be, or do as a life's work?
Your parents' names?
Father's occupation?
Is your mother employed outside the family?
Are your parents Christian?
How many brothers and sisters do you have?

The practical value of such information should be obvious to
all teachers. Detailed and intimate knowledge of your pupils will
greatly help you in studying your lessons. You can plan lessons to
meet pupil needs. That is the important thing. Your Bible materials
and other materials can be more skillfully selected and more
appropriately adapted. The attention and interest of your class
can be more effectively secured by tying in the lesson with pupil
interests and needs. Surely more fruitful results will follow, the
lost will be won to Christ, and greater service will be realized.

6. *Of the Laws of Teaching.* In addition to all of the above
factors, each teacher should know and practice the laws of teaching.
Only in this way can he carry out fully his function as a teacher.
These laws provide him with the skill so necessary in the process
of teaching. Because of the extreme importance of these laws,
particular attention and treatment of them is provided in the
section which follows. Perhaps the finest source of information
along this line is given in the classic, *The Seven Laws of Teaching*
by Gregory.

C. THE TEACHER AND THE LAWS OF TEACHING

1. *The Law of the Teacher.* This first law is the law of
PREPARATION — the teacher must know that which he would teach.
Only a thoroughly prepared teacher can be the truly successful
teacher. This kind of preparation takes two directions: (1) the
teacher needs to know the *content* of the lesson being taught, and
(2) he must prepare himself to *communicate* the content and
message in the lesson.

To know the content of a Sunday school lesson requires a

thorough knowledge of the Scriptures. This in turn demands careful and thorough study. A teacher's study processes, therefore, determine to a large extent his teaching effectiveness. Thus it behooves each teacher to be systematic in his study processes.

Much experience has taught us that methodical lesson preparation demands several phases of study and preparation. They are:

1. Personal study of the lesson content
2. Thorough planning of the teaching process
3. Careful selection of teaching materials
4. Adept selection of teaching methods
5. Thorough development of teaching procedures

Thorough Sunday school teachers will begin their lesson study early in the week, even on Sunday afternoon. The obvious advantages of this procedure are many. Early study gives time to prepare adequately for the coming Sunday. Appropriate materials and methods can be selected and thought through far enough in advance to provide some evaluation ahead of time. The lesson can be adapted to the meeting of pupil needs when the teacher has time to meditate on these things. No teacher should wait until Saturday night to prepare his lesson.

It has been the experience of many teachers that the same place for study used over and over again is helpful in setting the stage for concentration. He becomes accustomed to both sights and sounds.

A good teacher will need proper tools for his study. Space does not allow a lengthy discussion of study tools, but the following list should prove suggestive.

1. A good teachers' Bible, with appropriate helps, such as maps, charts, references, etc.
2. A good Bible dictionary
3. A Bible atlas
4. Commentaries
5. Concordance
6. Webster's dictionary
7. A book on Bible customs and archaeology
8. Various versions and translations
9. A topical reference
10. Lesson quarterly
11. Scrapbook
12. Pencil and paper

In addition to such tools, books on Bible study, child psychology, and Sunday school work will prove helpful from time to time.

Once having selected his place and tools for study, the teacher is ready to begin the actual study process. As always his first duty is to pray, to ask God's blessing and the anointing of the Spirit both upon the lesson itself and the whole study procedure.

One of the first and most helpful steps in studying the lesson, particularly at the beginning of the quarter, is to preview all 13 lessons for the quarter. By knowing what lies ahead, the teacher is enabled to prepare each lesson more thoroughly, select materials and methods more appropriately, and review most effectively.

Following a thorough preview comes the preparation of the individual lesson. In doing this the teacher should read over the lesson in the Bible *first*. Do not read the quarterly until later. Personal Bible study allows an opportunity to discover fresh truth which can be applied to the meeting of pupil needs as only the teacher knows them. Furthermore, he gives God a chance to speak through him.

Notice the subject of the lesson and, as you read, meditate on the subject in the light of the whole lesson. Keep pencil and paper handy to jot down the thoughts which occur to you as you read; meditate and pray. Give yourself plenty of time for this part of your preparation. Notice the Golden Text as you read — this is the central thought of the lesson. Notice the book of the Bible from which the lesson is taken. Acquaint yourself with the facts of the book — its author, time, purpose, outline, events, etc. You can often find such information in summary form in the back of your teacher's Bible. Read the chapters before and after the text which contains the lesson itself. If the book is short, read the entire book. Such study provides you with information in the context of the lesson.

As you read the lesson, write down the spiritual truths as you see them in the lesson. Bear in mind the spiritual needs of your pupils, their circumstances, problems, etc. These matters will prove helpful in planning applications of lesson truths.

Ask such questions as: What does the text mean? What does the lesson as a whole teach? What does the lesson teach in particular? Read the lesson for its story, for the incidents and events it contains, for the persons involved. All these things will provide clues and suggestions for points to develop in the lesson.

During all of this kind of study, be sure to write down your impressions. Surely they will be your own discoveries. As such they will prove extremely beneficial to you.

After you have thus thoroughly studied and recorded your notes, *then* turn to the quarterly and other helps. See if your own thinking agrees with the commentators and writers. You may want to combine some of your points with those of the nice outline in the lesson quarterly. By so doing you may come up with an outline which is better in the long run. It may be that further study in lesson helps will throw more light on the lesson. In any event you have studied early, far in advance, and thoroughly. You have an outline which you feel will be greatly helpful to you in teaching the lesson and meeting the needs of your class. Once this first step is complete, the teacher can move to the second phase of preparation — that of planning the lesson for classroom use.

The study process concerns the personal mastery of the lesson on the part of the teacher. Lesson planning, however, is concerned with the preparation of the lesson for the pupil, getting it ready for the classroom.

Lesson planning is particularly important, not only for the sake of efficiency in lesson presentation, but primarily that the lesson might be adapted to the age level being taught and in order that specific needs might be met in the hearts and lives of the pupils.

Several ways have been advocated for lesson study and planning, but it is generally accepted that the *written lesson plan* is the best. In such a plan the teacher lays out on paper a blueprint of procedure, a teaching plan. His work, therefore, is planned from the very opening moments of the Sunday school hour to the close. Many plans have been worked out in the past. The following is a sample of what can be done along this line.

MY TEACHING PLAN

Lesson topic: _____

General theme and purpose of the quarter: _____

My teaching aim for this lesson: (Note: be guided by knowings, feelings, willings)

My procedure for teaching the Lesson: _____

Materials I need for teaching (such as Bibles, pupil's quarterly, maps, supplies, etc.)

How I plan to begin the lesson (Note: appeal to intellectual interests of pupils)

Main points which I shall emphasize: _____

    1. _____

    2. _____

    3. _____

(Note: Show truth which satisfies needs: urge acceptance and show the way of truth)

How I plan to encourage class participation: _____

How I plan to close the teaching session: _____

(Note: here appeal to the will; decision; action!)

Carry-over suggestion

Assignment for next lesson

Following the suggested procedure in the teaching plan above, we note that the teacher should write down first the lesson topic for the day and the general theme and purpose for the quarter. This has the practical advantage of keeping the teacher "on the beam" in both study and teaching. Individual lessons generally form one part of a series of lessons for the quarter which are developing a general theme for that period. It is important that the connections of lessons be kept in mind as the quarter advances so that the theme for that period can be thoroughly developed in the classroom.

Actually, the first step in the lesson plan is the particular aim for the day's lesson. Such aims can be worked out by bearing in mind the great general objectives of Christian education pointed out in Chapter 1. However, the practical advantage of a lesson aim resides in its directional ability in guiding the teacher to teach the lesson in order that specific pupil needs can be met. In order, therefore, to set up practical aims for lessons, the teacher must know intimately the needs of the pupils in his class. To accomplish this it has been suggested that the teacher should work out a "set" of aims to meet a variety of needs represented in the class. Some needs will be mental, others emotional, others volitional, and some will take the form of problems. Following is a list of five practical questions each teacher should ask about aims. Answers to these questions will provide him with plenty of purposes for the day's lesson.

1. What do I want my pupils to know?
2. What do I want my pupils to feel?
3. What do I want my pupils to do?
4. What choices do I want my pupils to make?
5. What kind of character should my pupils manifest?

Answers to these questions should be written down so that they can be fitted into the lesson at the proper points.

Next, the lesson plan calls for the selection of proper materials for teaching the lesson. This should not be left to chance. Instead, each teacher should list on his plan all necessary materials he intends to use in teaching the lesson, such as Bibles, quarterlies, maps, supplies, etc.

It is also wise to select the methods through which the lesson will be presented. Shall it be by question and answer, lecture, recitation, supervised study, or research? Bear in mind that there is no one best method. A variety of methods seems to be the best approach. Remember too that the age of the pupils helps to determine the methods to be employed — for example: storytelling and flannelgraph for children, research and discussion for youth, lecture and discussion for adults. Experience will also teach the instructor much about proper methods for his class.

Once all these things have been gathered and laid out on the lesson plan, it remains for the teacher to strategically plan how to use them in the actual teaching situation. Here is where your outline will assume great importance. A good lesson plan will show just where the materials and methods affect each point on the outline. In other words, the teacher should take his outline which he developed during his study period and ask himself these questions about each point in it: (1) What bearing does this point have on my *purposes?* (2) What *materials* can I use to illustrate this particular point? and (3) What will be the best *method* of getting the point across to the class? Thus the lesson plan will show first the lesson point to be stressed and what materials and methods will be used to get the point across to the members of the class. For illustrations of this procedure, the reader may refer to Appendix VII, Sample Lesson Plan.

Before leaving this point, it may be well to list some of the most commonly used materials and methods employed by the average teacher at all levels.

Suggested Materials	*Suggested Methods*
1. Pictures	1. Lecture
2. Objects	2. Storytelling
3. Flannelgraph	3. Recitation
4. Projected Aids	4. Discussion
5. Clippings	5. Question and answer

The lesson plan is not complete, however, until several other important considerations are observed. Careful thought needs to be given on how the lesson will be presented. This involves an introduction, development, and conclusion to the lesson. These steps all involve the use of both materials and methods, so the teacher should include notes on procedure for these steps on his lesson plan.

Still another consideration is the procedure for the whole process. This involves the time devoted to the lesson period, how the pupils will be used during the class, and the relative amount of time which will be needed for the development of each point during the lesson presentation. All these matters should be carefully thought through before the class period so that important points can be stressed and the lesson covered adequately.

Bear in mind, however, that you cannot possibly present everything in one lesson. Eliminate those things which do not apply to the class and select only the material which will help to carry out your aims. Provide for illustrations and applications under each point of your outline. Also stop on each important point or Scripture passage and ask some good questions. Plan to draw your class into participation as much as possible. Remember, you are teaching pupils, not just lessons.

2. *The Law of the Pupil.* Formally stated, this law is: the pupil must attend with interest to the material being taught. This law involves attention on the part of the pupil. Attention may be flitting, requiring no effort of will to direct it; it may be purely voluntary, the kind given through force of will; or it may be absorbing, that kind in which the pupil is so absorbed in study that he is oblivious to his surroundings. This last kind is real interest. It is the kind that every teacher strives to attain.

Every teacher has a threefold task in focusing the consciousness of the pupil upon the lesson being taught. First, he has to gain the attention of the pupil, retain that attention, and then seek to turn attention into real interest. Only in this way can real learning take place. It is commonly known now that the wider the scope of attention, the less lesson content is retained. The purpose of the teacher, therefore, is to narrow the scope of attention so that the pupil is fully focused on the subject of study.

The duty of the teacher is essentially not that of a driver or taskmaster but rather that of a counselor and guide, for in no other way can he hope to gain the right kind of attention.

There are many problems which confront the teacher in the matter of gaining and holding attention. The length of attention fluctuates according to the age of the pupil. This necessarily must be borne in mind if the greatest results are to be achieved in the classroom. It becomes important therefore for the teacher to bear in mind this problem, particularly when dealing with children, for teachers may know whether pupils are interested by the amount of attention given by them. Teachers are also faced with the problem of competing attractions of many kinds, such as a variety of discomforts arising out of the environmental situation, distractions of various sorts inside and outside the classroom, disturbances resulting from intrusions of many kinds, and discipline problems. Then too, knowledge cannot be communicated simply by transfering thoughts from one mind to another as one would pass an object from one hand to another. Ideas must be made attractive enough to the pupil's mind for him to grasp them personally because he wants to do so and because he feels a need for them. In other words, the pupil must be motivated to receive the truth being taught.

These problems can be overcome through careful planning of the teaching situation on the part of the teacher. As far as possible, all outward hindrances must be removed and the best possible learning environment established, free of distractions and disturbances. Wherever possible the lessons should be connected to the natural interests of the class members. Attention can also be attained through the use of real enthusiasm for the work, appropriate facial expressions, gestures, audio-visual aids, and a variety of methods.

3. *The Law of the Language.* This law requires that the language being used in teaching must be common to both teacher and pupil. The same meaning must be evident to both before good communication is possible. This means that the vocabulary of the teacher must be adapted to that of the pupil. Otherwise, the use of words foreign to the pupil's understanding will prohibit the pupil from receiving the message of the lesson.

The teacher can practice this law in a variety of ways. First, he should be sure that his language is simple, that his sentences are short, and that his pronunciation is clear and loud enough to be heard. More important, however, is the language of the pupil. All pupils should be encouraged to speak, to enter into class discussions, for it is often through observation of the pupils' words that the teacher can determine the *extent* of their learning as well as the depth of learning. Teachers should secure from their pupils statements of expression on the lesson in order to learn both their ideas about the lesson and their means of expressing their thoughts. In this way he not only can guide them in comprehension but can also frequently correct false impressions along the way.

Where new words crop up in the development of the lesson, teachers should explain their meaning. This can be done by presenting the idea involved in the work, or it can be illustrated in some way by the use of natural objects or pictures.

The real test of this law is found in the ability of the pupils to retell the lesson in their own words and apply it to their lives. Herein resides the great importance of pupil participation in the lessons being taught.

4. *The Law of the Lesson.* This law requires that the truth to be taught must be learned through truth already known. This is based on the well-known psychological principle of apperception which requires that new truths must be connected in some way with old truths before understanding is possible. The mind comes to know through finding something in past experience which will explain and make meaningful the new experience.

Jesus practiced this law continually by teaching new truths in the light of those things with which His listeners were thoroughly familiar. His parables are good illustrations of this. He taught new and unfamiliar truths in terms of what the people already knew. For example, He compared spiritual water or eternal life with physical water; He compared doors with Himself as the way to heaven.

Every successful teacher today must use this law for effective teaching. It becomes his duty to find out what his pupils already know, both factually and spiritually, so that he can explain the new truths of the Scriptures to them. Such knowledge can be acquired through constant association and fellowship with his pupils, through playing with them, observing them at work and play, talking to former teachers and employees, listening to the language they use, and referring to books on psychology.

This law is particularly useful in lesson preparation and planning. The teacher must try to discover factual and spiritual truths in the lesson which might prove to be unknown to his class and then make plans to clarify them.

Still further, this law is quite helpful in lesson presentation. By using illustrations and applications which fall within the present knowledge and experience of the class, the teacher can gain and hold attention much more effectively. The total result will be greater interest and more effective learning. It goes without saying that better student participation in class work will also result when the teacher plans to use assignments which fall within the scope of the pupil's interest and experience.

5. *The Law of the Teaching Process.* It has been pointed out that one function of the teacher is to motivate and guide the pupil. In doing this the teacher must awaken and set in motion the mind of the pupil, arousing his self-activities. Thus, the fifth law of teaching demands that the teacher excite and direct the self-activities of the pupil and, as a rule, tell him nothing that he can learn for himself. In other words, make the pupil a discoverer of truth — make him learn for himself.

The teaching process demands pupil participation. For a long time it has been felt that the use of the question on the part of the teacher is one of the best ways of accomplishing this. Carefully designed question are greatly helpful in stimulating the thought processes of the pupil. They are also helpful in the development of the truths within the lesson. This questioning process must work in at least two directions: from teacher to pupil, and from pupil to teacher. It is helpful also for pupils to ask one another questions from time to time. In fact, the teacher should strive to keep the questioning atmosphere alive as long as possible in class discussions. This he can do by expecting pupils to participate and setting the kind of classroom climate which makes questions and questioners welcome. Quite often questions can be answered by raising further questions. Or questions might be referred to other members of the class for further study and research.

Pupils should be encouraged to ask questions of themselves, particularly in the study process. Such questions as What? Why? How? When? Where? and Who? are quite helpful in the discovery of truths in the lesson.

Careful assignments result in good student participation.

Since pupils learn by doing, teachers should not only tell pupils what to do but how to do it. Be sure, however, that such doing has a constructive purpose and is closely related to the lesson under consideration.

Guidance in the doing of research is helpful to pupils. Here they learn how to use study tools, such as concordances and dictionaries, in their search for Biblical truth. Thus through individual study the pupils are led to practice the principles of self-activity.

Careful assignments in the way of class projects will develop stewardship attitudes and habits. Participation in the church program leads to the development of Christian service habits and vision among classes of young people.

Following is a list of some of the ways teachers can get action and participation in the use of the Bible and class members during the lesson period:

Use of the Bible

1. The lesson may be read by the teacher
2. The lesson may be read by a *prepared* pupil
3. Give the gist of the lesson by selected verses
4. References may be read at intervals
5. Point out the fulfillment of prophecies which are read
6. Underscore precious promises
7. Quote Scripture from memory
8. Read the lesson in unision
9. Answer questions with Bible verses

Use of the Pupils

1. To tell the lesson story
2. To conduct a quiz
3. Assign problems to be solved
4. Outline lesson on the board during discussion
5. Spelling bee for review
6. Dramatize a lesson
7. Assign opportunities to practice the truth of the lesson
8. Develop a questionnaire; bring questions of their own on the lesson
9. Share personal experiences
10. Organize the class
11. Let a member teach a part of lesson
12. Forums, discussions, debates, models, and projects

Space does not allow the discussion on how to teach the various age groups in the Sunday school. Teachers can refer to a wide variety of departmental manuals now on the market for this information.

Before we leave this subject, one additional word is necessary. To be effective the teaching process should touch the lives and daily living of the pupils. Teachers should teach where their pupils live. This means that teachers should draw from the life-situations of their pupils the materials to use in class instruction, connect these with the Word of God, and then make applications of the truths involved in actual life situations. In this way teaching will be accomplished which will meet needs and will be directly connected to the daily lives of the pupils. In this way greatest effectiveness will be seen in the things that happen in the hearts and lives of the class.

6. *The Law of the Learning Process.* This law concerns the pupil's response to the teacher's efforts. In the teaching process we looked at the efforts of the teacher to motivate the self-activities of the pupil. The law of the learning process concerns the manner in which such activities are used. Therefore, this law demands that the pupil must reproduce in his own mind the truth to be learned. He should not be satisfied with being a "sponge." Knowing comes through thinking, not by simply being told.

Gregory, in *The Seven Laws of Teaching,* points out that there are at least five steps in the learning process:

1. Memorization
2. Understanding
3. Expressing the thought
4. Giving evidence for beliefs
5. Application of knowledge in daily life

Through memory the pupil stores up the facts of knowledge in his mind, but this does not guarantee an understanding of them. Although memorization of the lesson facts is important, it is more important for the student to understand and comprehend that which he memorizes. When he is able to express the thoughts of the lesson in his own words, he has theoretically climbed a step higher in the learning process. Still greater progress is manifested when a pupil can exercise reasoning powers in giving evidence for what he believes about the lesson, to express his convictions and the Scriptural evidence for them. The point of wisdom, however, is not really reached until the student is able to use the truths he has studied in his own life situations.

This law is not only exceedingly practical for the teacher but it is also helpful to the pupil, particularly in his study process. In keeping with the theory of learning expressed in the five steps above, it is useful for the pupil to bear in mind the following list of questions during his period of study:

1. What does the lesson say? (Facts to memorize)
2. What does the lesson mean? (Understanding)
3. How can I express the lesson in my own words?
4. Do I believe what I read? If so, Why? If not, why not?
5. How can I use this knowledge? (Application)

In the final analysis, the lesson has not really been learned until it bears fruit in the hearts and lives of the pupils. Some of the places where the teacher and pupil should expect to see some fruit of their teaching and study includes home relationships, play relationships, social relationships, work situations, and service in the Lord's vineyard. The question is not so much how pupils have grasped lesson truths intellectually but how Christlike they are becoming.

7. *The Law of Review and Application.* This law demands that the completion, test, and confirmation of the work of teaching must be made by review and application. This law is based on the demands of the mind for frequent reviews of the lessons learned. By returning to old truths, one can frequently gain new and vivid understandings of them. This is particularly true of the Bible, which is an inexhaustible resource of truth. It is often the experience of those who read and study its passages over and over again that they see things they never saw before.

Frequent reviews are practical to both teacher and pupil. To the teacher reviews often reveal gaps in both teaching and learning. They may reveal places where greater emphasis is needed than formerly realized, or they may disclose the need for correction of false impressions. They certainly provide the teacher with a means of testing and measuring the results of both teaching and learning. To the pupil, reviews obviously correct memory, deepen the powers of recall, and make available a ready store of knowledge for continued use. Reviews most certainly reveal to both teacher and pupil the various relationships between the lessons of the past, present, and future.

Reviews may be used frequently, in fact at almost any time during the teaching-learning process — at the beginning, in the middle, or at the end of the lesson period. The teacher should determine largely by the relative importance of lesson content how often this should be done.

The process of reviewing may be carried out in a wide variety of ways. Some teachers use written tests for this purpose. Others require a periodic written summary of the lesson. Still others use recitation, oral questions and answers, discussion, and oral summaries.

Too little review work is done in Sunday school teaching. It should be the determination of each teacher to check up at least occasionally on how well he has taught and how thoroughly the pupil has learned.

D. THE TEACHER AND CREATIVE METHODS

1. *Current Trends.* New and exciting things are happening in educational circles both inside and outside the church, particularly in the field of early childhood education. These developments are beginning to revolutionize both theory and practice in church education. New and exciting possibilities largely undreamed of among children have now opened up a new world of learning. The result is that our attitudes toward children's ability to learn are changing. There is now a strong recognition that the learning capacity of the person begins at an early age. Witness to this is seen in the recent developments among public school educators in the Headstart Programs. There is strong recognition now also of the priority which should be given to the home and the way parents can educate their children, preparing them for later instructional experiences in school. We are learning that the first two years of a child's life are the most significant, that he probably learns more during these years than at any other time in his life. Such learning capacity will decrease slightly up to age five and probably levels off at age seven.

These findings are particularly significant for church education both in terms of the Church school and in the home. The young child will learn most at home from mother (or someone else), particularly if that home is Christian. The implications are crystal clear. We must learn to train parents to observe how their children learn and instruct them how to observe this.

We are also learning that the ways we have taught in the past have not always been compatible with the real ways that children learn. We have often imposed adult methods on them, characterized by the statement "Sit still while I instill." Perhaps it will be helpful at this point to contrast the more traditional ways of teaching with those of the more creative ones:

Traditional	*Creative*
1. The teacher is teller	1. The teacher is guide
2. The pupil listens	2. The pupil discovers
3. Content — stresses facts	3. Stress laid on principles
4. Methods — story-telling and lecture	4. Methods — discussion, play, many activities, groupings
5. Physical arrangement — in rows	5. Small and large groups; variety; circle arrangements; activities

If the church is to use some of the more creative techniques there must be a restructuring of the organizational patterns, the development of leadership skills, the improvement of organizational units, the provision of proper facilities geared to open-room concepts, and the expansion of leadership and teacher-training programs — all geared to the new concepts of teaching and learning.

2. *New Developments in Learning Theory.* Many of the changes now being proposed in church education are based on greater knowledge of, and skill in the use of, new discoveries in educational psychology. In 1964 Benjamin Bloom of the University of Chicago proposed the thesis that at least half of all human intelligence is developed by age four. This was reflected in the book *Stability and Change in Human Characteristics.* This thesis was very largely supported by White and Watts at Harvard and revealed in the book *Major Influences on the Development of Young Children.* This view has gained rather wide acceptance among educators in this country.

Major questions were raised: What must we teach? How are we to educate? What is child learning? Many answers to these questions were supplied by Jean Piaget, the famous European psychologist. For more than fifty years he has been studying the development of intelligence in children. His work had its greatest impact in the domain of the new curricula that were the main educational thrust of the sixties. One illustration of this is the "new math." Less well known, perhaps, but equally important, are the implications of his work for the practice of teaching. His main theory in working with children was in the "semiclinical interview," a relatively nondirective open discussion with a child that deals with a particular issue or problem. He used questions posed by the children themselves as a starting point. He thus discovered their real interests. This has led to what may be called "thematic education," that is, instruction in all subjects by relating them to a common theme. This is one of the features of the current emphasis on the open classroom. Piaget also stressed the importance of starting where the child is in terms of language and conceptual development. This focuses on the importance of keeping verbalisms and abstractions to a minimum in working with children. In early years children need to concretize their language by relating words to things. They also need close personal relationships in learning experiences.

One of the emphases in Piaget, however, that some American psychologists differ with is his denial of the ability of the child to do abstract thinking until he reaches age seven. Because of extreme cultural factors in our society many believe that our children are able to do abstract thinking long before age seven. Among those advocating this possibility is Jerome Bruner who says that young children are often underestimated in their ability to learn. He advanced the premise that "any subject can be taught effectively in some intellectually honest way to any child at any state of development," at least among school age children.[1] Significant work to support this thesis is currently underway at several places in the United States. Oscar Moore at the University of Pittsburgh found that three-year-old children can learn to write stories on a coded key typewriter with the use of pictures. Significant work has been revealed on experiments at the High/Scope Research Foundation, Ypsilanti, Michigan, which show that educators and parents are learning how to give even crib-bound infants an educational head start. Thus, some form of school can and should be provided for small children.

Dr. Kagan at Harvard did research on the power of infants to think and found that babies react much like adults when confronted with new situations. Burton White, also at Harvard, points out that year two is very critical for the child. At the Harvard Pre-School Project, 1965, they discovered through experiments that three-year-olds have relatively the same cluster of abilities as do six-year-olds. In fact, they discovered that the period between ten months and eighteen months is the most significant period in the child's life. The role of the mother becomes very significant in guiding the child's learning experiences. From all of this we learn that the single most critical factor in any child's learning is the home and the role played by the mother or any other caretaker.

Great significance for church education and the Christian home are apparent. The great need, therefore, is to help prepare parents to be Christian and to give their young children the right kind of general and Christian instruction at a very early age.

The way this new theory is coming out in educational practice can be seen in current usages of the open classroom. Such usage is based on the premise that most of what we know has come through the pursuit of our interests and through our relations with those with whom we live and work. Perhaps curiosity and its satisfaction may have a better claim to time than does the typical routine of a controlled class situation as practiced under the more traditional situations. In the open classroom children do learn the basic skills. They may learn by lying down or curling up. Others may learn through projects involving carpentry, artwork, or weaving. For small children, play activities provide the natural settings for learning.

The basic premise of the open classroom is a faith in the child's desire to learn and in his ability to assume responsibility for choice. This will require more emphasis on guidance and less on teacher control. Children learn better from guides and fellow explorers than from authoritarian leaders. Greater freedom leads to greater interest and more involvement, and thus to better learning. To educate children who love to learn, we must recognize

[1]Jerome S. Bruner, *The Process of Education* (Cambridge, Mass.: Harvard University Press, 1960).

that both love and learning flow from the conditions of real life — the possibilities of choice, self-responsibility, and the freedom to relate to the people around us.

The way all of this comes out in the teaching-learning process might be pictured as follows:

For children:[2]

Listening	– get attention, interest – focusing on	knowledge
Exploring	– involves searching and involvement	understanding
	– provides options, choices, cooperation	
Discovery	– sees meaning and value under the leadership of the Holy Spirit	
	– involves self-discovery, not telling	attitudes
Appropriating	– makes learning personal	appreciations
	– implications for own life, behavior	
Responsibility	– lives the truth, uses it	action

For youth and adults:[3]

Familiarization	– deals primarily with facts – gives	information
	– student rather passive at this point	
Feedback	– tests information	
	– the student responds, inquires	understanding
	– use of questions, alternatives	
Exploration	– more pupil participation	attitudes
	– discovery through small groups	appreciations
	– search for meaning	appropriation
Responsibility	– applications of truth, usage	
	– pupil fully active	action
	– deals with meanings, applications	

Let us not forget that in all of these learning processes the work of the Holy Spirit is apparent. He is present to activate the teaching and the learning, bringing motivation, enlightenment, and application to the heart and life.

3. *Teaching Methods and Creativity.* In general, older and traditional methods of teaching have been largely teacher-centered with pupils on the periphery. The teacher is active and the pupils primarily are passive. The teacher works and the pupils listen and observe. The teacher is expected to prepare thoroughly through study and planning, and this is expected to result in capturing and holding the attention of the pupils.

In the more creative approach to teaching and learning, the teacher guides effective learning activities. The situation is oriented to the learner rather than to the teacher. Instead of using a mere handful of methods, such as stories, memory work, music, visual aids, and workbooks (good in themselves), a wide variety of methods and groupings are used. These will be referred to again.

This newer concept of teaching has been called *total session teaching.* Three aspects of function characterize this approach. (1) The entire department time is given to teaching and setting

[2]See Charles T. Smith, *Ways to Plan and Organize Your Sunday School,* chapter 2 for more details on this.
[3]See David A. Stoop, *Ways to Help Them Learn.* Gospel Light Publications, chapter 3 for more details on this.

the stage for learning. (2) All the learning activities for each session are related to one subject. This shows the thematic aspect of the work. (3) The objective in each session is to involve the pupils in learning by discovery. Teaching techniques in this plan call for team teaching on the part of the department leader and all the other workers in the unit.

In the traditional way of doing things, teaching sessions are divided roughly into two parts. The first part of the session is devoted to an assembly or an opening exercise which runs from five to twenty minutes in length. The second part of the period is devoted to teaching the lesson in classes very largely separated permanently from the rest.

USING THE FAMILIAR FACILITIES

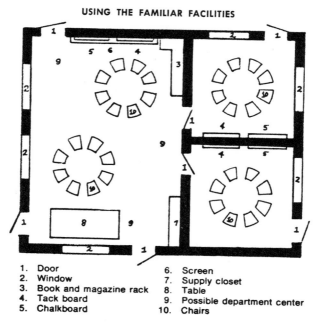

1. Door	6. Screen
2. Window	7. Supply closet
3. Book and magazine rack	8. Table
4. Tack board	9. Possible department center
5. Chalkboard	10. Chairs

In the more creative approach to teaching the open room concept is employed together with team teaching procedures. The time involved may be used in two general ways. In one approach the session is divided (at least for children) into three parts: (1) Bible study, (2) Bible sharing/planning, and (3) Bible-learning activities. In the first block of time children are divided into small rather permanent class groups. The moment the pupil arrives at Sunday school he starts to learn. He listens to the Bible story and its application to his life is contemplated. This builds readiness for Bible learning.

OPEN ROOM ENVIRONMENT

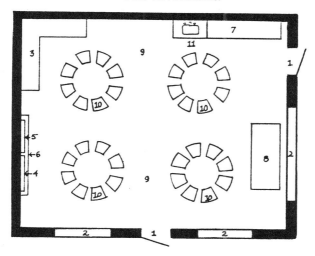

1. Door	7. Supply closet
2. Window	8. Table
3. Book and magazine rack	9. Possible department
4. Tack board	center
5. Chalkboard	10. Chairs
6. Screen	11. Sink

From this period the child joins a large group (not over 25-30) for activity in which he enjoys worship experiences and makes plans for the third part of the session. Both the Bible story and the Bible materials will be related to a chosen activity during the third part of the session in which nonpermanent groups start work on Bible-learning activities designed to reinforce the Bible study period. Pupil selection of activities will be made on the basis of personal interests. Such activities may touch a wide variety of experiences which utilize all the "senses" a child has. In a home-centered world, for example, the child plays out familiar experiences where he feels at home and learns about God's family and what it means to obey his parents. At a nature table he learns about God's wonders and comes to see that all things were made by Him. Sharing experiences and materials at an art center helps the pupil to learn to share with others. Block building yields opportunities for learning cooperation, developing talents and concepts, and teaching Bible life. Concepts of sharing, cooperation, love, kindness, helping, creation, and thankfulness can be taught and learned.

For those who want to follow the more traditional line of approach, or who have space problems, the teaching session may be divided into two parts instead of three. The first half could combine the Bible story with Bible-learning activities, involving small groups, and the second half could be devoted to Bible-sharing activities, involving the large groups. This plan can be used to adapt the more creative methods recommended here to a building where space is limited and more traditional curriculum materials are used.

The same general principles apply to the operation of teaching sessions for youth and adults. Under the old plan, classes meet for assembly and then go to separate rooms for teaching periods. The creative approach involves youth and adults in "total hour" experiences. Both large and small groups are used in this approach. Worship, study, and fellowship are all correlated into one unified session. Teachers and pupils move from one group (large or small) to other groups as called for by the purposes involved. Thus, the use of a wide variety of groupings for youth and adults provides for the same freedom of choice, participation, flexibility, and involvement as those methods employed among the children.

Procedures recommended above call for the use of open room situations.

In churches where permanent walls and rooms are already present, the open room situation can be achieved either by removing nonweight-bearing walls and/or removing doors permanently to leave open spaces which will allow open observation and freedom of movement in the room.

It is also important to note that creative methods and open room techniques require team teaching and careful advance preparation on the part of workers. Weekly sessions of workers in department meetings to plan Sunday sessions become imperative if proper cooperation and correlation of teaching precedures is to be achieved.

For those teachers who are interested in exploring teaching methods more creative in character consult the lists of teaching methods contained in Appendix VIII.[4]

E. THE TEACHER AND HIS DUTIES

1. *In General.* Much of what was said on the importance of the teacher and his work will apply directly at this point, but perhaps a general listing of such duties will be helpful:

[4]For more details on these matters consult the ICL teacher and leader manuals published by Gospel Light Publications, Glendale, California.

1. Keep in training for your task by keeping physically fit, mentally alert, and spiritually alive
2. Have a definite time, place, and object of study
3. Cooperate with all officers of the school
4. Attend all monthly departmental meetings possible
5. Attend church services and prayer meetings
6. Stay in touch with absentee workers and members
7. Visit the sick, careless, and indifferent
8. Get your class members to visit also
9. Keep your eyes open for new pupils
10. Walk with God; be natural, friendly, cheerful, cordial, tender, patient, serious, but enthusiastic
11. Be loyal to God and to the church
12. Do not become discouraged

2. *On Sunday.* Sunday provides the teacher with his greatest opportunities. He should make the most of them. Included in his list of duties for that day are:

1. Be present at least 15 minutes early
2. See that your room is in order; get your nerves quiet
3. Greet your pupils as they come and be alert for any needs
4. Plan carefully your pre-session activities
5. Sit with your class during opening assembly
6. Take an active part in the services
7. If your class has the program, join in with them
8. March to the room with your class
9. Organize your class to get things done
10. Stay "on the beam" and teach the Word
11. Teach for a verdict; do not be side-lined
12. Introduce all visitors and new pupils
13. Where used, sit with your class during closing assembly
14. Be sure class officers perform their duties
15. Report absentees to proper authorities

3. *During the Month.* The teacher should be busy through the month with his work and his class. This involves certain duties, such as:

1. Be present at workers' conferences
2. Attend departmental sessions
3. Check on literature for your class
4. Visit the members as much as possible
5. Read, study, and prepare yourself for your great work
6. Attend conferences, institutes, and conventions as your time will allow
7. Cooperate with your superintendents
8. Always be ready with a report of your work
9. Write notes and letters to pupils who are sick and absent

4. *The Organized Class.* While the duties of a Sunday school teacher fall into the above categories already discussed, it is also true that many duties have to do with the class as a whole. Obviously, the teacher cannot perform the many duties of classes and class officers, so it becomes necessary to organize the class for most effective results.

Beginning with juniors, teachers will find it possible to get good results from organized classes. Obvious advantages include the realization of better cooperation, training in leadership responsibility, greater service, enlarged enrollment, increased attendance, and fellowship. Some disadvantages are the dangers of classes becoming independent and the usurping of teaching time with formalities. Strong leadership on the part of the teacher, however, can obviate the difficulties.

There appear to be two general ways to organize classes: informal and formal systems. Entzminger (see page 47) suggests an informal system where the teacher, president, secretary and group leaders comprise the organization. The president presides at all meetings. Class work is done during the week and is comprised primarily of visitation and soul winning. Group leaders guide their respective groups in the work of the class. Very little social life engages the attention of classes under this plan.

Peirce and Honderick (see page 125ff) have suggested a more formal plan for class organization. In small schools with very small classes, officers are comprised of teacher, president, secretary-treasurer, group captains for 3-6 members, and a few committees as needed. A class of 30-60 members will need a teacher, president, vice-president in charge of membership, secretary, treasurer, enrollment secretary, committees as needed, and group captains for every 3-6 members.

Large classes will call for major officers and committees but greater organization of members. Group captains can head large segments of the class and group leaders work with 3-6 members in each segment.

The organized class will also choose a name, a motto, a Bible text, and will operate by a class constitution.

5. *Maintaining Discipline.* The problem of discipline actually is everyone's problem, but it centers largely in the classroom. This focuses attention on the need for the teacher to have a good approach to it.

The best approach to the solution of discipline problems in the Sunday school is a preventative one — that is, maintain a program and leadership of such high caliber that discipline problems will be the exception rather than the rule in Sunday school. A well-planned, efficiently-organized, and well-run school ordinarily will witness a minimum of discipline cases.

The general approach to the solution of discipline problems has been suggested as follows:

1. Study the problem thoroughly first
2. Establish law and order in the program
3. Correct administrative procedures where necessary
4. Improve the curriculum
5. Insist on adequate and thorough teacher preparation
6. Improve facilities and equipment where needed
7. Get parents to cooperate
8. Be faithful with prayer, genuine love, and praise

Thorough study to get the facts in the case demands an identification of the causes involved. Such causes are often more far-flung than realized at first. The following list helps to illustrate this:

Causes Among Personnel

1. Untrained teachers and workers
2. Bad teacher-pupil relationships
3. Poor teaching techniques
4. Lack of proper supervision
5. Unconscious favoritism shown
6. Odd mannerisms, peculiarities in speech and dress
7. Tardiness and talkativeness
8. Bad attitudes

Causes in the Facilities

1. Shortage of space and equipment
2. Rooms which are too small
3. Rooms which are too large
4. Improper ventilation
5. Lack of provisions for wraps
6. Lack of attractiveness
7. Lack of neatness and cleanliness
8. Poor seating arrangements

Causes in Administration

1. Improper age groups
2. Improper assignment of workers
3. Neglect of law and order
4. Improper curriculum
5. Disturbances and distractions permitted
6. Poor management of supplies, records, and officer personnel

Causes in the Pupil

1. Derives more satisfaction from wrong conduct
2. Full of energy and curiosity
3. Desires more recognition
4. Never has been taught what is right
5. Fails to see importance of Sunday school
6. Might have come without eating breakfast
7. Home background difficult
8. Not popular with other pupils
9. Poor physical conditions

Individual teachers might try some of the following suggestions in dealing with specific cases:

1. While you teach, stand by the pupil who is disturbing the class
2. Direct questions to the disturbing pupil
3. Pause until quiet is restored
4. Have a private talk with the pupil
5. Have a private talk with the parents
6. Let the class make rules for handling discipline problems
7. Insist on good order
8. Be patient but firm, yet gentle
9. Consider the age of the pupil
10. Try to discover and understand the cause

11. Turn disturbing situations into teaching situations by relating them to the lesson

12. Above all, let your pupils know that you love them

SUGGESTED READING — CHAPTER 7*

Anderson, *Charting the Course*

Benson, C. H., *The Christian Teacher*
     Introduction to Child Study

Betts, *How to Teach Religion*

Bowen, *Strange Scriptures that Perplex the Western Mind*

Byrne, *My SS Handbook, For the Teacher*, No. 1

Caldwell, *Teaching That Makes a Difference*

Campbell, *When Do Teachers Teach*

Corzine, *Look at Learning*
     Teaching to Win and Develop

Dobbins, *The Improvement of Teaching in the Sunday School*
     The School in Which We Teach, Chapter 8

DuBois, *The Point of Contact*

Eavey, *Principles of Teaching for Christian Teachers*

Edge, *Teaching for Results*

Eggleston, *The Use of the Story in Religious Education*

Entzminger, *How to Organize and Administer a Great Sunday School*, Chapter 7

ETTA, *A Guide for pedagogy*, Unit V
     Apt to Teach
     Teaching Techniques for Sunday School, Unit V, revised

Gettys, *How to Teach the Bible*

Gregory, *The Seven Laws of Teaching*

Gunderson, *The Great Opportunity of the Sunday School*

Horne, *The Master Teacher*

Hurst, *And He Gave Teachers*

Lawrance, *My Message to Sunday School Workers*, Chapters 3-10

Lebar, *Children in the Bible School*

Pearlman, *Successful Sunday School Teaching*

Peirce and Honderick, *Going with the Gospel*, Chapter 4

Plummer, *The Soul Winning Teacher*

Price, *Jesus the Teacher*

Sutherland, *How to Run a Sunday School*, Chapters 4-9, 11-15

Traina, *Methodical Bible Study*

Vieth, *Teaching for Christian Living*
     The Church School, Chapter 9

* See updated Bibliography at back of book.

CURRENT BOOKS — ARRANGED BY AGE GROUPS

*Books recommended for church libraries

Early Childhood

Axline, Virginia. *Dibs in Search of Self*. Boston: Houghton Mifflin, 1966.

Chamberlain, Eugene, Robert Harty, Saxe Adams. *Preschoolers at Church*. Nashville: Convention Press, 1969.

Dreikurs, Rudolf. *Children: The Challenge*. New York: Duell, Sloan, and Pearce, 1964.

*Ginott, Haim G. *Between Parent and Child*. New York: Macmillan Company, 1965.

*Heron, Frances Dunlap. *Kathy Ann, Kindergartner*. Nashville: Abingdon Press, 1955.

Hymes, James L., Jr. *The Child Under Six*. Englewood Cliffs, N. J.: Prentice-Hall, Inc., 1966.

Hymes, James L., Jr. *Teaching the Child Under Six*. Columbus: Charles E. Merrill Publishing Co., 1968.

Kellogg, Rhoda and Scott O'Dell. *The Psychology of Children's Art*. San Diego: CRM-Random House Publications, 1967.

LeShan, Eda. *The Conspiracy Against Childhood*. New York: Atheneum, 1967.

Lowenfeld, Margaret. *Play in Childhood*. New York: John Wylie and Sons, 1967.

Children

*American Sunday School Union. *The Teacher Taught*. Philadelphia: American Sunday School Union, 1861.

Ashby, La Verne. "Primaries and Church Membership." *Baptist Training Union Magazine*, March 1970, pp. 56-59.

*Baker, Delores and Rives, Elsie. *Teaching the Bible to Primaries*. Nashville: Convention Press, 1964.

Barnes, Albert. *Barnes' Notes on the New Testament*. Grand Rapids: Kregel Publications, 1962.

Barth, Roland S. "When Children Enjoy School." *Childhood Education*, Vol. 46, no. 4, January 1970, pp. 195-200.

Bayly, Joseph. *Christian Education Trends*. Elgin, Ill.: David C. Cook Publishing Co., June 2, 1969.

*Bolton, Barbara. *Ways to Help Them Learn, Children: Grades 1-6*. Glendale, Calif.: Regal Books, 1971.

Broman, Betty L. "Too Much Shushing—Let Children Talk." *Childhood Education,* vol. 46, no. 3, December 1969. pp. 132-134.

*Bowman, Locke E. *Straight Talk About Teaching in Today's Church.* Philadelphia: Westminster Press, 1968.

*Butler, J. Donald. *Religious Education. The Foundation and Practice of Nurture.* New York: Harper and Row Publishers, 1962.

*Chamberlain, Eugene and Fullbright, Robert G. *Children's Sunday School Work.* Nashville: Convention Press, 1969.

Clendinning, B. A., Jr. ed. *Family Ministry in Today's Church.* Nashville: Convention Press, 1971.

Clouse, Bonnidell. "Psychosocial Origins of Stability in the Christian Faith." *Christianity Today.* September 25, 1970, pp. 12-14.

*Cober, Kenneth L. *The Church's Teaching Ministry.* Valley Forge, Pa.: Judson Press, 1964.

Cooperative Curriculum Project. *A Design for Teaching-Learning.* St. Louis: Bethany Press, 1967.

*Cully, Kendig Brubaker, ed. *Basic Writings in Christian Education.* Philadelphia: Westminster Press, 1960.

DeJong, Norman. *Education in the Truth.* Nutley, N. J.: Presbyterian and Reformed Publishing Co., 1969.

*Doan, Eleanor L., ed. *431 Quotes from the Notes of Henrietta C. Mears.* Glendale, Calif.: Regal Books, 1970.

*Eavey, C. B. *History of Christian Education.* Chicago: Moody Press, 1964.

Fraser, David W. "What's Ahead for Preadolescence?" *Childhood Education,* vol. 46, no. 1, September-October, 1969, pp. 24-28.

Frymier, Jack R. *Learning Centers: Children on Their Own.* Washington, D.C.: The Association for Childhood Education International, 1970.

*Gregory, John Milton. *The Seven Laws of Teaching,* Revised Edition. Grand Rapids: Baker Book House, 1962.

*Harty, Robert A. *Children in Church Training.* Nashville: Convention Press, 1969.

*Horne, Herman Harell. *Jesus—The Master Teacher.* Grand Rapids: Kregel Publications, 1964.

*Ingle, Clifford. *Children and Conversion.* Nashville: Broadman Press, 1970.

*Jaarsma, Cornelius. *Human Development, Learning and Teaching.* Grand Rapids: Wm. B. Eerdmans Publishing Co., 1959.

*Jackson, B. F., Jr., ed. *Communication-Learning for Churchmen, Volume 1.* Nashville: Abingdon Press, 1968.

James, Howard. *Children in Trouble: A National Scandal.* New York: David McKay Co., 1970.

Jaroff, Leon, ed., Michaelis, Ingrid and others. "The American Family: Future Uncertain," *Time,* December 28, 1970, pp. 34-39.

Larson, Bruce. *No Longer Strangers.* Waco: Word Books, 1971.

*LeBar, Lois E. *Education That is Christian.* Westwood, N. J.: Fleming H. Revell Co., 1958.

*Lederach, Paul M. *Reshaping the Teaching Ministry.* Scottdale, Pa.: Herald Press, 1968.

LeShan, Eda J. *The Conspiracy Against Childhood.* New York: Atheneum, 1967.

McNeil, Elton B. "The Changing Children of Preadolescence." *Childhood Education,* January 1970. pp. 181-185.

MollenKott, Virginia Ramey. "Teachers, Students and Selfishness." *Christianity Today.* April 24, 1970, pp. 13-15.

Osborn, D. Keith and Hale, William. "Television Violence." *Childhood Education,* Vol. 45, no. 9, May 1969, pp. 505-507.

Pearce, Lucia. "Environmental Structure: A Third Partner in Education." *Educational Technology,* September 15, 1968, p. 13.

*Price, John M. *Jesus the Teacher.* Nashville: Convention Press, 1946.

*Rozell, Ray. *Talks on Sunday School Teaching.* Grand Rapids: Zondervan Publishing House, 1956.

Scripture Press Ministries, Christian Education Division. *Research Report on Sunday School Teachers.* Wheaton, Ill.: Scripture Press Publications, 1971.

*Solderholm, Marjorie. *Explaining Salvation to Children.* Minneapolis: Free Church Publications, 1962.

Smith, Wilbur. "Yesterday, Today and Forever." *Decision* magazine, May 1971, pp. 1, 12.

Terbeek, William R. *Frontiersman of Faith.* "Story of the Prophets." Teacher's Study Guide and Manual, Cathedral Films, n.d.

*Ulich, Robert. *A History of Religious Education.* New York: University Press, 1968.

Warner, Wayne M. "Making Moving More Meaningful." *Home Life,* August 1970, pp. 28-30.

*Wyckoff, C. Campbell. *Theory and Design of Christian Education-Curriculum.* Philadelphia: Westminster Press, 1961.

*Zuck, Roy. *The Holy Spirit in Your Teaching.* Wheaton: Scripture Press Publications, 1963.

*Zuck, Roy B. and Getz, Gene A. *Christian Youth, An In-Depth Study.* Chicago: Moody Press, 1968.

Youth

*Benson, Dennis. *The Now Generation.* Richmond: John Knox Press, 1969.

*Bowman, Locke E., Jr. *Straight Talk About Teaching in Today's Church.* Philadelphia: Westminster, 1967.

*Burton, Janet. *Guiding Youth.* Nashville: Convention Press, 1969.

Duvall, Evelyn M. *Today's Teen-Agers.* New York: Association Press, 1966.

Erikson, Erik H. *Identity: Youth and Crisis.* New York: W. W. Norton and Co. 1968.

*Ezell, Mancil. *Youth in Bible Study/New Dynamics.* Nashville: Convention Press, 1970.

Gesell, Arnold, Ilg, Frances L., and Ames, Louise Bates. *Youth: The Years from Ten to Sixteen.* New York: Harper and Brothers, 1956.

*Joy, Donald M. *Meaningful Learning in the Church.* Winona Lake: Light and Life Press, 1969.

Leonard, George B. *Education and Ecstasy.* New York: Delacorte Press, 1968.

*Leypoldt, Martha M. *40 Ways to Teach in Groups.* Valley Forge: Judson Press, 1967.

*Little, Sara. *Learning Together in the Christian Fellowship.* Richmond: John Knox Press, 1956.

McBurney, James H. and Mills, G. E. *Argumentation and Debate.* New York: McMillan, 1964.

McLuhan, Marshall. *Understanding Media: The Extensions of Man.* New York: McGraw-Hill Book Co., 1964.

Mead, Margaret. *Culture and Commitment.* New York: Doubleday and Co., 1970.

*Murphree, T. Garvice and Dorothy. *Understanding Youth.* Nashville: Convention Press, 1969.

*Rogers, Carl R. *Freedom to Learn.* Columbus: Charles E. Merrill Pub. Co., 1969.

Schaeffer, Francis A. *The God Who Is There.* Downers Grove, Ill.: Inter-Varsity Press, 1968.

*Sisemore, John T. *Blueprint for Teaching.* Nashville: Broadman Press, 1964.

*Snyder, Ross. *Youth and Their Culture.* Nashville: Abingdon, 1969.

*Stewart, Chas. W. *Adolescent Religion.* Nashville: Abingdon, 1967.

Strang, Ruth. *The Adolescent Views Himself.* New York: McGraw-Hill, 1957.

*Strommen, Merton P. *Profiles of Church Youth.* St. Louis: Concordia, 1963.

*Wald, Oletta. *The Joy of Discovery.* Minneapolis: Bible Banner Press, 1956.

*Zuck, Roy B. *The Holy Spirit in Your Teaching.* Scripture Press, 1968.

*Zuck, Roy B. and Getz, Gene. *Christian Youth: an In-Depth Study.* Chicago: Moody, 1968.

Adults

Brown, James W., at al. *AV Instruction: Media and Methods.* New York: McGraw-Hill Book Company, 1969.

*Coleman, Lyman. *Groups in Action.* Newton, Pennsylvania: The Halfway House, 1968.

*Edge, Findley. *Helping the Teacher.* Nashville: Broadman Press, 1959.

*———————.*Teaching for Results.* Nashville: Broadman Press, 1956.

*Ford, LeRoy. *Primer for Teachers and Leaders.* Nashville: Broadman Press, 1963.

*———————. *Tools for Teaching and Training.* Nashville: Broadman Press, 1961.

*———————. *Using the Case Study in Teaching and Training.* Nashville: Broadman Press, 1970.

*———————. *Using the Lecture in Teaching and Training.* Nashville: Broadman Press, 1968.

*———————. *Using the Panel in Teaching and Training.* Nashville: Broadman Press, 1971.

*Howard, Walden, ed. *Groups That Work.* Grand Rapids: Zondervan Publishing House, 1967.

Larson, Bruce. *Dare to Live Now.* Grand Rapids: Zondervan Publishing House, 1967.

*———————. *The Emerging Church.* Grand Rapids: Zondervan Publishing House, 1970.

———————. *Living on the Growing Edge.* Grand Rapids: Zondervan Publishing House, 1971.

———————. *Marriage is for Living.* Grand Rapids: Zondervan Publishing House, 1968.

———————. *No Longer Strangers.* Grand Rapids: Zondervan Publishing House, 1971.

———————. *Setting Men Free.* Grand Rapids: Zondervan Publishing House, 1967.

*Leypoldt, Martha. *Forty Ways to Teach in Groups.* Valley Forge: Judson Press, 1967.

*———————. *Learning Is Change.* Valley Forge: Judson Press, 1971

Miller, Keith. *Habitation of Dragons.* Waco: Word Books, 1970.

*————————. *The Second Touch.* Waco: Word Books, 1967.

————————. *The Taste of New Wine.* Waco: Word Books, 1965.

*Morrison, Eleanor. *Creative Teaching.* Prentice Hall, 1963.

*Pierce, Rice A. *Leading Dynamic Bible Study.* Nashville: Broadman Press, 1969.

*Richards, Lawrence. *Creative Bible Teaching.* Chicago: Moody Press, 1970.

*Wald, Oletta. *The Joy of Discovery.* Minneapolis: Bible Banner Press, 1956.

THE WORK OF THE DIRECTOR OF
SOCIAL LIFE AND FELLOWSHIP

OUTLINE FOR CHAPTER 8

(Social Life, Recreation, Fellowship)

A. SOCIAL LIFE AND RECREATION IN THE CHURCH
1. The Need for a Church Program of Social Activities
2. The Close Relationship of Spiritual and Social Life
3. The Place of the Sunday School As a Social Institution
4. To Have or Not to Have
5. Leadership

B. THE DIRECTOR OF SOCIAL LIFE AND FELLOWSHIP
1. Qualifications and Selection
2. Guiding Principles for the Director

C. THE PROGRAM OF SOCIAL LIFE AND RECREATION
1. A Written Program and Calendar
2. Play As a Teaching Method
3. Evaluation of the Program
4. In Small Churches
5. Principles in the Social Program
6. Planning Social Activities

D. FELLOWSHIP AND SOCIAL LIFE
1. Definitions
2. Christian Love and Social Life
3. Methods of Developing Fellowship
4. Other Concerns

8 | THE WORK OF THE DIRECTOR OF SOCIAL LIFE AND FELLOWSHIP

(Social Life, Recreation, Fellowship)

A. SOCIAL LIFE AND RECREATION IN THE CHURCH

1. *The Need for a Church Program of Social Activities.* Most peoples have sought some type of recreation. In the satisfaction of this desire, men have often chosen that which destroys rather than that which re-creates. One need only recall what history records of Nero and his destruction of human life to see an example. Today the modern bullfight illustrates this, although this form of recreation is not as common as a generation ago. These things show that the desire for recreation is certainly strong in mankind and many times this desire is misdirected, today as it has been in the past.

Our modern civilization has brought with it problems along this line which need to be solved. These problems will either defeat society or society will have to defeat them. First, shorter working hours mean more leisure time, and leisure creates the problem of its proper use. Since much leisure will be spent in some type of recreational activity, it is important to channel it toward worthy ends.

Second, the monotony of work in this machine age gives little opportunity for self-expression. Recreation and social life with its wide variety of offerings provides many opportunities for self-expression. Where these are not readily available, many force the means through which to channel their initiative.

Third, modern means of communication put us in contact with multitudes of busy, nervous people and thus we have moved farther from native tranquility into a mode of life characterized by strain and turmoil. These are some of the reasons why, more than ever before, people need and are seeking various forms of recreation.

The real problem, however, is that this need has resulted in misdirected use of leisure, either in idleness or in means of recreation which are detrimental to the individual as well as to society. Idleness leads to listlessness, apathy, and indifference, and this must be taken into account when a program of recreation is being considered for the church. Certainly this presents a challenge.

Furthermore, the movie industry has capitalized on providing entertainment for a recreation-hungry public. Millions attend the theaters every week spending millions of dollars. Dance halls are crowded night after night and roadside "dine and dance" places are the common thing of our day. We have had evidence from the director of the Federal Bureau of Investigation, J. Edgar Hoover, that this type of entertainment has definitely lowered the moral tone of our society and has been directly responsible for thousands of crimes. These facts should cause our Sunday schools to awaken to the need and to plan to do something definite to curb this onslaught of evil.

2. *Close Relationship of Spiritual and Social Life.* We have considered the effect of recreation upon the individual and society from the negative side. Now we shall consider something of the positive side of this subject. Professor Norman Richardson states that: "The permanency of Christian or any other form of civilization is directly dependent upon its ability to use its leisure for morally constructive purposes. To create leisure involves the responsibility of making it a spiritual asset."[1] It is impossible for one to be engaged in morally hurtful recreation and to enjoy sweet fellowship with Christ at the same time. Since this is true, it is the duty of the Sunday school to supply a positive Christian atmosphere for a recreational program. Let us consider some of the steps to accomplish this aim.

First, the pastor, Sunday school superintendent, and the presidents of other church organizations should meet and formulate policies and make plans to see that the organizations receive proper consideration. In this way, there should be proper balance in recreational activities and in their expression in the various groups within the church. It must be remembered that the Sunday school should play a dominate role in the program, once it is set up, but that the activities must not overlap and duplicate where some other church agency is functioning.

Secondly, the social program should be planned for the entire year and adopted at the church's first business meeting of the year. This will avoid confusion and give definite aim and direction to every department of the church work. It might be well to have a church calendar which will inform the entire congregation as to the year's program.

Third, it must be understood by all that the program of recreation is to be subservient to the deeper spiritual needs of the church. It is not only to serve as a "drawing card" to win outsiders but it is primarily to fill a real need for the Christians already within the church. So many are apt to think of recreation in terms of a specific entity divorced from any vital connection with the ultimate goal

[1]Norman E. Richardson, *The Church at Play* (Nashville, Tenn.: The Abingdon Press, 1922), p. 25.

of the church. For this reason, the social-life program of the church should be well in hand at all times and under definite church control.

3. *Place of the Sunday School As a Social Institution.* Weigle has suggested that the Sunday school can play a very vital role in the spiritual development of social consciousness. He has listed several things which can be done to make the Sunday school a social institution.

1. It can provide social life and enjoyment
2. It can maintain a social motive and atmosphere in its work of instruction
3. It can give its pupils a concrete understanding of social facts, and develop within them high social ideals (through study of Christian biographies, Church history, missions, social conditions and problems)
4. It can give its pupils something to do, and organize them in actual social service[2]

4. *To have Or Not to Have.* Whether or not a church should plan an extensive recreational and social program is dependent upon a number of factors. Certainly the need which actually exists in the community and church should be considered. These needs might be recognized as playgrounds and areas both inside and out. Of course the leadership available is a second important factor, not to speak of the ability of each church to finance the entire project.

These factors will help the local church determine the scope of its program. It may be that a gymnasium is unnecessary or it may be a duplication of a program already available through some other channel, such as schools and youth groups. It is quite possible that the church can cooperate with some other semi-religious group in providing certain facilities. It may be found possible to provide homemade equipment for the program.

Where the local church decides to provide a program, adequate financing should be given in the church budget. Where this is not possible, perhaps special donations, contributions, or pledges can be secured from other sources.

Each church will have to make a decision about questionable recreational practices and should avoid all practices which are not in harmony with Biblical and Christian principles and ethics.

5. *Leadership.* It goes without saying that all leadership in this area should be thoroughly Christian. In addition, leaders need to be adequately trained for the task. This means not only a well-trained and qualified director or committee, but the many helpers

[2]Luther A. Weigle, *The Pupil and the Teacher* (New York: Eaton and Mains, 1911), p. 186 ff.

and assistants in the program study should as well. Areas for such study and training should include the Christian philosophy of play, recreation and social life, methods, materials, and skills.

B. THE DIRECTOR OF SOCIAL LIFE AND FELLOWSHIP

1. *Qualification and Selection.* The point of greatest weakness with many church programs of recreation is found in the lack of effective supervision. In order to obtain good supervision, there should be a director who is responsible for carrying out the program which the pastor and church officers have outlined. The director should not only be qualified in this field but he should also be in love with the work. It follows naturally that he should be both an officer and member of the church. This should give him the proper attitude toward the importance of his job.

In considering the director of recreation it is needless to say that such a job requires one's full time. Naturally, in smaller churches the director is a volunteer worker, but in the larger churches he should be a paid member on the working staff. Many churches, who have had their eyes opened as to the importance of this department, have looked favorably upon it because it is one of the soundest investments the church can make in an attempt to retain its young people throughout the crucial intermediate years. By this plan they are made ready at maturity to be directed, as trained young men and women, into the adult congregation of the church, where they can continue in the same spirit of enthusiasm and cooperation, adding new life and vitality in the work of the kingdom of God.

Regardless of whether the director is on a paid staff or is serving on a volunteer basis, or whether they are a man or woman, there are some things that are essential to every leader of this kind. The first and most important is that he be born again and spiritually committed. Second, he must have a passion for lost souls and manifest an enthusiastic cooperation with the evangelistic program of the church. Richardson has commented at length on the responsibilities of the director by saying that:

> The director of social and recreational activities in a local church has a distinct responsibility and opportunity. He needs to see his task as a whole. He should also study it in its relation to all of the other aspects of the program of the church. It is not a mark of the highest leadership to drive ahead with his social and recreational program regardless of other allied interests. What wholesome play does for the individual the play program he directs should do for the local church. The prosperity of the entire organization, and not merely the success of his own plans, is his ultimate objective.

THE DIRECTOR'S RESPONSIBILITY

The first responsibility of the director is to formulate a clear conception of just what he proposes to do. Before beginning to carry out his plans, a written statement of what he expects to accomplish should be submitted to the pastor and to the appropriate committees. No program should be inaugurated until it has been understood and approved by those who are responsible for the entire work of the church. Social and recreational activities should be integral parts of the whole program of worship, study, service, and play. The time to solve practical problems and to avoid misunderstandings is while the plans are being made and not after they have been put into operation.

The director of recreational and social life is the recreational specialist of the local church and often for the community. If his judgment is to be trusted, he should give serious consideration to the study of the theory and practice of recreational leadership. Much of the best literature in this field is written from the standpoint of physical education or welfare. He must reinterpret much of it if he would use it to fit into the program of the church. In carrying out his program he will face many situations that are unlike anything he has previously encountered. His firm grasp of the general principles of play supervision and organization alone will make it possible for him to proceed without blundering and embarrassment.

A fourfold task. As director his duties may be summed up in the four words, visualize, organize, deputize, and supervise or administer. (1) He must first see the possibilities and needs in the situation; that is, he must define his objectives or make up his mind as to what ought to be done. (2) Then he must perfect or use without modification such organizations as are needed to achieve his purpose. (3) This done, his next task is to man the organization. As far as practicable, it is his function to assign to all available workers tasks suited to their abilities. (4) Finally, as supervisor, he is responsible for seeing that the various recreational projects succeed. Volunteer leaders need to be trained. He must check up on what is being done. The careful supervision of play is needed because of the inexperience or lack of reliability on the part of some young people and because of the erratic enthusiasm of others. He cannot just start things going and then go off and leave them. The point of greatest weakness with many church programs of recreation is found in this lack of effective supervision.[3]

In many cases churches have channeled large sums of money into the construction of gymnasiums and the purchasing of expensive athletic equipment, with little concern for efficient leadership. The natural outcome of this procedure could only be failure. Often in the dismal groans of this failure the congregation condemns the program of recreation because bricks and dumbbells didn't convert their children to the Christian way of life, while the real failure was on their part for going into such a program without giving due consideration to leadership and organization.

The leadership question should be given the first consideration. With effective leadership the program can start from the present circumstances and grow from there. Even if it is only a social room with a ping-pong table, it is a beginning that in itself can be effective. The supervision and administration of the program cannot be neglected.

[3]Richardson, *op. cit.*, p. 75.

2. *Guiding Principles for the Director.* In planning for an office of recreation in the churches, there are at least twelve general principles which should be observed.

1. The director of recreation should be an officer in the church. He should be given both responsibility and the authority to conduct his duties.
2. The play program should be graded. That is, it should be suited to the changing capacities, interests, and needs of the immature and also of the mature persons who make up the entire constituency of the church. The arguments in favor of graded lesson material and departmental organization in the Sunday school are equally valid for a graded play program.
3. The active enlistment of all. Strive to secure the active participation of the entire church constituency rather than of the favored few. The recreational director is not concerned primarily in meeting the needs of those who are most easily reached.
4. Maintain a balanced program. Find the golden meaning between variety or novelty and simplicity or familiarity. As far as practicable appeal to the entire range of play motives.
5. Make play recreative. In order to achieve its purpose, recreational plans must take into account the programs of work and of play in which the participants are already engaged.
6. Individual variation in play interests and needs. The temperaments or types of personalities of those who are to participate in the play program need to be taken into account.
7. Take into account the seasons of the year.
8. Use existing organizations. As far as possible, the existing organizations of the church should be used rather than new ones created.
9. Develop volunteer leaders. The discovery of and training of volunteer leaders is an important phase of the director's responsibility.
10. Provide adequate equipment. See to it that ample and suitable equipment is provided.
11. Cooperate with community agencies. The community is the natural unit for many of the most valuable forms of recreation. Hence cooperation with community agencies is a practical necessity.
12. Restrict the use of artificial motives. Prizes, awards, and merits may be used to reinforce or stimulate play motives. They should never be used, however, in such a way as to supplant or destroy real or true motives.[4]

C. THE PROGRAM OF SOCIAL LIFE AND RECREATION

1. *A Written Program and Calendar.* The director should construct a written program that accurately shows the plans and participation of the people. The program should be detailed enough to show at any time what group may be meeting, where they are meeting, what kind of recreation they intend to participate in, and the theme or devotion that should highlight the program. On the other hand, the program should be large enough to show the recreational functions of the entire church for a period of one year. This program is carefully constructed and made according to a scheduled calendar. A detailed schedule will save many mis-

[4]*Ibid.*, p. 77.

understandings and disappointments as to the allotting of equipment and social rooms. The following material will be of great value as an introduction to the responsibility of planning a program.

The Program

The Church is responsible for recreation. For a long time to come there is very little danger of the church's doing too much for its own members or for the community in providing recreation. Even in the city, where the schedule of the average young person is crowded with a multitude of activities, there still remains an unique and indispensible place for church centered recreation. And for thousands of smaller communities the church has the primary responsibility to serve as the center for wholesome social recreation. While religious agencies are trying to decide who shall provide constructive recreation for a rapidly increasing amount of leisure time, the forces of commercialized amusements have stepped in and are setting the standards and providing low forms of recreation on a stupendous scale.

It is the exceptional church which provides more than one recreational period a month for all its members, to say nothing of serving the needs of the community. The average program has been pitifully meagre. The church which provides only one recreational program a month, or a total of 30 or 40 recreation hours a year, is leaving 95% of the time open for other agencies or for potential commercial exploitation. The Church certainly has a right to claim more than 3% or 4% of the time of its members and must offer more than a three hours' recreation program a month to young people with a hundred hours to spend. 15% to 25% of leisure time centering in church activities would seem to be the minimum in which to develop sound recreational ideals and habits in growing youth. This means the planning of 150 to 400 hours of recreative leisure-time activities per member per year.

Standards for a Church Recreation Program

Keeping in mind the goal of a comprehensive recreation program, what can be used to supplement the customary meagre "monthly social" and occasional church supper? Before attempting to list the multitude of activities and interests which may be proposed, it will save confusion to set some guide by which to measure the program as a whole.

A two-fold task faces the leader who would plan the leisure-time activities for young people: (1) to meet the needs of the members of the group, and (2) to meet the best standards of good taste and the ideals of the church. The specific standards of the program of recreation as a whole might be essentially as follows:

IT IS INTERESTING

1. It meets the needs and interests of the members of the group. It contains elements of surprise and adventure.
2. It is capable of winning ultimate popularity with participants.

IT IS PHYSICALLY RECREATIVE

3. It provides for healthy physical activity; it develops unused muscles and functions.
4. It rests weary muscles and nerves. It conserves a surplus of energy. It does not lead to undue fatigue or dissipation.

IT IS SOCIALLY CONSTRUCTIVE

5. It furnishes ample opportunity for wholesome social contacts.
6. It gives young people a chance to make new friends of both sexes.
7. It develops courtesy and ease in making social contacts.
8. It is democratic. It provides activities which all ages and all classes can enjoy.

9. It develops sportsmanship and fair play.
10. It develops self-control.
11. It develops the art of living together.

IT IS EDUCATIONAL

12. It is mentally stimulating. It develops alertness.
13. It cultivates appreciation of the value of time.
14. It teaches recreation habits which do not interfere with vocational duties.
15. It maintains a proper balance between work and play.
16. It cultivates an appreciation of the value of money. It does not lead to profligate expenditures.
17. It teaches an individual to make his recreation choices wisely.

IT IS ESSENTIALLY SPIRITUAL

18. It appeals to higher impulses rather than merely to sensual desires. Its appeal is more than merely physical.
19. It is consistent with Christian ideals and in harmony with church membership.
20. It is governed by ethical standards in both individual and social implications.

IT IS CULTURAL

21. It is conducted amidst attractive surroundings conducive to social conduct. It cultivates aesthetic appreciation.
22. It utilizes the best in music, drama, art, and the beautiful in nature.

IT IS SELF-EXPRESSIVE

23. It encourages the active participation of all.
24. It offers varied opportunity for individual self-expression.
25. It provides for rhythmic expression.
26. It encourages the use of faculties ordinarily unused.
27. It stimulates ingenuity. It teaches the individual to create his own recreation.

THE SCOPE OF A RECREATIONAL PROGRAM

The well balanced program of Church Recreation would be built around at least five centers of interest (which are not mutually exclusive).

1. Out-of-doors activities (Sports, camping, picnics, outings, skating, nature study, etc.).
2. Socials and parties (Special programs planned around a central idea, using group games, stunts, music, singing and refreshments).
3. Fellowship meetings (Dinners, banquets, feeds and informal suppers, home hours and group meetings for conversation, discussion, and sociability).
4. Cultural interests (Cultivation of tastes for good reading, good music, great pictures, fine drama, and the beautiful in nature).
5. Community activities (Cooperating with schools and civic groups, neighborhood playgrounds and social centers, lyceums, and community celebrations and entertainments).[5]

In addition to these suggestions, the director will possibly find that he can use the values of some of the following activities:

1. Hobbies to encourage creativeness. Four types of activities might be used: a hobby exhibit, a hobby night, a hobby workshop, and a hobby club.
2. Dramatics which provide teaching situations and inspiration. Types to use will include suggested dramatics, spontaneous dramatics, game dramatics, and stunt dramatics.

[5]Lynn Rohrbough, "Hardy" (Chicago: Church Recreation Service, 1928), p. D-3, 4.

3. Christian movies, slides, and filmstrips.
4. Team games.
5. Hikes.
6. Reading.

A director will find that this outline will serve as a guide in planning his material, but there are still many important matters that he will face. These include yearly schedule, operating budget, raising and distributing recreational funds, replacement of equipment. The operation of such a program makes it as complicated as any business enterprise. If this program is not maintained and conducted in a strict business-like manner, it can only end in failure.

2. *Play As a Teaching Method.* It has been evident for a long time that instruction in the small children's classes can be conducted through play. Play is a part of the lives of children, a very large part. It is only natural that it should be used instrumentally in teaching the Gospel. Many teachers have found that "playing the story" has been the most effective way of teaching.

The teaching effectiveness of play, however, is not confined to the children's division. Other divisions are finding many values of the "spirit of play" through such activities as pageants and dramatics, as well as social gatherings.

The writer is convinced that there is much to be done even during recreational and social periods to teach the Gospel. For example, the game of dodge ball can be used to teach the Scriptures. By substituting the person in the middle with a Bible character such as the giant Goliath, many little Davids can throw the ball to see if they can hit the giant. A variation of this is to set up some problem as the center of attention and to throw various solutions at it. The possibilities are unlimited along this line. It will take imagination and creativeness for this to happen, but we must come to it.

Just as it is important for lesson material to be graded, so it is important that play should be graded. That which the primary department would enjoy could hardly be expected to meet the need of the young people's department. Not only should recreation be graded on the basis of age groups but also on the basis of differing interests and needs of individuals within the groups. The type of work and recreation in which people are already engaged should also be considered. If variety is maintained in an evening's social — that is, quiet games and active games are interspersed — it should meet the needs of all concerned. The director should keep these things in mind in the administration of his duties. Furthermore, the church should provide the director with sufficient though not elaborate equipment.

It is important that definite and thorough plans be made for every social occasion. This is the director's responsibility. The following are some things that should be taken into consideration:

(1) the nature of the occasion; (2) the persons who are to be present; (3) how much time ought to be consumed; and (4) the conditions under which the program is to be carried out. This gives definite direction for each recreational function.

3. *Evaluation of the Program.* In evaluating the recreational program one can visualize the appalling circumstances of seeing a large plant with a hull of a gymnasium full of deteriorating equipment, dark and useless, because it is void of leadership. For most of the week the building is vacant because the program is not efficient enough to adequately utilize it.

On the other hand, one can see a program that started with an objective and is now effective and efficient. The effective program would have been drawn up in the light of theories and motives, with centralized leadership maintained through high Christian principles and moral standards. In place of the cold and darkness of a large recreational plant, there is laughter and fellowship under the lights of the church basement, indicating that an effective program has been conducted. Bear in mind that the true aim of play is not increasing enrollment and attendance but rather the development of Christian character.

4. *In Small Churches.* While it is recognized that only the larger churches can afford a paid and full-time director of recreation and social life, small churches may find it possible to use a qualified person on a part-time, voluntary basis. Others may find it necessary to appoint a church-wide committee to plan the work. Tully has listed some of the responsibilities of such a person or committee as follows:

1. Co-ordinate the social functions of the church through a calendar of activities
2. Leading all-church functions, such as picnics
3. Provide resource suggestions
4. Recreation librarian
5. Research — local needs, abilities, interests
6. Training of leaders[6]

5. *Principles in the Social Program.* It is in this field that the greatest amount of just criticism is directed against the recreational program of the church. These accusations are just if the accuser can prove that there is no difference between the recreational program of the church and that of the secular school. In other words, if a boy who has played on the secular school's team is now playing on the local church team, says, "There in no difference in the motives behind the two teams," he exposes that the church

[6]Chapter 14, by Bob Tully, in *Orientation in Religious Education*, edited by Philip H. Lotz. Copyright 1950 by Pierce and Smith. Used by permission of Abingdon Press.

team is a "flop," irregardless of how good the ball club may be. Or if a girl who has attended the school Halloween party attends a church Halloween party and comes away saying she could see no difference in the two socials, then the church program would be open for criticism.

Why should a tax-paying Christian who has to support a school recreational program turn to his church and support a like program with his tithes! If the motives of both programs are the same, he would do better to let the tax-supported institution take care of the recreational needs and send his tithes to the mission field. Chances are that the tax-supported program will have more advantages — as in funds and supervision boards — in securing better equipment and more highly trained leadership. It is evident, therefore, that the church should find other motivations for its social program.

> The task of the church is not to supply recreation and still more recreation for young people who already are over-privileged in this regard. Nor is it that of furnishing the easiest and cheapest forms of amusement for those whose recreational training has been wholly neglected. It is, rather, that of so directing the play life of all the people, both young and old, that their lives will count for the most in carrying on the work of the Kingdom of God.[7]

Leaders need to stress the value of the spiritual emphasis in the social. This does not mean that a sermon must be preached in every social, but it does mean that time should be given to a devotional period, hymn singing, or prayer, where God is recognized along with the salvation that comes to lost souls through the blood of Jesus Christ. Further, the Holy Spirit should be recognized and accepted as being present and in the midst of every game that is played and every story that is told. That which Wells pointed out at the close of the last century is still true today.

> He should be present from beginning to end of every Christian Endeavor Social. We do not pray half enough over our socials, either while we are planning them or while we are carrying them out. Unless a social is a sort of silent prayer meeting, it is certain to be a failure. And the chief thing we should pray for is that Christ should be there. Have you read Dr. Gordon's book, "When Christ Came to Church"? Read it, and it will move you profoundly, and will open your eyes, perhaps, to see our blessed Lord in the midst of his people, when they are playing as well as when they are praying.
> How if the carpenter, dropping saw and hammer from weary hands, should in visible form enter your next social should ask, "What are you playing, my children?" should beg, "Let me join in your game"? Would you wish the game something different? Would you like to change the spirit in which the game is played? This consideration affords the only possible answer to the common question, What games are proper for Christian Endeavor socials? The answer is, Any game in which Christ would join, — the loving, the pure, the manly, the joyous Christ.[8]

[7]Richardson, op. cit., p. 69.
[8]Amos R. Wells, Social to Save (Boston: United Society of Christian Endeavor, 1895), p. 11.

If one is going to have a church social, then let it be a church social, not a worldly social held in a church basement. It is appalling to see a group of people who ridiculously think that they can have a social under the auspices of the church, which is the Bride of Christ, without reverence for the presence of the Saviour.

Some will probably think that this will take all the fun out of the social, but that is not true. The last ten minutes is the most important time that should be reserved for devotional purposes. This truly enhances the program by putting the correct godly emphasis on the benediction of the program.

> The closing moments of a social offer an unusual opportunity for informal expression of Christian fellowship. Reserve and self-consciousness are entirely absent and the hour of play has welded the group into a unit, willing to follow the leader in any move.
>
> The secret of bridging the apparent gulf between a spirit of rollicking and often boisterous fun and an attitude of reverence and worship is simply in recognizing that there is no fundamental antithesis between them. Worship, like play, is an expressional activity; the one ministering to the spiritual and emotional nature and the other to the physical and mental nature.
>
> The technique of leading a worship service at the close of an evening of recreation consists in simply leading the crowd by easy stages from one mental attitude to the other. This part of the program must have the most careful preparation. Better never attempt it than bungle it. Use candle light, illuminated pictures, etc., to change the atmosphere.
>
> The same leader who has led the group in the fun must lead the group in the devotional close. The good will and loyalty of the crowd to him cannot be transferred at the last minute to another. A sincere straight from the shoulder talk, story, or short prayer, and a benediction, not only eliminates the "free for all rough-house" that characterizes the close of so many socials, but stamps the Church social as sincere and worthwhile, holds the crowd together as a unit to the last moment, and sends them home with a definite and pleasant "good-bye." The leader who thinks he can not close a social with the devotional ten minutes, needs only to try it once to be convinced of the charm and pull it holds.[9]

6. *Planning Social Activities.* Good social and recreational events require careful planning for success. The following items will provide a general outline for such planning:

1. Theme — the subject or idea which will be dominant
2. Time
3. Place
4. Crowd — size and nature

In addition to general planning there needs to be specific planning for the particular social and recreational event. Some of the items to be considered include:

[9]Rohrbough, *op. cit.*, p. D-22.

1. Invitations
2. Decorations — simple and inexpensive but appropriate
3. Refreshments — not necessary but well planned when used
4. Program
    a. Activities for first comers
    b. Mixer: get acquainted and ice-breaker period
    c. Social activities, the program itself which should call for participation and movement within a wide variety of elements
    d. Refreshments — at well-planned time
    e. Climax — worship to fit the theme
5. Clinic — time for evaluation of results

D. FELLOWSHIP AND SOCIAL LIFE

1. *Definition.* "Fellowship," as defined by Webster, is a community of interest activity, feelings, etc. It is friendliness and comradeship. Any union or association, especially a company of equals or friends, constitutes fellowship. It is communion or mutual relations between members or branches of the same church.

"Social" is that which is spent, taken, or enjoyed in the company of one's friends or equals as agreeable social relations. Man is gregarious by nature and habit — he is by nature a social creature.

The Scripture demands that the church meet the needs of men. Christianity therefore added benevolence to ethics. Fellowship and social life stem from benevolence.

2. *Christian Love and Social Life.* In the twenty-second chapter of Matthew, Christ was asked to summarize the law. He said, " 'You must love the Lord your God with your whole heart, your whole soul, and your whole mind' This is the great commandment, and is first in importance. The second is like it. 'You must love your neighbor as you do yourself.' The essence of the whole law and the prophets is packed into these two commandments.' "[10]

Jesus tells us who our neighbor is by giving us the parable of the "Good Samaritan." He defines what love for our neighbor is in Matthew by telling us about the "day of judgment."

> When the Son of Man comes in His splendor, and all the angels with Him, He will take His seat on His splendid throne, and all the nations will be gathered before Him, and He will separate them from one another, just as a shepherd separates his sheep from his goats, and He will put the sheep at His right hand and the goats at His left. Then the King will say to those at His right, 'Come, you who are blessed by my Father, take possession of the kingdom prepared for you from the creation of the world. For when I was hungry, you gave me something to eat, when I needed clothes you put them on me, when I was sick you looked after me, when I was in prison you came to see me.' Then the upright will answer, 'Lord, when did we ever see you hungry and give you something to eat, or thirsty, and give you something to drink? When

[10]Matthew 22: 34-40 (Williams' Translation).

did we ever see you a stranger and welcome you to our homes, or needing clothes, and put them on you? When did we ever see you sick or in prison, and come to see you?' And the King will answer them, 'I solemnly say to you, every time you did a good deed to one of these most insignificant brothers of mine, you did a good deed to me.' "[11]

There are tests of love found in the first epistle of John — the "apostle of love." No one, save Jesus, was more qualified to define our relationship to the God of love than the apostle John. He said, "We know that we have passed from death unto life, because we love our brothers" (I John 3:14).

In the seventeenth verse of the same chapter we read, "But if anyone has this world's means of supporting life and sees his brother in need and closes his heart against him, how can love to God remain in him? Dear children, let us stop loving with words or lips alone, but let us love with actions and in truth." John insists that brotherly love finds its practical test in things of common need.

James is moved upon by the Holy Spirit to say the same thing in a different way. "My brothers, what good is there in a man's saying that he has faith, if he has no good deeds to prove it? Such faith cannot save him, can it?" (James 2:14).

Again John writes, "If anyone says, I love God, and yet habitually hates his brother, he is a liar; for whoever does not love his brother whom he has seen cannot love God whom he has not seen" (I John 4:20).

Man demands justice, brotherhood, liberty, and the chance for a human way of life. He expects us to be willing to help him get what is good and fight what is wrong. We must not burn our energies fighting mere results of sin rather than attacking the cause of the problems represented. We must not help men to fight for something that they will consume on their own lusts. However, they deserve our aid to do what is right in matters of spiritual warfare. We need to help them and then show them a "more perfect way."

Our love must be adapted to the social needs represented in the church. Single young adults have a special desire to fellowship with others just like themselves. Newly married couples want fellowship with other young married couples. Married couples with young children need fellowship activities suited to the schedules demanded of them.

3. *Methods of Developing Fellowship.* We can meet the demands represented through organized classes, studying together, worshiping together, and providing other opportunities for fellowship and social life.

We organize our classes because teachers need help and

[11]Matthew 25:31-46 (Williams' Translation).

leaders in our classes need to serve. An adult Bible class should have a president, a vice-president, a group leader for every five members, and a secretary.

Since class officers have a definite spiritual ministry to perform, it is essential that they should meet certain standards. Class officers should:

Have a genuine Christian experience.
Be loyal members of the church in which they are to serve.
Be genuinely co-operative with the church program.
Love the Bible and be students of it.
Be vitally interested in the salvation of the unsaved.
Be willing to work at the job assigned.
Be willing to prepare themselves for their task.
Continuously seek to deepen their own spiritual lives.

Smaller classes may find it convenient to have "class outings" at least once a quarter. Others may prove their interest in social gatherings which include a wide variety of activities, such as eating, singing, music, readings, talks on popular themes, birthday parties, etc. Some schools have followed the procedure of using a joint committee to plan social gatherings for two or more classes.

We need to study our problems together. It is best to find out what vitally concerns the group that we are working with. For an adult class, it is well to make up an interest indicator such as the ones in Appendix VI.

We need to worship together. A sense of real and vital fellowship with God is a need of everyone. The extent to which this is realized is dependent almost entirely on the church. The real purpose of our teaching is to explore the concerns of our class in relation to the material in use for that session. For a time of worship, occasionally it would be well to pick out a series of hymns on the subject, "What We Believe." A discussion or project method would work nicely for class presentation.

Other opportunities for fellowship and social life must be provided through Christian service projects. This benefits the served and the ones serving. Truly it is in giving that we receive. Opportunities for service are found in special classes in weekday schools, Bible clubs, child evangelism fellowship, vacation church school, camps and conferences, and of course in all other activities that call for leadership.

Success in these projects demands that the officers take the lead in setting a proper example. They should be congenial and friendly in their own personal relations. Some schools develop this through periodical social gatherings, luncheons, and suppers for their workers. Other schools make provision for an occasional extra meeting of the workers for the express purpose of recreation and relaxation. Some superintendents make a habit of entertaining the workers once a year either at a banquet or social evening. Such meetings should not be so formal that the real purposes involved are overlooked.

4. *Other Concerns.* In Chapter 1, under the discussion devoted to the matter of *enthusiasm* or fellowship as one of the church's objectives, it was suggested that in addition to social life and recreation other concerns should attract our attention in the program. These concerns are genuine burden bearing, the use of leisure time, Christian ethics, social etiquette, morale, and Christian culture.

The superintendent of social life and fellowship may not possess all the skills necessary to the realization of these factors in his program, but he should try to locate people who have the abilities necessary to serve in these areas. The matter of bearing one another's burdens should be given particular study, especially within the immediate framework of the local congregation. Definite suggestions for use of leisure time for all age groups is becoming increasingly important in this day of science and technology. Many good suggestions may be secured from materials available in public libraries. The matter of Christian ethics can be cared for through the use of special study classes on Christian conduct and standards. Social etiquette can be stressed particularly among classes of youth and women and the various organizations outside the Sunday school. A program of Christian recreation may incorporate the use of skills among those who specialize in the fine arts. Talent cannot only be found within the local congregation but many good sources are available in the community.

Further suggestions along this line may be consulted in the following chapter in the section devoted to special ministries.

SUGGESTED READINGS — CHAPTER 8*

Barclay, *The Church and a Christian Society,* Chapter 11
Chalmers, *The Church and the Church School,* Chapter 7
Clemens, et. al., *Recreation and the Local Church*
Cope, *Religious Education in the Church,* Chapter 11, 17
Flake, *The True Function of the Sunday School,* Chapter 10
Heim, *Leading a Sunday Church School,* Chapter 12
Henderson, *Make Sunday School Interesting,* Chapter 6
Jacobsen, *The Why and How of Social Programs for Adult Classes*
Lotz, *Orientation in Religious Education,* Chapter 14, 25
Price, *Survey of Religious Education,* Chapter 20
Weigle, *The Pupil and the Teacher,* Chapter 19

---

* See updated Bibliography at back of book.

THE WORK OF CHRISTIAN EDUCATION
IN WIDER RELATIONSHIPS

OUTLINE FOR CHAPTER 9

RELATIONSHIPS

(Extension)

A. A COMPREHENSIVE PROGRAM OF CHRISTIAN EDUCATION
1. A Comprehensive Program
2. Beyond the Local Church

B. CHILDREN'S DIVISION
1. A Total Program
2. Expanded Sessions
3. Junior Church
4. Sunday Evening Program
5. Vacation Church School
6. Weekday Church School and Activities
7. Camping

C. YOUTH DIVISION
1. A Total Program
2. Sunday Evening Sessions
3. Weekday Activities
4. Camping and Conferences

D. ADULT DIVISION
1. A Total Program
2. Sunday Evening Program
3. Weekday Activities
4. Summer Activities
5. Christian Family Education
6. Extension Department

E. SPECIAL MINISTRIES
1. The Pastor's Class
2. Ministry of Music
3. Ministry to College Students
4. Ministry to Servicemen
5. Exceptional People
6. Drama and Art
7. Special Schools
8. Christian Literature
9. Counseling
10. Social Problems
11. Ministry to Foreign Students

F. OUTSIDE AGENCIES
1. Community Relations
2. City and State Organizations
3. National and International Groups

9 | THE WORK OF CHRISTIAN EDUCATION IN WIDER RELATIONSHIPS

(Extension)

A. A COMPREHENSIVE PROGRAM OF CHRISTIAN EDUCATION

1. *A Comprehensive Program.* A comprehensive program of Christian education is based on the *total church* concept of Christian education. This means that the program must embrace elements not only within the traditional Sunday school but also outside it. While it is true that the Sunday school is the primary instructional agency of the program, the needs of all ages in the church demand the use of a great many agencies in the development of a total church program. A survey of possibilities for each division of the program is given in this chapter.

2. *Beyond the Local Church.* The church is a world-wide fellowship. A comprehensive program of Christian education, therefore, will not only involve the total congregation within the bounds of the church as a local congregation, but it will make an effort to reach out beyond the walls of the local group in an effort to minister to the needs of a lost world.

Efforts beyond the local church will not only embrace the denominational program but also agencies beyond the denomination as such. This will not only include the use of a good extension department but will include many special areas, such as the ministry to retarded children, servicemen, etc., and cooperation with various kindred agencies to the church. The second purpose of this chapter, therefore, is to lift up some of the opportunities for Christian education provided by situations beyond the local congregation.

B. CHILDREN'S DIVISION

1. *A Total Program.* The total program for children in the church includes all that the church is doing for children from birth through eleven years of age. It includes not only activities carried on in the Sunday church school but also those comprehended in the home, worship services, expanded sessions, weekday activities, and vacation time.

The program will be a unified one, avoiding duplication on the one hand, but on the other hand incorporating a good balance, thus leading to the creation and development of a well-rounded Christian personality. This means that some type of committee

303

or council, composed of officers and teachers, will meet periodically to plan the total program for children. It might also mean one person who will assume the directorship of children's work. He would be responsible to the director of Christian education.

In addition to the Sunday school, such a program will make provisions for wider contacts with other departments and groups in the church, the observance of special days and seasons together with other groups, sufficient time for instruction, home and church cooperation, child care at church, extra teaching sessions occasionally for children, vacation church school sessions, a summer program, weekday religious education, and possibly a weekday kindergarten program.

All these activities can be coordinated in the program through the adoption and use of a calendar of activities for the year.

2. *Expanded Sessions.* Expanded sessions for children represent an extension of the Sunday school time for instruction. Such a program will vary in length, depending on the length of church services, and generally is conducted during the Sunday morning period which traditionally embraces Sunday school and church services. The entire period is planned as a unit and provides a well-rounded program of worship, study, fellowship, and service.

Some churches make available special teaching materials for this kind of program. Others incorporate suggestions for this period in the regular Sunday school lesson materials. Some groups allow children to worship with parents in the sanctuary for at least part of the worship service, returning to their rooms for additional activities.

3. *Junior Church.* Some churches make provision for a separate worship program for children on Sunday mornings during the adult worship service. Such a service is often called "Junior Church", "Children's Church," or "Junior Congregation." Where expanded services are well-planned and administered, the need for this group is largely diminished.

The primary purpose of a junior church is worship; therefore unless it is properly organized and conducted, the real value is lost and people will not respond in seeing that their children participate. While there is no set pattern for this group, definite steps should be taken to see that the spiritual needs of the children are met, that their spiritual relationship to God is strengthened, and that they are trained in the art and techniques of public worship. Readers are referred to the publication by Eleanor Doan on *How to Plan and Conduct a Junior Church* in the reading list at the end of the chapter.

4. *Sunday Evening Program.* A few church groups make provisions for children in the program for Sunday evening just before the church service. A particular illustration of this is the

junior fellowship for children 9-11 years of age. This is an extension of the youth fellowship idea. It has the advantage of making provision for the whole family to get some training on Sunday evening.

It is obvious that where this plan is used, an early evening hour should be used for children. A nursery group could meet in its own Sunday school quarters and supplementary lessons be used for them. Beginner children can participate in a similar program either with special materials or supplementary vacation Bible school materials adapted for evening programs.

Where an expanded session is not used for primary and junior children, materials used during this period can be drawn from the Sunday school program. Of course there are special materials also available for this purpose. Some denominations provide junior programs for this group of children.

A school of missions for children is conducted in some churches.

5. *Vacation Church School.* High on the list of children's activities and ranked next to the Sunday school perhaps in importance is the vacation church school. While its general function is largely the same as that of the other parts of the program for children, it has many unique advantages of its own that make it extremely important for each church to conduct a school of this type.

If a church cannot conduct a local school of its own, then it should look for opportunities to unite with other churches to provide a school of this kind for children. A special committee subject to the Board of Christian Education should assume the responsibility for planning and conducting of the school. In the main, the same leaders who work with children on Sunday can work with them in the vacation church school, although this is not absolutely necessary. The period covered should comprehend at least two weeks and longer if possible. Most denominations have developed teaching materials for these schools and many independent publishing houses can supply good materials.

6. *Weekday Church School and Activities.* This type of school can be conducted in the local church or be united in a program involving several churches. In many communities the children are released from public school classes and given an opportunity to attend special classes.

In some churches other weekday activities are carried on among primary and junior children for the purpose of developing Christian character and growth. Such activities include Bible clubs, scout programs, and recreation groups.

A relatively new venture for some churches is the weekday nursery school. This type of weekday activity is particularly helpful in communities where public school education for small children is not available. The program consists of a half-day schedule for nursery and kindergarten children. It is useful also in connection with Christian day schools and in situations where a great many mothers work to supplement the family income. In most states, schools of this kind are required to be licensed by the State Board of Education or the State Welfare Board.

Here again the school of missions can be included in a week-day program instead of on Sunday. At least two periods of six weeks' length are necessary for an adequate program.

7. *Day Camping.* Some churches are using day camps to supplement the vacation church school and summer program. Day camping enables the church to sponsor a camping program at home. The program runs from morning to late afternoon, allowing children to be home at night. Older primaries, juniors, and junior high children participate. The best program incorporates a five-day week for at least three weeks. The program consists of study, worship, crafts, and recreation in an outdoor setting. The advantages of activities carried on in a nature-environment are many and obvious.

Other types of camps call for an all-day program and overnight accommodations. These camps are sponsored by national headquarters' groups of various denominations and call for professional personnel to administer them.

C. YOUTH DIVISION

1. *A Total Program.* The youth division of the church embraces young people in the junior high, senior high, and older youth groups and comprehends all their activities in the church and Sunday school. While the Board of Christian Education will bear the responsibility for planning the total church program, it is best to delegate the actual administration of the youth division to a youth council or committee on youth work. At least one of this group who is particularly burdened for the work should serve as chairman of the committee and director of all youth work.

The youth committee will plan and coordinate all youth work. This will include all departments in the youth division of the Sunday school. The personnel will include all youth leaders, the general superintendent, and the pastor. An annual calendar of activities will coordinate the program.

The best plan is to provide one total program for youth in the church. This will call for at least three groups — junior high, ages 12-14; senior high, ages 15-17 or 18; and older youth, about 18-24, generally unmarried. Ideally each group will have a superintendent and an adviser. The morning and evening sessions are parts of one program in this plan. Superintendents will be largely responsible for adult workers in each group while the advisers will have the primary responsibilities of working with the youth themselves.

The young people will also have a strong hand in planning and directing the program in this plan. This can be accomplished through an organized youth cabinet for each youth group. The general officers from each youth group form a youth council to coordinate the total youth program in the church.

2. *Sunday Evening Sessions.* In addition to Sunday school classes and departments for youth, a total program will provide for additional sessions for youth on Sunday evenings. These have traditionally been known as youth fellowship meetings.

The values of these Sunday evening sessions are many. The main purposes are to provide inspiration, information, fellowship, training, spiritual life, and leadership for youth. All these can be provided in a setting of social life and spiritual atmosphere. Training opportunities in such a program will embrace the program elements of conducting worship experiences, prayer life, service, expression, music, drama, and many Christian service skills.

While many policies will be determined by the committee on youth work, through advisers, the actual program planning for evening sessions will be accomplished by the youth themselves.

In small churches one youth meeting may be enough but even then wherever possible, after an opening period of worship and fellowship, separate sections should be conducted for the major part of the program.

3. *Weekday Activities.* A total program for youth will make room for a wide variety of weekday activities for youth. Some churches provide missions groups for boys and girls. Others organize club groups of various types centered around natural interests, hobbies, recreation, etc. In some areas churches are active in the promotion of scout work.

Where a released time program is allowed, the weekday church school gives additional opportunities to instruct youth in the elements of our Protestant heritage. Often this proves to be a cooperative venture between several church groups in a community.

The vacation church school should have provision in its program for youth classes. This can perhaps be accomplished most easily when class sessions are held in the evening hours.

Following is a list of possible programs to investigate:
A. Bible Clubs in Schools — independent
B. High School Groups
    1. Born-againers
    2. Youth for Christ Bible Clubs
C. College Groups — Inter-Varsity Christian Fellowship

    D. Cooperating Organizations
       1. Boy Scouts
       2. Girl Scouts
       3. Christian Service Brigade
       4. Pioneer Girls
       5. Sky Pilots
    E. Local Church
       1. Home Bible Clubs
       2. Friendship Clubs
       3. Bible Study Classes
       4. Story Hours
       5. Red Shield and Torchbearers
       6. Christian Endeavor
       7. Christ's Ambassadors
       8. Crusaders
       9. Overcomers
      10. Combinations
      11. Arts
      12. Crafts
      13. Hobbies

4. *Camping and Conferences.* Some denominations have developed permanent camp sites for their members and provide a full summer program. Camps specialize in an outdoor setting, using nature as part of the curriculum and stressing Bible study, leadership training, and fellowship.

Conferences may be conducted on a camp site but often use indoor settings as well. The curriculum stresses leadership training, classes, fellowship, counseling, and Christian social values.

The many values derived by the young people and the church make it definitely worthwhile for a church to plan for its youth to attend camps and conferences. The Board of Christian Education, therefore, should recruit promising youth, make available funds for this purpose, and urge church support. They will find a sub-committee to do this kind of planning very helpful.

As with children, leaders of youth are finding opportunities to supplement the offerings of Sunday school and vacation church school for youth through day camping. A camp atmosphere and setting prevails during the day and the youth spend the nights at home. The program consists of Bible study, crafts, fellowship, singing, hiking, recreation, nature lore, and other activities. A five-day week for three weeks seems best.

City parks, Y.M.C.A. camps, scout camps, or a private piece of property are often made available for day camping purposes. In a few places *winter day camps* have become popular. These are usually conducted on weekends. Winter sports are used for recreational purposes during the day and evening hours are devoted to study, discussion groups, and worship.

D. ADULT DIVISION

1. *A Total Program.* A comprehensive program for adults will embrace more than Sunday school classes. Definite plans will be laid to serve adults of the church and community. It is the opportunity and responsibility of the leaders of adults to discover the desires, longings, and interests of the persons they may reach through the church and to plan activities which will give adults satisfying opportunities for creative Christian living. This will involve an expanding program for young adults, middle adults, and older adults.

The Board of Christian Education has direct responsibility for planning the expanded program for all adults. The superintendent of the adult division will see that the wishes and plans of the board are executed. He is also chairman of the adult council of workers. This council comprehends the Sunday school and all adults outside the Sunday school. In larger churches special directors of adult work may be appointed to direct such areas as worship, study, recreation, evangelism, missionary education, Christian service, and family education. These directors will work closely with officers and teachers to provide an adequate program.

All activities in the division should be coordinated in the program through the use of a calendar of activities for the year.

2. *Sunday Evening Program.* Sunday evenings are favorable times for adults to meet for study and discussion groups. These groups take the form of training sessions or popular adult education classes. The primary advantages of Sunday evening meetings lies in getting whole families to church for these occasions. While children and youth engage in their activities, parents can be profitably engaged in theirs. All this contributes to better church attendance in the evening as well.

Sunday evening study groups may be divided according to various adult interests. They are not usually organized on a permanent basis. Elective courses with a wide variety of subjects and procedures are possible. Forums, lectures, discussions, panel presentations, and workshops are possibilities. Often such programs are entitled "College of Life," or "School in Christian Living."

3. *Weekday Activities.* The most obvious weekday activity in many evangelical churches is the midweek program. The traditional one-hour service devoted to Bible study and prayer is common. Other opportunities are provided through occasional schools of missions, stewardship, evangelism, and leadership training. At times the program may start with the evening meal and incorporate a period of recreation.

On other weekdays a wide variety of activities may be carried on. Women's groups and men's brotherhoods provide opportunities for stressing service, stewardship, and fellowship.

Some churches are finding ways to help parents by providing study and discussion groups for parents on Christian homemaking and Christian living. Study topics include items such as child-rearing, use of time and money, use of the Bible, prayer life, etc. A few churches sponsor mothers' clubs which meet regularly to study child needs.

Parent-teacher meetings are conducted at least quarterly in some churches. Here stress is laid on the relations of home and church. Parents and teachers can meet regularly to make plans for the common task of giving attention to the spiritual welfare of children.

Specialized groups are used by some churches to minister to adults. These include clubs for older people, Christian recreation groups, athletic teams, hobby clubs, craft groups, and drama clubs.

4. *Summer Activities.* Many churches are finding special opportunities for leadership training and Christian fellowship during the summer. Combining the vacation spirit with a camping atmosphere is proving greatly helpful and attractive to scores of adults during summertime. These situations enable church leaders to use people of outstanding ability and wide experience to train adults.

5. *Christian Family Education.* To face the stark realities of the breakdown of family life in America and to bolster the strength of genuine Christian family life, the church is faced with the responsibility of making provisions for Christian family education in the program of the adult division. This means that specific provisions for parent education are necessary. Such education must revolve around the parents' basic responsibilities for rearing their children in the home — a home which is genuinely Christian.

The early Hebrews and Christians insisted upon parental teaching of children. In early America parents taught religion to their children. Today the church cannot rely solely on sermons, parents' classes, and reading materials to do the job. Systematic study is needed. Parents and church school workers must face this problem squarely and plan a definite program.

Such a program will incorporate parents' nights, monthly church-family conferences, sex education, parent-teacher meetings, courses of study on child study, family altar, Christian ethics, etc., mothers' or parents' clubs for study and fellowship, books and library materials on marriage and the Christian home, and the observance of "Christian Family Week." Parent-teacher cooperation can be solicited through visitation in the homes, letters sent to parents, parental visitation in the classes, regular reports sent to the home, parent-teacher conferences, and other ways. Much can be accomplished through cooperation with other churches and community agencies.

6. *Extension Department.* This department provides adults with practical opportunities for carrying out the Great Commission and for real home mission work. As such, the extension department is that part of the program of Christian education which is organized to take the ministry of the Gospel to all people who are permanently or temporarily unable to attend the church and school. In a real sense it provides the same situation as that of the early church recorded in Acts 5:42: "And daily in the temple, and in every house, they ceased not to teach and preach Jesus Christ."

Some of the objectives are:

1. To minister to all who cannot attend because of age or health or Sunday work
2. To enlist each in regular Bible study and prayer
3. To win the lost to Christ and the saved to church membership
4. To encourage each to tithe his time, talent, and money
5. To be a connecting link between the church and the home

An outstanding superintendent is necessary to make this department a real success. The number of workers needed will be determined by the size of the church and the number of prospects. Older people and particularly young people will find a special opportunity for ministry in this department.

Some of the people to be reached in this ministry will include:

1. Aged people too feeble to attend services
2. Shut-ins, both the infirm and those ministering to them
3. People confined to institutions such as county homes, jails, etc.
4. Families living in rural districts out of reach of the church
5. Children in neighborhoods out of reach of the church; under-privileged families
6. Sunday workers, such as nurses, firemen, policemen, trainmen, gasoline attendants, hotel, restaurant and hospital employees, utility workers, public transit workers, watchmen, factory shift workers, etc.
7. Expectant mothers and children in the home; new mothers
8. Non-residents
9. People without a church home

E. SPECIAL MINISTRIES

1. *The Pastor's Class.* Many educational opportunities are presented to pastors of churches who conduct annual classes in training for church membership. While it is recognized that preparation for church membership is preparation for participation in the total life of the church, and while the average pastor's class

is devoted to matters of belief and doctrine, yet there are self-evident and wide-open opportunities for the pastor to engage in real Christian education and evangelism. Some of the important matters which need to be included are Christian experience, belief, doctrine, Christian home, worship, church history and polity. Emphasis, of course, will be determined by the age group being dealt with.

2. *Ministry of Music.* Music not only has charms, it has a vital place in the Ministry of the church. Along with this are many educational opportunities.

Not the least of such opportunities is the choir. Choirs minister to congregations and to the individuals who sing in them. They provide the ministry for all age groups. Values are derived, not from money or prestige but rather from service and Christian training. Participation in choir work affords each individual not only training in vocal and instrumental skills but a knowledge of church music, the art of worship, and acquaintance with the rich heritage of sacred music. It is obvious that children's and youth choirs give valuable preparatory experience for adult choirs.

3. *Ministry to College Students.* It is important for churches to minister to college age students. Home churches should give particular parting attention to those going away to school, to prepare them for college and to keep them church conscious. This can be done by observing Christian education emphases to include young people, by sending high school seniors on tours of church colleges, by planning an off-to-college day, by writing denominational people at the college to give attention to youth who will come to them, and by keeping them on the Sunday school roll.

When youth get to college, special attention can be given to them by writing and notifying churches in the college town of their presence.

When they come home, use them, particularly during the summer. Some of their activities might include:

1. Helping in Sunday school
2. Assisting in other age groups as counselors
3. Teaching in daily vacation Bible school
4. Assisting with census
5. Aid in visitation
6. Revise or start a church library
7. Lead in church-sponsored recreation
8. Improve church property and equipment
9. Give recreational help
10. Singing in choir or special numbers
11. Help in youth camps
12. Help with mission projects

4. *Ministry to Servicemen.* The Southern Baptists instituted their "Military Service Membership Plan" of the Sunday school in 1953. The plan calls for counting service men as active enrollees in Sunday school. Enrollment cards are sent to the men and women in service. When the cards are returned, they are counted as military members of the home Sunday school. Sunday school literature and church bulletins are sent out regularly to each one. Monthly letters from the minister go out and each quarter a newsletter is circulated among them. Members are also encouraged to write personal letters. Special attention is given to service personnel in prayer groups.[1]

5. *Exceptional People.* Any variation from the normal or average person on the part of certain individuals serves to stamp them as exceptional people. They may be handicapped, mentally retarded, frustrated, rebellious, emotionally disturbed, even mentally superior. Whatever the condition, the church should understand these people and serve them wherever possible.

The National Council of Churches has made some recommendations to local churches which should prove helpful. They are reported by Virgil E. Foster as follows:[2]

1. It is important that a church establish communication with the families in its community that have members with physical or mental handicaps.
2. In extending friendly counsel to such people it is important that church leaders have a clear understanding of what are the responsibilities of society to exceptional persons.
3. It is suggested that churches consider as one of their most important responsibilities that of public interpretation.
4. Wherever possible it is recommended that exceptional persons be assimilated into regular groups in the church.
5. It must be recognized that in individual cases an exceptional person is not ready for assimilation. Here special groups are needed.
6. Churches are urged to take advantage of the consultation services available from state and private agencies working with exceptional persons.
7. It is strongly recommended that churches make serious study of their buildings and equipment to discover what special provisions need to be made so that handicapped persons will not face physical barriers to participation.[3]
8. It is recommended that exceptional persons be assimilated in regular church camps whenever possible, but also that churches be sure their camps conform to the highest standards of health and safety.
9. It is recommended that churches take seriously the training of leaders for work with exceptional persons.
10. Greater study should be given to the problems involved under the guidance of competent professionals.

[1]Gainer E. Bryan, Jr., "Ministry to Servicemen Bears Fruit," *Sunday School Builder* (January 1956), p. 44.
[2]Virgil E. Foster, "Exceptional Persons Need the Church, Too," *International Journal of Religious Education* (January 1958), p. 16.
[3]Information is available from the National Society for Crippled Children and Adults, Inc., 11 South La Salle Street, Chicago 3, Illinois.

11. Exceptional persons should be given opportunity to become a part of the church activities and program.
12. It is strongly recommended that the needs of exceptional persons be faced by churches working together and working in cooperation with specialized agencies.

6. *Drama and Art.* As mediums of worship and instruction drama and art have been very popular and are widely used in some church circles. Drama has a way of making religion a living reality and has values for both participants and observers. Color, movement, and the spoken word all combine the obvious values of audio-visual aids and are very effective in getting the message of the Gospel across to people. Types of drama suitable for churches include dramatized Bible stories, plays, pageants, shadow plays, tableaux, pantomines. The test of drama in the church is not only that its content must be Biblical and spiritual, but also what its effect on the audience is. An exaltation of spirit and a deeper sense of religious fellowship with God and man must be achieved before drama is essentially Christian.

Art has long been the handmaid of religion. In fact it was Christianity which actually saved art, preserving it until the present day. The two most obvious places where art is used in the church is in worship and instruction. In worship it is used to amplify spiritual concepts. In instruction its primary function is to illustrate. Art has been found useful in architecture, in specialized uses of religious pictures, poster making and design work, modeling, chalk talks, moving pictures, filmstrips, and handicrafts.

7. *Special Schools.* The church has long been interested in school work. In fact the history of education for long periods was inextricably connected with the church. Beginning with the early catechumenal, catechetical, and cathedral schools of early centuries and moving into the Reformation period where denominational schools became prominent in the perpetuation of religious principles, the church has demonstrated its use of schools of instruction of one sort or another until today schools of many kinds are being operated under the sponsorship of the church.

Several years ago a survey was made in an effort to determine the characteristics of a Christian school. It was determined that a Christian school will have at least the following minimum distinctives:

A Christian objective, aim, purpose
A Christian faculty and Christian teaching
A Christian viewpoint
A Christian spirit, atmosphere, life
A Christian program
A Christian product[4]

[4]J. M. Price, et. al., *A Survey of Religious Education* (New York: Thomas Nelson and Sons, 1940), p. 295.

In addition to maintaining a Christian witness in the field of education, schools under church sponsorship should be expected to train Christian leaders, Christian layworkers, Christian writers and research workers, ministers, and missionaries.

Some of the schools now being sponsored by churches include Christian nursery schools, day schools (both elementary and secondary), Bible institutes, Bible colleges, Christian liberal arts colleges, and a few graduate schools.

In all these schools Christian education is expected to take place, and in this modern day they are becoming increasingly strategic in the perpetuation of the church and the spread of the Gospel around the world. These schools must deal with all truths as it relates to modern life, but more than that they must give the Christian interpretation to all truth. Only in this way can the Christian school be made to function in the thought and conduct of men. Only in this way can genuine *Christian* education be achieved.

8. *Christian Literature.* One of the great, if not the greatest, mediums of communication is the printed page. Communism is proving that. Books, magazines, and papers by the millions are molding the thoughts and conduct of men and nations.

Christian literature has become one of the most important channels for Christian education. Literature for this purpose is produced in church school periodicals, books, weekly and monthly journals, missionary magazines, bulletins, pamphlets, leaflets, tracts, curriculum materials, newspapers, fiction and other forms. One of the greatest challenges in this field which comes to the church is reaching untold millions on the mission field through missionary papers. A parish paper should not be overlooked.

9. *Counseling.* Countless people today are streaming into the offices of psychiatrists, psychologists, and ministers to obtain counseling services in an effort to solve the problems arising out of the pressures, tensions, and social situations of our day.

While some may consider counseling rather unrelated to Christian education, yet the very act of communicating in an interview provides the counselor with opportunities to supply the spiritual and religious help needed at the right moment. Not only so, but counselors in the church can explain the values and opportunities of counseling to their people and enable them to see the wisdom in securing this kind of help. In this they are performing an educational function.

10. *Social Problems.* The many evils present in community life demand action on the part of the church in an effort to cleanse the community. The church cannot afford to blind itself to the presence of corruption in the form of roadhouses, beer joints, burlesque shows, sex and crime motion pictures, houses of prostitu-

tion, drinking, gambling, and other social evils, including salacious literature.

Churches not only need to educate their membership regarding the harm and sin involved in such evils, but they can unite in community-wide information campaigns and even engage in united efforts to eliminate such evils from the community, at least on a legal basis. This is Christian education by way of preventing unsavory situations to exist.

The Women's Christian Temperance Union and other temperance organizations can supply churches with up-to-date information on alcohol problems and education. The primary sources of visual aids materials on temperance are:

Encyclopedia Britannica Films, Wilmette, Illinois
American Automobile Association
W.C.T.U., Evanston, Illinois
Society for Visual Education, Chicago, Illinois
The California Temperance Federation has an excellent bibliography

11. *Ministry to Foreign Students.* The Federal Government has issued permission to thousands of young people from foreign countries to study in the United States. This presents the church with an unusual opportunity to minister. In fact, what we do with these students may well affect not only their attitudes toward our country but toward Christianity for many years to come. An example of the extent of this opportunity is illustrated in only one school. Indiana Technical College of Fort Wayne, Indiana, enrolls over 300 foreign students annually.

The church should contact these students and enroll them in Christian education situations to teach them the Word of God and evangelize them wherever possible.

F. OUTSIDE AGENCIES

1. *Community Relations.* In addition to the work within its own walls and to its own individual constituency, the church has a ministry to the community as well. By "community" we mean the limited geographical area immediately surrounding the church and its immediate constituency. The extent of each community in a particular situation depends on the resources of the churches involved. As far as possible the life and ministry of the church should influence the community and bring the light of the Gospel to the great issues of community life. In doing this the church will act as a moral force, not to gain privilege or power, but to achieve spiritual, moral, and social ends.

Some of the responsibilities to be assumed by the church in this area include training people to feel their responsibilities for expressing Christianity through citizenship, seeking solution to community problems through the application of Christian principles, witnessing to civic leaders on moral, social, and spiritual issues, studying Christian implications in the practice of vocations, and practicing Christian ethics.

There are wide-open opportunities for inter-church cooperation in community action. Some of the possibilities would embrace community-wide fellowship, ecumenical education, cooperation with public education, developing favorable public opinion on the need for religious education, cooperation in weekday religious education programs, cooperating with community character-building agencies, such as scouting, Y work, etc., cooperative community social action, and community recreation.

2. *City and State Organizations.* In some situations denominations have combined their interests in local councils of Christian education in cities and states. Here a loosely knit organization makes it possible for churches to cooperate in accomplishing certain aspects of their common mission. Common problems are attacked and cooperation in community projects is made possible.

In other situations local churches cooperate in the establishment and conducting of Sunday school associations and conventions in cities and at the county, township, and state levels.

3. *National and International Groups.* Evangelical churches through the National Association of Evangelicals have been instrumental in reviving the National Sunday School Association. Among other churches the Division of Christian Education of the National Council of Churches renders helpful assistance in the field of Christian education. Still others find help from organizations like the Religious Education Association, the United Christian Youth Movement, and the World Council of Christian Education.

SUGGESTED READINGS — CHAPTER 9*

Bailey, *The Use of Art in Religious Education*
Blankenship, *Our Church Plans for Children*
Davis, *Extension Department*
Doan, *How to Plan and Conduct a Junior Church*
Domingos, *Working With Children in the Small Church*
Eastman and Wilson, *Drama in the Church*
ETTA, *Vacation Bible School*, Unit XI
Fordham, *Our Church Plans for Youth*
Gillett, *At Work With Children in the Small Church*
Harner, *The Educational Work of the Church*, Chapters 4, 6, 7, 9, 10
Jacobsen, *How to Succeed with Your Home Department*
Jones, *Our Church Plans for Adult Education*
Lerrigo, *The Mentally Retarded and the Church*
Lotz, *Orientation in Religious Education*, Chapters 18, 19, 24, 27, 33, 34, 35, 36, 37

* See updated Bibliography at back of book.

McCarty, *The Church Plans for Children*
McCraw, *The Extension Department*
Parker, *The Sunday School Reaches Out*
Person, *An Introduction to Christian Education*, Chapters 7-9, 11-15
Price, *A Survey of Religious Education*, Chapters 14-19, 22, 23
Taylor, *Religious Education, A Comprehensive Survey*, Chapters 10-13, 19-22, 27, 28, 30-34
Vieth, *The Church and Christian Education*, Chapters 5, 7, 8

APPENDICES

APPENDIX I

Functional Organization and Administration of the Program

of Christian Education

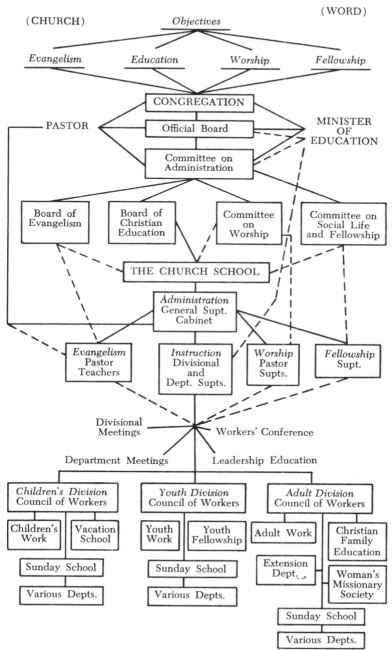

APPENDIX II

PLANNING A YEAR'S PROGRAM IN THE SUNDAY SCHOOL

SEPTEMBER

Educational Evangelism (Sunday School Enlistment Month)

1. Christian Education Week, with a retreat for the teachers and officers of the Sunday school. Plan your year's program at this time.
2. Begin to strengthen the Sunday school.
3. Provide "echo meetings" for camp testimonies.
4. College-Seminary Day — Sponsored by the Board of Christian Education.
5. Promotion Day — sponsored by the Board of Christian Education. This is to be held on the last Sunday in September (Installation Day).
6. Plan for November (Enlargement month and Rally Day).
7. September — last Sunday — Check up time — make a critical evaluation of your Sunday School.
8. Robert Raikes Birthday — September 8.
9. School usually begins this month.

OCTOBER

Church Loyalty Month (Enlargement Month)

The Sunday School Year Begins

1. World Wide Communion Sunday
2. Sunday School Loyalty Sunday
3. Loyalty in church attendance (for the Sunday School)
4. Reformation Sunday
5. Sunday school emphasize loyalty crusade with special Sunday emphasis for men, for women, and for children
6. Rally Day
7. Missionary Day
8. Columbus Day
9. World Temperance Sunday
10. Halloween
11. United Nations Day
12. Laymen's Day
13. National Bible Week
14. This is a good month to emphasize enlargement
15. Promote December activities in October
16. Promote Thanksgiving plans
17. Check on Sunday school material for the year
18. Monthly Workers' Conference (lay plans for future meetings)
19. Thanksgiving to Christmas Bible readings should be distributed
20. Evaluate the Sunday school program for the last year

NOVEMBER

Emphasis on Prayer and Thanksgiving (Bible Month)

1. Denominational loyalty Sunday
2. Continue the Sunday school evangelism program
3. Cooperate in the church emphasis on prayer and thanksgiving
4. Armistice Day
5. Thanksgiving Day
6. Missionary Day

322

7. Decision Day
8. All-Saints Day?
9. Good month to emphasize the Bible
10. Continue work on the Christmas plans and program
11. Plan for the workers' conference
12. Plan for the workers' training class
13. Promote in November what you have to have in January

DECEMBER

World Missions Emphasis
1. Universal Bible Sunday
2. Christmas program
3. Student Recognition Sunday
4. Installation Service — on the last Sunday in December by the Board of Christian Education
5. Missionary Sunday
6. Promote future training plans for the Sunday school staff
7. Monthly workers' conference
8. Promote the February Sunday school plans
9. Bill of Rights Day
10. First Day of Winter, December 21st
11. December 31 — last day of the old year — can be used to your advantage not only in the Sunday school work but by the church as well

JANUARY

Youth Evangelism   (Training Month)
1. First Week — Week of Prayer
2. Second Week — Evangelism Sunday
3. Third Week — Pioneer Day — under the direction of the Board of Pensions
4. Fourth Week — Youth Week — Sponsored by the Board of Christian Education — Cooperate with the "Win My Chum" Campaign
5. Epiphany Sunday
6. Missionary Sunday
7. New Year's Day— Organize a watch night to precede this day, or cooperate with the church in this function
8. Monthly workers' conference
9. "A Trained Teacher in Every Classroom" — this is a good time for teacher training programs
10. Plan the March work

FEBRUARY

Visitation
1. Visitation campaign is to be organized and carried out by the whole church
   a. Prepare prospect and assignment cards from the Sunday school
   b. Conduct visitation evangelism training school
   c. This is under the direction of the Board of Evangelism, but the entire church must be cooperating if it is to be successful. Sunday school teachers make wonderful callers, especially when they contact the families of their own class
2. Boy Scouts Sunday
3. Lincoln's Birthday
4. Washington's Birthday
5. Valentine Day
6. National Freedom Day
7. Plan Easter activities
8. National Smile Week
9. Missionary Sunday
10. Monthly workers' conference

11. Prepare your work for April
12. Promote a regional Sunday school convention in your denomination
13. National Crime Prevention Week

MARCH

Spiritual Enrichment Month

1. Revival meetings are held — They must be Sunday school supported. An excellent idea is to make them a "Sunday School Revival"
2. Palm Sunday — Decision Day in the Sunday school
3. Easter ingathering
4. Promotion of May program
5. Plan a loyalty campaign for April (avoiding the Easter slump)
   a. Prevents absenteeism
   b. Adds new members
   c. Encourages faithfulness
   d. Grows spiritually

APRIL

Worship and Assimilation

1. Easter to Pentecost — conservation program
2. Plan for June
3. Good Friday
4. Easter Sunday
5. Arbor Day
6. Loyalty Campaign through the last Sundays of April and the first Sundays of May. (The Assemblies keep this going for five Sundays)

MAY

Family Emphasis

1. Christian Family Week — For the Sunday school and the church. A good slogan: "The whole family together in Sunday school"
2. Promote family worship in the Sunday school
3. Cooperate with church emphasis on stewardship
4. Observe Pentecost Sunday (the start of the Christian Church)
5. Plan for July
6. Plan for Sunday outing
7. May Day
8. "I Am an American" Day
9. National Flag Day

JUNE

Child Evangelism Month   (Daily Vacation Bible School Month)

1. Promote Daily Vacation Bible school
2. Evangelism of children through the Sunday school
3. Plan for summer evangelism program through retreats and camp attendance
4. Children's Day — sponsored by the Board of Christian Education, (emphasizing the children's work)
5. Plan for August
6. Father's Day
7. Last Sunday of June — Decision Day

JULY

Summer Camp Month

1. Enlist boys and girls and young people to attend the summer camps if possible
2. Plan an "echo service" for the Sunday school
3. Missionary Sunday
4. Workers' conference
5. Plan for September — Get vacationers back into Sunday school as soon as they get home
6. Independence Day

AUGUST

Camp Meeting Evangelism Month
1. Plan and promote attendance at the family camp
2. Friendship Day
3. Workers' conference
4. Missionary Sunday
5. Homecoming Sunday — last Sunday
6. Decision Day
7. Plan for October — appoint enlargement committees

APPENDIX III

Number 1

CHECK LIST FOR EVALUATING EFFECTIVENESS OF LEADERSHIP EDUCATION AGENCIES IN A LOCAL CHURCH

The following check list is taken from *A Guide for Presbyterian Church Schools*, Chapter 3. [1] For convenience in scoring, a total of 100 is assigned to this chart and each question is given as nearly as possible a properly proportioned value.

A. *Leadership Enlistment* (20)

1. Is a survey of leadership needs made annually? (5) _____
2. Is a survey of available leadership personnel made annually? (5) _____
3. Is a "challenge to service" made personally to such potential leaders? (5) _____
4. Is preliminary training provided for prospective teachers? (5) _____

B. *Workers' Conferences* (20)

1. Do the officers, teachers, and leaders of the church school meet for study and inspiration at least nine times a year, either all together or by age groups represented? (5) _____
2. Are at least two-thirds of the officers, teachers, and leaders present at each meeting? (5) _____
3. Do teachers of each department meet for the specific planning of each unit of lessons? (5) _____
4. Is at least 45 minutes taken at each workers' conference for educational and inspirational programs, carefully planned in advance on the basis of discovered needs? (5) _____

C. *Leadership Schools and Classes* (20)

1. Does the school make available at least one leadership course annually to its workers, either in separate classes or schools? (3) _____
2. Do you maintain a continuing leadership class through the year? (3) _____
3. Do at least half the officers and teachers earn at least one credit annually? (5) _____
4. Do you send one or more leaders annually to a summer leadership school? (3) _____
5. Is a leadership course on the duties of church officers offered at the time new officers are elected? (3) _____
6. Does the school cooperate in at least one interdenominational school annually where practicable? (3) _____

D. *Pre-Service and In-Service Training* (20)

1. Are individual teachers and leaders urged and provided opportunities to consult frequently with the pastor, the director of religious education, or other qualified local leaders, with a view to improving the quality of their teaching? (4) _____
2. Are teachers urged and provided opportunities for calling in regularly qualified "teacher consultants" for personal conferences, where such consultants are available? (3) _____
3. Are the teachers urged and enabled to visit "training centers"? (3) _____

[1] By David B. Walthall. Used by permission of John Knox Press.

4. Is apprentice training provided for new teachers and leaders? (3) _____
5. Do at least one-third of your officers and teachers attend an annual church school institute where such is provided in your presbytery? (4) _____
6. Have you ever held a "church school clinic" under the guidance of your regional director? (3) _____

E. *Resource Materials* (20)

1. Does the school maintain a leadership library with new books added annually? (5) _____
2. Do at least two-thirds of the leaders and teachers read at least one book annually on Christian education? (5) _____
3. Do the leaders and teachers read regularly the articles in *Presbyterian Action, The Earnest Worker,* and other good magazines on Christian education? (5) _____
4. Are leadership education audio-visuals such as the LEAV Kit used in workers' conferences or other meetings of leaders? (5) _____

TOTAL SCORE (possible 100) _____

Number 2

TEACHER SELF-RATING CHART

	Possible Score	Your Score
A. WORSHIP:		
1. Do you attend at least one worship and preaching service a Sunday, unless hindered by some valid reason?	5	_____
2. Do you make the worship service of your department one of real worship for yourself, and so conduct yourself that you would be willing to have the pupils follow your example?	5	_____
3. Do you practice personal fellowship with God, with at least some moments of each day dedicated specifically to this purpose?	5	_____
B. LESSON PREPARATION:		
1. Do you devote a minimum of at least one hour a week to lesson preparation, getting thorough understanding of the content for yourself and for your individual pupils?	12	_____
2. Do you make a written teaching plan to use in the presentation of your lesson?	8	_____
C. COOPERATION:		
1. Do you relate your work to the whole church program, and are you interested in the other church activities of your pupils?	5	_____
2. Are you open-minded in giving and receiving suggestions in conferences with your officers?	5	_____
D. PERSONAL RELATIONSHIP TO PUPILS:		
1. Do you keep personal information about your pupils, such as addresses, phone numbers, birthdays, etc., and such other information about their work as will at all times give an accurate picture of each individual?	5	_____
2. Are you a real friend to your pupils, greeting them on the street, playing with them when the opportunity offers, visiting them when sick, and taking an interest in their affairs?	5	_____

3. Do you visit the homes of your pupils at least once a year, and is each absence checked by yourself or some responsible person? 5 _____

E. FAITHFUL ATTENDANCE:
   1. Do you regularly attend the monthly workers' meetings and all departmental meetings? 10 _____
   2. Are you always present 15 minutes early in order to meet the first comers to your class? 10 _____
   3. Do you always give ample notice of necessary absence? 10 _____

F. GROWTH IN EFFICIENCY:
   1. Do you read regularly at least one good magazine on your work? 2 _____
   2. Do you make use of available library facilities, reading at least one good book a year on your work? 2 _____
   3. Do you complete one or more courses in leadership training class each year? 6 _____

TOTAL SCORE (possible 100) _____

It is suggested that visiting the corresponding grade in public schools is very helpful for growth in efficiency. Better still, visit some other Sunday school class.

Number 3

A CHECK-CHART FOR TEACHERS

A. PREPARATION
   1. Do I plan my work far enough ahead?
   2. Do I spend enough time upon each lesson?
   3. Do I set a goal for each quarter (some definite objective I want to reach)?
   4. Can I state, in a simple sentence, what I am setting out to do in each lesson?
   5. Do I make suggestions to my class for outside reading and preparation so that each lesson is not approached "cold"?
   6. Does every member of the class have adequate preparation materials and helps?

B. TEACHING METHODS
   1. Do I strive for variety:
      a. By alternating between the discussion and lecture methods? Others?
      b. By using charts, maps, posters, blackboards?
      c. By arranging for dramatization of some of the lessons?
   2. Do I open the class period with prayer?
   3. Are my opening statements challenging, interesting, clear, and heard by all?
   4. Do I stick to the lesson? Do I apply it to life?
   5. Do I summarize in an endeavor to tie together all loose ends, so as to make one definite, lasting impression?
   6. Do I link my thoughts and lessons together, so as to make a complete picture?
   7. Do I do all the talking?
   8. Do I argue?
   9. Do I listen to the opinions of others?
   10. Am I attempting to do the teaching rather than presenting the teachings of Jesus Christ and the Bible?

C. THE CLASS
   1. Is my class made up as nearly as possible of people of the same age and interests?
   2. Is my classroom attractive and comfortable?
   3. Is my class too large? Too small?

D. THE TEACHER
    1. Do I start and close the period on time?
    2. Do I use all the time to advantage, or do I waste time? ·
    3. Am I friendly?
    4. Do I make my class feel at home?
    5. Do I get my students acquainted with each other?
    6. Am I personally concerned for the spiritual welfare of every pupil?
        a. Do I pray for them?
        b. Do I encourage them to come to church?
        c. Do I try to help them outside of the class period?
        d. Do I keep check on their spiritual welfare?

Number 4

STANDARD FOR A WORKERS' TRAINING PROGRAM IN THE LOCAL CONGREGATION[2]

I. GENERAL PROVISIONS FOR WORKERS' TRAINING   150
    1. Is some person made definitely responsible for recruiting and
       training workers in the congregation?   10
    2. Is a careful canvass made each year of young people (as well
       as older) who show promise of ability but are not now active?   5
    3. Is there an assistant-teacher plan whereby young people learn
       to be teachers or officers through apprenticeship?   15
    4. Is adequate opportunity given young people in class, depart-
       ment, or society to conduct their own affairs under guidance?   10
    5. Are all workers given a democratic share in considering and
       determining policies and plans of the church?   20
    6. Does a sense of mission, the consciousness of a great and
       sacred task to be accomplished, pervade the church and its
       membership?   25
    7. Is the congregation properly appreciative of the efforts of its
       lay workers?   5
    8. Is there an annual public installation and consecration of
       officers and teachers?   5
    9. Is there a workers' library, with some new books added each
       year and with a definite plan of reading for the workers?   10
    10. Is there a plan whereby the workers receive regularly a good
        magazine on Christian education?   5
    11. Does each worker read at least one Christian education journal
        regularly and at least one book on Christian education each
        year?   5
    12. Is there a plan whereby each worker makes a worth-while visit
        to another church twice a year?   5
    13. Do the workers consciously set goals for themselves through
        the annual use of teacher-standards or teacher rating scales?   5
    14. Is the work of the church of such high caliber that both
        present workers and the children and young people as well are
        learning the best methods through actual experience? (Stand-
        ard B is the guide in answering this question so far as the
        church school is concerned)   20
    15. Are courses on the history and the present program of the
        church offered young people in church school, young people's
        society, or church membership class?   5
II. WORKERS' CONFERENCES   120
    1. Does the school have a workers' conference approximately ten
       times a year?   15
    2. Do all the workers attend these conferences?   10

[2]From *The Educational Work of the Church*, copyright 1939 by Nevin C. Harner, pp. 193-196. Used by permission of Abingdon Press.

    3. Is an educational topic provided as the main feature of the workers' conference?   15
    4. Is this topic, as a rule, concrete and specific?   10
    5. Does the program provide for participation by the workers?   10
    6. Are these programs planned as carefully as a session of a training class?   10
    7. Do the conferences as a rule end in some definite plan of action?   5
    8. Are the substitute or apprentice teachers participants in the conferences?   5
    9. Do members of the official board meet at least four times a year in conference on topics relating to their work?   20
   10. Are these programs planned and conducted as carefully as a session of a training class?   20

III. SUPERVISION   90
    1. Is some person made definitely responsible for supervising?   15
    2. Does each worker have the benefit of two supervisory visits and conferences a year?   20
    3. Would the supervisor's training and experience in Christian education qualify him to be an accredited instructor in the Standard Training Curriculum?   20
    4. Is his personality and high Christian purpose such as to make his visits and guidance welcome to the leaders?   15
    5. Do the conferences deal with such specific matters as: the needs of the persons under the worker's care, the methods employed, the materials employed, the worker's religious beliefs, etc.?   15
    6. Is the supervisory plan running without undue friction?   5

IV. TRAINING CLASSES AND SCHOOLS   80
    1. Does the church conduct or co-operate in conducting at least one Standard Training Class or School each year?   15
    2. Is a syllabus constructed for each course which builds primarily upon the problems and interests of the class members and only secondarily on the text?   20
    3. Is discussion amply provided for?   10
    4. Is actual practice amply provided for before, during, and after the course?   10
    5. Does the number of credits earned annually in this fashion plus those earned in summer camps and schools equal one half of the number of active workers in the church?   15
    6. Are these credits earned chiefly by persons who now are or soon will be active workers in the church?   10

V. CO-OPERATION WITH REGIONAL OR DENOMINATIONAL AGENCIES   60
    1. Are one to six persons — depending on the size and the financial ability of the church — sent to training camp or summer school each year?   20
    2. Are these delegates carefully chosen?   10
    3. Is the camp or school of sufficiently high educational level to have its courses accredited by the International Council of Religious Education?   10
    4. Does the church send official delegates to at least two conventions or institutes each year?   10
    5. Are these delegates carefully chosen for their ability to profit by the convention and to embody suggestions made there in the life of the church?   5
    6. Do the conventions or institutes devote the major part of their sessions to thinking through several education problems which are real to the delegates?   5

                                                500

Number 5
LIST OF WORKERS NEEDED

A. OFFICERS AND COMMITTEES
1. *Pastor* — An ordained leader in the local church and in every phase of its program.
2. *Assistant Pastor* — Ordained for the same duties of a pastor, but with special responsibility for program planning, calling or religious education.
3. *Director of Religious Education* — Has charge of the teaching program, teacher training, and leadership counsel for each age group.
4. *Office Secretary* — General secretarial work, such as typing, mailing, receptionist's duties, church roll, mimeographing, sometimes giving full time to financial matters.
5. *Full-time Music Director* — Planning of all music, leading one or more choirs, serving at the organ and piano, giving vocal lessons to choir; man or woman.
6. *Assistant to the Pastor* — A church secretary with more responsibility.
7. *Educational Assistant* — Assisting the pastor in teaching program.
8. *Director of Youth Work* — Commissioned in large church to guide study, worship, and recreation in youth groups.
9. *Director of Children's Work* — Commissioned in large church to guide activities of children up through 12.
10. *Deaconess* — Ordained to help parish underprivileged, calling, teaching or religious education.
11. *Church Social Worker* — Commissioned to case work or group work in parish or church-sponsored settlement house.
12. *Church Sexton or Custodian* — Employed to keep church and parish buildings clean.
13. *Class Leader* — A spiritual leader who encourages his brethren, visits the sick, and has charge of the class.
14. *Assistant Class Leader* — Aids the class leader and takes charge in his absence.
15. *Trustees* — Have care of the property and see that order is maintained during worship.
16. *Stewards* — They promote the practice of Christian stewardship and provide the elements for the Lord's Supper.
17. *Financial Secretary* — Receives and records all monies from individual contributors, keeping an accurate account.
18. *Church Treasurer* — Administers all funds for ministerial support and purely local expenses.
19. *Missions and Benevolence Treasurer* — Administers all missions and benevolence monies.
20. *Committee on Evangelism* — Are responsible for all missions and benevolence monies.
21. *Committee on Missions* — Are responsible to the local church in the missionary task.
22. *Committee on Christian Education* — Seek to improve the program.
23. *Committee on Social Action* — Study and make recommendations concerning attitudes and activities pertaining to social conditions.
24. *Committee on Stewardship* — Study ways of creating an intelligent conception of the fundamental principles of Christian stewardship.
25. *Committee on Finance* — Have charge of the financial program of the church.
26. *Committee on Church Property* — Are responsible for the care and protection of the property.
27. *Committee on Music* — Guide in the selection of and the supervision of the work of the choir, the chorister, the organist, and other musical leaders.
28. *Committee on Ushering* — Guide in selection and training of ushers, and serve as a committee to welcome visitors.

29. *Committee on Christian Literature* — Place denominational literature in the Sunday school and homes.
30. *Committee on Publicity* — Have charge of all publicity in the local church.
31. *Committee on Audit* — Annually audit the books of all treasurers of the local church and its organizations and report to the Church Council of Administration the financial status of the local church.

B. DENOMINATIONAL WORKERS IN NATIONAL OR AREA PROGRAM
1. Denominational executives of national boards
2. Denominational editors and lesson writers
3. Area denominational executives
4. Expert in radio, films, and T.V.
5. Publishing house managers; printers, salesmen, office and plant personnel
6. Book-store managers and clerks
7. Office secretary or clerical workers

C. WORKERS IN INTER-CHURCH NATIONAL OR AREA PROGRAM
1. Council of churches executive
2. Educational executive in state or city council
3. Social service director and staff
4. Director of research and survey
5. Institutional chaplain
6. Director of public relations and finance
7. Week-day church school teacher, or supervisor
8. Office secretaries and clerical workers

D. CAMPUS, INSTITUTIONAL, AND MILITARY WORKERS
1. College or prep school chaplain
2. Denominational chaplain
3. College or prep school teacher of religion
4. Professor in theological seminary
5. Student movement secretary
6. House parent
7. Full time hospital or jail chaplain
8. Worker in church institution for special groups (children, old people, handicapped, etc.)
9. Community "Y" secretary
10. Military chaplain

E. WORKERS IN MISSIONS (All mentioned above plus:)
1. Evangelist in missions
2. Mission teacher in grade or high school
3. Mission seminary teacher
4. Medical missionary teacher
5. Missionary dentist
6. Missionary nurse
7. Missionary social worker
8. Missionary dietitian
9. Overseas relief worker
10. Other missionary jobs

F. DEPARTMENT WORKERS
1. *Sunday School*
   a. Sunday school superintendent
   b. Associate superintendent
   c. Secretary
   d. Treasurer
   e. Librarian
   f. Chorister
   g. Pianist
   h. Divisional superintendent
   i. Department superintendent

      j. Teachers
      k. Assistant teachers
      l. Class secretary

2. *Youth Fellowship*
   Intermediate 12 - 14   Senior 15 - 17   Young People 18 - 24
   a. President
   b. Vice-president
   c. Secretary
   d. Treasurer
   e. Adult counselor
   f. Commission on Worship and Devotional Life
   g. Commission on Evangelism and Stewardship
   h. Commission on Missions and Social Action
   i. Commission on Recreation and Leisure

3. *Adult Christian Endeavor League*
   a. President
   b. Vice-president
   c. Secretary
   d. Treasurer
   e. Membership committee
   f. Devotional committee
   g. Service committee
   h. Fellowship and recreation committee

4. *Men's Fellowship*
   a. President
   b. Vice-president
   c. Secretary
   d. Treasurer
   e. Commission on Devotional
   f. Commission on Christian Training
   g. Commission on Christian Service
   h. Commission on Christian Fellowship

5. *Women's Society of World Service*
   a. President
   b. Vice-president
   c. Secretary
   d. Treasurer
   e. Flower committee
   f. Music director
   g. Director of Christian Education
   h. Age group directors

SUMMARY OF WORKERS NEEDED

G. CLASSIFICATIONS:
  1. Administrators
  2. Teachers
  3. Counselors
  4. Persons to share in community and world-wide enterprises
  5. Leaders of worship
  6. Musicians
  7. Leaders of recreation and leisure time activities
  8. Church visitors
  9. Supervisors
  10. Leaders for special groups and activities
  11. Persons skilled in publicity

Number 6

ENLISTMENT BLANK
(Used by the Oregon City, Oregon, EUB Church in 1954)

Trusting the Lord to use me in His service to the upbuilding of the work in this church, I make the following commitments, and by God's grace I will endeavor to keep them: (Please check items for which you will offer your service and talent.)

CHURCH
( ) calling on the sick; absentees ( )
( ) calling on new prospects
( ) personal work
( ) choir, orchestra ( )

GENERAL
( ) property maintenance; repairing, etc.
( ) ushering
( ) secretarial work;
  ( ) mimeographing
  ( ) church bulletins
  ( ) publicity, mailing
  ( ) telephoning

SUNDAY SCHOOL
( ) teacher; ( ) age desired
( ) calling, writing, addressing
( ) personal work
( ) car for pupil pickups

YOUTH WORK
( ) choir; orchestra ( )
( ) advisor
( ) personal work

OTHER
( ) _____
( ) _____

Make all decisions after prayer; place in offering plate or hand to the pastor.

NAME _____

CHRISTIAN SERVICE INVENTORY
(Published by Division of Christian Education, NCCC, 79 E. Adams St., Chicago 3, Ill.)

(Front of card)

GENERAL CHURCH SERVICES
____Officer
____Usher
____Group work
  ____Boys
  ____Girls
  ____Youth
  ____Women
  ____Men
____Leading music
____Instrumental music
Instrument____
____Vocal music
Voice____
____Evangelism
____Finances
____Inter-church cooperation
____Missions
____Peace
____Public speaking
____Social action

CHURCH SCHOOL
____Officer
____Dept. supt.
  ____Children
  ____Youth
  ____Adult
____Nursery roll
____Home dept.
____Teacher
  ____Children
  ____Youth
  ____Adults
____Vacation Bible School
____Weekday C. S.
____Greeter
____Librarian
____Pianist
____Secretary
____Work with Families

SOCIAL INTERESTS AND SERVICES
____Art work
____Audio-visual education
____Calling
  ____worship
____Community welfare
____Cooking
____Waiting tables
____Correspondence
____Crafts
____Dramatics
____Folk games
____Industrial relations
____Intergroup relations
____Mimeographing
____Typing
____Nature
____Nursing
____Photography
____Projectionist
____Publicity
____Transportation
____Radio-television
____Recreation
____Storytelling
____Telephoning

(On back side a message, appeal, challenge, and place to sign)

Number 7

AND NOW TO WORK

As a steward of God, I am interested in:
(Check those offices in which you feel you could serve best and would be willing to serve.)

Check Office

Give experience here

——Working with cradle roll_____
——Working in nursery_____
——Teaching in kindergarten_____
——Teaching primaries_____
——Teaching juniors_____
——Teaching intermediates_____
——Working with young people_____
——Teaching adults_____
——Working in home department_____
——Being pianist_____
——Leading singing_____
——Providing special music_____
——Singing in choir_____
——Visiting in homes_____
——Visiting the sick_____
——Helping in jail services_____
——Working with church finance_____
——Working with Boy Scouts_____
——Working with Girl Scouts_____
——Being librarian_____
——Ushering _____
——Publicizing the church_____
——Helping with bulletins and mailings_____
——Typing _____
——Being church secretary_____
——Working in missionary society_____
——Planning picnics and socials_____
——Preparing special programs (Christmas, Easter, etc.)_____
——Directing recreation_____
——Directing dramatics_____
——Distributing tracts_____
——Decorating the church_____
——Working in the kitchen_____
——Cleaning _____
——Carpentry _____
——Electrical work_____
——Other activities not included here_____
Are you willing to prepare to do this work?_____
If selected, can we count on you to be dependable?_____
Name_____ Address_____

Number 8

ENLISTMENT

"We are laborers together with God" (I Cor. 3:9)

DESIRING to enlist as a LABORER in the work of the Kingdom of God, as a MEMBER (_____), FRIEND (_____) of the _____
E. U. B. Church, I will to the best of my ability perform the following if and

when I am called upon:

1. Support the work and worship of this church by prayer_____.
2. Support financially _____; and register myself as a tither_____.
   I will not give less than 75% of my tithe to the program of my
   Church _____.
3. By serving as a teacher of a S.S. class; Adult_____; Youth_____;
   Children_____.
4. By serving as an assistant S.S. teacher, or secretary of records_____.
5. As a pianist_____; in the choir_____ (Alto_____, Tenor_____,
   Soprano_____, Bass_____, Sing Special Music_____.)
6. Serve as an advisor to youth groups; Junior_____; Intermediate_____;
   Young people_____.
7. Serve as an usher_____; help build a men's program in the church
   _____.
8. Serve at church dinners_____ or in connection with other church
   functions_____.
9. Work with boys_____ or girls_____ in club work.
10. Serve upon a church decoration committee for special occasions
    _____.
11. Serve on the Trustee Board; Stewards_____; Music Committee_____;
    Evangelism Committee_____; Social Action Committee_____; Com-
    mittee on Missions_____; Christian Education_____.
12. Serve on a committee for the visitation of the sick_____.
13. Do visitation in the interest of the church_____; SS class_____;
    auxiliary_____.
14. Give an extra night a month for the visitation of men_____;
    women_____; youth_____.
15. Help in the church office with mailing_____; filing_____; secretarial
    work_____.
16. Use my car to bring people to Sunday school_____; church_____.
17. Work on special committees of the church_____; Sunday school
    _____; Youth Fellowship_____.
18. Open my home to visiting workers (evangelists, etc.) _____.
19. Open my home to cottage prayer meetings _____.
20. Do occasional repair work about the church_____.
21. I have had experience as a bookkeeper_____, secretary_____, file
    clerk_____, public stenographer_____, school teacher_____, business
    executive_____, personnel director_____, foreman_____, salesman
    _____, building maintenance man_____, professional experience
    _____, Other_____.
22. I should like to show my interest in the work of Christ's kingdom by
    doing the following:

SIGNED: _____

ADDRESS: _____

    If under 21, please give age _____
    Please return this fact-finder by mail, or hand it
    to your UNIT LEADER when he calls on you.

Number 9

RECRUITING LEADERSHIP FOR THE LOCAL CHURCH

NAME _____

ADDRESS _____

CITY _____ STATE _____

HOME TELEPHONE _____ BUSINESS TELEPHONE _____

CHURCH MEMBERSHIP _____

SUNDAY SCHOOL _____

OCCUPATION _____

EMPLOYER _____

ART
( ) I do art work
( ) I do lettering
( ) I do poster work
( ) I am interested in arranging flowers
( ) I am interested in decorating church for special occasions
( ) My hobby craft specialty _____

BUSINESS
( ) Good knowledge of insurance
( ) Good knowledge of real estate
( ) Good knowledge of advertising
( ) I am in _____ business or profession and would be glad to use my influence in this respect for the good of the church

HOSPITALITY
( ) I (we) would open our home to entertain delegates, conference personnel, etc.
( ) We can provide lodging for _____ (number) persons
( ) We would like to open our home occasionally for
    ( ) Prayer groups
    ( ) Youth groups

KITCHEN AND DINING ROOM SERVICE
Food Preparation
I am willing to assume the responsibility of planning°
( ) large church dinners
( ) small church dinners
( ) refreshments for large receptions
( ) refreshments for small receptions
I am willing to *assist* in the planning of
( ) large church dinners
( ) small church dinners
( ) refreshments for large receptions
( ) refreshments for small receptions
    (Planning covers the menu planning, figuring quantity and cost of food needed and ordering of same)
( ) I would cook for large dinners
( ) I would cook for small dinners

DINING ROOM
( ) Interested in decorating tables
( ) Would serve as a waitress
( ) Would set tables
( ) Would supervise dining room

DISH WASHING
( ) I am willing to wash dishes with a group

LEADERSHIP
BOYS' CLUBS
( ) Have had experience with boy club work
( ) Would serve as a leader
( ) Would serve on a committee
( ) Would transport boys occasionally

GIRLS' CLUBS
( ) Have had experience in girls' club work
( ) Would serve as a leader
( ) Would serve as a committee member
( ) Would serve as a driver to take girls home following weekly meeting

LEADERSHIP
YOUTH WORK
( ) Would like to be a leader for a youth group
( ) I have had experience in working with groups (give added information) _____

( ) As a couple (husband and wife), we would be interested in being sponsors or counsellors for a youth group. Age group preferred _____

LIBRARY
( ) Would enjoy working as a church librarian
( ) Would like to be a book reviewer for the library
( ) Would like to serve as a committee member
( ) Have library experience

MUSIC
Singing Voice
( ) Alto
( ) Bass
( ) Soprano
( ) Tenor
Interested in the following
( ) Choir
( ) Ensemble
( ) Male chorus
( ) Male quartet
( ) Mixed quartet
( ) Ladies' trio
Instrumental
I play _____ (instrument)
( ) do solo work
( ) would like ensemble work
( ) would like to play in a string band
( ) would like to play in an orchestra

Piano
( ) I play the piano
( ) read music readily
( ) could serve as a pianist where less difficult music is used

Organ
( ) Play the pipe organ
( ) Play an electric organ
( ) feel qualified to serve as an assistant

Directing
( ) do song-leading
( ) could direct an orchestra
( ) could direct children's choirs
( ) would like to be a music librarian

OFFICE WORK
( ) accountant
( ) bookkeeper
( ) write shorthand
( ) typist
( ) mimeograph operator
( ) would be willing to learn mimeographing
( ) would do telephoning from my home
( ) work on mailings
   ( ) addressing in longhand
   ( ) folding and stuffing

RECREATION
(_____) Preferred recreation or sport
Would like to direct recreation for following group
( ) Men
( ) Senior high boys
( ) Junior high boys
( ) Grade school boys
( ) Please list sports trained and experienced in _____
_____
( ) Enjoy planning games, etc., for children's parties and events
( ) Interested in directing recreation for women and girls

TRANSPORTATION
( ) I have a chauffeur's license
( ) I would drive the Sunday school bus
   ( ) regularly
   ( ) occasionally
( ) I would be willing to use my car when transportation is needed
   ( ) to transport guest speakers
   ( ) to pick up children outside Sunday school bus route and located near me

SKILLS
( ) Cabinet-maker
( ) Carpenter
( ) Electrician
( ) Interior decorator
( ) Mason
( ) Mechanic — auto
( ) Painter
( ) Plumber
( ) Practical nurse
( ) Registered nurse
( ) Photographer
( ) Radio technician
( ) Seamstress
List your specialty not named above _____

SUNDAY SCHOOL
( ) I have had formal teacher training
   ( ) Bible school or seminary
   ( ) College
( ) Evening school, etc.
( ) I have had experience as a teacher
(_____) age group preferred
Check any of the following you are particularly interested in doing.
( ) teaching
( ) superintending a department
( ) superintending children's church
( ) assisting in teaching
( ) assisting in children's church
( ) general secretary of the Sunday school
( ) supply secretary
( ) department secretary
( ) missionary education for children
( ) Memory work projects for children
( ) song leading
( ) playing piano
( ) leading worship services for children
( ) assisting in nursery during church services
( ) would ride Sunday school bus to supervise children
( ) supervise picnics or outings
( ) assist in planning picnics, etc.
( ) PRAY regularly for workers and pupils _____

WRITING
( ) Editorial ability
( ) Write poetry
( ) Write plays or skits
( ) Like reporting for a paper
( ) Have had experience in reporting
( ) Know the printing business

VISITATION
Would serve
( ) in a community canvass
( ) as a personal worker in visitation work team

( ) to call on the sick
( ) to do general calling
( ) Have had experience in personal soul-winning

Perhaps you have a talent or ability which is not named above. Please feel free to add that to the questionnaire. Also, make any comments you wish in making your answers clear.

Number 10

A CALENDAR FOR A PROGRAM OF LEADERSHIP EDUCATION IN THE LOCAL CHURCH

AUTUMN

Small Church

Annual Recognition and Dedication Service
Christian Education Week observed
Monthly workers' conferences
Participation in a standard training school
Weekly training class as a part of Sunday school program
Acquaint workers with home study plan

Large Church

Annual Recognition and Dedication Service
Christian Education Week observed
Monthly workers' conferences
Standard training school
Weekly training class as a part of Sunday school program
Acquaint workers with home study plan

WINTER

Monthly workers' conference
Weekly training class a part of Sunday school program
Home study
Emphasize reading
 Books of missions
 Books on Christian education
School of missions or a conference on missions

Monthly workers' conference
Weekly training class as part of Sunday school program
Home study
Emphasize reading
 Books on missions
 Books on Christian education
Midweek night training school with classes to meet the particular needs of the local church. Consider a school of missions

SPRING

Monthly workers' conference
Midweek night class on church membership and beliefs
Home study
Plan for Christian Education Week

Monthly workers' conference
Home study
Weekly training class as part of Sunday school program
Plan for Christian Education Week

SUMMER

Monthly workers' conference
Home study
A training class within the vacation church school
Assemblies, camps, and conferences
Summer leadership training schools

Monthly workers' conference
Home study
Weekly training class as part of Sunday school program
A training class within the vacation church school
Assemblies, camps, and conferences
Summer leadership training schools

Number 11

MODEL INSTALLATION SERVICE

1. Opening Hymn: "My Faith Looks up to Thee"
2. Read the Roll of Officers and Teachers elect
3. Hymn: "Stand Up, Stand Up for Jesus"
   (Have officers and teachers come forward)
4. Prayer — by the pastor
5. Admonitory Scripture Reading: I Cor. 12:4-12; II Tim. 2:14-21
   Led by the pastor or one appointed by him
6. Questions to the Officers and Teachers elect
   a. Do you freely accept the position as officer or teacher to which the church has called you?
   b. Will you endeavor faithfully to discharge the duties pertaining to it?
   c. Will you strive earnestly to set before your scholars a good Christian example in all things?
   d. Will you give diligence to Bible study and preparation for teaching, as opportunity allows?
   e. Will you faithfully attend the various meetings which the superintendent may call unless you are providentially hindered?
7. The Covenant of Office (Leader reading it clause by clause; officers and teachers repeating after)
   "I do solemnly devote myself, in the fear and by the favor of God, to my Sunday school work. I will study my Bible thoroughly and strive to govern and to teach my scholars intelligently and faithfully. I will endeavor to be a loyal and exemplary member of my church, and an example to my scholars in the use of the means of grace. I will counsel spiritually with my scholars at home and elsewhere and will give such portion of my time as is possible to my Sunday school duties. I will strive to be punctual and present at school and at all meetings of teachers. In the presence of God and His people, and by the grace of Jesus Christ. Amen."
8. Benediction
9. Brief address
10. Closing Hymn: "I Love Thy Church, O God"

Number 12

TEACHER'S AGREEMENT
(Sample)

In consideration of my appointment by the _____
Sunday school and of the opportunity offered me to participate in the sacred work of teaching the religion of our Lord and Master, as a teacher in the Sunday school, I agree on my part that:

1. I will accept and faithfully perform the duties of that office, from this date to the following December 31.
2. I will make it a practice to attend the sessions regularly, and if for any real reason I am prevented from coming, I will notify my department superintendent, or the general superintendent, and help to provide a substitute who is mutually acceptable. If I am absent more than 10 Sundays in the year, or 3 Sundays without notice, I understand that my office shall be considered vacant.
3. I will make it a practice to come on time to the sessions, which I interpret to mean that as a teacher I am to be present at least 10 minutes before the opening of the session.
4. I will prepare thoroughly for each session, maintain discipline, help to create an attitude of reverence and a spirit of loyalty and cooperation, and, with the help of God, set a good example in Christian living.
5. I will cooperate with the officers of the school, my department superintendent, and my fellow teachers; I will welcome constructive criticism and

helpful suggestions, and will at all times abide by such rulings as may be made for the best interests of the whole school.

6. I will regularly attend the meetings of teachers and officers, known as the workers' conference, and participate in the work of the conference.

7. I will broaden my knowledge of and experience in my task through reading and study. I will read regularly a magazine dealing with my work, study good books, or take a training course — all three if possible.

8. I will make a careful study of the "Self-Rating Chart" used in our school, and make a conscious effort to measure up as high as possible in each of the points.

9. In case I find it impossible to continue my services for any reason, I will notify the superintendent in writing at least two weeks in advance.

Signed: _____

The_____day of_____, 19_____

Number 13

OUTLINE FOR A JOB ANALYSIS
(Teacher, Administrator, or Director, Supervisor)

A. SCOPE AND OBJECTIVES OF THE PROGRAM
What are the aims or objectives of the program for which the worker is engaged?

B. DESCRIPTION OF POSITION
1. For what type of job is the worker needed? Is it a single or combined job such as teacher, supervisor, director, consultant, director-teacher, supervisor-teacher, or director-supervisor? Define the type of position for which the person is employed.
2. What type of person is needed for this job? Describe the type of person in terms of personality and character, education, and experience.
3. Working conditions
   a. What is the salary and plan of salary increase?
   b. What is the length of term of employment?
   c. What provisions are made for social security, insurance, annuity, etc.?
   d. What is the plan for vacations, sick leave, and substitute teachers? (Usually follows local publc school practice)
   e. How many classes and pupils will the teacher have? What grades will he teach? What will be the size of the classes? What will be the length of the class periods?
   f. What provision is made for mimeograph materials and other supplies, equipment, transportation, and necessary expenses?
   g. What kind of contract will you have with the worker; formal or informal (letter)?

C. RESPONSIBILITIES RELATED TO THE TEACHING
1. What preparation for daily teaching is expected?
2. Which of the following activities will he be expected to carry on: Bible study, worship, service project, creative activities, and other materials and experience.
3. How much time and attention shall he give to individual guidance? What arrangements are made for a time for personal counseling?
4. What home contacts should the teacher make? Should he do home visitation, consultation, reports, letters, etc.?
5. What church contacts should the teacher make? To what extent should he visit the churches, confer with church officials concerning pupils and program?
6. In what forms of in-service training will the teacher be expected to engage? What assistance will the council provide?
7. Will you provide opportunity for teachers to attend state and national Christian education conferences, by providing substitutes, transportation, and part of expenses?

8. In what ways will he be expected to cooperate with the administrator and the governing board? What regular conferences will he be expected to attend? What records and reports will he be asked to make?

D. RESPONSIBILITIES RELATED TO ADMINISTRATION
   1. What are the responsibilities of the worker in planning for the housing, including arrangements for —
      a. Heat and janitor service
      b. Equipment
      c. Other supplies (visual aids, etc.)
   2. What are his duties in enrolling pupils?
   3. What is his part in working out schedules for both teachers and pupils?
   4. With whom and to what extent does he work in building, evaluating, and revising the curriculum?
   5. To what extent and with whom does he plan the budget?
   6. To what extent will he be responsible for promoting and publicizing the program?
   7. What will be his specific responsibility in employing and directing the personnel?
   8. To whom should his regular reports be made?
   9. What provision for secretarial help is given?
   10. What should be his duties in relationship to —
       a. Churches of the community
       b. Other faiths
       c. Public school
       d. Homes
       e. Other community agencies

E. RESPONSIBILITIES RELATED TO SUPERVISION
   1. What are his responsibilities in explaining the purpose and nature of the curriculum?
   2. What are his duties in evaluating and improving the quality of teaching?
   3. How much time will be given in his schedule to the study and improvement of working conditions?
      a. Of the pupils — such as attractive rooms, teacher attitudes, etc.?
      b. Of the teachers — such as a sense of personal security?
   4. How much of his time should be given to personal conferences with teachers, guiding their reading, planning the curriculum, and setting up general conferences?
   5. To what extent will he be encouraged and enabled to attend state and national conferences for professional enrichment?
      (Through release of time and provision of expenses.)

F. OTHER RESPONSIBILITIES
   What other responsibilities will the worker have? Define them clearly.

APPENDIX IV

CHURCH SCHOOL TEACHER AND OFFICER
INFORMATION BLANK*

1. Occupation (school teacher, housekeeper, etc.) _____
2. Male _____ Female_____
3. At what age did you begin to teach? _____
4. Your present age _____
5. Department _____
6. Officer? _____
7. Teacher? _____
8. Years in present S. S. position _____
9. What schools have you attended?
   Elementary — No. of yrs.? _____ Teachers' College — No. of yrs.? _____
   High School — No. of yrs.? _____ College, University — No. of yrs.?____
   Business College — No. of yrs.? Other School _____ No. of yrs.?
   _____
10. Check the following courses you have had in college or university:
    Educational Psychology _____   Principles of teaching religion _____
    School Management _____   History of religion _____
    History of Education _____   Biblical literature _____
    Principles of Teaching _____   Missions _____
    Organization and Adm. of   Bible History _____
    Church Schools _____
    Other courses _____
11. Indicate courses taken at the following schools:
    (a) Courses taken in local church training school:
        Course _____No. of lessons _____
        Course _____No. of lessons _____
    (b) Courses taken in community training school or summer school:
        Course _____No. of lessons _____
        Course _____No. of lessons _____
12. How many years have you taught in the following schools?
    Sunday school — years _____   Daily Vacation Bible school _____
    Public or private school _____   Other school? _____
    Week-day religious school _____
13. List some books on religious education recently read: _____
    _____
14. What religious educational periodicals or magazines do you read regularly?
    _____
15. What conventions, institutes, training classes have you attended regularly?
    or recently? _____
16. What do you consider to be the types of service you are best qualified
    to undertake? _____

* From Frank M. McKibben, *Improving Religious Education Through Supervision*, p. 211.

343

Number 2

GUIDE FOR OBSERVING A CHURCH SCHOOL SESSION

I. HOW TO OBSERVE
   A. Things for the supervisor or observer to remember
      1. It is difficult for the teacher to teach children in the presence of observers or supervisors
      2. The teacher is quite conscious of being observed and evaluated
   B. Suggestions for supervisors and observers
      1. Arrive early
         a. Give the teacher time to explain to you the purposes and plans for the lesson before the pupils arrive
         b. Remember that this is only one session in a series
      2. Remove hat and wrap and stay in an inconspicuous place during the entire session unless requested by the teacher to move
      3. Remain quiet; do not laugh at comments or actions of pupils
      4. Take time to talk to the teacher after the class session

II. WHAT TO OBSERVE
   A. The physical conditions
      1. Is the room inviting and attractive? Heat? Cleanliness?
      2. Is the room adequate in size? Well lighted? Ventilated?
      3. Are the chairs, tables, and other furnishings appropriate for the age group?
      4. What provision is made to create an atmosphere of beauty, worship, work, and friendliness?
      5. Is there a place for work (or play) materials so that pupils can have access to them?
      6. Is there a place for the teacher to keep his supplies?
      7. Are pictures appropriate for the age group? To the unit being used? Are they appropriately placed?
      8. Is there a place for wraps for both teachers and pupils?
   B. Routine factors
      1. Does the teacher arrive early? How much?
      2. Does the teacher remove his hat and wrap and get busy on arrival (saving visiting with others until after the session)?
      3. What method is used to get started? Taking roll? Seating and passing? Offering? Distributing supplies? Handling materials and apparatus?
      4. Do the pupils and teachers feel at ease and at home with each other?
      5. Are individual needs and interests recognized?
      6. Is there a spirit of cooperation among the pupils? Between the teachers and the pupils?
      7. Do the teachers speak in quiet voices? Meet interruptions calmly? Enter into the pupils' conversation and work joyfully?
   C. Discipline and order
      1. Means?
      2. Skill? Occasions?
   D. Class Procedure
      1. Is there evidence of a definite aim or purpose to the lesson?
         a. Can you detect the kinds of knowledge or information which the teacher planned to give to the class?
         b. Can you detect what attitudes and feeling responses the teacher tried to encourage?
         c. What applications to the students' life and conduct were made during the course of the lesson?
      2. What evidences of the use of materials or subject matter did you observe?
         a. Were stories used?
         b. Were pictures or object lessons used?

    c. What kind of prayers were used?
    d. Music?
    e. Handwork or other forms of expression material
3. What methods were used?
    a. What types of teaching were used? Storytelling? Questions? Drama? Discussions? etc.
    b. Were assignments made?
    c. Was a review of the previous lessons given?
    d. How was the interest of the students engaged?
    e. Do all participate in the lessons?
    f. How were the following used in the session?
      (1) Bible
      (2) Other books
      (3) Stories
      (4) Conversation
4. What general principles of teaching were violated, if any?
5. How did the teacher use questions?
6. Did the teacher use any methods of evaluation, such as tests, examinatons, rating scales, standards, etc.?

Number 3

SUPERVISOR'S CHART

Thank you for your hospitality. I was glad for the privilege of visiting your class in order to learn to know your pupils better and to become better acquainted with the work being done in your department.

I liked a lot of things about your class on _____.
Among these were:

_____ Your personal appearance, which was neat and showed thoughtful consideration for your important work.

_____ The pleasant, friendly atmosphere which you create in your classroom.

_____ The manner in which you interest and gain the attention of your pupils and the way in which they respond to you.

_____ The evidence that you meet the children at other times than during your class session — by visiting them in their homes or seeing them in other places.

_____ The resourceful way in which you had prepared for many activities through which your pupils might learn the Christian way of life and the necessary skills and information by which to live the good life.

_____ The obvious fact that you study books and magazines which will help you to do a better teaching job in your work of helping to build the kingdom of God.

I did think your work would probably be more effective if you:

_____ Would have your class sessions a little more carefully planned, with your aim a little more accurately thought through.

_____ Would have more variety of method in your class sessions. (Perhaps you do change your method from Sunday to Sunday — this helps your pupils to come to your class in an expectant mood.)

_____ Would provide for more activities (purposeful ones, not too difficult) through which your pupils can gain knowledge and Christian skills.

_____ Would plan your questions so they would require more thought for answering — avoid questions that can be answered with one word, except on written quizzes.

_____ Would improve the physical appearance of your classroom — look about and see what you yourself could do about it.

_____ Would give more attention to the ventilation, temperature, seating, lighting, and other physical comforts of your pupils.

_____ Would arrive earlier in your classroom and plan for some interesting pre-session activities for your pupils.

A personal note:

Signature: _____

Number 4

MIDTERM EXAMS FOR OUR CHURCH SCHOOL — An Evaluation

How Do We Know When We Have an Adequate Program
Of Christian Education?

I. The Church school must serve under the direction of a church board or committee on Christian education, For the church school is not an independent agency; it is the school of the church.

_____ 1. Do we have a Committee on Christian Education authorized and appointed by the church?

_____ 2. Do its elected members serve in rotation so that each year there is some new life in the Committee?

_____ 3. Does the nominating committee choose them with care to include people with a religious interest, an educational background, an understanding of childhood and youth?

_____ 4. Does this committee really function — not in matters of detail, but in determining policies?

II. The educational program of the church must include all ages.

_____ 5. Do we offer study opportunities for men and women?

_____ 6. Is provision made for older young people and young adults?

_____ 7. Do we have a nursery class for the three-year-olds, meeting by itself in the Sunday church school?

_____ 8. Is our home-nursery roll (from birth to the age of three) something more than a "roll"? Through it does your church help young parents in their task of Christian training?

_____ 9. Do we have the following departments (or in a small church combination of these groups): Nursery, Kindergarten, (Beginner), Primary, Junior, Junior High (Intermediate), Senior, Post-High School (Young People), Adult?

III. The choice of the class curriculum is important, and when selected this material is used faithfully.

_____ 10. Is the decision as to curriculum materials made by the Committee on Christian Education, with advice from mothers who are concerned?

_____ 11. Does our committee consider first its own denominational curriculum suggestions?

_____ 12. If a teacher is critical of a course of study, does he suggest to the Christian Education Committee that a change be made and that they confer about the matter rather than being free on his own initiative to change to another course?

_____ 13. Is there an occasional curriculum conference that helps workers to see the plan as a whole, to look forward to their teaching task with a sense of unity, and to receive help in any problems they face?

IV. Worship is an important part of the church school program.

_____ 14. Is every worship service planned in advance, and not made a quick task for Sunday morning after arrival at the church?

_____ 15. Do our leaders have a sense of graded worship so that, for example, there is a clear difference between worship in the Primary Department and worship for Junior High boys and girls?

16. Are there times and places when training is given in the elements of worship so that members of the school learn hymns, learn Scripture passages appropriate to their age, learn prayers, and have the experience of writing their own prayers?

17. Are our pupils actual participants in the worship service, rather than silent and passive listeners?

18. In our thought does Christian education include the leadership of worship so that as pupils mature they are having an increasing experience in the leadership of worship?

V. Giving is a Christian grace, concern for others is a basic element of Christianity, and service experiences are essential in Christian education.

19. Does our school include training in the Christian use of money? Can we point to definite grades and times when this is found in our program?

20. Do the members of our school use the envelope system so that they are being trained in the habit of regular and systematic giving to the church and the world-wide work of the church?

21. Are our pupils guided into experiences of service in their own community, carefully chosen so that such experiences are appropriate to the age of the participants?

22. Are they brought face to face with service opportunities for others in other parts of America and other parts of the world (suggested, perhaps, by one of our denominational agencies) so that they will have the experience of sharing and will enjoy a growing feeling of world fellowship?

VI. The teaching staff is of primary consideration in bringing about a successful church school.

23. Do we have a plan for securing teachers so that the more competent are asked, and asked personally, for a definite task and a definite time, so that our staff for the year ahead is practically completed by June?

24. Do we follow a plan for the training of prospective teachers that includes (a) an on-going training class for this one purpose, and (b) a system of apprenticeship in which one may serve as assistant to an experienced teacher?

25. Do we follow a plan for the training of those now serving as teachers, including (a) regular teachers' and officers' conferences with educational programs, (b) local church or community training schools offering standard courses, and (c) the sending of some of our workers to summer laboratory schools or leadership education conferences?

26. Is a conscientious effort made to have every teacher prepare a lesson plan before each teaching session and to develop teaching skills in such fields as storytelling, creative activities, and leading a discussion?

27. Do we recognize our church school workers (a) by a service of dedication at the beginning of the year, and (b) by some concrete occasion of appreciation before the end of the school year?

VII. The best possible equipment is an aid in realizing our purposes.

28. Do we have separate class rooms or, if that is financially impossible, do we separate classes by the use of screens or curtains?

29. Are we utilizing all available space, e.g., an old room that might be transformed into a room for an adult class?

30. Can we honestly say that when the school assembles Sunday morning the total appearance is one of cleanliness and neatness?

_____ 31. Do we have adequate closet space and storage space for materials with up-to-date materials, arranged in orderly fashion?

VIII. The home must be the basic institution in Christian training.

_____ 32. Do we have at least one conference a year for parents and teachers, with a program that makes clear the church's plans for Christian training and recognizes the common responsibility of both?

_____ 33. Do we have an occasional "Family Festival" or a "Family Day at Church" or something of the kind?

_____ 34. Do as many as half of our teachers call in the homes of pupils?

_____ 35. Do we have a study group — even a short course for six weeks during some period of the year — for the parents?

_____ 36. Is it our custom to send something to the homes — other than requests for help — at least once a year, e.g., a report on the pupil's progress, book suggestions, or helpful material on child development or the Christian home?

IX. One hour a week is scarcely enough for Christian education.

_____ 37. Did we conduct a vacation church school this past summer?

_____ 38. Has our committee given serious consideration to the extension of the Sunday school time from one hour to one and one-half hours or two hours?

_____ 39. Do we have weekday religious education on released time in our community? If not, has our church taken the lead in holding a conference with other churches to consider its feasibility?

_____ 40. Does at least one of our departments have some kind of service or social or study activity during the week that we consider valuable from the standpoint of Christian education?

X. We need to cultivate the learning habit among our leaders, and minds open to new ideas.

_____ 41. Do we have a workers' library, kept fairly up-to-date?

_____ 42. Do as many as half of our workers draw books from it and read them during the year?

_____ 43. Do we try to find out about other church schools that are doing an excellent piece of work? During the past year has some one from our church visited such a school in search of new ideas?

_____ 44. Is our church usually represented at summer schools of religious education and at institutes held within a reasonable distance?

XI. We should be able to see results in the lives of pupils from our church school.

_____ 45. Do we keep records that indicate not only information about the family and attendance on Sunday, but also mastery of the subject matter of the course and the teacher's estimate of the pupil's growth in Christian character, his attitude, and his participation in the life and work of the group?

*By John Leslie Lobingier, from *International Journal of Religious Education* (March, 1953), p. 6.

APPENDIX V

SAMPLE SUNDAY SCHOOL STANDARD

Goal I — CURRICULUM — A Bible-Centered school.
1. The Bible is the textbook for all classes 2
2. Bible-centered lesson materials and literature that are approved by the National Sunday School Board 2
3. Well-planned departmental worship periods 2
4. Pupils provided with opportunity to use their Bibles 2
5. A minimum of 40 minutes devoted to each class session .. 2   10

Goal II — LEADERSHIP — A faithful staff.
1. Officers and teachers give evidence of salvation; are exemplary in life, and in full harmony with the doctrine and policy of the   (denomination)   3
2. All workers regularly attend church services, including Sunday morning and evening, prayer meetings and revivals .. 3
3. All workers are present in Sunday school at least 46 Sundays 2
4. All workers are present in Sunday school at least 10 minutes ahead of the opening time 2
5. In case of necessary absence, teachers and officers report to the superintendent as early as possible 2
6. An annual installation service for all teachers and officers .. 2
7. The teacher or class visitor contacts each pupil's home at least once a year 2   16

Goal III — LEADERSHIP TRAINING — A trained staff.
1. The Sunday school shall provide at least one leadership training course per year using materials that are approved by the national Sunday school office of the (denomination) 4
2. At least 60 per cent of the teachers, including the superintendent and pastor, shall attend the course 3
3. Literature for the stimulation of new ideas and education for effective teachers shall be provided for the officers and teachers 2   9

Goal IV — WORKERS' CONFERENCE — A planned program.
1. There shall be at least 10 conferences per year 4
2. At least 75 per cent of the workers shall be present at these meetings 3   7

Goal V — ORGANIZATION — A competent school.
1. The school shall be properly graded and departmentalized as size and space permit 4
Cradle Roll .... Birth to 2 years
Nursery .... 2 - 3 years
Beginners .... 4 - 5 years
Primary .... 1st, 2nd, 3rd, grades
Junior .... 4th, 5th, 6th, grades
Junior high .... 7th, 8th, (9th) grades
Senior high .... (9th), 10th, 11th, 12 grades
Young people's .... 18 - 24 years
Adult group .... 25 years and up
(Grading a Sunday school does not require the organization of the pupils into units with separate rooms. The principle

349

of grading can be applied in the one room school. The purpose of grading is to identify the natural grouping of pupils and to encourage the staff to meet their individual needs as an age group.)

  2. There shall be a proper amount of officers, including general superintendent, assistant superintendent, department superintendents, secretaries, treasurer, and other officers as needed 3

  3. There shall be an annual calendar of all church related events 2   9

Goal VI — RECORDS — An alert school.

  1. Maintain weekly record of pupil attendance, making reports to the Sunday school secretary by class or department 2

  2. The school shall maintain a master file with a permanent record card for each member 3

  3. The school shall adopt and maintain the 4 - 6 point record system 2

  4. The school shall maintain a definite visitor and absentee record and follow-up system 3

  5. There shall be a monthly study of records by teachers and officers to measure progress 2   12

Goal VII — EVANGELISM — A ministry.

  1. The superintendent or pastor shall give frequent opportunities for pupils to receive Christ and confess Him publicly . 3

  2. Teachers shall seek to lead each unsaved pupil to Christ by personal contact 3

  3. The school shall acquaint the pupils with the (denominational) missionary projects, and make an annual contribution for missions giving each pupil an opportunity to contribute 3

  4. The school shall promote a definite system of visitation to secure new members and prospects 3

  5. The school shall encourage its youth to dedicate their lives for service 2

  6. Each member shall be encouraged to be a witness for Christ 2   16

Goal VIII — CHURCH RELATIONSHIP — A church school.

  1. At least 75 per cent of those attending Sunday school above 8 years of age shall remain for the morning worship service 3

  2. An effort shall be made to lead converts into baptism and church membership — especially juniors and older pupils .. 3   6

Goal IX — FINANCES — A giving school.

  1. The school shall encourage regular offerings. (Regular giving shall be taught on the principle of the tithe belonging to the Lord) 3

  2. There shall be an annual Sunday school budget 2   5

Goal X — COOPERATION — A cooperating school.

  1. The Sunday school shall actively participate in the program of our National Sunday School Council (denominational) 5

  2. The school shall contribute annually to the National Sunday School fund (denominational) not less than twenty-five cents per enrolled member. (This offering is to be sent in during the Fall Sunday School Advance) 5   10

      Grand Total   100

APPENDIX VI

Number 1

INTEREST INDICATOR*

Check List to Discover Interests

What subject do you want to explore with other interested adults? CHECK YOUR FIRST, SECOND, AND THIRD CHOICES.

	First Choice	Second Choice	Third Choice
Getting Acquainted with the New Testament A thirteen-lesson unit designed to awaken an intelligent, devotional and eager use of the New Testament			
Daniel and Revelation. A study of apocalyptic literature			
Toward Understanding the Bible. Deals with some reasons why persons should know the Bible as the Word of God and understand how it came to be			
Understanding Myself and Others. A nine-lesson unit on problems of personality adjustment in the light of Christian faith			
Achieving a Christian Home Today. A thirteen-lesson unit on vital problems of home building			
Our Children Ask About God. An eight-lesson unit that aims to help parents and other adults find wisdom to answer the eager or shy questions children ask about God			
Christianity and Our World. A study of the place Christianity occupies in the modern world			
(Write in any other subject you prefer)			
CHECK THE TIME AT WHICH YOU PREFER TO MEET Sunday morning, church school period			
Sunday evening, preceding preaching service			
Midweek service			

Are you interested in a monthly forum devoted to a consideration of public affairs?

Yes _____ No _____

Name _____

Address _____

*From Leo M. Rippy, *Adult Work in the Church School*, The Methodist Publishing House, Chicago, Illinois, No. 4500-BC, Price, 35 cents.

351

Number 2

RECREATIONAL INTEREST INDICATOR*

Name _____ Address _____

I should like to participate in the following recreational activities in our young adult groups. Please check activities which interest you.

DRAMATICS

Play reading ( )
Putting on plays ( )
Choric speech ( )

HOBBIES

Hobby nights ( )
Hobby programs ( )
Hobby fair ( )
Craft shop ( )
Photography ( )
Painting ( )
Sketching ( )
Collecting stamps, etc. ( )

OPEN HOUSE AND GAME ROOM

OUTDOOR ACTIVITIES

Picnics ( )
Hikes ( )
Star study ( )
Bird study ( )

LITERATURE

Reading club ( )
Reviews ( )
Poetry club ( )
Writer's club ( )
Storytelling programs ( )

MUSIC

Listening to programs ( )
Choral or glee clubs ( )
Musicales ( )
Community sings ( )

PARTIES

Big theme party
Quarterly ( )
Monthly ( )

ACTIVE GAMES

Folk games ( )
Bowling ( )
Skating ( )

I should like to help make recreational experiences successful by volunteering to do the following work: ( ) Plan parties; ( ) help decorate; ( ) lead singing; ( ) direct games and recreational events; ( ) serve refreshments; ( ) notify others.

Check below any area of recreational activity in which you may have some training for leadership:

_____ Dramatics   _____ Music
_____ Hobbies   _____ Outdoor activities
_____ Literature   _____ Directing parties

*Source unknown

APPENDIX VII

LESSON PLAN FOR FIRST YEAR JUNIOR
(LENGTH OF SESSION, ONE HOUR)

Aim

To help the pupils to discover the heart of Jesus' message in the Kingdom of love and to lead them to consecration to the ideals of the Kingdom.

Materials

Construction paper; pictures for illustrating hymn; notebooks; scissors; paste; pencils; "The Children's Bible" (Each pupil has his own).

Procedure

Pre-session

Finish booklets illustrating the hymn, "We Would See Jesus, Lo! His Star is Shining." Preparation of notebooks for section on the New Testament.

10:00

Conversation; stories; supervised study; pictures; dramatization.
1. What is the Kingdom?
   a. Ruled by a King.
   b. Made up of people who are loyal to the King.
   c. Governed by laws, policies, or rules (Why are there rules for a game? laws of a country?)
      The Kingdom of love (Jesus' purpose was to help God to establish this Kingdom, not just in one country, but throughout the world.)
2. Rules of the Kingdom of love (to be developed in class discussion)
   a. Love God
      (Supervised study: "The Children's Bible" page 312, "The Two Great Commandments" Matt. 22:35-40 in the Bible.)
   b. Love your neighbor as yourself
      (Same as above; to be studied)
   c. Have your treasure in heaven, not on earth
      (Tell the story "How to Use Money" from "The Children's Bible" pp. 313, 314)
   d. Help those in need.
      (Tell the story of Grenfell)
   e. Love your enemies.
      (Study the parable of the Good Samaritan and, if time permits, tell the story of Stephen; possibly dramatize the story of the Good Samaritan.)
   f. Be modest, not proud
      (Study from "The Children's Bible," pages 327, 328, "Jesus Tells How One May Become Great." Tell the story "King Robert of Sicily" in "Tales of a Wayside Inn" by Longfellow)
3. Does this Kingdom make a difference in life?
   a. In Jesus' Day
      "Except ye . . . . become as little children" See Mark 10:13-16. Jesus makes Zacchaeus his friend. (Tell the story in "The Children's Bible" page 328.)
   b. In our day
      What kind of world would this be if everyone should live by the rules of the Kingdom? Who are some people who have lived by these rules? (Jesus, Father Damien, Lord Staftsbury, etc.)

10:45 Notebook work — write rules of Kingdom. Add story to help you remember them.

APPENDIX VIII

Number 1

SUGGESTED TEACHING METHODS

I. Teaching by *Discussion*
  A. General discussion — free interchange of opinion.
  B. Panel discussion — a group of people freely discuss a matter, then the chairman summarizes and draws conclusions.
  C. Symposium — members of a group present prepared statements.
  D. Forum — one speaker makes a presentation and answers questions for the class.
  E. Hearing — similar to court procedures.
  F. Public conversation — a "host" and a "guest" engage in conversation before the class.
  G. Seminar — assigned topics are reported on by members of the class, followed by a discussion.
  H. Round table — general discussion is conducted around a table, using forms of discussion mentioned above.
  I. Debate — two sides of a controversial issue are presented.
  J. Clinic — "Experts" examine a "case" in question, followed by general discussion.
  K. Buzz groups — subdivision of group into small groups of four to six people for a limited period of discussion.
  L. Question and answer period.
  M. Interview.
  N. Film forum — a film is shown, followed by discussion.
  O. Brainstorming — dreaming up of new ideas.
  P. Listening teams — the group is divided into teams to listen to a talk or watch a film to answer some particular question and then report opinion through a spokesman.
  Q. Circular response — the chairman proposes a question and the group in a circle answers by turns.
  R. Committee work — a cooperative, problem-solving group that seeks concensus of opinion in a face-to-face (informal) situation.

II. Teaching Through *Action*
  A. Projects — an undertaking that is selected, studied, planned, carried out, and judged by the class.
  B. Dramatization — reproduction of an event in order to express its original meaning.
  C. Deputation — a small selected group is sent to perform a certain service.
  D. Research — investigation of the unknown in an effort to add to human knowledge.
  E. Pageantry — inspirational religious drama.
  F. Cells — a division of a large group into smaller groups to plan and carry out a project.
  G. Visitation — calls on individual and/or groups and situations for a wide variety of reasons.
  H. Work groups — similar to buzz groups but of much longer duration.
  I. Role playing — brief acting out of situations in which groups or individuals identify with other groups or individuals in an effort to understand how someone else feels.
  J. Field trips.
  K. Coaching.
  L. Laboratory work.
  M. Demonstrations.

III. Teaching Through *Other Methods*

  A. Lecture.
  B. Directed study — assigned study under the direction of a leader.
  C. Personal counselling.
  D. Storytelling (illustrations).
  E. Personal conferences.
  F. Audio-visual aids.
  G. Tutorial plan — following a lecture the class is divided into groups under the guidance of a tutor or mentor.
  H. Personal evangelism.
  I. Life situations — problems for group discussion.
  J. Inductive method.
  K. Scripture search — topical collation.
  L. Notebook.
  M. Problem census.
  N. Opinionnaire — responses to questions or questionnaire.
  O. Monotorial.
  P. Expanding panel — 15-30 minute presentation by a panel; expanding for the rest of the period to include whole class.
  Q. Sermon forum — 15-30 minute sermon; audience discusses its significance; follow-up in S. S. Class.
  R. Colloquy — an audience panel of resource people, with audience representation, follow-up of speech, problem evaluation, or needs. Divide into groups to discuss the issue, each group appointing one representative for the group. Then come together to discuss the issue with the help of the resource panel.

Number 2

TEACHING METHODS FOR CHILDREN

Arranged according to Senses

Hearing

Bible verse games
Bible stories
block printing
books
box puppets
brainstorming
buzz groups
case study
choral speaking
creating songs
creative writing
curios
discussion
dramatization
face-mask puppets
fact games
field trip
films
filmstrips
flash card games
flip chart
finish it
formal games
free association quiz
hymn study
hymn singing
interview
lecture-forum
letter writing
listening teams

listen-forum
litany
map study
marionettes
match-the-halves game
match-the-word game
monologue
music
musical instruments
newspaper puppets
newspaper writing
painting
panel-forum
paper-bag puppets
papier-mâché puppets
poems
print making
problem solving
puppets
questions and answers
quiz games
research
review games
role playing
singing
skill games
stick puppets
story writing
stocking puppets
strategy games

symposium forum
table-top scenes
time lines

Seeing

Bible verse games
block printing
blueprinting
books
box puppets
cartooning
case study
charts
clay modeling
collage
creating songs
creative writing
curios
diorama
displays
dramatization
drawing
face-mask puppets
fact games
field trips
fill-in-the-blank
films
filmstrips
finger painting

finish it
flash card games
flat map
floor scenes
formal games
free association quiz
frieze
globe
interview
learning hymns
map study
marionettes
match-the-halves game
match-the-word game
mobiles
modeling
models
montage
mosaic
mural
musical instruments
newspaper puppets
newspaper writing
painting
panorama
pantomime
paper-bag puppets
paper cutting
paper tearing
paper-mask puppets
peep box
photography
picture posing
pictures
poems
posters
print making
puppets
quiz games
relief map
research

review games
role playing
skill games
slides
spatter painting
stick puppets
stocking puppets
story writing
strategy game
table-top scenes
time lines
writing

Smelling

field trips

Tasting

field trips

Touching

Bible verse games
block printing
blueprinting
books
box puppets
cartooning
charts
clay modeling
collage
creative songs
creative writing
curios
diorama
dramatization
drawing
face-mask puppets
fact games
field trip
fill-in-the-blank

finger painting
finish it
flash card games
flat maps
flip charts
floor game
formal games
free association quiz
frieze
globes
learning hymns
map study
marionettes
match-the-halves game
match-the-word game
mobiles
modeling
models
montage
mosaic
mural
musical instruments
newspaper puppets
newspaper writing
painting
panorama
pantomime
paper-bag puppets
paper cutting
paper tearing
peep boxes
picture posing
posters
quiz games
relief map
review games
scenes
skill games
stick puppets
string painting

Now after you have analyzed your teaching by determining the senses involved, look at some broad categories of learning projects. In each unit of study, there should be a balance among the types of learning experiences. Use a worksheet similar to the one below and list (write in) the learning projects for your next unit of study. Perhaps it will point up some areas of weakness, omission, or duplication.

Category

Art
Books
Creative writing
Displays (models)

Drama
Group vocals
Interviewing
Learning games, puzzles
Map study

Music
Nature
Projected visual aids
Research
etc.

Number 3
TEACHING METHODOLOGIES FOR YOUTH AND ADULTS

Teaching and Learning Methods
Reading and Listening

1. note taking plus talk-back
2. group lecture
3. informal visual aid

4. conversation reading
5. retelling a sequence
6. question and answer search
7. memorization
8. listen teams plus "feed back"

Versatile Discussion
1. formal discussion
2. informal discussion
3. conversation — free talk
4. circular response
5. brainstorming
6. buzz session
7. informal debate
8. case study
9. group interview
10. evaluation

Assignment — Resource
1. symposium
2. panels
3. formal debate
4. interview
5. assignment plus report
6. personal experience
7. storytelling

Paper Plus Pencil
1. creative writing
2. Bible parable paraphrase
3. note book
4. opinions plus response
5. testing — quizzes

Group Learning — Drama
1. role play
2. sociodrama

3. spontaneous drama
4. playreading plus analysis
5. discussion starter
6. monologues
7. tableau and pantomime
8. plays
9. slides and home movies
10. commercial movies — filmstrips
11. Radio-TV format
12. choral readings

Group Learning — Art
1. collage and montage
2. murals
3. poster making
4. exhibits — displays
5. hanging visuals
6. map making
7. photography
8. art study
9. charts and graphs

Group Learning — Music
1. music resource center
2. records
3. hymn-text study
4. hymn reading
5. group singing
6. lyric writing
7. ensemble productions

Number 4
YOUTH AND ADULT METHODOLOGIES
ARRANGED ACCORDING TO GOAL

Development of Knowledge
1. purposeful reading
2. lecture
3. audio-visuals
4. field trips
5. question and answer
6. exhibits
7. recitations
8. research projects
9. depth Bible encounter
10. symposium dialogues
11. panels
12. book reports
13. inductive Bible study
14. assignments
15. biographies
16. brainstorming
17. buzz groups
18. colloquy
19. debates
20. film — talk-back
21. interview-forums
22. lecture-forum
23. listening teams
24. magazine research
25. neighbor nudging

26. newspaper research
27. oral reports
28. programmed learning
29. reaction panel
30. seminar
31. discussion
32. workshops
33. triads
34. time line
35. group response team
36. screened speech

Problem-solving
1. brainstorming
2. buzz groups
3. case study
4. chain-reaction forum
5. couple buzzers
6. play-reading talk-back
7. role playing
8. simulation games

First-Hand Experience
1. action parable
2. field trips
3. mini-plunge
4. workshops

Attitudes and Interest

1. role playing
2. free discussion
3. feedback
4. counseling
5. field trips
6. exhibits
7. visits
8. group reports
9. biographies
10. seminars
11. interviews
12. agree-disagree
13. circle response
14. creative drawing
15. creative writing
16. creative drama
17. music forum
18. psycho-drama

Skills

1. problem solving
2. case studies
3. writing assignments
4. demonstrations
5. role playing
6. drill
7. practice teaching
8. observations
9. lab experiments
10. brainstorming
11. buzz groups
12. creative drawing
13. creative writing
14. debates
15. games
16. projects
17. work groups
18. clay modeling
19. college creation
20. creative drama
21. modern parables
22. music-art happening
23. pantomiming
24. rythmic movement
25. structuring
26. celebration
27. worship

To Gain Opinions

1. talk-backs
2. discussions
3. panels and debates
4. circle response
5. film — talk-back

Arranged According to Groupings
For Small Groups

1. brainstorming
2. buzz groups
3. case study
4. circle response
5. couple buzzers
6. discussion
7. inductive Bible study
8. projects
9. work groups
10. time line
11. question and answer
12. creative arts
13. creative writing

For Large Groups

1. debate
2. demonstrations
3. drama
4. play reading
5. spontaneous drama
6. film — talk-back
7. interview
8. field trips
9. lecture
10. visual aids
11. overhead projection
12. listening teams
13. research and report
14. role playing
15. symposium
16. panels

Lecture Ideas

1. always use a visual
2. students can
   — take notes
   — complete work sheet
   — listening teams
   — summarize lecture
3. tape it and play it
4. use charts and outlines
5. lecture followed by
   — open forums
   — listening teams-questions
   — reaction panel

To Encounter Bible Truths

1. charting
2. choral reading
3. depth Bible encounter
4. inductive Bible study
5. marginal notes
6. multiple readings
7. paraphrasing
8. picture conversation

Number 5

SPECIFIC SUGGESTIONS ON THE USE OF THE BIBLE WITH ALL AGE GROUPS

Nursery Children — ages 4 and under
1. Use action stories — simple drama, short, full of conversation.
2. Use real-life objects to illustrate the Bible story.
3. Workers should demonstrate the Bible truths.
4. Use learning aids which appeal to the senses.
5. Use the Bible itself.
   a. Hold it while you tell the story so the children can see the connection.
   b. Be reverent in attitude toward the Bible.
6. Repetition is very useful for this age.

Beginner Children — ages 4 and 5
1. Tell Bible stories — simple, short, avoid time and symbolism.
2. Use spontaneous dramatization —take turns, use much repetition.
3. Draw the story — use large crayons, colored paper.
4. Use happenings in the classroom as teaching situations.
   a. Connect the story to these events.
   b. Some of these can be planned.
5. Use Bible story books — colorful, posterlike, a picture on each page.
6. Pictures should be simple and within their experience.
7. Use the Bible itself (same as for nursery).
8. Repetition is useful.

Primary Children — ages 6, 7, 8 and grades 1, 2, 3
1. Continue to use stories — can be longer, a little more abstract.
   a. Stories may be told; a greater number may be used at this age too.
   b. Stories may be read — older ones may help read them.
2. Use the Bible itself — large type.
   a. Stress that it is the special book through which God speaks to us.
   b. Emphasize its use in study and worship and as a daily guide. .
3. Memory work can be started in this age group — use verses in connection with their activities.
4. Introduce units that furnish knowledge of Bible background.
5. Dramatization is greatly useful at this age.
6. Tests, riddles, and games are enjoyable for this group.
7. Third graders can organize speaking choirs — e.g., recite Ps. 100 in unison.
8. Connect the Bible story with the whole passage. Let the children know that the story is a part of broader Scripture — e.g., Samuel in the Temple.
9. Relate the Bible and Bible material to everyday life of children.
   a. Love neighbor — this may mean to welcome a new playmate into a tight circle of friends.
   b. Worship — "He has made everything beautiful in his time" (Eccl. 3:11).

Junior Children — ages 9, 10, 11 and grades 4, 5, 6
1. Since they are very active, give Juniors *experiences* with the Bible — active Bible study about active people. Stress drama.
2. Emphasize stories with heroes of good qualities, but do not hesitate to point out the qualities that are not so good.
3. Be sure to explain difficult words and customs.
4. Memorize accurately and understandingly.

5. This group can study Bible backgrounds, maps, etc.
6. They may learn the books of the Bible as they study the text.
7. Stress the Bible as the inspired Word of God.
8. A wide variety of methods can be used with Juniors.
   a. Bible passages can be read in connection with nature settings,
   b. Passages can be marked.
   c. Use of Bible concordance, dictionary, and other tools.
   d. Murals on the life of Jesus and Paul can be made.
   e. Make use of the Bible in connection with special days and
      occasions.
   f. Book reports can be made on Bible stories.
   g. Bible exhibits can be set up.
   h. Pictures, bookmarks, maps, handwork, and newspaper clippings
      are among materials which can be used.
9. Be sure to relate Bible verses and lessons to the problems of children; judge current events and community news in the light of
   Bible principles.

Young People and Adults

1. Key passages can be read by the class members. Vary this. Passages may be read in concert, alternatively, or responsively. Or
   you may select passages for group reading together or dramatically.
2. Raise questions and require that answers be given by reference to
   verses.
3. Let difficult or disputed meanings be interpreted by reference to
   related passages found elsewhere in Bible.
4. Let members point out truths which they have found especially
   helpful to them personally.
5. Reports can be made, based on previous assignments, by designated
   members — on geography, history, etc.
6. Undertake an interesting project which grows out of the class
   itself — such as maps, notebooks, service projects, etc.
7. Initiate a Scripture search — e.g., the word "comfort." Use concordances.
8. Different translations may be used with discretion.
9. Avoid the verse-by-verse method of explaining, if possible.
10. Use silent reading sometimes.
11. Make duplicate copies of twenty-five choice portions of the Bible
    and encourage members to memorize these.
12. Use written exams on the Bible occasionally.
13. Use charts to outline Bible lessons.
14. Put key questions on the chalkboard and use the Bible to find the
    answers.
15. Older young people should study "How We Got the Bible." Study
    the materials — papyrus, vellum, and paper — and the various manu-
    scripts and translations.

BIBLIOGRAPHY

*Books recommended for church libraries.

A. Books and Magazine Articles

*Adair, Thelma, and Elizabeth McCort. *How to Make Church School Equipment.* Philadelphia: Westminster Press, n.d.

*Althoff, Leona. *Church Library Manual.* Nashville: Sunday School Board of the Southern Baptist Convention, 1937.

*American Baptist Convention. *This We Can Do in Church School Administration.* Philadelphia: American Baptist Convention. Department of Church School Administration, 1958.

*Anderson, Mavis L., editor. *Charting the Course.* Harrisburg, Pennsylvania: Christian Publications, Inc., 1955.

*Anderson, Philip. *Church Meetings That Matter.* Philadelphia: United Church Press, 1965.

*Armstrong, Hart H. *Manual For All Workers in Sunday School Administration and Organization.* Springfield, Missouri: Gospel Publishing House, 1950.

*Atkinson, C. Harry. *Building and Equipping for Christian Education.* New York: National Council of the Churches of Christ in the U.S.A., 1955.

—————. *How to Get Your Church Built.* New York: Doubleday, 1964.

Audio-Visual Resource Guide. Division of Christian Education New York: National Council of Churches of Christ, annual.

Bailey, Albert E. *The Use of Art in Religious Education.* New York: Abingdon Press, 1922.

*Barnard, Floy M. *Drama in the Churches.* Nashville: Broadman Press, 1950.

*Barnett, J. N. *A Church Using Its Sunday School.* Nashville: Broadman Press, 1937.

*—————. *The Place of the Sunday School in Evangelism.* Nashville: Broadman Press, 1945.

*Barrett, Mrs. E. R. *A Guide for Sunday School Evangelism.* Wheaton, Illinois: Evangelical Teacher Training Association, 1942.

*Belew, M. W. *Churches and How They Grow.* Nashville: Broadman Press, 1971.

*Benson, Clarence II. *A Guide for Child Study.* Volume IV.

Wheaton, Illinois: Evangelical Teacher Training Association, 1935.

*——————. *A Guide for Pedagogy*, Volume V. Wheaton, Illinois: Evangelical Teacher Training Association, 1953.

*——————. *A Guide for Sunday School Work*, Unit VI. Wheaton, Illinois: Evangelical Teacher Training Association, 1947.

*——————. *Techniques of a Working Church*. Chicago: Moody Press, 1946.

*——————. *The Christian Teacher*. Chicago: Moody Press, 1950.

*——————. *The Sunday School in Action*. Chicago: Moody Press, 1941.

*Benson, Erwin G. *Ideas for Sunday School Growth*. Kansas City, Missouri: Beacon Hill Press, 1954.

*——————. *Planning Church School Workers' Conferences*. Boston: W. A. Wilde, 1952.

*Benson, Erwin G. and K. S. Rice. *How to Improve Your Sunday School*. Kansas City, Missouri: Beacon Hill Press, 1956.

Betts, George H. *The Curriculum of Religious Education*. New York: Abingdon Press, 1924.

Bielby, A. R. *Education Through Worship*. London: SCM, 1970.

*Blankenship, Lois. *Our Church Plans for Children*. Philadelphia: The Judson Press, 1951.

*Board of Education, *A Program of Leader Development*, revised edition. Presbyterian Church, U.S., 1953.

*Board of Education, Presbyterian Church, U.S. *Christian Family Education*. Richmond, Virginia: John Knox Press, 1952.

*Bogardus, LaDonna. *Planning the Church Camp for Juniors*. New York: NCCC, 1955.

Bowen, C. E. *Lesson Materials in the Church School*. Nashville: Cokesbury Press, 1929.

Bower, Robert K. *Administering Christian Education*. Grand Rapids: William B. Eerdmans Publishing Company, 1964.

Bower, William C. *Christ and Christian Education*. New York: Abingdon-Cokesbury, 1943.

——————. *Religious Education in the Modern Church*. St. Louis: Bethany Press, 1929.

*Boyd, Robert M. *Recreation for Churches*. Nashville: Broadman Press, 1967.

*Breck, Flora E. *Special Day Programs*. Boston: W. A. Wilde Co., 1951.

Brubacher, John S. *A History of the Problems of Education*. New York: McGraw-Hill Book Co., Inc., 1947.

*Burke, Verdia. *Building a Better Sunday School*. St. Louis: Bethany Press. 1950.

*————————. *The Workers' Conference.* St. Louis: Bethany Press, 1954.

*Burnett, Sibley C. *Better Vacation Bible Schools.* Nashville: Convention Press, 1957.

*Byrne, Herbert W. *My Sunday School Handbook, For the Board of Christian Education.* Ft. Wayne: Ft. Wayne Bible College, n.d.

*————————. *My Sunday School Handbook, For the Local Church,* No. 2. Ft. Wayne: Ft. Wayne Bible College, n.d.

*————————. *My Sunday School Handbook, For the Pastor,* No. 3 Fort Wayne: Fort Wayne Bible College, n.d.

————————. "The Ministry of Teaching," *Asbury Seminarian* (Winter, 1956), p. 36.

*Campbell, Oscar P. *The Superintendent Wants to Know.* Philadelphia: The Judson Press, 1937.

Camp Director's Manual. Wheaton: Scripture Press, 1965.

*Clark, Ruth A. *Vacation Bible School,* Unit XI. Wheaton, Illinois: Evangelical Teacher Training Association, 1959.

*Clemens, F. et. al. *Recreation and the Local Church.* Elgin, Illinois: Brethren Publishing Company, 1956.

*Clemmons, Robert S. *Dynamics of Christian Adult Education.* New York: Abingdon, 1958.

————————. *Education for Churchmanship.* New York: Abingdon, 1966.

*————————. *Young Adults in the Church.* New York: Abingdon, 1959.

*Cober, Kenneth L. *Evangelism in the Sunday Church School.* Philadelphia: Judson Press, 1955.

Colson, Howard P. and Cook, Melba. *The Sunday School at Work.* Nashville: Broadman Press, 1969.

Conover, Elbert M. *The Church School and Parish House Building.* New York: The Interdenominational Bureau of Architecture, 1950.

Cooperative Curriculum Project. *The Church's Educational Ministry.* St. Louis: Bethany Press, 1965.

Cooperative Curriculum Project. *Tools of Curriculum Development for the Church's Educational Ministry.* Anderson, Indiana: Warner Press, 1967.

*Crossland, Weldon. *Better Leaders for Your Church.* Nashville: Abingdon Press, 1955.

*————————. *How To Build Up Your Church School.* Nashville: Abingdon-Cokesbury, 1948.

*Cully, Iris V. *The Dynamics of Christian Education.* Philadelphia: Westminster Press, 1958.

*Cummings, Oliver DeWolf. *Christian Education in the Local Church.* Philadelphia: Judson Press, 1950.

*——————. *The Youth Fellowship.* Chicago: Judson Press, 1956.

*Dale, Edgar. *Audio-Visual Methods in Teaching,* revised edition. New York: Dryden Press, 1954.

*Danford, H. G. *Creative Leadership in Creation.* Rockleigh, N. J.: Allyn and Bacon, 1970.

Davey, J. A. *God is the Superintendent.* Harrisburg, Pa.: Christian Publications, 1969.

*Davis, George and Billie. *Extension Department.* Springfield, Missouri: Gospel Publishing House, 1952.

*DeBlois, Austen K. and Donald R. Gorham. *Christian Religious Education.* New York: Fleming H. Revell Company, 1939.

DeBoer, John C. *Let's Plan.* Philadelphia: United Church Press, 1970.

Department of Leadership Education. *A Program of Leader Development,* revised edition. Richmond 9, Virginia: Board of Christian Education, Presbyterian Church, U. S.

Dillingham, John. *Making Religious Education Effective.* New York: Association Press, 1935.

Division of the Local Church. *Methodist Church School Superintendents.* Nashville: The Methodist Publishing House, No. 502-H.

*Doan, Eleanor. *How to Plan and Conduct a Junior Church.* Grand Rapids: Zondervan Publishing House, 1954.

*Dobbins, Gaines. *Learning to Lead.* Nashville: Broadman Press, 1968.

*——————. *The School in Which We Teach.* Nashville: Broadman Press, 1934.

*Domingos, Ann Marie. *Working with Children in the Small Church.* Nashville: Methodist Publishing House, 1952.

*Duckert, Mary. *Help! I Run a Sunday School.* Philadelphia: Westminster Press, 1971.

*Eakin, Mildred M. and Frank. *The Pastor and the Children.* New York: Macmillan Company, 1947.

*Eastman, Fred. *Drama in the Church.* Chicago: Willett, Clark and Company, 1933.

*Eavey, C. B. *Principles of Teaching for Christian Teachers.* Grand Rapids: Zondervan Publishing House, 1940.

*——————. *The Art of Effective Teaching.* Grand Rapids: Zondervan Publishing House, 1953.

Edge, Findley B. *Does God Want You as a Minister of Education.* Nashville: Broadman Press, 1951.

*——————. *Helping the Teacher.* Nashville: Broadman Press, 1959.

*——————. *Teaching for Results.* Nashville: Broadman Press, 1956.

*Elicker, Virginia W. *Biblical Costumes for Church and School.* New York: The Ronald Press Company, 1953.

Ensberger, David J. *A Philosophy of Adult Christian Education.* Philadelphia: Westminster Press, 1959.

Entzminger, Louis. *How to Organize and Administer a Great Sunday School.* Wichita: The Wichita Publishing Company, 1949.

*Evangelical Teacher Training Association. *Church Educational Agencies.* Wheaton: ETTA, 1968.

*Fakkema, Mark. *Christian Philosophy: Its Education Implications.* Chicago: Christian Schools Service, Incorporated, 1952.

*Faut, David J. *All About the Sunday School.* New York: Christian Publications, Incorporated, 1947.

Fidler, James E. *Our Church Plans for Leadership Education.* Valley Forge: Judson Press, 1962.

*Flake, Arthur. *Building a Standard Sunday School.* Nashville: Broadman Press, 1950.

*————————. *Sunday School Officers and Their Work.* Nashville: Broadman Press, 1952.

*————————. *The True Functions of the Sunday School.* Nashville: Broadman Press, 1936.

*Ford, G. L. *Manual of Management for Christian Workers.* Grand Rapids: Zondervan Publishing House, 1964.

*Fordham, Forrest B. *Our Church Plans for Youth.* Philadelphia: The Judson Press, 1953.

*Forsyth, Nathaniel F., editor. *The Minister and Christian Nurture.* Nashville: Abingdon Press, 1957.

Foshee, Howard B. *The Work of Church Officers and Committees,* Convention, 1968.

Foster, Marcus A. *Making Schools Work.* Philadelphia: Westminster Press, 1971.

*Foster, Virgil E. *Christian Education is Where the Learning Is.* New York: Prentice Hall, 1968.

*————————. *How a Small Church Can Have Good Christian Education.* New York: Harper and Brothers, 1956.

*Gable, Lee J. *Christian Nurture Through the Church.* New York: Publication Office of NCCC, 1955.

*————————, editor. *Encyclopedia for Church Group Leaders.* New York: Association Press, 1959.

*Gaebelein, Frank E. *The Pattern of God's Truth.* New York: Oxford University Press, 1954.

*Gage, Albert H. *Increasing Church School Attendance.* Grand Rapids: The Zondervan Publishing House, 1939.

*Gangel, Kenneth O. *Leadership for Church Education.* Chicago: Moody Press, 1970.

*Gettys, Joseph M. *How to Teach the Bible.* Richmond, Virginia: John Knox Press, 1949.

*————————. *Teaching Pupils How to Study the Bible.* Richmond, Virginia: John Knox Press, 1950.

*Getz, Gene A. *Audio-Visuals in the Church.* Chicago: Moody Press, 1959.

Geyer, Nancy. *Team Building in Church Groups.* Valley Forge: Judson Press, 1970.

*Gillet, Edith L. *At Work With Children in the Small Church.* Valley Forge: Judson Press, 1940.

*Glasscock, Elizabeth. *Childrens' Work in the Local Church,* revised. Richmond, Virginia: Department of Children's Work, Presbyterian Church, U.S., n.d.

Greater Chicago Sunday School Association. *The Key to Sunday School Achievement.* Chicago: Moody Press, 1965.

*Gregory, John M. *The Seven Laws of Teaching.* Grand Rapids: Baker Book House, 1957.

*Griffin, Dale E., comp. *New Ways to Learn.* St. Louis: Concordia Publishing House, 1970.

————————. *The Subject Is Persons.* St. Louis: Concordia Publishing House, 1970.

————————. *What Has God Done Lately?* St. Louis: Concordia Publishing House, 1970.

————————. *Well, What Is Teaching?* St. Louis: Concordia Publishing House, 1970.

*Gunderson, Vivian D. *The Great Opportunity of the Sunday School.* Chicago: Moody Press, 1953.

*Gwynn, Price H., Jr. *Leadership Education in the Local Church.* Philadelphia: Westminster Press, 1952.

*Haburn, W. B. *Christian Education File Outline.* 1925 Junction Avenue, El Cerrito, California, 1967.

*Hanson, Joseph J. *Family Camping Enriches Family Living,* pamphlet. Philadelphia: American Baptist Convention, n.d.

————————. *Serving Senior Adults in Your Church,* pamphlet. Philadelphia: American Baptist Convention, n.d.

————————. *The Successful Adult Class,* pamphlet. Philadelphia: American Baptist Convention, n.d.

————————. *Vitalize Your Home Department,* pamphlet. Philadelphia: Baptist Convention, n.d.

————————. *Young Adult Work in Your Church.* Philadelphia: American Baptist Convention, n.d.

————————. *Your Church and Christian Family Life,* pamphlet. Philadelphia: American Baptist Convention, n.d.

*Harner, Nevin C. *The Educational Work of the Church.* Nashville: Abingdon Press, 1939.

*————————. *Youth Work in the Church*. Nashville: Abingdon-Cokesbury Press, 1949.

*Harner, Nevin C. and David D. Baker. *Missionary Education in the Church*, revised edition. New York: Friendship Press, 1950.

*Harper, Albert F. *The Nazarene Sunday School*. Kansas City, Missouri: Beacon Hill Press, 1952.

Harper, W. A. *The Minister of Education*. Ashland, Ohio: The University Post Publishing Company, 1939.

*Harrell, William A. *Planning Better Church Buildings*. Nashville: Broadman Press, 1947.

*Heck, J. Arthur. *The Workers' Conference*. Dayton, Ohio: Otterbein Press, 1937.

*Heim, Ralph D. *Leading a Church School*, rev. ed., Philadelphia: Fortress Press, 1968.

*Hensley, J. Clark. *The Pastor As Educational Director*. Kansas City, Kansas: Central Seminary Press, 1950.

*Herrick, Cheesman A. *Outstanding Days*. Philadelphia: Union Press, 1920.

*Hoiland, Richard. *Planning Christian Education in the Local Church*, rev. ed., Philadelphia: Judson Press, 1949.

Horn, Purl. *Practical Methods for Building Sunday Schools.* Pasadena, California: Clementine Publishing Company, 1952.

Howard, J. Gordon. *The Successful Sunday School*. Dayton, Ohio: Otterbein Press, 1943.

Howse, W. L. *The Sunday School and Missions*. Convention, 1957.

Hughes, Ray H. *Workers Training Course, No. 1*. Cleveland, Tennessee: National Sunday School Board Church of God, 1955.

*Hurst, D. V. *And He Gave Teachers*. Springfield, Missouri: Gospel Publishing House, 1955.

*————————, et. al. *Operation Sunday School*. Springfield, Missouri: Gospel Publishing House, 1957.

Hyde, Floy S. *Protestant Leadership Education Schools*. New York: Bureau of Publications, Teacher's College, Columbia University, 1950.

*Jaarsma, Cornelius. *Human Development, Learning and Teaching*. Grand Rapids: William B. Eerdmans Publishing Company, 1959.

*Jacobsen, Henry. *How to Succeed With Your Home Department*. Wheaton: Scripture Press, 1956.

*Jacobsen, Marion L. *The Why and How of Social Programs for Adults*. Wheaton, Illinois: Scripture Press, 1958.

*Jones, Iris W. *Our Church Plans for Adult Education*. Philadelphia: Judson Press, 1952.

*————————. *The Superintendent Plans His Work.* Philadelphia: Judson Press, 1956.

Jones, Phillip S. *The Church School Superintendent.* Nashville: Abingdon-Cokesbury Press, 1939.

*Johnson, Marian S. *Promoting Your Church Library.* Minneapolis: Augsburg Publishing House, 1968.

Judy, Marvin T. *The Multiple Staff Ministry.* Nashville: Abingdon Press, 1969.

*Kelley, D. M. *Why Conservative Churches are Growing.* New York: Harper & Row, 1972.

*Knight, Cecil B. *Keeping the Sunday School Alive*, No. 5. Grand Rapids: Baker Book House, Sunday School Workers' Training Course, 1960.

*Knowles, Malcolm and Hulda. *How to Develop Better Leaders.* New York: Association Press, 1955.

*Kraft, Vernon R. *The Director of Christian Education in the Local Church.* Chicago: Moody Press, 1957.

Kramer, Adolph H. *Sunday School Leader's Handbook.* St. Louis: Concordia Publishing House, 1952.

*Kramer, E. J. *Equipment and Arrangement for Children's Groups in the Church.* Nashville: Methodist Publishing House, 1950.

Leavell, C. S. *The Successful Sunday School at Work.* Nashville: The Sunday School Board of the Southern Baptist Convention, 1924.

*Leavitt, Guy. *How to Conduct the Workers' Conference.* Cincinnati: Standard Publishing Company, 1953.

*————————. *Superintend With Success.* Cincinnati: Standard Publishing Company, 1960.

*————————. *Teach With Success.* Cincinnati: Standard Publishing Company, 1956.

*Lebar, Lois. *Called to Teach.* Wheaton, Illinois: Evangelical Teacher Training Association, 1958.

*————————. *Children in the Bible School.* Westwood, New Jersey: Fleming H. Revell, 1952.

*————————. *Education That Is Christian.* Westwood, New Jersey: Fleming H. Revell, 1958.

*————————. *Focus on People in Church Education.* Revell, 1968.

*Lerrigo, Marion O. *The Mentally Retarded and the Church,* Booklet. International Journal of Religious Education, December, 1958.

*Leslie, R. C. *Sharing Groups in the Church.* Nashville: Abingdon Press, 1971.

Lessell, William M. *Church Publicity.* Camden, New Jersey: Thomas Nelson, Inc., 1970.

*Lindhorst, Frank A. *The Minister Teaches Religion.* Nashville: Abingdon Press, 1955.

*Lobingier, John L. *The Better Church School.* Boston: The Pilgrim Press, 1952.

*London, A. S. *The Sunday School Challenge.* Butler, Indiana: Higley Press, 1958.

*Lotz, Phillip H., editor. *Orientation in Religious Education.* New York: Abingdon Press, 1950.

*Martin, A. W. *Worship in the Sunday School,* revised by O. W. Moerner. Nashville: Abingdon Press, 1943.

*Mason, Harold C. *Abiding Values in Christian Education.* New York: Fleming H. Revell Company, 1955.

Maves, Paul B. *Older People and the Church.* New York: Abingdon, 1949.

Meadows, Thomas. *Psychology of Learning and Teaching Christian Education.* New York: Pageant Press, Inc., 1958.

*Milhouse, Paul W. *Enlisting and Developing Church Leaders.* Anderson, Indiana: Warner Press, 1946.

Miller, Randolph C. *Education for Christian Living.* Englewood Cliffs, New Jersey: Prentice-Hall, Inc., 1956.

Milson, Frederick. *Group Methods for Christian Leaders.* Religious Education Press, 1965.

*Morsch, Vivian S. *The Use of Music in Christian Education.* Philadelphia: Westminster, 1956.

Munro, Harry C., editor. *Protestant Nurture.* Englewood Cliffs, New Jersey: Prentice-Hall, Inc., 1956.

—————————. *The Church As a School.* St. Louis: Bethany Press, 1929.

—————————. *The Director of Religious Education.* Philadelphia: Westminster Press, 1930.

—————————. *The Pastor and Religious Education.* New York: The Abingdon Press, 1930.

*Murch, James D. *Christian Education and the Local Church.* Cincinnati: Standard Publishing Company, 1945.

McCarty, Margie. *The Church Plans for Children.* Nashville: Methodist Publishing House, 1953.

*McGraw, Mildred C. *The Extension Department Lifting Through Love.* Nashville: Broadman Press, 1952.

McKay, Joy. *Creative Counseling for Christian Camps.* Wheaton: Scripture Press, 1966.

McKibben, Frank. *Christian Education Through the Church.* Nashville: Abingdon-Cokesbury Press, 1947.

*—————————. *Guiding Workers in Christian Education.* Nashville: Abingdon Press, 1953.

——————. *Improving Religious Education Through Supervision.* Nashville: Abingdon-Cokesbury Press, 1931.

McMarrissy, Lester W. *Handbook on Christian Education in the Inner City.* New York: Seabury Press, 1966.

McMichael, Jack B. *The New Superintendent.* Richmond, Virginia: John Knox Press, 1950.

*National Council of Churches. *A Guide for Curriculum in Christian Education.* Chicago: Special Committee on Curriculum Guide, Division of Christian Education, 1955.

*——————. *Evaluation and Christian Education.* New York: Office of Publication and Distribution, 475 Riverside Drive, 1960.

National Council of Churches of Christ. *Home and Church Work Together,* Education Bulletin No. 423. Chicago: Office of Publishing, 1940.

*——————. *The Organization and Administration of Christian Education in the Local Church.* Chicago: Division of Christian Education, 1951.

*Noland, Emma. *The Six Point Record System and Its Use.* Nashville: Broadman Press, 1952.

Olson, Ove S. *Administration of the Church School.* Rock Island, Illinois: Augustana Book Concern, 1943.

*Parker, J. Fred. *The Sunday School Reaches Out.* Kansas City, Missouri: Beacon Hill Press, 1953.

Paulk, Earl P. *Workers' Training Course, No. 4, Sunday School Evangelism.* Cleveland, Tennessee: National Sunday School Board, Church of God, Pathway Press, 1958.

*Paulson, Irwin G. *The Church School and Worship.* New York: The Macmillan Company, 1940.

*Peirce, Willard C. and L. C. Honderick. *Going With the Gospel.* Springfield, Missouri: Gospel Publishing House, 1949.

*Person, Peter P. *Introduction to Christian Education.* Grand Rapids: Baker Book House, 1956.

*——————. *The Minister in Christian Education.* Grand Rapids: Baker Book House, 1960.

*Potts, Edwin J. *Evangelism in the Sunday School.* Chicago: National Sunday School Association, 1960.

*Powell, Robert R. *Improving Your Church School.* New York: Abingdon Press, 1949.

*Price, J. M., et. al. *A Survey of Religious Education.* New York: Thomas Nelson and Sons, 1940.

Prince, Darek. *A Christian's Guide to Leadership.* Chicago: Moody Press, 1966.

Prugh, Marcella. *The Parish Director of Christian Education.* Greenwich, Connecticut: The Seabury Press, 1952.

Raffety, W. Edward. *How to Lead a Bible School.* Cincinnati: Standard Publishing Company, 1936.

——————. *The Smaller Sunday School Makes Good.* Philadelphia: American Sunday School Union, 1927.

*Ramsey, William M. *Cycles and Renewal Trends in Protestant Lay Education.* Nashville: Abingdon Press, 1969.

Rein, R. C. *Building the Sunday School.* St Louis: Concordia Publishing House, 1950.

*Reisinger, D. K. *Sunday School Success.* Wheaton: Evangelical Teacher Training Association, 1958.

—————— and Clate A. Risley. *Apt to Teach.* Wheaton, Illinois: Evangelical Teacher Training Association, 1957.

Research Report on Church Education Ministries. Wheaton: Scripture Press, 1970.

Rice, Kenneth S. *How Sunday Schools Grow.* Kansas City, Missouri: Nazarene Publishing House, 1964.

——————. *Sunday School — The Growing Edge.* Boston: Beacon Press, Inc., 1964.

——————. *The Department Supervisor.* Kansas City, Missouri: Beacon Hill Press, 1955.

Richardson, Norman E. *The Church at Play.* New York: Abingdon Press, 1922.

Riggs, Ralph. *A Successful Sunday School.* Springfield, Missouri: Gospel Publishing House, 1934.

Ross, Charles M. and G. McRae. *The Superintendent Faces His Task.* St. Louis: Bethany Press, 1946.

*Rumpf, Oscar J. *The Use of Audio-Visuals in the Church.* Philadelphia: The Christian Education Press, 1958.

Russell, J. Elmer. *The Up-to-Date Sunday School.* New York: Fleming H. Revell, 1932.

Sandt, Eleanor. *Variations of the Sunday School.* New York: Seabury Press, Inc., 1967.

*Santa, George F. *Youth Leader's Handbook.* Redondo Beach, California: Christian Workers' Service Bureau, 1955.

*Schisler, John Q. *Christian Teaching in the Churches.* Nashville: Abingdon Press, 1954.

Schreyer, George M. *Christian Education in Action.* New York: Comet Press, 1957.

Shaver, Erwin L. *The Worker's Conference Manual.* New York: Abingdon-Cokesbury Press, 1938.

*Sisemore, John T. *The Ministry of Visitation.* Nashville: Broadman Press, 1954.

Sloyan, Gerald S. *Speaking of Religious Education.* New York: Herder & Herder, 1968.

*Smart, James D. *The Teaching Ministry of the Church.* Philadelphia: The Westminster Press, 1954.

Smith, Frank W. *How to Improve Your Sunday School*. New York: Abingdon Press, 1924.

Smith, Irene C. *Solving Church School Problems*. Anderson, Indiana: Warner Press, 1944.

*Smith, Leon. *Family Ministry Through the Church*. New York: Abingdon-Cokesbury Press, 1967.

Smithe, Henry G. W. *The Pastor at Work in Christian Education*. Philadelphia: Judson Press, 1935.

Smither, Ethel L. *The Use of the Bible With Children*. New York: Abingdon-Cokesbury Press, 1937.

Squires, Walter A. *Educational Movements of Today*. Philadelphia: Board of Christian Education, Presbyterian Church, U.S.A., 1930.

Stuart, George W. *A Guide to Sunday School Enlargement*. Convention, 1968

Sutherland, Angelyn B. *How to Run a Sunday School*. New York: Fleming H. Revell, 1956.

*Swearingen, Tilford T. *The Community and Christian Education*. St. Louis: Bethany Press, 1950.

Sweazy, Carl M. *The Ministry of the Saints* (Effective Visitation Evangelism). Los Angeles: Challenge Publishing Co., 1952.

*Taylor, Marvin J., editor. *Religious Education, A Comprehensive Survey*. Nashville: Abingdon Press, 1960.

The Sunday School Form Folio. Los Angeles: Cowman Publications, Inc., n.d.

Todd, Wayne. *Library Services in the Church*. Convention, 1969.

*Tovey, Herbert G. *Music Levels in Christian Education*. Wheaton, Illinois: Van Kampen Press, 1952.

*Tower, Walter. *The Assistant Superintendent's Manual*. Nashville: Methodist Publishing House, 1953.

*Townes, Elmer L. *Evangelize Through Christian Education*. Wheaton: Evangelical Teacher Training Association, 1970.

*————————. *Successful Church Libraries*. Grand Rapids: Baker Book House, 1971.

*————————. *The Ten Largest Sunday Schools*. Grand Rapids: Baker Book House, 1969.

*Vieth, Paul H. *Improving Your Sunday School*. Philadelphia: The Westminster Press, 1930.

*————————, editor. *The Church and Christian Education*. St. Louis: The Bethany Press, 1947.

*————————. *The Church School*. Philadelphia: Christian Education Press, 1957.

*Wald, Oletta. *The Joy of Discovery*. Minneapolis: Bible Banner Press, 1956.

Wallin, LaVose A. *Keys for the Sunday School Superintendent and Officers*. Los Angeles: Cowman Publications, 1955.

Westmoreland, R. A. *A Guide to Church Publicity.* Austin, Texas: Sweet Publishing Company, 1971.

*Widber, Mildred C. *Focus: Building for Church Education.* Philadelphia: Pilgrim Press, 1969.

Williams, Mrs. A. J. *The Master Sunday School Guide.* Butler, Indiana: The Higley Press, 1942.

Woodworth, Reginald O. *How to Operate a Sunday School.* Grand Rapids: Zondervan Publishing House, 1961.

*Wyckoff, D. Campbell. *The Gospel and Christian Education.* Philadelphia: Westminster Press, 1959.

B. MAGAZINES AND PERIODICALS

Bethany Guide, Christian Board of Publication, Beaumont and Pine Boulevard, Box 179, St. Louis 6, Missouri.

The Biblical Archaeologist, American Schools of Oriental Research, 409 Prospect Street, New Haven 11, Connecticut.

Children's Religion, Pilgrim Press, 14 Beacon Street, Boston, Massachusetts.

Child Evangelism, P.O. Box 156, Grand Rapids, Michigan.

Child Study, Child Study Association of America, 221 West 57th Street, New York 19, New York.

Christian Educator, 1009 Sloan Street, Crawfordsville, Indiana.

The Christian Home, Methodist Publishing House, 810 Broadway, Nashville 2, Tennessee.

Christianity Today, 1014 Washington Building, Washington 5, D.C.

Christian Life, 33 South Wacker Drive, Chicago 6, Illinois.

The Christian Scholar, 257 Fourth Avenue, New York 10, New York.

Christian School Guide, Christian Schools Service, Incorporated, 10119 Lafayette Avenue, Chicago 28, Illinois.

Christian School Life, Christian Schools Service, Incorporated, 10119 Lafayette Avenue, Chicago 28, Illinois.

The Christian Teacher, National Association of Christian Schools, 10201 South State Street, Chicago 28, Illinois.

Church School Builder, 2923 Troost Avenue, Box 527, Kansas City 41, Missouri.

Educational Screen, 64 East Lake Street, Chicago 1, Illinois.

Eternity, 1716 Spruce Street, Philadelphia 3, Pennsylvania.

The Free Methodist, Free Methodist Publishing House, Winona Lake, Indiana.

International Journal of Religious Education, 79 East Adams, Chicago 3, Illinois.

Moody Monthly, 820 North LaSalle Street, Chicago, Illinois.

NSSA Link, 175 North Franklin, Chicago 6, Illinois.

Presbyterian Action, 8 North Sixth Street, Richmond 9, Virginia.

Religious Education, Religious Education Association, 20 West

Jackson Boulevard, Chicago 4, Illinois.

Sunday School Builder, 127 Ninth Avenue, North, Nashville 3, Tennessee.

Sunday School Times, 325 North 13th Street, Philadelphia 5, Pennsylvania.

World Christian Education, The World Council of Christian Education and Sunday School Association, 156 Fifth Avenue, New York.

Consult other denominational journals.

For addresses of denominational publishing houses and agencies, see Lotz, Henry L., editor, *Orientation in Religious Education.* Nashville: Abingdon Press, 1950, p. 586 ff.

For information on audio-visual materials, equipment, and aids, see Getz, Gene A., *Audio-Visuals in the Church.* Chicago: Moody Press, 1959, p. 241 ff.

SUBJECT INDEX

Administration
    A comprehensive program, 242
    And department superintendent,
        182
    And Director of Religious Educa-
        tion, 107
    And general superintendent, 131
    Committee of, 42, 140
    Functional plan of, 44, 47
    Needed, 43, 46
    Of small church, 46
    Of the pastor, 76
    Principles of, 48

Adults
    Extension department, 311
    Family education, 310
    Program for, 309
    Summer activities of, 310
    Sunday evening sessions, 309

Attendance
    Depends on, 211, 212
    Increasing, 213

Attention
    Gaining it, 260
    Holding it, 260

Audio-visuals
    Committee of, 238
    In the curriculum, 238

Board of Christian Education
    And the program, 57
    Committees of, 56
    Constitution of, 54
    Duties of, 61
    Function of, 53
    Importance of, 53
    In small churches, 65
    Meetings of, 63
    Membership of, 54, 55
    Officers of, 56
    Organization of, 54, 56
    Place of, 53
    Relationships of, 64
    Responsibilities of, 57, 87
    Size of, 55

Calendar
    Master calendar, 82
    Of total program, 78, 79

Camping
    For children, 306
    For youth, 308

Children
    Camping, 306
    Expanded sessions, 304
    Junior church, 304
    Program of, 303
    Sunday evening sessions, 304
    Vacation church school, 305
    Weekday classes, 305

Christian Character
    Goal of, 20

Christian Education
    Organization of, 33
    Total program of, 22, 291
    Pattern for, 26
    Purposes of, 23

Church
    And the pastor, 41
    Character goal of, 20
    Early church, 17
    Function of, 17
    Nature of, 17
    Objectives of, 20
    Origin of, 17
    Program of, 22, 27
    Prophetic goal of, 21
    Purpose of, 18, 19
    Social goal of, 20, 21
    Teaching ministry of, 21
    Total program of, 22

Classes
    Meetings of, 141
    Organization of, 274

Consecration
    As a purpose, 24

Committees
    Of administration, 42, 134
    Of Board of Christian Education,
        56
    Of evangelism, 92
    On audio-visuals, 238
    On worship, 204

375

NOTES

NOTES

NOTES

NOTES

NOTES

NOTES